T0214301

Lecture Notes in Computer Science 12243

More information about this series at http://www.springer.com/series/7412

Lucio Tommaso De Paolis ·
Patrick Bourdot (Eds.)

Augmented Reality, Virtual Reality, and Computer Graphics

7th International Conference, AVR 2020
Lecce, Italy, September 7–10, 2020
Proceedings, Part II

Editors
Lucio Tommaso De Paolis ⓘ
University of Salento
Lecce, Italy

Patrick Bourdot
University of Paris-Sud
Orsay, France

ISSN 0302-9743   ISSN 1611-3349   (electronic)
Lecture Notes in Computer Science
ISBN 978-3-030-58467-2   ISBN 978-3-030-58468-9   (eBook)
https://doi.org/10.1007/978-3-030-58468-9

LNCS Sublibrary: SL6 – Image Processing, Computer Vision, Pattern Recognition, and Graphics

This Springer imprint is published by the registered company Springer Nature Switzerland AG
The registered company address is: Gewerbestrasse 11, 6330 Cham, Switzerland

Preface

Virtual Reality (VR) technology permits the creation of realistic-looking worlds where the user inputs are used to modify in real time the digital environment. Interactivity contributes to the feeling of immersion in the virtual world, of being part of the action that the user experiences. It is not only possible to see and manipulate a virtual object, but also perceive them via different sensorimotor channels, such as by using haptic devices and 3D audio rendering.

Augmented Reality (AR) and Mixed Reality (MR) technologies permit the real-time fusion of computer-generated digital contents with the real world and allow the creation of fascinating new types of user interfaces. AR enhances the users' perception and improves their interaction in the real environment. The virtual objects help the user to perform real-world tasks better by displaying information that cannot directly detect with their own senses. Unlike the VR technology that completely immerses users inside a synthetic environment where they cannot see the real world around them, AR technology allows the users to perceive 3D virtual objects superimposed upon the real environment. AR and MR supplement reality rather than completely replacing it, and the user is under the impression that the virtual and real objects coexist in the same space.

This book contains the contributions to the 7th International Conference on Augmented Reality, Virtual Reality and Computer Graphics (SALENTO AVR 2020) organized by the Augmented and Virtual Reality Laboratory (AVR Lab) at University of Salento, Italy, during September 7–10, 2020. This year the event was rescheduled as a virtual conference to ensure the welfare of the community.

The conference series aims to bring together the community of researchers and scientists in order to discuss key issues, approaches, ideas, open problems, innovative applications, and trends on VR and AR, 3D visualization, and computer graphics in the areas of medicine, cultural heritage, arts, education, entertainment, military, and industrial applications. We cordially invite you to visit the SALENTO AVR website (www.salentoavr.it) where you can find all relevant information about this event.

We are very grateful to the Program Committee and Local Organizing Committee members for their support and for the time spent to review and discuss the submitted papers and doing so in a timely and professional manner.

We would like to sincerely thank the keynote speakers who willingly accepted our invitation and shared their expertise through illuminating talks, helping us to fully meet the conference objectives. In this edition of SALENTO AVR, we were honored to have the following invited speakers:

- Massimo Bergamasco – Scuola Superiore Sant'Anna, Italy
- Mariano Alcañiz – Universitat Politècnica de València, Spain
- Emanuele Frontoni – Università Politecnica delle Marche, Italy
- Mariolino De Cecco – Università di Trento, Italy
- Domenico Prattichizzo – Università di Siena, Italy

SALENTO AVR 2020 attracted high-quality paper submissions from many countries. We would like to thank the authors of all accepted papers for submitting and presenting their works, for making SALENTO AVR an excellent forum on VR and AR, facilitating the exchange of ideas, and shaping the future of this exciting research field.

We hope the readers will find in these pages interesting material and fruitful ideas for their future work.

July 2020   Lucio Tommaso De Paolis
                                                              Patrick Bourdot

Organization

Conference Chairs

Lucio Tommaso De Paolis   University of Salento, Italy
Patrick Bourdot   CNRS/LIMSI, University of Paris-Sud, France
Marco Sacco   CNR-STIIMA, Italy

Scientific Program Committee

Andrea Abate	University of Salerno, Italy
Giovanni Aloisio	University of Salento, Italy
Giuseppe Anastasi	University of Pisa, Italy
Selim Balcisoy	Sabancı University, Turkey
Vitoantonio Bevilacqua	Polytechnic of Bari, Italy
Monica Bordegoni	Politecnico di Milano, Italy
Davide Borra	NoReal.it, Italy
Andrea Bottino	Politecnico di Torino, Italy
Pierre Boulanger	University of Alberta, Canada
Andres Bustillo	University of Burgos, Spain
Massimo Cafaro	University of Salento, Italy
Bruno Carpentieri	University of Salerno, Italy
Sergio Casciaro	IFC-CNR, Italy
Marcello Carrozzino	Scuola Superiore Sant'Anna, Italy
Mario Ciampi	ICAR-CNR, Italy
Pietro Cipresso	IRCCS Istituto Auxologico Italiano, Italy
Arnis Cirulis	Vidzeme University of Applied Sciences, Latvia
Mario Covarrubias	Politecnico di Milano, Italy
Rita Cucchiara	University of Modena, Italy
Yuri Dekhtyar	Riga Technical University, Latvia
Giorgio De Nunzio	University of Salento, Italy
Francisco José Domínguez Mayo	University of Seville, Spain
Aldo Franco Dragoni	Università Politecnica delle Marche, Italy
Italo Epicoco	University of Salento, Italy
Ben Falchuk	Perspecta Labs Inc., USA
Vincenzo Ferrari	EndoCAS Center, Italy
Francesco Ferrise	Politecnico di Milano, Italy
Dimitrios Fotiadis	University of Ioannina, Greece
Emanuele Frontoni	Università Politecnica delle Marche, Italy
Francesco Gabellone	IBAM ITLab, CNR, Italy
Damianos Gavalas	University of the Aegean, Greece
Osvaldo Gervasi	University of Perugia, Italy

Luigi Gallo	ICAR-CNR, Italy
Viktors Gopejenko	ISMA University, Latvia
Mirko Grimaldi	University of Salento, Italy
Heiko Herrmann	Tallinn University of Technology, Estonia
Sara Invitto	University of Salento, Italy
Fabrizio Lamberti	Politecnico di Torino, Italy
Leo Joskowicz	Hebrew University of Jerusalem, Israel
Tomas Krilavičius	Vytautas Magnus University, Lithuania
Salvatore Livatino	University of Hertfordshire, UK
Silvia Mabel Castro	Universidad Nacional del Sur, Argentina
Luca Mainetti	University of Salento, Italy
Eva Savina Malinverni	Università Politecnica delle Marche, Italy
Matija Marolt	University of Ljubljana, Slovenia
Daniel R. Mestre	Aix-Marseille University, CNRS, France
Sven Nomm	Tallinn University of Technology, Estonia
Fabrizio Nunnari	German Research Center for Artificial Intelligence (DFKI), Germany
Roberto Paiano	University of Salento, Italy
Giorgos Papadourakis	Technological Educational Institute (TEI) of Crete, Greece
Gianfranco Parlangeli	University of Salento, Italy
Gianluca Paravati	Politecnico di Torino, Italy
Nikolaos Pellas	University of the Aegean, Greece
Eduard Petlenkov	Tallinn University of Technology, Estonia
Roberto Pierdicca	Università Politecnica delle Marche, Italy
Sofia Pescarin	CNR ITABC, Italy
Paolo Proietti	MIMOS, Italy
Arcadio Reyes Lecuona	Universidad de Malaga, Spain
James Ritchie	Heriot-Watt University, UK
Giuseppe Riva	Università Cattolica del Sacro Cuore, Italy
Andrea Sanna	Politecnico di Torino, Italy
Jaume Segura Garcia	Universitat de València, Spain
Paolo Sernani	Università Politecnica delle Marche, Italy
Danijel Skočaj	University of Ljubljana, Slovenia
Robert Stone	University of Birmingham, UK
João Manuel R. S. Tavares	Universidade do Porto, Portugal
Daniel Thalmann	Nanyang Technological University, Singapore
Nadia Magnenat-Thalmann	University of Geneva, Switzerland
Franco Tecchia	Scuola Superiore Sant'Anna, Italy
Carlos M. Travieso-González	Universidad de Las Palmas de Gran Canaria, Spain
Manolis Tsiknaki	Technological Educational Institute of Crete (TEI), Greece
Oguzhan Topsakal	Florida Polytechnic University, USA
Antonio Emmanuele Uva	Polytechnic of Bari, Italy
Volker Paelke	Bremen University of Applied Sciences, Germany

Aleksei Tepljakov   Tallinn University of Technology, Estonia
Kristina Vassiljeva   Tallinn University of Technology, Estonia
Krzysztof Walczak   Poznań University of Economics and Business, Poland
Anthony Whitehead   Carleton University, Canada

Local Organizing Committee

Ilenia Paladini   University of Salento, Italy
Silke Miss   XRtechnology, Italy

Contents – Part II

Applications in Education

Applications in Industry

Contents – Part I

Mixed Reality

3D Reconstruction and Visualization

Applications in Cultural Heritage

Technologies to Support Tourism Innovation and Cultural Heritage: Development of an Immersive Virtual Reality Application

Alisia Iacovino[1]([⊠]), Lucio Tommaso De Paolis[2]([⊠]), and Valentina Ndou[2]([⊠])

[1] Department of of Cultural Heritage, University of Salento, Lecce, Italy
alisia.90@libero.it
[2] Department of Engineering for Innovation, University of Salento, Lecce, Italy
{lucio.depaolis,valentina.ndou}@unisalento.it

Abstract. Recent advances in technology and its applications have impacted fundamentally the tourism industry. Technological progress and innovations have for many years worked in facilitating the development of tourism [23, 31]. More recently, the emergence of new advanced technologies such as multimedia technologies, virtual reality (VR) and augmented reality (AR) have become key tools for tourism promotion and development. The use of these tools enhance travelers' richness and interaction and provide them a simulated real visit and virtual experience before visiting the destination or the attraction [20].

Especially, VR technologies offer to travelers the possibility to get immersed in the digital world, and to navigate the real situations through a virtual environment [20]. As such these technologies have also created new opportunities for promotion and marketing of different tourism products such as destination cultural heritage, museums, parks etc [5, 11, 21, 28].

Following these developments in this paper we aim to present a technological solution that could be an innovative and valuable tool for tourism promotion of the area. In particular, the technological tool consists in the development of an app that uses Erasmus students as ambassadors for the promotion of the destination by providing tourists with a real immersive virtual reality experience.

Keywords: Virtual reality · 360° immersive virtual reality · Tourism promotion · Cultural heritage Erasmus students · Project management canvas

1 Introduction

The rapid dissemination of technology has created new opportunities for tourism firm's innovation, management, promotion, marketing and value creation [29].

Advanced technologies are providing unprecedented tools for travelers to get informed, to co-create products and services, to co-create experiences, boost tourists' attitude toward a destination, as well as to create the brand, market and increase the value for tourism operators [8, 10, 24].

© Springer Nature Switzerland AG 2020
L. T. De Paolis and P. Bourdot (Eds.): AVR 2020, LNCS 12243, pp. 3–14, 2020.
https://doi.org/10.1007/978-3-030-58468-9_1

Meantime, the emergence of new advanced technologies such as multimedia technologies, virtual reality (VR) and augmented reality (AR) have become key tools for tourism promotion and development. The use of these tools enhance travelers' richness and interaction and provide them a simulated real visit and virtual experience before visiting the destination or the attraction [20].

More and more tourism companies are using VR and AR to provide tourists with immersive and interactive experience, to offer them new innovative ways for getting informed and experiencing a specific attraction or place [22] before trip or also after trip.

Different research studies have demonstrated the uses and advantages of AR and VR applications in the tourism industry, related with the positive impact for travelers' intention to visit a specific place or attraction, the increasing of web presence to a destination, benefits related to providing travelers with real experiences, offering interactive, customized and entertainment experiences [17, 24, 34].

While the use of these tools for promotion is well known and widely used, the combination of the use of these solution by a specific and novel group of tourists, that are 'Erasmus students' has not been considered. These group of people could be ambassadors for the promotion of tourism destination, and they could have a great level of influence for other travelers.

Another, novel element to consider is that Erasmus students could be co-creators of the AV app solution, being that their experiences in the location are used as information base for constructing and updating the Virtual experience of the destination.

Therefore, in this paper we present the technological solution consisting in an application that uses 360° immersive virtual reality that allows its users (Erasmus students and tourists) to take a virtual tour of the city of Lecce with particular content that will cheer up the trip.

This paper is structured as follows. In the first part there are the related works, i.e. examples of similar, but not identical works to the proposed solution. The work design of the application is then described.

Then follows the description of tourism and the new ways in which it is used today. The application is then described in its structure and in its technical and stylistic design; its main functions and features are listed. At the end the test phase and the implementation of the application are provided, including the resolution of the problems encountered.

The conclusion underlines the importance and the contribution that the application can provide to tourism and technology; they also take shape some ideas for possible future developments and follow up of the proposed work.

2 Related Works

The way how tourism companies and destination promote their services and products are constantly changing. While tourism competition grows exponentially, the marketing strategies and tools are changing radically in the aim to send to travelers' specific image in correlation with extra destination value [15, 18, 30].

New marketing opportunities are being offered by new technologies related to VR and AR. VR and AR technologies are finding extensive uses in all fields such as in military, in education, in healthcare, in entertainment, in fashion, in tourism and heritage, in business, in engineering, sport, in media, scientific visualization, in telecommunications, in construction and in film [2, 10].

The purpose of Virtual Reality is to make the user experience a complete immersion in real or imaginary environment, and to interact with the elements present in the scene, by the movement of the head only or with the help of a general various controllers [1].

Such experiences are especially valuable for confidence products such as tourism ones that are not possible to be tested in advance [35]. Therefore, these technologies are being used extensively in the tourism industry for creating virtual experiences for theme parks, for destinations and for the cultural heritage sector [24].

An example of the use of virtual reality in tourism is the application of Virtual tour 360° Hotel Meliá Barcelona Sky; The 4-star Superior Hotel has created a virtual tour of its rooms and the attic and the terrace on the top floor of the skyscraper. By visiting the website, tourists can explore every corner of the place having a more realistic perception and booking with more security and awareness [26].

Another example is the Camino de Santiago 360°. With this App you can wear interactive boots. Using glasses for VR, you can enter like in the skin of a pilgrim.

The application combines document function in interactive guide format.

Camino de Santiago 360° is useful for virtually making the Camino, to prepare the pilgrimage or remember everything once after doing it [9].

Technology is revolutionizing cruise ships too. So, another example is the MSC virtual tour. MSC created an application called MSC for me. The app allows guests of MSC cruises to communicate with the crew and the ship immediately, book with a click excursion, dinner table. It also allows the client to see the interior of the ship in all its spaces through a virtual tour 360°, viewable with PC or mobile devices [27].

Another example is Visual Italy; it is an immersive tourism platform ad it has been applied to the region of Lombardy and Apulia, creating a 360° map of the area's attractions.

Visual Italy allows to identify on the map both the natural and cultural beauties and the economic operators connected to tourism [33].

It also includes virtual immersive tours of the present or of the past. It is possible to compare 360° photos with tridimensional reconstruction of the same area. This technological solution is applicable to the past, for example to present the ancient aspect of archaeological sites, and for the future to visit real estate complexes or urban interventions.

In this case the user lives a visual and sound experience, but he can also interact with the environment through gamepads, special game controllers, technological gloves or other tools that produce vibrations and tactile feedback.

The VR projects allow users to live adventures and experiences in first person, breaking down geographical barriers and simulating any environment.

Today the experience of virtual reality is mainly provided through the use of a viewer or headset. The viewer can show an environment through a display placed in front of the eyes using panoramic images at 360° or stereoscopic videos [34].

3   Work Design

In this paper we present a technological solution that could be an innovative and valuable tool for tourism promotion of the area. This constitutes an innovative solution, that puts together multiple technologies with the aim of increasing and encouraging a local tourism promotion and uses Erasmus students as ambassadors for the promotion of the destination by providing tourists with a real immersive virtual reality experience.

For the design, definition and development of the solution the project management canvas framework was adopted, which includes five logistic blocks of the Canvas considered useful to the guide of the realization from the application [25].

The first phase of the methodology consists in the preliminary identification of the context in which the project is born and develops. Attention is focused on the subject or the target subjects of the result and on all those who are interested in the project itself. It is also part of what the design process will bring as a result.

Customers, stakeholders and project output are then identified with all its characteristics. The second phase foresees the analysis of the entire life of the project; that is, it is decomposed and analyzed in all its phases identifying the timing as well as the duration and characteristics of each sequence [6].

Then, we followed with the identification and specification of the all the tools necessary for the development of the application as software, computer tools for the acquisition of photos to 360° and for the final development of the prototype [21].

In the world of information technology, Virtual Reality (also known as VR or Virtual Reality) has undergone, in recent years, an unparalleled development, also linked to the continuous evolution of software and technological devices. It is in the 2000s that viewers and other VR technologies are known and used by a very large audience.

Today the experience of virtual reality is mainly provided through the use of a viewer, or headset.

The viewer can show an environment through a display positioned in front of the eyes using 360° panoramic images or 360° stereoscopic videos. In this case, the user experiences a visual and sound experience, but there can also be interaction with the environment via gamepads, special game controllers, technological gloves or other tools that produce vibrations and tactile feedback.

Some examples of viewers used today are: Oculus Rift, HTC Vive, Oculus Go, Oculus Quest.

To develop and make the application usable, we have chosen to use immersive virtual reality and google cardboard as a tool.

360° immersive virtual reality is perfect to give the user a view of the city and to allow him to take a real tour of the streets and monuments of the city.

The choice of google cardboard as a visualization tool is equally prudent as it has nothing to envy to the performance of other viewers and has a decidedly low cost which makes the usability of the application easier and cheaper.

In fact, the user can independently assemble the instrument and insert his own mobile phone, in which the application was downloaded, to immerse himself in an engaging virtual tour [16, 32].

4 An Alternative Tourism Promotion

The application realized allows the user to view, within a viewer or a cardboard, some places in Lecce in 360° immersive modes. There are two different tours inside: one designed specifically for Erasmus students and the other for tourists. Following the tour, the user can also view some audio, textual and photographic contents according to the chosen path.

The Erasmus photos will have double significance: they will represent the sweet memories of the students once they return home and will be the potential storytelling of the place in question, the keystone of the tourist promotion and word of mouth in the corresponding countries of residence of the Erasmus students [3].

All the contents together replace technologically what can be a standard tourist guide, with the added immediacy of visual content and the surprise that often only technology can infuse.

The proposed application aims to focus its promotion on a particular target, namely that of Erasmus students. Erasmus is now a growing phenomenon throughout Europe and not only that, and the innovation of the proposed solution lies in making Erasmus students true ambassadors of tourism promotion. Through the technological and immersive vision of the city, students, as well as tourists (another target audience) can have historical and useful information about the city and can relive the memories of the past days in those places and the emotions experienced between those monuments.

According to a survey carried out by the Erasmus+ Agency, Italy is at the 3rd place in the European ranking after France and Germany with about 8,000 young people left in 12 months, 20% more than the previous year [7].

Inevitably, the mobility of Erasmus students increases and moves the economic sector, creating an opportunity for the host country.

Erasmus students in particular are a suitable target for increasing tourism promotion. The keystone of the promotion will be in the period after the Exchange Studio.

Once the experience is over, back in their countries, the students will bring with them all the memories, emotions and information regarding what was their home for several months. Through their stories, impressions, experiences and opinions expressed during their stay, they will be able to carry out a tourist promotion in all respects, using a powerful tool today (and always) as the Word-of-Mouth (word-of-mouth).

In addition, thanks to the innovative solution proposed, they can also remember and relive their memories, through music and photos and share them with people they care most, with family, friends and acquaintances. They can encourage and advise other Erasmus students and encourage them to travel and/or go to the very place that has been their home for so long.

Anyone who has done an Erasmus knows what it's like to return: a combination of contrasting emotions mixed with a strong nostalgia. The application will help to remember the highlights of that wonderful experience, putting in action an important promotion system.

Exchange study students have been identified as a segment of the international student market that has significant growth potential. [8]

5   Development of a Virtual Reality Application for Tourism: Reviver

The project was born mainly as a result of the analysis of the problems inherent in the Italian and Apulian cultural tourism and the lack of an application that allows you to live a 360° tour of the city of Lecce permitting (to Erasmus students and tourists) to see memories and add more [4].

It is important that both Italy and the Apulia region keep up with the times and create a tourist experience adapted to the technological level and the demand as well as the tourist offer proposed by other nations in Europe and in the world. In a world where technology dominates every sector, an immersive experience through viewers and suggestive projections allows you to experience emotions and get lost in a timeless journey; an immersive experience, where you can interact with the recreated environment and the objects present in it. Being able to see a place through a viewer in an immersive reality and be able to interact with the surrounding environment is certainly exciting and intriguing, is able to attract a greater number of tourists including age groups of the most diverse. This would make it possible to involve young people and adults and bring them closer to know the history and monuments of the city.

In this context the idea of the innovative solution Reviver develops.

It was born to be able to live Lecce through a virtual tour of 360°. By wearing a headset, the user can fully immerse himself in some of the most famous places in the city by observing the environment and its monuments in their details.

All this is accompanied by some information and photos visible within the view to 360°. In detail, the textual contents will give some information about the local history and art; the historical photos (in black and white) will show how the places visible today were so different in the past years. Erasmus photos will have double value: they will represent the sweet memories of the students once they return home and will be the potential storytelling of the place in question, the keystone of tourist promotion and word of mouth in the corresponding countries of residence of the children. The audio content, chosen appropriately for each route will accompany the user in this journey time and emotional.

All the contents together replace technologically what can be a standard tour guide, with in addition the immediacy of visual content and the surprise that often only technology can "infuse".

Among all the types of headsets existing and present on the market, we have chosen to use as a means of visualization of the application the Google Cardboard: It has nothing to envy to other viewers from the point of view of performance but has a much lower market cost than the other archetypes.

6   Structure and Operation of the Innovative Solution

Reviver was designed to favor 360° immersive virtual reality.

The development of the project has been punctuated by various macro-phases.

FIRST PHASE: statistical research and information on Italian and Apulian tourism. Study of the state of the art of existing technologies and applications similar to the innovative solution proposed.

SECOND PHASE: collection of material for the development of the application (creation of 360° photos collection of ancient photos and Erasmus photos, collection of artistic cultural information, choice of places etc.).

THIRD PHASE: development of the application through the graphic engine Unity
FOURTH PHASE: testing and implementation of the application.

The research conducted during the first phase has shown, as already mentioned, that it is important for our country to take a step towards the high-tech landscape offered by other nations and employed in the tourism sector, that offers tourists a multitude of different technological and innovative experiences that encourage them to travel and to go to certain places to visit them. After a careful analysis and study of the current situation of tourism in Italy and the Apulia region and after choosing the target audience, the state of the art study of existing applications similar to the proposed solution has been carried out in order to make it as innovative as possible on the reference market.

We then moved to the collection of photographic and content material for the development of the application.

Three places were chosen in Lecce that were representative of the city to be able to implement a tour with 360° view.

The selected places are: "Piazza Duomo", Roman amphitheater and "Piazza Sant' Oronzo".

The choice fell on these spaces of the historic center as they qualify as symbolic and emblematic both from the historical point of view content, artistic and from their being places assiduously frequented by Erasmus students, as well as visited by tourists.

The next stage was to take 360° photos of the established locations.

They were then taken photos with some boys and girls who are doing Erasmus in Lecce, in collaboration with the association ESN Erasmus Lecce.

Through the help of the web was also collected the rest of the photographic and content material. Selected some black and white photos of the city of Lecce related to the places chosen for the virtual tour: users will thus be able to view in immersive reality mode at 360° how the city looks today and through such photos as the same places were shown in a completely different period that is the first years of the 900 about.

The historical-artistic contents related to the places and monuments present in them have been chosen. It can be noted that the various texts intended for the application have been reworked and made synthetic in order to communicate a few important information, in order not to weigh down the use to the user.

A Menu has been created with a special legend in order to create buttons that the user will find located in the virtual tour. These buttons can be activated by the user (specific info in the next paragraph) and each show its own content that is visual, musical etc.

In the third phase, the application was developed.

It was developed with the Unity graphics engine. Unity is a multi-platform graphics engine developed by Unity Technologies that enables the development of video games and other interactive content, such as architectural visualizations or real-time 3D animations.

To create a tour with 360° visualization we start from the reaction of a 3D Object or a geometric sphere inside which the 360° photo is inserted as a shader.

It is necessary to place the main camera exactly in the center of the sphere, so you will have the impression of being "immersed" in the place of the photo.

It was decided to create a small tour for each of the three selected places: two spheres were placed with 360° images for each of them (Fig. 1).

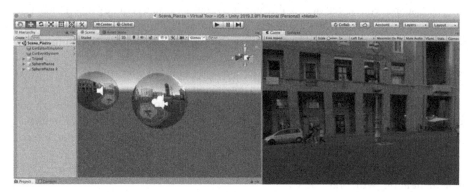

Fig. 1. Unity interface, view balls with 360° photo shader

Once created the scene it is implemented inside with some objects with which the user can interact, such interaction is made possible by the union of Game Object and the appropriate associated scripts. For each object or action inserted in the application have been created the methods and the functions implemented, with its associated script:

Interaction. It was made to allow the interaction of the cursor when approaching an object. It is used the pointer function Enter that is interaction without the need to click, being this an application to be displayed in the viewer (Fig. 2).

Fig. 2. Unity interface, interaction with a button.

Change of scene. In order to create a link between the two spheres it is necessary to make a move to the camera that through a Script, all interaction with a button (an arrow) will move from the first to the second sphere (Fig. 3).

Fig. 3. Unity interface, scene change.

Home. In this case, through the interaction of the cursor with a button (home), you can stop the tour and return to the home or the first scene of presentation of the app (Fig. 4).

Fig. 4. Unity interface return to home.

The choice of the graphics and design of the application is aimed at being able to offer the user a good visual communication in line with the message and the content that the project wants to convey.

The use of colors is not random and is traceable to the color theme established for the reviver logo. The design of the buttons, their location in the scene, the selected images as well as the choice of music, are aimed at arousing certain emotions in the user and to guide and accompany him on his tour in all its details, leaving nothing to chance.

The first scene of the application allows the user to choose the tour to be completed that is: the tour of the Erasmus memory, designed for Erasmus students, or the historical tour specifically designed for tourists. It consists of a sphere at the center of which is placed the main camera, so as to get an immersive view in VR, once entered into the Play mode. Selected the tour you access the Menu where there are panels in which you can start the tour by selecting the various places to visit: "Piazza Duomo", Amphitheatre, "Piazza Sant' Oronzo". Through symbolic icons you can access the next screens. There are then, in the part below a panel where you can play the audio guide describing the city and a panel at the top that allows the user to return to the first scene.

The scene consists of a cube and each of the faces consists of a panel with a photo. The main camera is placed in the center of the cube. After the tour it will be possible to return to the initial scene.

7 Testing the Innovative Solution

The last phase was the test and implementation of the application. The reviver prototype has been tested and implemented several times throughout the development period.

From a purely technical point of view, after various tests, 3 main problems were found and implemented:

1 sensitivity and durability in the interaction of the cursor with the buttons 2 duration of the scene change 3 arrangement of buttons and their contents.

These issues were almost fully implemented and resolved following subsequent testing cycles.

As for the graphic aspect, we tried to make more balanced the ratio and the intonation of color of the buttons: some in black to be more visible within the scene, others, where possible, the color that recalls that of the logo of the application.

Textual contents have been minimized in order to make a fruition of an immediate understanding without unnecessary repetitions.

We then tried to make the first scene (related to the choice of the tour) quite synthetic and understandable: it was used as a background the color of the logo and were inserted in addition to the logo itself, an audio with the word 'hello'. in 10 different languages and two 3D objects to which has been added a simple rotation animation in order to make the scene understandable, dynamic at the right point and harmonious in the style and layout of the contents.

The tests were an important stage of development as they supported the progress and implementation of the application.

The technical-specific description and graphics of the application are intended to present reviver in all its aspects and to make known its potential and the possible innovation in the field of tourism promotion.

8 Conclusions and Future Developments

The paper concludes by articulating some ideas for possible future developments and follow up of the proposed work.

The first step to develop the application would be to adapt the application to any place and city of Italy, Europe and the world.

Every Erasmus student could receive and have information about the city in which he wants to carry out his journey and his adventure.

Therefore, another aspect to implement would be related to the languages with which the app is made usable.

The app would present a panel in which the user can choose their own language. Another step that can accompany the developments of the application could be to test the application to users and collect all the feedback of users.

In fact, a beta version could be created, that is, a non-definitive version, but already tested by experts, which could be made available to a greater number of users, trusting precisely in their unpredictable actions that could bring to light new bugs or incompatibilities of the software itself.

Reviver is therefore able to confer benefits to its users whether they are Erasmus students or tourists.

The application is able to provide a complete city tour guide with historical artistic text content, ancient photos, souvenir photos and audio content (audio guide and background music). It is configured as an alternative, innovative and surprising guide tour that through technology allows you to visit a place even before you went, during your stay and after through memories and nostalgic emotions.

References

1. Anisetti, M., Carmigniani, J., Ceravolo, P., Damiani, E., Furht, B., Ivkovic, M.: Augmented reality technologies, systems and applications. Multimed. Tools Appl. **51**(1), 341–377 (2011)
2. Azuma, R.: A survey of augmented reality. Presence: Tele-Oper. Virtual Environ. **6**(4), 355–385 (1997)
3. Baggio, R., Cooper, C., Scott, N., Corigliano, M.A.: Advertising and word of mouth in tourism, a simulation study. In: Tourism Marketing Conference, Bournemouth (2009)
4. Becheri, E., Ciccarelli, M.: Destinazione Puglia, Oltre il turismo che non appare, per New Mercury Tourism Consulting, Firenze (2018)
5. Benckendorff, P.J., Sheldon, P.J., Xiang, Z.: Tourism Information Technology. Cabi, Boston (2019)
6. Bove, A.: Project Management: la metodologia dei 12 Step. Hoepli, Milano (2008)
7. Brown, L., Aktas, G.: The Cultural and Tourism Benefits of Student Exchange. University World News, USA (2012)
8. Buhalis, D., Foerste, M.: SoCoMo marketing for travel and tourism: empowering co-creation of value. J. Destin. Mark. Manag. **4**, 151–161 (2015)
9. Camino de Santiago 360° Homepage. http://caminosantiago360.com
10. Chung, N., Han, H., Joun, Y.: Tourists' intention to visit a destination: the role of augmented reality (AR) application for a heritage site. Comput. Hum. Behav. **50**, 588–599 (2015)
11. Cirulis, A., De Paolis, L.T., Tutberidze, M.: Virtualization of digitalized cultural heritage and use case scenario modeling for sustainability promotion of national identity. Procedia Comput. Sci. **77**, 199–206 (2015)

12. Cisternino, D., Gatto, C., De Paolis, L.T.: Augmented reality for the enhancement of Apulian archaeological areas. In: De Paolis, L.T., Bourdot, P. (eds.) AVR 2018. LNCS, vol. 10851, pp. 370–382. Springer, Cham (2018). https://doi.org/10.1007/978-3-319-95282-6_27

13. Cisternino, D., et al.: Virtual portals for a smart fruition of historical and archaeological contexts. In: De Paolis, L.T., Bourdot, P. (eds.) AVR 2019. LNCS, vol. 11614, pp. 264–273. Springer, Cham (2019). https://doi.org/10.1007/978-3-030-25999-0_23

14. Crotts, J.C., Gupta, S.K.: Innovation and Competitiveness in Hospitality and Tourism. Kaniska Publishers, New Delhi (2013)

15. Del Vecchio, P., Ndou, V., Passiante, G.: Turismo digitale e smart destination: Tecnologie, modelli e strategie per la crescita di un sistema turistico integrato. Franco Angeli, Milano (2018)

16. De Paolis, L.T., Aloisio, G., Celentano, M.G., Oliva, L., Vecchio, P.: A virtual navigation in a reconstruction of the town of Otranto in the middle ages for playing and education. Int. J. Adv. Intell. Syst. 4(3&4), 370–379 (2011)

17. Diemer, J., Alpers, G.W., Peperkorn, H.M., Shiban, Y., Mühlberger, A.: The impact of perception and presence on emotional reactions: a review of research in virtual reality. Front. Psychol. 6, 26 (2015)

18. Ejarque, J.: WARNING! Cambio di ciclo nel turismo. Luci ed ombre per imprese e destinazioni turistiche, in ftourism online (2019)

19. Gemini, L.: In viaggio. Immaginario, comunicazione e pratiche del turismo contemporaneo. Franco Angeli, Milano (2008)

20. Guttentag, D.A.: Virtual reality: applications and implications for tourism. Tour. Manag. 31(5), 637–651 (2010)

21. Hale, K.S., Stanney, K.H.: Handbook of Virtual Environments: Design, Implementation, and Applications, 2nd edn. CRC Press, Boca Raton (2014)

22. Han, D.I., tom Dieck, M.C., Jung, T.: User experience model for augmented reality applications in urban heritage tourism. J. Herit. Tour. 13(1), 46–61 (2018)

23. Hjalager, A.M.: A review of innovation research in tourism. Tour. Manag. 31(1), 1–12 (2010)

24. Huang, Y.C., Backman, S.J., Backman, K.F., Moore, D.: Exploring user acceptance of 3D virtual worlds in travel and tourism marketing. Tour. Manag. 36, 490–501 (2013)

25. Margherita, A., Elia, G., Secundo, G.: Project Management Canvas. Franco Angeli, Milano (2018)

26. Meliá Barcelona sky Homepage. https://www.melia.com/it/hotels/spagna/barcellona/melia-barcelona-sky

27. MSC Virtual Tour Homepage. http://virtual-tours.msccruises.com/MSC-Seaside

28. Nayy, A., Dac-Nhuong, L., Bandana, M., Suseendran, G.: Virtual reality (VR) & augmented reality (AR) technologies for tourism and hospitality industry. Int. J. Eng. Technol. (SPC) 7, 156–160 (2018)

29. Ndou, V., Del Vecchio, P.: Empowering tourists to co-create services. Projects and Forms of the European Digital Citizenship, pp. 129–143 (2014)

30. Šerić, N., Marušić, F.: Tourism promotion of destination for Swedish emissive market. Adv. Econ. Bus. 7(1), 1–8 (2019)

31. Tanti, A., Buhalis, D.: The influences and consequences of being digitally connected and/or disconnected to travellers. Inf. Technol. Tour. 17(1), 121–141 (2017)

32. Vidal, B.: Turismo e Tecnologia: come il digital sta rivoluzionando il settore turistico. In: WAM (We Are Marketing) (2018)

33. Visual Italy Homepage. http://www.visual-italy.com/IT

34. Wei, W.: Research progress on virtual reality (VR) and augmented reality (AR) in tourism and hospitality. A Critical Review of Publications from 200 to 2018, Orlando (2018)

35. Yung, R., Khoo-Lattimore, C.: New realities: a systematic literature review on virtual reality and augmented reality in tourism research. Curr. Issues Tour. 22(17), 2056–2081 (2019)

An Augmented Reality Tour Creator for Museums with Dynamic Asset Collections

Alexander Ohlei$^{(\boxtimes)}$, Toni Schumacher$^{(\boxtimes)}$, and Michael Herczeg$^{(\boxtimes)}$

IMIS, University of Lübeck, 23562 Lübeck, SH, Germany
{ohlei,schumacher,herczeg}@imis.uni-luebeck.de

Abstract. In this contribution, we present the architecture and implementation of an Augmented Reality (AR) system that enables museum professionals to create and edit AR tours inside their exhibitions without programming knowledge. Museum professionals can use content created during their regular digitization projects and transform them into rich AR content. To create and edit AR tours a web-based frontend called the Ambient Learning Spaces (ALS) Portal has been developed. The media and metadata are stored in a semantic database inside the Network Environment for Multimedia Objects (NEMO) backend and middleware system. To present the tours to the visitors, the platform-independent mobile AR app InfoGrid has been implemented. The content of AR tours can consist of text, audio, video, and 3D objects. Additionally, we added the option to use the new dynamic overlay type Asset Collection as an AR element. This allows the museum staff to dynamically add animated interactive 2D/3D objects into the AR tour at runtime. The system has been applied and evaluated in the context of a natural history museum.

Keywords: Augmented Reality · Authoring · Usability study and digital exhibition design

1 Introduction

Augmented Reality (AR) is a technology that integrates virtual objects into real environments in real-time [1]. To see these virtual objects, special glasses (e.g., Microsoft HoloLens, Magic Leap) or mobile devices (smartphones and tablets) can be used. This implies that everybody, who owns a smartphone with sufficient processing power, can use AR in the sense of *"Bring your own Device" (BYOD)*.

Google and Apple provide AR frameworks as an integrated part of their mobile operating systems (e.g., ARCore or ARKit). This close integration with the OS indicates a shift for AR from a marginal technology that was only supported by third-party developers and researchers to an integral part of all future mobile devices. The logistics industry (e.g., DHL vision picking), the retail industry (e.g., Ikea), and the game industry (e.g., Pokemon Go), among others, have already successfully implemented applications using AR on a daily basis.

AR is very suitable to support arts and cultural education, e.g., in museums. While museum visitors watch the artifacts, AR can provide an additional virtual information

© Springer Nature Switzerland AG 2020
L. T. De Paolis and P. Bourdot (Eds.): AVR 2020, LNCS 12243, pp. 15–31, 2020.
https://doi.org/10.1007/978-3-030-58468-9_2

layer. This way, AR does not replace or obscure the exhibits but keeps them in the center of attention. With AR on mobile devices, visitors can use their own devices (BYOD), which they are familiar with and museums can save on expensive AR hardware. Additionally, museums save time and money on charging, maintenance, and cleaning of the devices. Many museums are running digitization projects and already have started to store semantic information – often called metadata in this context – describing their collections in specialized database systems (e.g. MuseumPlus, CatalogIt) [2]. Depending on the scope of the digitization project, they also collect information on the semantic relations between elements of their collection.

In the area of AR authoring, many research questions exist regarding content creation, content editing, and content placement. The research question we address in this publication can be found in the area of content creation. We want to find out how to design a system in a way that interactive and animated AR elements can be dynamically placed inside an AR tour even at runtime by users without programming skills. Therefore, we first present the implementation of the ALS framework for the generation of AR tours. Then, we will present the concept of a new overlay type we call *Asset Collection*. These can include all kinds of assets, e.g. models, textures, audio clips, animations, and dynamic behavior. In our solution, such collections can be created like media content itself independently of the InfoGrid AR app. After creation, they can be loaded dynamically at runtime by the mobile AR app and directly used in an interactive tour. This way it is not necessary to update the InfoGrid app in the Android or iOS store when new content is published. Using *Asset Collections,* tours that are more complex can be created. These tours can also adapt to the user's interest. The system architecture can also be used as platform for the evaluation of AR settings. Finally, we evaluate the users' view of the system and assess the usability through sample elements.

2 Related Work

A lot of research has been carried out in the area of technical aspects of AR. An important part is an improvement of tracking methods [3] and the enhancement of tracking with techniques like combining image targets with *Simultaneous Localization and Mapping (SLAM)* [4].

Another research area focuses on the positive effects of learning with AR. The work of Alakärppä et al. has shown that using AR the learning experience increases in comparison to paper-based learning [5]. Other work has shown positive effects on learning attitudes, learning performance [6], and improvements in vocabulary learning [7]. Interior design students also validated higher learning effectiveness [8] when using AR. The publication of Albuquerque et al. has shown that AR can be used to display invisible physical forces in education environments [9].

A different research area deals with research on the development of AR apps inside the museum. One of the first AR tours was created by the DNP Museum Lab inside the Louvre - created for museum visitors in an Islamic art exhibition [10]. Tracking available mobile devices with RFID they added virtual contents for six exhibits. Using RFID detection, the animation started 2 to 3 m away from the exhibit. The platform displayed 3D objects described in the VRML97 standard. Therefore, the team that created the animations could work independently from the technical team.

Today, based on the results of scientific research many museums started using AR inside their exhibition. The National Museum of Singapore created the installation Story of the Forest [11] using AR to transform 69 drawings into animated 3D objects. Until April 2018 the Art Gallery of Ontario had a similar exhibition called ReBlink [12] which was used to show a modern representation of paintings in AR. The Smithsonian National Museum of Natural History in Washington D.C. is using the app Skin & Bones [13] created an AR app that adds virtual content to bones inside the exhibition of the museum.

Another part of the research analyzes the digitalization of cultural content and providing it for Augmented and Virtual Reality applications. Rahaman et al. describe the workflow from a photo to 3D objects into a mixed reality environment [14]. They present several open access and proprietary software packages and services that can be used for automatic 3D reconstruction. 3D reconstruction laser scanning [15] and photogrammetry [14, 16] are widely used techniques. Barsanti et al. formulate that 3D models are useful to preserve the information about historical artifacts, the potential of these digital contents are not fully accomplished until they are not used to interactively communicate their significance to non-specialists [17]. Radosavljević et al. say that the number of visitations will not be increased solely by digitization. To increase the number of visitors, new technologies should be properly implemented into the marketing strategies [18].

Researchers of the *EMOTIVE: virtual cultural experiences through personalized storytelling* project implemented and evaluated tools to support the cultural and creative industries in creating personalized storytelling [19]. The project created tools for computer programmers to create AR content through visual programming mechanisms, wizards, and a scripting editor. Recently, Vargas et al. published an overview of the scientific development of AR in museums evaluating and comparing cultural heritage AR studies [20]. In summary, there is much work on AR technology, learning effectiveness, evaluations of AR systems in cultural heritage, and content digitalization for AR and VR but little work on AR authoring in a cultural heritage context. The latter is what we will focus on in the following sections about our ALS system architecture.

3   The Ambient Learning System (ALS)

In our research project *Ambient Learning Spaces (ALS)* we develop digitally enriched body- and space-related learning environments for schools and museums [21, 22]. In these environments, users can interact with applications running on multiple interconnected display devices in physical space to learn collaboratively (see Fig. 1). In the context of ALS, body- and space-related human-computer interaction combined with Cross-Device Interaction (XDI) [23] builds the conceptual foundation. In the backend, the *Network Environment for Multimedia Objects (NEMO)* is the platform for all ALS applications. Inside NEMO, all media are stored in a context-specific semantic model. Additionally, logic elements for ownership, storytelling, and interactivity are stored in the NEMO as well. Therefore, all ALS applications on mobile and stationary devices can access NEMO as a contextualized media and logic repository.

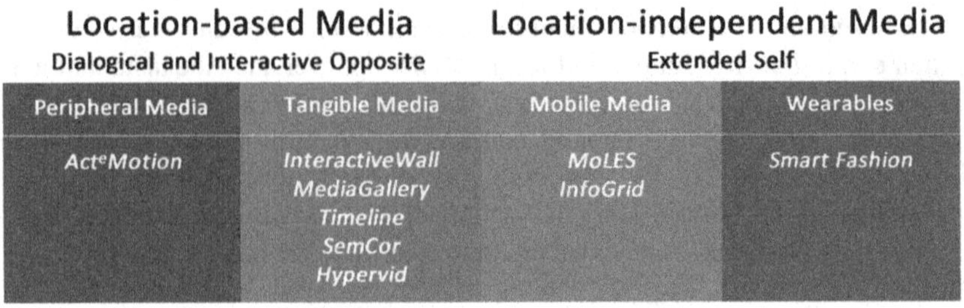

Location-based Media Dialogical and Interactive Opposite		**Location-independent Media** Extended Self	
Peripheral Media	Tangible Media	Mobile Media	Wearables
Act^eMotion	*InteractiveWall* *MediaGallery* *Timeline* *SemCor* *Hypervid*	*MoLES* *InfoGrid*	*Smart Fashion*

Fig. 1. ALS teaching and learning applications sorted by media type [22].

We designed the system in a modular way so that museum professionals can use multiple frontend applications developed in previous work to enable visitors to access the exhibits' information layers through different media types such as tangible or mobile media as well as interactive Multitouch displays. We developed tools for museum professionals to easily create and edit media files such as videos and 3D objects [16, 22] and to setup AR tours [24]. Using the *Asset Collections* described in this publication, static 3D objects created by e.g. photogrammetry can be animated. Furthermore, interactivity and effects can also be added to the objects.

3.1 ALS System Architecture

The system architecture of the ALS learning applications consists of three main logical subsystems. The first subsystem includes the data creation and the AR tour construction systems, which can be used by the museum professionals. The second subsystem is the backend system, which stores media files in a semantic database. The third subsystem consists of the frontend applications for the museum visitors (see Fig. 2). To add and remove media files the web-based ALS Portal can be used. All data uploaded through the ALS Portal is stored inside the connected NEMO instance.

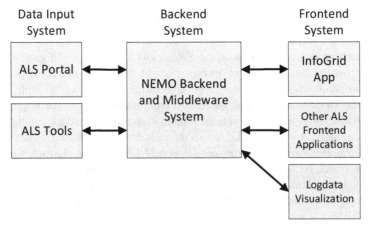

Fig. 2. ALS system architecture with a focus on the AR app InfoGrid. All parts of the ALS infrastructure are connected by a web services infrastructure.

The ALS Tools can be used to edit media and create new media from existing sources, such as videos and 3D objects. Media files created with the ALS tools are automatically stored inside NEMO and can also be accessed through the ALS Portal.

The *InfoGrid* AR application downloads prepared tours from NEMO and displays the information to the user. User actions are anonymously logged through the app and stored in NEMO. To analyze the log data the ALS Portal provides a log data visualization application. The communication with NEMO runs through https-secured web-service connections. NEMO, the ALS Portal, and parts of the ALS Authoring Tools are developed with ASP.NET and WCF. We developed the InfoGrid mobile app with Unity 2019 and the Vuforia vision framework.

3.2 ALS Portal

The ALS Portal is used to create and edit information for all ALS learning applications through a regular web browser. The form inside the ALS Portal for the creation of InfoGrid tours takes *name, description,* and *institution* as parameters for a new tour (see Fig. 3). Furthermore, a target database needs to be uploaded. The target database can be created through the webpage of the AR framework provider *Vuforia.* The target database contains features of up to 100 image targets along with their name and scaling parameters. We also implemented an option for museum professionals to add tour-related information as *start options* that will be displayed at the start of the tour. They can contain a *textual description,* a *thumbnail,* and a *video file,* which are used to welcome the visitor, introduce the exhibition, and show where and how to find the targets in physical space.

Fig. 3. ALS Portal view which shows the page for adding a new InfoGrid project.

After saving the new tour, the ALS Portal redirects the user to the tour elements definition page (see Fig. 4) showing a list of all available targets. This list is extracted from the previously uploaded target database. Towards each target, an AR overlay function can be defined from a dropdown list.

The currently implemented overlay types are:

Deactivated: No event will be triggered upon target recognition.
3D: A 3D object with texture and shaders can be uploaded as a zip file. It will be placed on top of the target image when the app recognizes it.
Audio: An audio file can be uploaded and will be played upon recognition of the image target.
VideoOverlay: A video file can either be selected from a list of videos available for the user, who is logged into the ALS Portal, or entered by URL. The video will be placed on the target image as a registered overlay fitted to the proportion of the original target.
VideoFullScreen: A video file can either be selected from a list of videos available for the user who is logged into the ALS Portal, or entered by URL. The video will be shown in full screen mode.
AssetCollection: Unity AssetBundles (iOS and Android) can be uploaded into this category. Section 3.3 describes the creation of AssetBundles inside the Unity development environment. They can consist of animated 3D objects with assigned Unity behavior such as interactivity and/or animations.

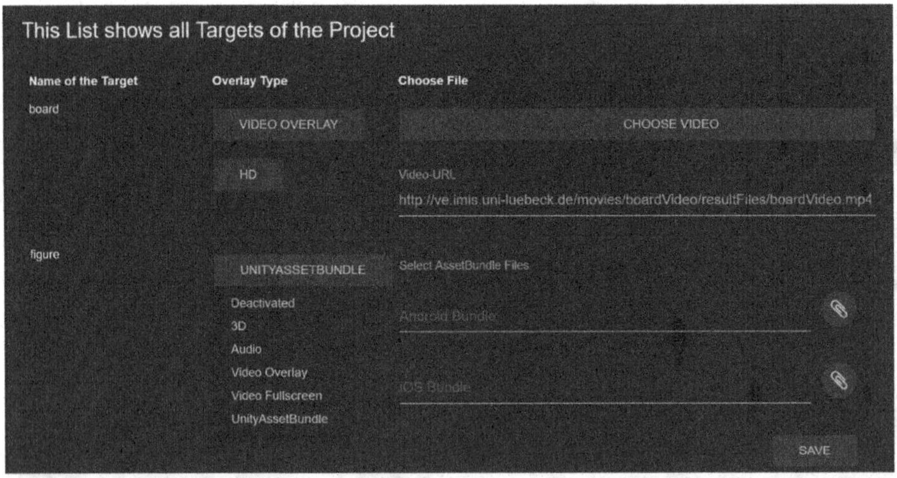

Fig. 4. ALS Portal page for editing tour elements. The view shows two targets. The *board* target will show a video file and the *figure* target will show an Asset Collection.

3.3 Asset Collections

The InfoGrid AR app along with the ALS-Portal and NEMO is a system for the generation of AR experiences. When designing AR tours making use of audio, video, and text augmentations, creators might have an interest in adding interactive elements. Most 3D modeling applications like Blender or 3ds Max support the creation and modification of 3D objects as well as creating complex animations. When the developer wants to add dynamic behavior, 3D development platforms like Unity or the Unreal engine can be used.

As described in Sect. 4 we developed InfoGrid with Unity 2019. Unity is a 3D development platform that can also be used to create Asset Collections. The concept of Asset Collections is not limited to Unity and can be implemented with any other AR/VR development platforms as well. To deliver Asset Collections to the users of InfoGrid we use a Unity internal file type called AssetBundle. An AssetBundle is a Unity specific archive file containing platform-specific assets (e.g., models, textures, animations, audio clips). Applications created with Unity can load these AssetBundles at runtime (see Fig. 5).

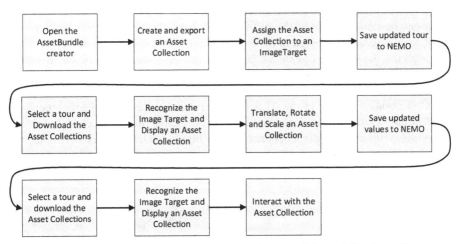

Fig. 5. Pipeline for the creation, implementation, and usage of Asset Collections. Content creators' steps for the creation of the assets (in yellow); museum professionals' steps for the assignment and transformation of the assets (in blue); museum visitors' steps for the retrieval and interaction with the Asset Collection (in green). (Color figure online)

To simplify the process of creating Asset Collections we developed a Unity add-on based on the AssetBundle Manager and AssetBundle browser from Unity. After opening the AssetBundle creator project, the add-on can be accessed through a new menu item in Unity (see Fig. 6).

The add-on adds the functionality to create Asset Collections platform-specific for Android and iOS devices with a few steps (see Fig. 7).

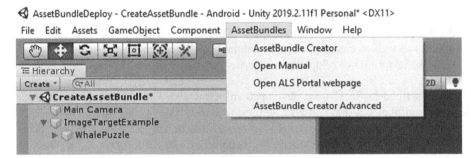

Fig. 6. Unity add-on AssetBundle creator integrated into the Unity editor. Adding a new menu item, the AssetBundle creator and the advanced version with extended logs and more AssetBundle deployment settings can be opened.

With the development of the Asset Collection creator, the process of creating AR content can be done outside of the InfoGrid AR app. Museums are now able to add content without getting involved in the development of AR technology and apps. They can as well use the services of external content creator service providers. The dynamic loading of Asset Collections is also used to reduce the AR app size. When starting a tour, only the currently defined tour-related Asset Collections will be loaded. Furthermore, Asset Collections uploaded in the ALS Portal are stored in a local NEMO repository to be distributed faster in the local area network. This deployment process is optimized for museums with limited internet connectivity or highly loaded network environments. Using dynamically loaded Asset Collections also assures that users will get the most recent versions of the augmentations without updating the AR app.

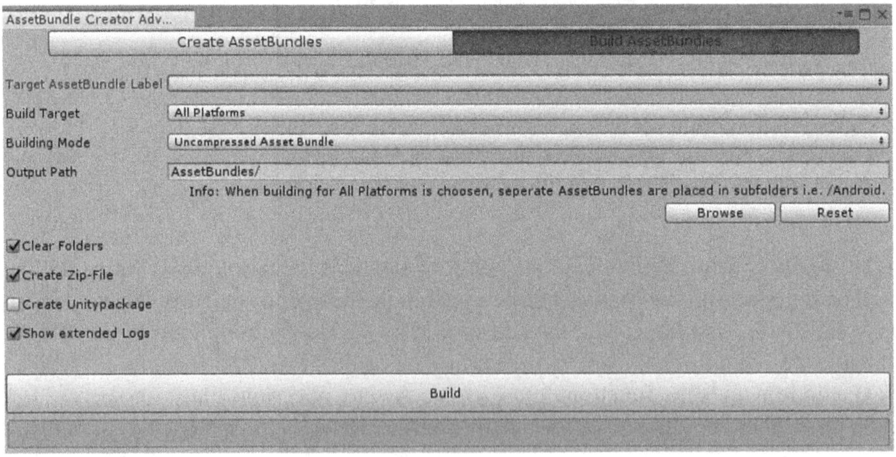

Fig. 7. The add-on window inside the Unity environment to build an AssetBundle providing several settings (e.g. build target platform, build mode, the path to store the AssetBundle)

To use AR functions, we provide an InfoGrid Application Programming Interface (API). The InfoGrid API contains events for the target detection (e.g., the camera detects the target; the camera lost the target). It also contains access to InfoGrid conform animations to interact with AR content (e.g., tapping on the screen, swiping in a given direction, rotating an object) and it contains access to a simplified process to export Asset Collections for the upload in the ALS Portal.

3.4   The InfoGrid AR App

InfoGrid has been developed with the Unity and the Vuforia image recognition framework. Users can download the app onto their Android or iOS mobile device to experience the AR content. The app download size is currently about 26 MB. InfoGrid downloads 3D objects and Asset Collections of the selected tours at runtime. This behavior keeps the file size of the store download small and assures that the users will get the most recent version of the tour.

Upon start, InfoGrid connects to NEMO and downloads a list of available tours. Once the user selects a tour, all 3D Objects and Asset Collections are transferred to the mobile device. The app then receives a list of all augmentations saved inside the tour. This list is internally parsed, and each target augmentation dynamically instantiated with predefined parameters. These parameters include the type of media and the file location, and additionally the translation, scaling, and rotation values. When the preparation is complete, the user can see an optional intro regarding the AR tour. When the mobile device is pointing to one of the prepared targets, the app calls the function *OnTrackable-Found* and shows the instance of the augmentation on the mobile device. In the case of audio and video augmentations, the app streams the audio and video data from the connected NEMO instance (see Fig. 8). When the target is out of camera focus the function *OnTrackableLost* is called. This function hides the augmentation and anonymously sends the name of the augmentation and on how long the interaction was to the NEMO backend as a logging mechanism for further analysis and user evaluations.

Fig. 8. The InfoGrid app displays a video overlay augmentation informing about the excavation site in *Groß Pampau* inside the Museum for Nature and Environment in Luebeck, Germany.

3.5 Placement of Interactive AR Elements

When a 3D object or an Asset Collection is uploaded into the ALS Portal its orientation, scale, and translation regarding the trackable target are set to a fixed initial setting. It includes a rotation of zero, a translation of zero, and a scale of 1. In most cases, virtual objects need to be aligned with the physical trackable target. Therefore, we developed an administration interface inside the InfoGrid app that enables the authors of AR tours to rotate, scale, and translate 3D Objects and Asset Collections using easy to perform direct manipulation methods. The new orientation, scale, and translation values are stored inside NEMO and each user of InfoGrid will automatically receive the new positional data when the tour is started inside the app [25].

3.6 ALS and InfoGrid in a Museum

The Museum for Nature and Environment in the City of Luebeck has been authoring an AR tour using InfoGrid. At the entrance of the museum, a poster and a video screen inform about the availability of the app. Visitors will also be informed about the app when purchasing their tickets. To download the app, visitors can either use their own mobile data connection or use the WiFi provided inside the museum. The app can be found by searching the Apple iTunes or Google Play store for *InfoGrid* or by scanning a QR code printed on the poster, which is displayed in the entrance area.

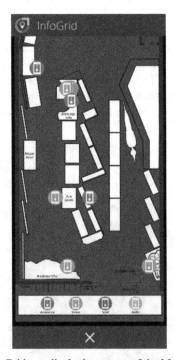

Fig. 9. Screenshot of the InfoGrid app displaying a map of the Museum for Nature and Environment in Luebeck with AR targets. Green icons represent video targets, blue elements represent 3D animations, red elements represent games and yellow represent audio files. (Color figure online)

When visitors start the app and select one of the tours of the museum, they can first watch an introduction video about the exhibition area. To find the AR targets inside the exhibition a map (see Fig. 9) can be opened inside the app. It shows where the augmentations are located. Tapping onto the icons shown on the map opens a detailed view providing information about the exhibit and a photo of the area where the target is located. The media files presented inside the museum include several videos telling about the excavation site and other parts of the exhibition. Meanwhile, several interactive elements for the exhibition have been developed. To integrate them into the tour, they were compiled with the Asset Collection creator described above.

The first element is an interactive puzzle. When visitors scan a certain area inside the museum, where unsorted whale bones are exhibited as shown in Fig. 10 (a), the app opens the puzzle shown in Fig. 10. (a) Area in the exhibition of the museum where bones of a whale are presented to the visitors. The bones lie unsorted and signs show what kind of bone it is. (b) Interactive puzzle, where visitors can sort parts of bones on their smartphones. The goal of the puzzle is to fit the different parts of the whale together. The puzzle's implementation is intended to provide a gamified reflection of the work of the people working in the excavation site. When the puzzle is completed successfully, the system will present the user information about baleen whales.

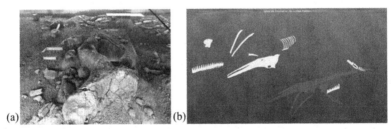

Fig. 10. (a) Area in the exhibition of the museum where bones of a whale are presented to the visitors. The bones lie unsorted and signs show what kind of bone it is. (b) Interactive puzzle, where visitors can sort parts of bones on their smartphones.

The second element is a virtual reconstruction of a Miocene dolphin. Inside the museum, bones of a Miocene dolphin are displayed. Of course, no photos of real animals of this time exist, but based on the bone findings a photo-realistic picture of a dolphin has been created (see Fig. 11 a). The picture served as a basis for the creation of an animated blender model (see Fig. 11 b). The swimming animation was taken from a current living

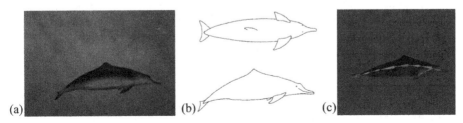

Fig. 11. (a) Painted picture of a Miocene dolphin (b) shape of the dolphin of (a) as a basis for the virtual reconstruction. (c) Blender model of the dolphin with its armature.

dolphin and mapped onto the reconstructed model. Visitors of the museum can point their mobile device towards the bones of the dolphin inside the museum and they will be able to see the reconstructed dolphin model with a swimming animation.

The third element shows a reconstruction of a duck-billed dinosaur. Inside the museum, a duck-billed dinosaur egg is part of the exhibition as show in Fig. 12 (a). To get an idea of how these dinosaurs look like, a reconstruction of the embryo has been created. When scanning the egg, the animated 3D model of the dinosaur shown in Fig. 12 (b) (c) is augmented over the physical egg. Through this, visitors can have a look inside the egg.

(a)   (b)   (c)

Fig. 12. (a) Egg of a duck-billed dinosaur inside the exhibition of the museum for Nature and Environment in Luebeck. (b) Reconstruction of a duck-billed dinosaur fetus. (c) Duck-billed dinosaur with skin texture.

4   Evaluation and Results

In previous work, we have evaluated the usability of the InfoGrid app with museum visitors using the SUS Questionnaire [26]. The study was carried out with a previous version of InfoGrid when the Asset Collection overlay type was not yet available. The resulting usability score of the SUS test was 86.04 (of 100; N = 31) which is interpreted as excellent usability [27].

In this publication, we focused on the evaluation of the usability of interactive elements. For the evaluation, printed images were taken as AR image targets. We had 37 participants (N = 37) between the age of 19 and 65 who took part in the study. Out of these participants, 25 were male, 11 female, and one person did not respond to the question. First, the participants were given a Samsung Galaxy S9+ smartphone with InfoGrid already running on it. Then they were asked to scan all three targets one after another and interact with them. Finally, they were asked to fill out a questionnaire.

For the Miocene dolphin AR element, the following statements were asked:

Q1. The movement of the dolphin was natural.
Q2. The dolphin shakes a lot when I move my cell phone.
Q3. I thought it was good to be able to see the dolphin from different perspectives.

Answers could be given on a 5-point Likert scale with values ranging from 0 to 4 (0 = totally disagree; 2 = neutral; 4 = totally agree). The results are shown in Fig. 13.

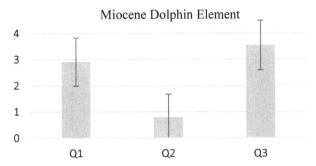

Fig. 13. Mean results of the feedback of the participants (N = 37) towards the questions regarding the dinosaur AR element (Q1: 2.91 SD = 0.91, Q2: 0.79 SD = 0.87, Q3: 3.54 SD = 0.94).

For the dinosaur element, the following statements were asked:

Q1. The movement of the dinosaur was natural.
Q2. The dinosaur shakes a lot when I move my cell phone.

Answers could be given on a 5-point Likert scale with values ranging from 0 to 4 (0 = totally disagree; 2 = neutral; 4 = totally agree). The results are shown in Fig. 14.

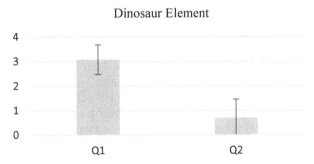

Fig. 14. Mean results of the feedback of the participants (N = 37) towards the questions regarding the Miocene dolphin AR element.

For the puzzle element, the following statements were asked:

Q1. The interaction was easy.
Q2. It bothered me that I only saw one side of the whale.
Q3. I did not realize what I had to do.
Q4. I have learned something new through the puzzle.
Q5. It bothered me that bone fragments were missing.

Answers could be given on a 5-point Likert scale with values ranging from 0 to 4 (0 = totally disagree; 2 = neutral; 4 = totally agree). The results are shown in Fig. 15.

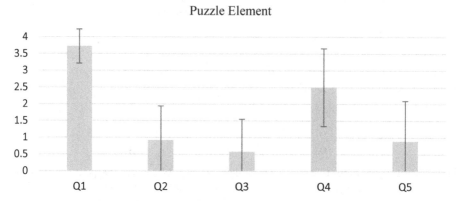

Fig. 15. Mean results of the feedback of the participants (N = 37) towards the questions regarding the puzzle AR element.

4.1 Discussion of the Results

The results show that users mostly agree that the augmentations looked quite natural. The users responded that during their trials a little shaking occurred. We found out that a combination of lighting issues and the number of visible features of the printed targets caused this behavior. In the museum context, it is therefore very important to test image targets for their quality and run tests on different devices, to make sure visitors have a good user experience. To improve the quality, it might be necessary either to improve the smoothness of the animation or to remove some shaking of the object completely.

Users sometimes reported problems with grabbing the smallest puzzle parts. Therefore, we suggest to only using bigger parts of the puzzle. If small parts were necessary for a puzzle, it would make sense to define a touch area around the element so that it becomes easier to grab. Another solution would be to leave it out of the puzzle by fixing it to the part where it belongs. Visitors stated that their learning progress was mostly neutral regarding the puzzle. This confirms our observation where we noticed that the participants did not spend attention on the information that was presented after finishing the puzzle. When the users completed a puzzle, we presented a random fact out of a list of facts on the screen regarding the whale. However, most users did not read the information. We assume that users also have not been aware that different facts are displayed if the puzzle is solved multiple times.

5 Conclusions and Future Work

In this paper, we presented the ALS system architecture with a focus on the InfoGrid AR learning application, its authoring tools, and the dynamic loading capabilities of Asset Collections. We build a fully working system architecture that can be used by museum professionals to create AR tours inside their museum without any programming knowledge. Using the system, museum professionals can create interactive animated AR tours to guide visitors through their exhibitions, personalize tours for groups of certain age, or provide tours in multiple languages. We have shown that it is possible to extend AR tours by creating Asset Collections and loading them at runtime. This enables museum professionals to add or change interactive animated 2D/3D elements into their tour at any time. Because of these dynamic runtime Assets Collections, museum professionals can ask widely available media developers to create specific interactive and animated media content for them and connect these themselves to their AR tour without any programming skills. We received positive feedback about the creation of Asset Collections from three groups of test persons that have used it to develop elements for the AR tour inside a museum.

We identified future work for the museum. InfoGrid provides a static map that shows the visitor where to find the AR contents inside the exhibition. It has shown that museum professionals also need to be able to edit this map without programming skills as well to manage the whole process of changing or extending the tour.

In the case of large-scale museum, databases with more than 100 image trackers do not fit into the smartphones' memories when using the Vuforia framework. Therefore, it would be interesting to find out, whether a cloud recognition engine can be used, where the camera image is processed on an external server. The results would be similar to the implementation of a beacon-aware AR application, which helps the app change the internal database based on the user's physical location. Results of different kinds of beacons like BLE or UWB [28] beacons could also be compared.

This architecture could also be used in other application areas, like city tours or scientific displays to save time in app development by using a generic app with dynamic asset loading and easy to use tour editing functions.

References

1. Azuma, R.T.: A survey of augmented reality. Presence: Teleoper. Virtual Environ. **6**, 355–385 (1997)
2. Barsanti, S.G., Guidi, G.: 3D digitization of museum content within the 3D ICONS project. ISPRS Ann. Photogramm. Remote Sens. Spat. Inf. Sci. **2**, 151–156 (2013)
3. Zhang, J., Gui, M., Wang, Q., Liu, R., Xu, J., Chen, S.: Hierarchical topic model based object association for semantic SLAM. IEEE Trans. Vis. Comput. Graph. **25**, 3052–3062 (2019)
4. Sernani, P., Angeloni, R., Dragoni, A.F., Quattrini, R., Clini, P.: Combining image targets and SLAM for AR-based cultural heritage fruition. In: De Paolis, L.T., Bourdot, P. (eds.) AVR 2019. LNCS, vol. 11614, pp. 199–207. Springer, Cham (2019). https://doi.org/10.1007/978-3-030-25999-0_17
5. Alakärppä, I., Jaakkola, E., Väyrynen, J., Häkkilä, J.: Using nature elements in mobile AR for education with children. In: Proceedings of the 19th International Conference on Human-Computer Interaction with Mobile Devices and Services, MobileHCI 2017 (2017)
6. Hwang, G.J., Wu, P.H., Chen, C.C., Tu, N.T.: Effects of an augmented reality-based educational game on students' learning achievements and attitudes in real-world observations. Interact. Learn. Environ. **24**, 1895–1906 (2016)
7. Ibrahim, A., Huynh, B., Downey, J., Hollerer, T., Chun, D., O'Donovan, J.: ARbis pictus: a study of vocabulary learning with augmented reality. IEEE Trans. Vis. Comput. Graph. **24**, 2867–2874 (2018)
8. Chang, Y.S., Hu, K.J., Chiang, C.W., Lugmayr, A.: Applying mobile augmented reality (AR) to teach interior design students in layout plans: evaluation of learning effectiveness based on the ARCS model of learning motivation theory. Sensors (Switzerland) **20**, 105 (2020)

9. Albuquerque, G., Sonntag, D., Bodensiek, O., Behlen, M., Wendorff, N., Magnor, M.: A framework for data-driven augmented reality. In: De Paolis, L.T., Bourdot, P. (eds.) AVR 2019. LNCS, vol. 11614, pp. 71–83. Springer, Cham (2019). https://doi.org/10.1007/978-3-030-25999-0_7

10. Miyashita, T., et al.: An augmented reality museum guide. In: 2008 7th IEEE/ACM International Symposium on Mixed and Augmented Reality, pp. 103–106. IEEE (2008)

11. National Museum of Singapore - Story of the Forest exhibition Homepage. https://www.nhb.gov.sg/nationalmuseum/our-exhibitions/exhibition-list/story-of-the-forest. Accessed 01 May 2020

12. Art Gallery of Ontario - exhibition ReBlink Homepage. https://ago.ca/exhibitions/reblink. Accessed 01 May 2020

13. Smithsonian Institution - exhibit Bone Hall Homepage. https://naturalhistory.si.edu/exhibits/bone-hall. Accessed 01 May 2020

14. Rahaman, H., Champion, E., Bekele, M.: From photo to 3D to mixed reality: a complete workflow for cultural heritage visualisation and experience. Digit. Appl. Archaeol. Cult. Herit. **13**, e00102 (2019)

15. Altuntas, C., Yildiz, F., Scaioni, M.: Laser scanning and data integration for three-dimensional digital recording of complex historical structures: the case of Mevlana museum. ISPRS Int. J. Geo-Inf. **5**, 9–12 (2016)

16. Bouck-Standen, D., Ohlei, A., Höffler, S., Daibert, V., Winkler, T., Herczeg, M.: Reconstruction and web-based editing of 3D objects from photo and video footage for ambient learning spaces. Int. J. Adv. Intell. Syst. **11**, 94–108 (2018)

17. Gonizzi Barsanti, S., Caruso, G., Micoli, L.L., Covarrubias Rodriguez, M., Guidi, G.: 3D visualization of cultural heritage artefacts with virtual reality devices. Int. Arch. Photogramm. Remote Sens. Spat. Inf. Sci. - ISPRS Arch. **40**, 165–172 (2015)

18. Radosavljević, Z., Ljubisavljević, T.: Digitization of cultural heritage as a potential for increasing museum attendance in Central Serbia. Bizinfo Blace **10**, 53–67 (2019)

19. Katifori, A., et al.: The EMOTIVE project - emotive virtual cultural experiences through personalized storytelling. In: CEUR Workshop Proceedings, vol. 2235, pp. 11–20 (2018)

20. Vargas, J.C.G., Fabregat, R., Carrillo-Ramos, A., Jové, T.: Survey: using augmented reality to improve learning motivation in cultural heritage studies. Appl. Sci. **10**, 897 (2020)

21. Winkler, T., Scharf, F., Hahn, C., Herczeg, M.: Ambient learning spaces. In: Méndez-Vilas, A. (ed.) Education in a Technological World: Communicating Current and Emerging Research and Technological Efforts, pp. 56–67. Formatex Research Center, Badajoz (2011)

22. Herczeg, M., Winkler, T., Ohlei, A.: Ambient learning spaces for school education. In: ICERI 2019 Proceedings, vol. 1, pp. 5116–5125 (2019)

23. Scharf, F., Wolters, C., Herczeg, M., Cassens, J.: Cross-device interaction : definition, taxonomy and application. In: Third International Conference on Ambient Computing, Applications, Services and Technologies, AMBIENT 2013, pp. 35–41 (2013)

24. Ohlei, A., Bouck-Standen, D., Winkler, T., Herczeg, M.: InfoGrid: an approach for curators to digitally enrich their exhibitions. In: Mensch und Computer 2018 - Workshop (2018)

25. Ohlei, A., Bundt, L., Bouck-Standen, D., Herczeg, M.: Optimization of 3D object placement in augmented reality settings in museum contexts. In: De Paolis, L.T., Bourdot, P. (eds.) Augmented Reality, Virtual Reality, and Computer Graphics : 6th International Conference, AVR 2019, Santa Maria al Bagno, Italy, June 24–27, 2019, Proceedings, Part II, pp. 208–220 (2019)

26. Brooke, J.: SUS-A Quick and Dirty Usability Scale. Usability Evaluation in Industry. CRC Press, Boca Raton (1996)
27. Ohlei, A., Bouck-Standen, D., Winkler, T., Herczeg, M.: InfoGrid: acceptance and usability of augmented reality for mobiles in real museum context. In: Mensch und Computer 2018 - Workshop (2018)
28. Cirulis, A.: Ultra wideband tracking potential for augmented reality environments. In: De Paolis, L.T., Bourdot, P. (eds.) AVR 2019. LNCS, vol. 11614, pp. 126–136. Springer, Cham (2019). https://doi.org/10.1007/978-3-030-25999-0_11

Interactive Archaeological Storytelling: Using Immersive Technologies to Visit the Ancient Site of Roca Vecchia (Lecce, ITA)

Ferdinando Cesaria[1]([✉]), Teodoro Scarano[2], Marina Cucinelli[1], Giuseppe De Prezzo[1], Nicoletta Spisso[1], and Italo Spada[1]

[1] CETMA, Cittadella della Ricerca S.S.7 Km. 706+030, 72100 Brindisi, Italy
{ferdinando.cesaria,italo.spada}@cetma.it
[2] Dipartimento di Beni Culturali, Università del Salento, Via Dalmazio Birago 64, 73100 Lecce, Italy
teodoro.scarano@unisalento.it

Abstract. Immersive technologies have the potential to significantly improve the way of presenting cultural heritage storytelling and conveying the results of the archaeological research to a wide generalist audience. This work describes the methodological approach we applied to develop an augmented realty and a virtual reality application to support the narrative of the archaeological site of Roca Vecchia (Lecce, Italy). Starting from the archaeological evidence, we virtually rebuilt the area as it was supposed to be at the time of the Middle Bronze Age and we developed immersive and interactive applications to let visitors vividly experience some of the historical events happened around the mid 2nd millennium BC. The methodologies described and the applications developed are the result of the ongoing collaborative research leaded by a multidisciplinary team made up of archaeologists, humanists, engineers and artists.

Keywords: Virtual reality · Augmented reality · Cultural heritage · Archeology

1 Introduction

The value of an archaeological site is inestimable for archaeologists and historians, but sometimes, cause the detrimental effect of time on the ruins' state of conservation, it can look uninteresting to many people. This is particularly true when the excavation shows only a minimal part of the original state of the finds. Non-specialist audiences can have some difficulties to understand the unseen and consequently to be interested in the archaeological assets. Therefore, cultural heritage sites must embrace new approaches to convey the results of the archaeological research in a synthetic, clear and engaging way. New ways of presenting narratives became crucial; telling stories can speak and connect different types of audiences engaging them in the attempt of understanding the past. In this regard, storytelling has burst into historical archaeology for more than thirty years, offering new efficient approaches of archaeological communication and analysis [7]. More recently, ICT tools and in particular innovative interactive technologies, such as

© Springer Nature Switzerland AG 2020
L. T. De Paolis and P. Bourdot (Eds.): AVR 2020, LNCS 12243, pp. 32–52, 2020.
https://doi.org/10.1007/978-3-030-58468-9_3

virtual and augmented reality, are emerging in different social areas, including cultural heritage. These technologies are able to enhance users' experience, allowing them to visit and interact with spaces and objects unreachable or that do not exist anymore.

In this paper, we study the use of immersive technologies, and specifically of virtual and augmented reality, as tools to enhance the evocative power of stories in cultural heritage. We describe the methodologies that lead us, starting from excavation data, to develop an augmented realty and a virtual reality application to support the narrative related to some special evidence such as the event of war and siege which took place at the Bronze Age walled site of Roca around the mid-2nd millennium BC. The suggestive coastal archaeological area of Roca Vecchia (Lecce, Italy), placed on the Adriatic coast of Puglia roughly 18 km north of Otranto, represents a unique heritage in the world. It was a very special location in the past because of the importance of its geographical position (at the narrowest passage - barely 70 km - of the Otranto Channel) and the richness in natural resources of its territory. It was a strategic harbour for the sailing routes between the Aegean and the Central Mediterranean at least from the 2nd millennium BC onwards; it was likely an iconic place which seems to have preserved over the centuries a distinct identity as a regional core-site probably mainly of religious nature. The Roca site was occupied without interruption from the Middle Bronze Age (17th century BC) to the Hellenistic Age (2nd century BC), and then in the Late Middle Ages (14th–16th century AD) [19].

Starting from the material evidence brought to light during the last decades archaeological investigations, we digitally rebuilt the area as it was supposed to be at the time of the Middle Bronze Age events in order to develop interactive and immersive applications for the use of visitors. The obtained result was possible thanks to collaborative research activities leaded by a multidisciplinary team made up of archaeologists, humanists, engineers, artists and with the essential support and collaboration of the Melendugno Municipality and the Superintendence authority (SABAP_LE - Soprintendenza Archeologia Belle Arti e Paesaggio per le Provincie di Brindisi, Lecce e Taranto).

2   The Archaeological Background

The Department of Cultural Heritage of the University of Salento carries out archaeological investigations at Roca Vecchia since the late '80s after the discovery in 1983 of Grotta Poesia cave-sanctuary [13]. It consists of two large karst cavities, known as "Grotta Poesia Grande" and "Grotta Poesia Piccola", both now invaded by seawater and open to the sky as a result of the collapse of their roofs, are situated 200 m south of the promontory on which the fortified protohistoric settlement stands. The smaller of the two caves counts as one of the most extraordinary archaeological monuments ever discovered: thousands of inscriptions and carvings cover its walls and attest to intense religious activity from the Neolithic to the beginning of the Roman Republican Age [14]. The fortified space, which was also imbued with a symbolic value, was certainly key to the spatial identity of the human settlement. However, in terms of why the location was chosen in the first place and why it was subsequently occupied for so many centuries might probably relate to the presence of the "Grotta Poesia" cave-sanctuary playing an essential role. These two factors, the fortifications and the cave-sanctuary, taking account of their immense social significance, constitute the central elements in the precise regional identity that this place acquired in the 2nd millennium BC.

The protohistoric settlement was situated on the current peninsula of Roca and throughout its existence was protected by a large fortification wall. At the moment of their destruction the size of the Middle Bronze Age fortifications were clearly in excess of what was required to demarcate and defend the settlement. Indeed, they had acquired a symbolic meaning, expressing political power and control of the territory. The desire to express the political and cultural status of the settlement and the community that inhabited it via the monumental character and sheer size of the defensive walls (the most striking feature seen by those approaching the settlement from outside) should also be seen as an indicator of social and territorial competition in the wider context of the fortified coastal settlements of the first half of the 2nd millennium BC along the Adriatic and Ionian coasts of Puglia [20].

The evidence from Roca may provide decisive clues for interpreting the historic scenario of which it was part and for gaining a deeper understanding of its functional and social aspects.

3 Immersive Technologies in Cultural Heritage

In the last years, interactive and immersive technologies have been increasingly used in cultural heritage. The release of new wearable hardware has increased the potential of these technologies providing new possibilities of experiencing the cultural assets as described in many projects and surveys [1, 2, 5, 6, 8, 9, 12, 23, 25].

Immersive technology is generally used to refer to technologies that extend or create a new reality through a digital or simulated world by creating a surrounding sensory feeling, thereby creating a sense of immersion. These technologies include virtual reality, augmented reality and mixed reality, whose relation is graphically shown in the reality-virtuality continuum representation (Fig. 1).

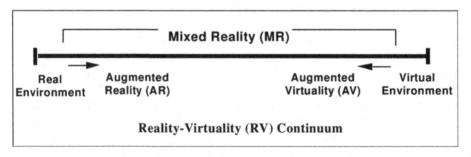

Fig. 1. Reality-virtuality continuum (Milgram-Kishino)

The reality-virtuality continuum describes the interval between real and virtual world, with Augmented Reality (AR) and Augmented Virtuality (AV) in between [11]. AR is close to the real world and AV is close to a virtual environment.

Virtual Reality can be described as a simulated world, in which a user can interact in realistic three-dimensional simulation. It can be also defined as a simulated environment in which a perceiver experiences telepresence [22] or, following one of the 52 definitions from Lanier, a "Hope for a medium that could convey dreaming" [10].

Augmented reality is defined as a variation of virtual environments where virtual objects are integrated into a real environment in real time. Virtual reality completely immerses a user inside a synthetic environment. While immersed, the user cannot see the real world around him. In contrast, AR allows the user to see the real world, with virtual objects superimposed upon or composited with the real world. Therefore, augmented reality supplements reality, rather than completely replacing it [1].

Mixed reality in the Milgram definition is the area between real and virtual environment, where both the real and the virtual are mixed. This consists of both augmented reality and augmented virtuality. However, in the last few years this term has adopted a different and more specific meaning, referring to the technology able to augment the reality with awareness of the physical environment, resulting in an accurate blend between the digital contents and the physical world. The latest is achieved with the use of specialized hardware that combines computer vision and SLAM techniques, typically used in augmented reality, with specialized sensors such as depth cameras.

In archaeological sites, the use of mobile augmented reality can be a very powerful tool to exploit high quality 3d models for dissemination [4, 15, 24].

The use of immersive technologies can enable a wide set of opportunities for archaeologists and heritage curators to present the cultural assets in more captivating ways. They can be a powerful instrument to show visitors what is not visible anymore and support the story telling related to a particular asset.

4   From Archaeological to Digital Interpretation

Information technologies allow the digital interpretation and an accurate reality-based reconstruction of archaeological sites, ancient landscapes and historical places by the visualization in Virtual Reality (VR) or in Augmented Reality (AR). However, it is essential that technological experts in digital production (e.g., digital makers, illustrators, graphic designers and video composers) are supported by cultural heritage scholars, who are able to scientifically validate the contents, the results of the individual production phases and the final reconstruction [3, 21].

Roca Archaeological Project is the result of a deep collaboration between experts of different fields of research, who worked with several ICT tools to the reconstructive phases of Roca's digital scenes and, more generally, to make the archaeological areas known to general public. Specifically, CETMA, is responsible for the digital reconstruction of ancient scenarios and the development of digital tools, Dr. Teodoro Scarano (University of Salento-Department of Cultural Heritage) has the scientific direction of the archaeological researches, Harald Meller (Landesamt für Denkmalpflege und Archäologie Sachsen-Anhalt) supported the investigations and funded the graphic illustrations of the Middle Bronze Age event of war by Karol Schauer, and the Superintendence authority supervised and coordinated the project collaborating with the Municipality of Melendugno (Lecce, Italy) as for the conservation and management of the archaeological area.

Each of these subjects has actively contributed in supporting CETMA in the digital interpretation of the different reconstructive levels of the Roca ancient site. The archaeological documentation from the excavation campaigns, the reconstructive hypotheses elaborated by the team of archaeologists, the interpretative drawings, the scientific papers and every single contribution from the subjects mentioned above were the basis for the reconstruction results.

The co-working activities carried out for the reconstruction of some daily life snapshots of Roca ancient site are the outcome of a collaboration between a team of archaeologists sharing the results of a field research project and a team of experts of new media and technologies for the communication of cultural heritage such as computer scientists, modelers and 3D animators. Defining a method of sharing and digital interpretation of technical data collected in about 35 years of investigations and studies at Roca Vecchia has been very complex.

First, it was crucial to define the points of interest (POI) on which focusing the development of the contents to be digitally treated. Each POI was selected among the archeological evidence documented at Roca on the base of some crucial factors: a) scientific importance; b) state of preservation in terms of architectural and/or material remains; c) possibility to be seen/understood by the visitors; d) potential value in terms of storytelling and emotional involvement; e) historical/landscape identity value. On these bases, as shown in the image below (Fig. 2), the points of interest selected for the digital translation were the following three:

Fig. 2. POI of Roca digitally reconstructed

- the Middle Bronze Age Fortifications
- the Final Bronze Age so-called "Hut/Temple"
- the Late Medieval Citadel.

In order to present an illustrative case study and thus outlining the methodological approach, the operative process and the results, this paper presents a special focus on the first POI that is the extraordinary archaeological evidence from the Middle Bronze Age fortification walls of Roca Vecchia.

The Bronze Age walled settlement of Roca Vecchia is currently one of the most important archaeological site all over Europe and the Mediterranean mainly because of the monumentality and state of preservation of the remains as well as the huge quality and quantity of the finds. When it was destroyed by fire around the mid-14th century BC, it was defended by a mighty fortification wall (up to 25 m thick) running from North to South across the isthmus of the peninsula and marking the settlement boundary along the landward side. The enceinte was not only a dry-stone masonry marking a line of defense between an exterior and an interior space; as a matter of fact it had corridors and chambers (whose walls included robust wooden frameworks supporting the roof), the plan included a main entrance and different postern gates in addition to a ditch [17].

In particular, the architectural complex of the Monumental Gate is one of the most important piece of testimony in the Mediterranean protohistory, in terms of both its planimetric complexity and its state of preservation. The archaeological investigations and the restoration works conducted on this monument during the last 20 years for reasons of both knowledge and conservation allow us to plan valorization and managing projects for public use. If on the one hand the results of the archaeological investigations carried out from the University of Salento in this area from the early '90s are very well known from the scientific community because of the many publications, on the other hand the architecture itself is currently almost completely invisible to the public because of the wooden formwork built to slow down the degradation of the dry-stone structures. This means that the archaeologist who investigated and studied the Middle Bronze Age Monumental Gate of Roca is able to tell the story of the siege and battle which took place exactly there at that time, describing (at least in part) the original aspect of this imposing architecture and illustrating the tragic end of some of the people who participated in these events, being intensively involved in what he is talking about. In contrast, who is listening the archaeologist cannot see almost anything among those ruins trying to imagine something which is completely unknown; that is the success of the knowledge transfer is completely addressed to the ability of the storyteller.

Since the main aim of an archaeological investigation is to tell a story lost in the past with both a scientific and a popular approach, it was important to project and develop experiential tools to allow users to visit the ancient site of Roca Vecchia by ensuring a long-term preservation of the monument. For this reason, it has started a collaboration with CETMA with the aim to rebuild a three-dimensional immersive model of the Monumental Gate that allows a virtual access to the archaeological evidence and to the related historical interpretation of the data resulting from the investigation. Starting from the study of scientific data, the main aims of computer experts and archaeologists were to define the methodological approach to create an ancient reality reconstruction which allows transferring to the end users, such as tourists and visitors, the historical interpretation of archaeological data in terms of both storytelling and sensory perception of the archaeological evidence. In this case, it means to make visitors to experience the event of war and siege which took place at Roca Vecchia around the mid 2nd millennium

BC. To achieve these objects, the project team agree that virtual reality and augmented reality are the most useful techniques to provide users a fully immersion in the historical place and to figure out in a few seconds the dynamics of a specific armed conflict otherwise of the whole siege of the site.

With reference to the excavation data collected over the years, in addition to the more recent discoveries from the investigations of the Middle Bronze Age fortifications carried out in the area of the Monumental Gate (Fig. 3), it was possible to hypothesize a sequence of some "archaeological events" which took place simultaneously during the temporal unit of the siege. In order to figure out how to visualize these historical events in detail by means of new technologies such as virtual reality and augmented reality, two parallel working groups have been defined: the first focused on the reconstruction of the whole scenario of the fortification walls besieged by the attackers (augmented reality), the second concentrated on the restitution of two specific scenes related to what happened during the event of war in the western end of the Postern C and in the southern tower of the Monumental Gate (virtual reality).

Fig. 3. The working sequence in the area of the Monumental Gate between 2016 and 2018

As a matter of fact, the outstanding archaeological evidence from these two areas of the fortifications (whose extraordinary state of preservation is in large part due to the suddenness of the destruction in the violent fire) allows us to say that in the latter case we are dealing with a battle scene since the skeleton of an armed young man unearthed underneath the rubble revealed that a conflict took place somewhere on top of this tower, likely involving at least 2 opponents according to the stab wounds identified on his bones. In the former case conversely, the investigation yielded a clear evidence that we are handling the testimony of a siege; it was unearthed indeed an impressive snapshot of what happened to a group of 7 unarmed people of both sexes and different ages who tried to take refuge in this narrow corridor after bounding its western end with a stone barricade and setting up all what they need to dwell inside for some time. Unfortunately, due to the fire in the fortification wall, they all died from asphyxia trying to hide themselves behind a heap of vessels [16].

The reconstruction of the Middle Bronze Age fortification walls and the Monumental Gate represented a very complex challenge for the Roca Archaeological Project team; notwithstanding an unusual state of preservation, the remains brought to light during the excavations carried out over the years (as well as the related current literature) refers, in the best case, only to about the 50% of the elevation of the original hypothetical architecture. For this reason, it has been very complex to define a reconstructive scheme of the entire monument for the 3D modeling team. The aim of the digital interpretation of the fortification scene was to reproduce the details of a still little known monument in virtual version. In addition, the steps of Roca reconstruction has enjoyed the support of Karol Schauer, an artist who, in occasion of the special exhibition "Krieg. Eine Archäologische Spurensuche" organized by Landesamt für Denkmalpflege und Ärchaologie Sachsen-Anhalt held in 2015 at the Landesmuseum für Vorgeschichte Halle-Saale (Germany), has created a series of illustrated tables of the different scenes telling the story of the Middle Bronze Age siege of Roca Vecchia [18].

Starting from the illustrated tables of Karol Schauer and comparing them to the recon-structive hypotheses provided by the archaeologists, it was possible to reconstruct the Middle Bronze Age fortifications and the Monumental Gate (Fig. 5). Having defined and validated the three-dimensional model of the architectures the CETMA team modeled the landscape that characterized the settlement. In addition, the rocks, the chromatic details and the entire digital context have been rebuilt with the support of valid spe-cialists. Figure 4 and Fig. 5 allow to see the reconstructive comparison between the illustrated tables (already the result of interpretation) and the three-dimensional model of the fortifications. Figure 6, instead, shows the details of the Monumental Gate.

Fig. 4. Reconstruction of the Middle Bronze Age fortress of Roca (illustration by Karol Schauer)

The idea is also to add the indigenous populations through an augmented reality app at the real scene. Therefore, it was very important to define both the 3D models of warriors who attacked Roca and of those who defended it. In addition, the continuous collaboration for research sharing and the mutual transfer of know-how between the scientific archaeological team and the CETMA production team allowed the correct digital interpretation of the characters represented in the siege scene. The reconstruction of clothes, weapons, movements and events are the results of a long sharing of knowledge. The visual result represents the efforts of years of studies. Actually, the user can see a reality based reconstruction of the ancient site with its defense structures during the Middle Bronze Age.

The availability of different skills among the workgroups operating for the recon-struction phases of the fortifications model, allowed the definition of a method for sharing

Fig. 5. 3D reconstruction of the Middle Bronze Age fortifications of Roca

Fig. 6. Details of the 3D reconstruction of the Middle Bronze Age Monumental Gate

information, that has been replicated for the other points to be displayed through AR and VR technologies in the same site. The international benchmark to which refer the visualization processes and outputs of the Roca Archaeological Project was The London Charter[1], whose set of principles is conventionally adopted by scholars challenging with 3D reconstructions in archaeological interpretation to ensure the intellectual and technical accuracy of the digital heritage visualization.

4.1   The Archaeological Documentation

As mentioned before, currently the state of preservation of the Middle Bronze Age fortification walls is unusual and stands alone all over the Mediterranean prehistory notwithstanding the ruins of this monument were largely damaged especially starting from the Late Medieval Age when the military citadel of Roca Vecchia was founded. Even though the analysis of the Middle Bronze Age fortification walls revealed different constructive phases probably starting at least since the late 17th century BC, the violent and sudden destruction by fire dated to the mid 14th century BC determined that everything (and everyone) was inside or close to the defensive walls was sealed in its functional situation that is most likely as it was a little before the destruction and the

---

[1] http://www.londoncharter.org/.

collapse of the upper parts of the masonry, so it was possible to record some unusual testimonies of this warlike event. The excavation of the archaeological contexts that were buried and protected by the collapsed walls has yielded a huge quantity of information useful for accurately determining the chronological and cultural aspects of this historic event.

According to the latest research [15, 17, 18], the late Middle Bronze Age fortification wall presents a slight curve along its entire length, approximately 200 m, with a maximum height of about 4 m and a maximum width of more than 23 m in correspondence with the Monumental Gate. The plan of the enceinte consisted of a monumental main entrance, at least five postern gates and a ditch excavated in the limestone bedrock (about 2.5 m wide and from 3 to 3.5 m deep) with a stone saved bridge for each entrance which, therefore, was not concealed. Inwards and outwards of the enclosure there were also structures of different shapes and dimensions such as towers, buttresses, cobbled paths, covered and uncovered environments or functional areas. Furthermore, the investigations carried out in the last few years in different areas of the external line of defense to the North of the Monumental Gate pointed out that the building front is still preserved in this section (more or less from 0,50 to about 1 m high) of the fortification and that small protruding rectangular towers (or buttresses) flanked the corridor entrances. The Monumental Gate is a building standing alone because of its dimensions and complexity; at the time of the siege, it was at least 25 m thick and its maximum height was probably from 8 to 10 m. A monumental and uncovered approaching path defended by a semicircular watchtower, the Corridor of the Orthostats, reached the centuries-old oak door of the gate controlled by two guardhouses; beyond the wooden door, the long covered Central Corridor arrived at the two opposed semicircular rooms placed within two imposing towers in the inner part of the gate.

Many of the postern gates were probably converted to refuges by small groups of people who set up all what they need (tens of pots, bone and stone tools, clay platforms or cooking stands) to dwell on the inside for the time of the siege. The most extraordinary discovery came from Postern C: the complete articulated skeletons (thus most likely preserving the positions of the bodies at the time of death) of seven individuals of both sexes and different ages (an adult male, an adult woman, two juveniles and four infants) were sitting or lying down close together, within a section at the western end of the corridor about 1,5 m long. This space was bounded to the South-West by a barricade made of stones, which probably served to blockade the outer entrance to the postern, and to the Northeast by a group of impasto vessels, mainly large closed-shape containers, arranged across the corridor and stacked one on top of the other. All these elements seem to indicate that the individuals found in Postern C were in danger and possibly were trying to hide behind the heap of vessels. Unfortunately, due to the fire in the fortification wall, they all died from asphyxia. The archaeological record from Postern C provided a unique opportunity to correlate the quantitative, qualitative and spatial data of the artefact assemblages with the people who brought those objects into the corridor, determined their spatial distribution, and used them. The location of the pottery within Postern C clearly attested two different functional areas: the first, at the western end of the corridor, was used mainly for the preparation and consumption of liquid and dry food, whereas the other, about 2 m to the North-East, was used for storing foodstuffs and possibly for cooking (as well as for sleeping and hiding).

To this date, the evidence collected from the other postern gates allows us to argue that many of them likely had an unusual function during the siege. Concerning with the Postern B and the Postern D, they both had rich assemblages of artefacts grouped in functional clusters as well as cooking structures on the inside. Additionally, the articulated complete skeleton of an infant was found in the Postern B. A smaller set of items was discovered in the Postern A in association with the complete articulated skeleton of a dog, whereas few artefacts were gathered from the Postern E.

On the other side, the Monumental Gate maybe kept its regular function throughout the course of the siege, although investigations revealed that it was a battle scene. The excavation of the southern semicircular room indeed led to the discovery of another very life-like archaeological context: the articulated skeleton of a young man (18–20 years old) was found in the lower part of the collapse layer. This individual would have died in a place somewhere above this room and then fallen down into it when the ceiling collapsed. The anthropological analysis confirmed this interpretation and revealed that the death was most likely due to some stab wounds on his back because of some clear unhealed marks on the bones. Two important artefacts were found in the same layer near the skeleton: an Aegean-type bronze dagger and the head of a bird made of hippopotamus ivory (this latter item probably refers to a Levantine-type duck pyxis). This further amazing snapshot from the siege of the Apennine fortification of Roca allows us to ask the question «Who was the warrior that owned these exotic artefacts? Was he an attacker or a defender?». A first answer could come from the currently ongoing isotope analysis. The battle and fire that destroyed the late-Apennine fortifications and settlement was a key event in the history of Roca and it was anything but an isolated occurrence since in most cases the coeval walled settlements in the region were also destroyed by fire around that time. The significance of this archaeological evidence could support the hypothesis of a possible large-scale cultural and maybe political turnover. Whatever happened something changed: it is the time (likely in the second half of the 14th century BC) of the archaeological transition from the Middle to the Recent Bronze Age. Many of these ruined settlements were nevermore rebuilt or anyway were not dwelled again before some centuries; those which went on to be occupied often reveal clear changes in material culture, architectures and funerary rituals even though preserving a local cultural identity.

During the last two decades the excavation of Recent Bronze Age levels (late 14th– 13th century BC) produced an impressive amount of Aegean and Aegean-type pottery: presently, the sample from Roca is far larger than those found anywhere else in Italy. This evidence indicates that Roca played a central role in the political and economic relationships between the indigenous communities of southeastern Italy and the Aegean seafarers. This was the result of the central role played by the site during the Bronze Age in the social and economic relationships with the Aegean traders. Two elements probably determined the importance of this site: the strategic value of its geographical location relative to the main sea-routes between the eastern and central Mediterranean, and the occurrence of the important cult place presently known as Grotta Poesia.

5   The Innovative Storytelling

As previously described, the main goal of the project was to vividly narrate to visitors of Roca archaeological site the event of the siege, which took place in the Bronze Age walled site around the mid-2nd millennium BC. Considering the current state of the site (Fig. 7), it was crucial to offer to non-specialist audiences instruments to understand the historical value of the surrounding.

Fig. 7. Roca Vecchia aerial view (ph. Teodoro Scarano)

After the digital translation of scientific data, starting from archaeological investigations to 3D modelling, the final step was to convey the information acquired to visitors (Fig. 8). This goal has been achieved with the use of immersive technologies to support the narration and the story telling, thus an augmented reality and a virtual reality applications were designed and developed.

5.1   Augmented Reality Application

The augmented reality application was designed and developed to present the Roca's siege of the Middle Bronze Age fortification wall. Visitors can access to the AR content when they are in front of the Monumental Gate remains. The Monumental Gate was the main passage to overcome the defence walls and probably, the theatre of some of the bloodiest battles. The content shows a sequence of the assault to the fortifications (Fig. 9).

The mobile augmented reality application was developed with Unity and deployed for Android mobile devices. The digital reconstruction was made with Autodesk Maya. As a first step, the 3D digital contents have been modelled with very high details. Therefore, the produced models have intrinsically a strong descriptive value. However, for the

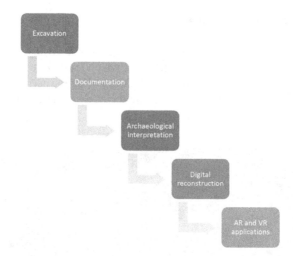

Fig. 8. From excavation to visitor use

Fig. 9. Frame of the assault to the Monumental Gate

mobile augmented reality app purpose, they could not be used as they were, due to the limited capabilities of mobile devices. One possible solution was to simplify the models in order to obtain less polygons in the scene, at the cost of less detailed meshes, and then to animate the scene in real time. Another solution was to render the scene animation offline, with all the details and high graphic fidelity, and afterwards aligned in real-time the 2D animation with the real environment. Since the aim of the project was to let visitors vividly and emotionally experience the historical events relative to the gates, the team decided for the most detailed and graphical appealing solution. Using the Arnold ray-tracing engine with Maya, the animation of the assault to the fortification was rendered as a sequence of png files with transparency, which allows blending the digital contents and the real world.

Afterwards the png sequence was imported in Unity (Fig. 10). A script controls the sequence and plays it at 30 fps when a fiducial marker is recognized.

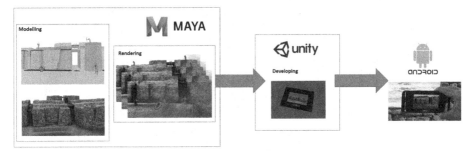

Fig. 10. Workflow

In order to obtain the correct alignment between the AR content and the real environment we placed two frames, serving as windows on the gate, at different height, both protected from the sun by a wooden structure (Fig. 11). The two frames were positioned at different heights in order to be of use for both adults and children.

Fig. 11. Windows on the Monumental Gate

The wooden structure represents the point of observation from where visitors have the best frontal view of the Monumental Gate and can take advantage of the AR application. Fiducial markers placed around the frame of the wooden windows trigger the contents (Fig. 12).

Fig. 12. Fiducial marker

In order to see the animation with the correct perspective, the user has to align a digitally drawn rectangle, triggered by the fiducial marker, with the frame (Fig. 13).

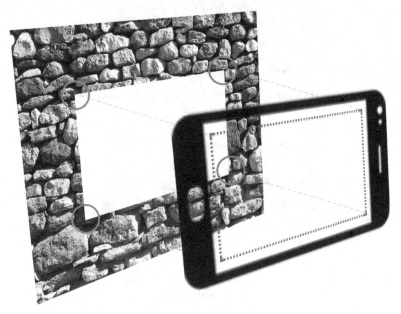

Fig. 13. AR alignment

Only after a close match between them, the sequence of the assault is showed (Fig. 14).

Fig. 14. The AR rectangle in red and the frame are aligned and the content is showed (Color figure online)

Finally, the visitors can enjoy the augmented reality content lined up with the remains of the walls. Digital and real contents are aligned and showed together thanks to the alpha channel presents in the images of the sequence (Fig. 15). The designed solution allowed solving a typical augmented reality problem regarding the outdoor alignment between digital contents and real big-sized objects.

In the setting up of the system, it was essential the support and collaboration of the Melendugno Municipality and the Superintendence authority (Soprintendenza Archeologia Belle Arti e Paesaggio per le Provincie di Brindisi, Lecce e Taranto).

5.2 Virtual Reality Application

The augmented reality app shows what happened on the fortifications and the exterior part of the Monumental Gate during the siege around the mid-2nd millennium BC. However, this is only one part of the story. From skeletons, bones and artefacts found in the area, archaeologists were able to reconstructs also the tragically events that led inhabitants of the area and warriors to death inside the defensive walls. In particular, it was possible to suppose the death by asphyxia of seven people inside one of the postern, and the fall of a young warrior from the wall to the inner room of the south tower after an armed fight.

Fig. 15. The assault on Roca's walls in augmented reality

In order to tell these detailed stories in a substantially evocative way a virtual reality app was designed and developed. The idea was to freeze the most dramatic moments of the two stories and put the visitor in the centre of the scenes.

As for the augmented reality system, the work started from the translation of archeologically data in digital models to be later adapted for virtual reality use (Fig. 16).

Fig. 16. Reconstruction of the Postern C evidence of siege.

In order to show the contents on site, the virtual reality application was developed for mobile system such as Samsung Gear VR. Thus, giving the performance limitation of these systems, and the goal of having a photorealistic result richness in details (Fig. 17), the two scenes had been pre-rendered as stereoscopic panoramic images. As for the AR application, the scenes were modelled and rendered in Autodesk Maya and imported in Unity for the VR development.

Fig. 17. High fidelity renderings

The stereoscopic effect was obtained rendering in Autodesk Maya two different images with two shifted virtual cameras, later displayed separately for each eyes in virtual reality as skyboxes created in Unity, (Fig. 18).

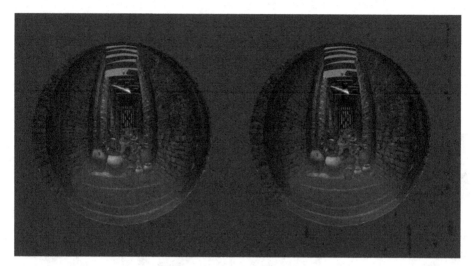

Fig. 18. Left and right skyboxes

The result is a stereoscopic panoramic view where the user is totally immersed in the scene, where he can look around with 360 degrees of freedom (Fig. 19). The user can choose what scene to explore in the Virtual Reality application thorough a 3D user interface, which connects the different views.

Fig. 19. VR application in use during a visit in the Roca archeological site

Visitors can use and enjoy the VR application inside the archeological site in a dedicated space not too far from the place where the stories narrate happened thousands of years ago.

6 Conclusion

In this paper, we described the methodology behind the realization of an augmented reality and a virtual reality application for the valorisation and communication of scientific results coming from archaeological investigations in the site of Roca Vecchia. This site, with its Bronze Age walled settlement, is currently one of the most important archaeological site in Europe, but despite the monumentality of the remains and the huge quality and quantity of the finds, the architecture itself is currently almost invisible to the public, as normal for ancient archeological sites of this age.

The main goal of the work illustrated was to offer to visitors of the site a way to have the chance to give a look and understand what is unseen and consequently to better engage with the heritage assets. In order to accomplish this objective, we developed a methodology that let us mold the archaeological investigations into vivid and immersive stories which were lost in a remote past. The methodology described underlines some key points, such as the choice of the points of interest in the site and the technologies for the realization, that take in account possible constraints such as limited budget and time. Furthermore, the workflow for the digital interpretation of the different reconstructive levels in Roca Vecchia site has been described in details. Finally, the obtained result showed the efficacy of a multidisciplinary teamwork made up of archaeologists, engineers, artists and supported by local public stakeholders such as the Melendugno Municipality and the Superintendence authority (Soprintendenza Archeologia Belle Arti e Paesaggio per le Provincie di Brindisi, Lecce e Taranto).

Thanks to the enthusiastic feedbacks from visitors, we consider this project the right starting point to design and develop more complete and advanced cultural experiences, and to set broader guidelines in order to simplify the transferability of the methodology described.

References

1. Azuma, R.T.: A survey of augmented reality. Presence: Teleoper. Virtual Environ. **6**(4), 355–385 (1997)
2. Bekele, M.K., et al.: A survey of augmented, virtual, and mixed reality for cultural heritage. J. Comput. Cult. Herit. (JOCCH) **11**(2), 1–36 (2018)
3. Demetrescu, E., et al.: Reconstructing the original splendour of the House of Caecilius Iucundus. A complete methodology for virtual archaeology aimed at digital exhibition. SCIRES-IT-SCI. RES. Inf. Technol. **6**(1), 51–66 (2016)
4. Dragoni, A.F., Quattrini, R., Sernani, P., Ruggeri, L.: Real scale augmented reality. A novel paradigm for archaeological heritage fruition. In: Luigini, A. (ed.) EARTH 2018. AISC, vol. 919, pp. 659–670. Springer, Cham (2019). https://doi.org/10.1007/978-3-030-12240-9_68
5. Fernández-Palacios, B.J., Morabito, D., Remondino, F.: Access to complex reality-based 3D models using virtual reality solutions. J. Cult. Herit. **23**, 40–48 (2017)

6. Gaitatzes, A., Christopoulos, D., Roussou, M.: Reviving the past: cultural heritage meets virtual reality. In: Proceedings of the 2001 Conference on Virtual Reality, Archeology, and Cultural Heritage (2001)
7. Gibb, J.G.: Imaginary, but by no means unimaginable: storytelling, science, and historical archaeology. Hist. Archaeol. **34**(2), 1–6 (2000)
8. Gonizzi Barsanti, S., et al.: 3D visualization of cultural heritage artefacts with virtual reality devices. In: 25th International CIPA Symposium 2015, vol. 40, no. 5W7. Copernicus Gesellschaft mbH (2015)
9. Kalay, Y., Thomas, K., Janice, A.: New Heritage, New Media and Cultural Heritage. Routledge, London (2008)
10. Lanier, J.: Dawn of the New Everything: A Journey Through Virtual Reality. Random House, New York (2017)
11. Milgram, P., Kishino, F.: A taxonomy of mixed reality visual displays. IEICE Trans. Inf. Syst. **77**(12), 1321–1329 (1994)
12. Noh, Z., Sunar, M.S., Pan, Z.: A review on augmented reality for virtual heritage system. In: Chang, M., Kuo, R., Kinshuk, Chen, G.D., Hirose, M. (eds.) Learning by Playing. Game-based Education System Design and Development. Edutainment 2009. Lecture Notes in Computer Science, vol. 5670. Springer, Heidelberg (2009). https://doi.org/10.1007/978-3-642-03364-3_7
13. Pagliara, C.: Santuari costieri. In: Proceedings of the 30th Magna Grecia Conference, pp. 503–526, Taranto (1991)
14. Pagliara, C.: La Grotta poesia di Roca (Melendugno, Lecce). Note preliminari. In: Annali della Scuola Normale Superiore di Pisa, vol. XVII, pp. 267–328 (1987)
15. Quattrini, R., et al. virtual reconstruction of lost architectures: from the TLS survey to ar visualization. Int. Arch. Photogramm. Remote Sens. Spat. Inf. Sci. **41** (2016)
16. Scarano, T.: Refuge or dwelling place? The middle bronze age fortification walls of Roca (Lecce): spatial and functional analysis of postern C. Rivista di Scienze Preistoriche **LXI**, 95–122 (2011)
17. Scarano, T.: Roca I. Le fortificazioni della media età del Bronzo. Strutture, contesti, materiali (Claudio Grenzi Editore, Foggia) (2012)
18. Scarano, T.: Die Belagerung der Bronzezeitlichen Befestigung von Roca. In: Meller, H., Schefzik, M. (eds.) Krieg. Eine Archäologische Spurensuche/War. Decoding its archaeological traces. Special exhibition catalogue, Landesamt für Denkmalpflege und Ärchaologie Sachsen-Anhalt, Landesmuseum für Vorgeschichte, Halle (Saale), pp. 309–311 (2015)
19. Scarano, T.: L'assedio di Roca. La guerra in un santuario costiero del Salento nel II millennio a.C. Archeologia Viva, Maggio/Giugno, pp. 40–53 (2016)
20. Scarano, T.: Gli insediamenti costieri fortificati della Puglia meridionale nella prima metà del II millennio a.C. In: Radina, F. (ed.) Studi di Preistoria e Protostoria 4, Preistoria e Protostoria della Puglia, pp. 965–969 (Firenze 2017)
21. Stefano, B.: The importance of being honest: issues of transparency in digital visualization of architectural heritage. Ippolito Alfonso. Handbook of Research (2017)
22. Steuer, J.: Defining virtual reality: dimensions determining telepresence. J. Commun. **42**(4), 73–93 (1992)
23. Tom Dieck, M.C., Jung, T.H.: Value of augmented reality at cultural heritage sites: a stakeholder approach. J. Dest. Mark. Manag. **6**(2), 110–117 (2017)
24. Vlahakis, V., et al.: Archeoguide: first results of an augmented reality, mobile computing system in cultural heritage sites. Virtual Reality Archeol. Cult. Herit. **9**(10.1145), 584993–585015 (2001)
25. Tscheu, F., Buhalis, D.: Augmented reality at cultural heritage sites. In: Inversini, A., Schegg, R. (eds.) Information and Communication Technologies in Tourism 2016, pp. 607–619. Springer, Cham (2016). https://doi.org/10.1007/978-3-319-28231-2_44

Promoting Awareness on Sustainable Behavior Through an AR-Based Art Gallery

Luca Turchet[(✉)] and Jhonny Hueller

Department of Information Engineering and Computer Science,
University of Trento, Trento, Italy
luca.turchet@unitn.it

Abstract. This paper presents "Augmented Gallery", an art gallery in the form of a networked, AR-based, audio-visual system, which was devised to convey the visitors a clear message about the urgency of taking action to address environmental threats such as pollution, climate change, and biodiversity loss. The system was designed to both entertain and educate the visitors, empowering them to understand how unsustainable behaviours may affect our lives in the future and emphasize the need to take relevant actions for building a more environmentally sustainable world. Augmented Gallery consists of an AR app running on networked smartphones used by visitors. The app displays, at visual and auditory level, scenes representing various healthy environments as well as, via user interactions, their counterpart affected by the consequences of an unaddressed climate change and unsustainable human behaviour, exposing predictions based on the Intergovernmental Panel on Climate Change climate report. A user study was conducted, where the gallery was evaluated during two public events. The results showed that opinions about Augmented Gallery were generally very positive. Furthermore, visitors admitted that attending the gallery increased their awareness on environmental issues and their consequences on the planet.

Keywords: Augmented reality · Sustainability · Persuasive technology

1 Introduction

Art has a unique power to convey messages and throughout history artists have intelligently exploited this power in their masterpieces. The recent advancements in Augmented Reality (AR) technologies are not only impacting contexts such as industry 4.0 or learning, but are also fostering new possibilities for artistic creation. In particular, the use of AR in the art experience is creating unique new opportunities to raise awareness and reach audiences about various topics. As of today, a very timely topic is that of climate change and its consequences. Various artists worldwide are using their craftsmanship, mastery and virtuosity to create awareness of environmental issues. This includes also AR-based art

© Springer Nature Switzerland AG 2020
L. T. De Paolis and P. Bourdot (Eds.): AVR 2020, LNCS 12243, pp. 53–65, 2020.
https://doi.org/10.1007/978-3-030-58468-9_4

forms (see e.g., exhibitions at Singapore ArtScience Museum's Climate S.O.S –
Season of Sustainability[1]).

Various studies have investigated the use of AR applications in cultural heritage [11], music performance [14,16], or other artistic contexts [9]. Whereas those
studies involved different hardware technologies (including handheld devices,
smart glasses, or AR-headsets [2,20]), common to all the developed systems is
the utilization of AR technologies to superimpose virtual content to a scene (e.g.,
annotations to a painting [15]), or objects (e.g., virtual objects superimposed to
items in museums [6,13]). However, to the best of authors' knowledge, little
attention has been devoted by the artistic and research community to the use
of AR technologies as a medium to augment an environment "as such", rather
than objects present in it. Indeed, despite this is not its primary use, AR has the
possibility to generate virtual content that instead of augmenting a real content,
substitutes it. This enables the virtual reconfiguration of a real environment into
a virtual one, which is nevertheless linked to the real scene.

On the other hand, various studies have investigated the experience of users in
interacting with AR technologies involved in contexts of museums or art galleries
(see e.g., [4,7,10]). However, thus far the specific topic of climate change has been
little addressed by the AR community dealing with art. According to Coen et al.
[5], AR has the potential to help educate people on climate change and promoting
sustainable behaviours. In recent years a handful of artists have employed AR
technologies to attempt to raise awareness of climate change, under the premise
that such a technological medium would help audiences better "experience" it
and its consequences.

In this paper, we first explore the concept of using AR in a mobile phone app
to enable the repurposing of environments into AR-based art galleries. Secondly,
we apply this concept to the artistic representation of the topic of climate change,
with the ultimate aim of educating and raising the visitor's awareness towards
this timely issue. We position our system, which we call "Augmented Gallery", as
a persuasive technology [8,12] because by allowing visitors to experience in novel
ways the environmental issues, it is intended to increase knowledge about them
and consequently modify users' attitudes or behaviours. Finally, we assess the
developed technology and its conveyed user experience via an ecologically-valid
user study conducted during a set of artistic exhibitions.

2 Augmented Gallery

Augmented Gallery is a networked AR-based system developed to convey the visitors a clear message about the urgency of taking action to address environmental
threats such as climate change and biodiversity loss. The system was designed
to both entertain and educate the viewers, empowering them to understand how
unsustainable behaviours may affect our lives in the future and emphasize the
need to take relevant actions for building a more environmentally sustainable

---

[1] https://www.unenvironment.org/news-and-stories/story/new-cleanseas-augmented
-reality-experience-merges-real-world-and-virtual.

world. To achieve this goal, Augmented Gallery uses interactive virtual objects to show to the viewer the consequences of an unaddressed climate change, exposing predictions based on the Intergovernmental Panel on Climate Change (IPCC) climate report[2].

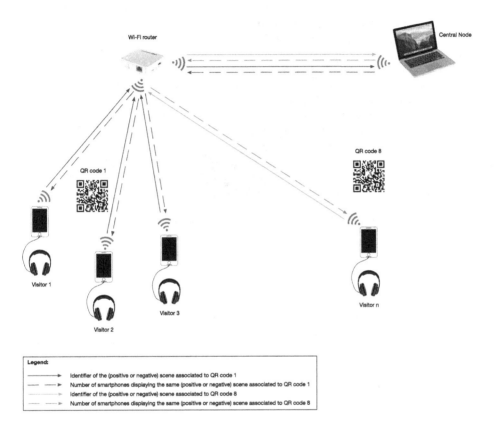

Fig. 1. A schematic representation of the networked architecture of Augmented Gallery, including its main components and data flow. Each QR code represents a scene.

Augmented Gallery is a networked system consisting of smartphones (used by the visitors), which run a dedicated audio-visual AR app (see Fig. 1). The app consists of eight scenes. Each scene is defined by a unique QR code, freely placeable on walls of whatever environment (see Fig. 2). The placement of the QR codes is arbitrary and each QR code can be placed independently from one another. The scenes represent various harmonious environments (the "positive environments") as well as their counterpart affected by the consequences of an unaddressed climate change and unsustainable human behaviour (the "negative

---

[2] Synthesis Report of the IPCC Fifth Assessment Report of 2014, https://www.ipcc.ch/.

environments"). The latter include scenarios like rising sea levels, droughts, acid rains, poisonous smog, and floods. Each negative environment was created from the positive one by changing it to reflect the outcomes of the climate change hypothesize by IPCC.

Fig. 2. A picture of a participant interacting with Augmented Gallery.

At visual level, the AR app is based on two types of metaphors. The first type consists of a window-like object (see Fig. 3). The QR code placed on a wall generates a window in which a small 3D environment is shown. The window is rendered so to hide a significant part of the virtual environment from the viewers, forcing them to change perspective to be able to see the whole environment: the app was designed to respond to various kinds of interactions of the viewers, who could get close or far, or move to left, right, top and bottom to change the angle of view (see Fig. 4). Another interaction is the user's touch onto the virtual glass of the window (i.e., onto the smartphone touchscreen), which enables the change of scene from the positive environment to the negative one, and vice versa. When the visitor encounters for the first time a QR code, the displayed scene shows an environment untouched by pollution and climate change or in harmony with human activities. Upon the user's touch, the virtual glass slowly brightens to the point in which it becomes a white opaque wall. At this point the scene is replaced with the corresponding negative environment. The glass slowly returns to its normal transparent state and the changed scene is displayed.

The second type of metaphor is diorama (see Fig. 5). Dioramas are miniature models of various scenes or objects, often encapsulated in a glass showcase. These items do not feature the same rendering effect of the scenes with windows metaphors, and all the scene is show instantly to the viewer. Moreover it has the possibility to grow or shrink with a pinch gesture on the touchscreen allowing the viewer to be able to see the details. The virtual dioramas also feature a changing

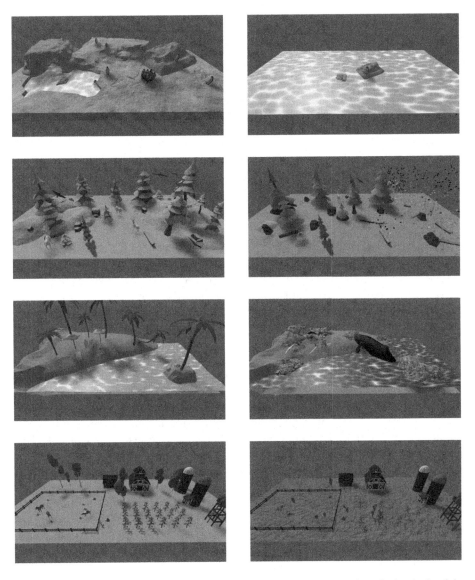

Fig. 3. Screenshots of the AR scenes based on the windows metaphor. Left: the healthy environment; right: the same environment affected by climate change consequences.

environment, which can be changed in the same fashion as the windows by touching the smartphone touchscreen.

At auditory level, the AR app provides a soundscape[3] for each of the positive and negative scenes described above. The soundscapes were ad-hoc composed

---

[3] The term "soundscape" refers to the sonic environment, the aural counterpart of the term landscape referred to visually-related items in an environment.

Fig. 4. Screenshots of different perspectives of one of the AR scenes. On the left the scene is shown from a front view, on the right the perspective is changed, which allows to see other parts of the environment not visible using the front view. The blue background was not rendered, but the real world tracked by the mobile camera was visible. (Color figure online)

[18,19] using audio content retrieved from the online repository Freesound.org [1]. The sonic material reflected the virtual content visually displayed on the smartphones screens. The soundscapes of the positive scenes were designed to be radically different from those of the corresponding negative scenes. The choice of using a sonic layer additional to the visual AR content was due to the aim of achieving a more immersive experience.

The smartphones present in the gallery are connected over a Wi-Fi link to a central node. The central node (which can be another smartphone or a computer) has the function to receive/route messages from/to the other smartphones. This network infrastructure is only utilized to create a dynamic soundscape, which varies in function of the number of visitors exploring a same scene (see Fig. 1). Specifically, in the default configuration (when only one visitor is in front of a scene), only one audio track is played back as soon as the QR code is recognized by the software and the scene is shown to the viewer. As soon as more visitors are exploring the same scene, a new audio track is played on top of the previous ones. This design choice of creating more complex soundscapes as a function of the number of viewers aimed at increasing social presence [17] leveraging the audio channel.

To enable communication among the devices in the network we utilized the Open Sound Control protocol (OSC) [21]. The AR app was created in Unity and was built only for Android-based mobile phones. It used the third party tool Vuforia, one of the best AR toolkit available for Unity, as well as the plugin OSCJack, a lightweight implementation of the OSC protocol. Only static IP were used (assigned by the router), which avoided to create a local network session within the Unity application that would have increased the burden on the hardware and, as a consequence, decreased the performances.

Fig. 5. Screenshots of the AR scenes based on the diorama metaphor. Left: the healthy environment; right: the same environment affected by climate change consequences.

Augmented Gallery was developed only for Android-based smartphones. The minimum and recommended requirements to run the app on Android-based devices are listed in Table 1.

Table 1. Minimum and recommended requirements to run Augmented Gallery on Android-based devices.

	Minimum requirements	Recommended requirements
Operating system version	Android 7 (Nougat)	Android 9 (Pie)
RAM	4 GB	6 GB
Memory	140 MB	140 MB
Resolution	720 × 1280 pixel	2340 × 1080 pixel
System chip	HiSilicon Kirin 659	Snapdragon 855
GPU	ARM Mali-T830 MP2	GPU Adreno 640

3 User Study

The user study aimed at investigating whether it is possible to convey a message about climate change and its consequences by means of an art gallery entirely based on AR and wireless network technologies. Augmented Gallery was tested twice was set up in two places: a coffee shop and at one of the halls of the University of Trento, which provided ecologically-valid settings for an art exhibition (see Fig. 2). A total of 24 visitors (aged between 18 and 40, mean age = 22.3) took part to the evaluation (13 males, 8 females, 3 preferred not to say their gender).

At the outset, visitors were asked to download and install the app on their smartphones as well as to wear the headphones. They were also instructed about the interactions afforded by the app. As the app could run only on Android-based smartphones, the participants using iOS-based smartphones were given a smartphone pre-configured with the app. Similarly, participants who did not have a pair of headphones were provided with them by the experimenter. Each participant was invited to freely explore the gallery, starting from a point in the gallery at his/her choice (in this way the order of the visited scenes was randomized).

After having explored the whole gallery, participants were asked to fill an ad-hoc questionnaire. The questionnaire comprised demographic information such as age and gender, as well as the level of familiarity with AR technologies and the degree of familiarity with the climate change topic (the last two items were evaluated on a 7-point Likert scale, with 1 = little familiar, 7 = very familiar). Moreover, the questionnaire comprised the following questions to be evaluated on a 7-point Likert scale (with 1 = strongly disagree, 7 = strongly agree):

- *[Learning.] I learned something new about climate change and its consequences thanks to this AR exhibition.*
- *[More Informed.] This AR exhibition made me more knowledgeable about the climate change issue and its consequences.*
- *[Motivation.] This AR exhibition stimulated my curiosity to learn new things about climate change and its consequences.*

- *[Awareness.] This AR exhibition improved my awareness of the climate change issue and its consequences.*
- *[Behavioural Change.] This AR exhibition can change the way I think or behave in relation to the climate change issue and its consequences.*
- *[Immersion.] I was very engaged with the AR exhibition.*
- *[Recommendation.] I recommend this AR exhibition to others.*
- *[Appreciation.] I appreciated this AR exhibition.*

In addition, participants were asked to answer the following open ended questions: *"What did you enjoy the most about the exhibition?"; "What did you enjoy the least about the exhibition?"*. Finally, participants were also allowed to leave an open comment about their experience. On average, participants took 30 min to complete the experiment.

3.1   Results

The responses of the questionnaire items "familiarity with AR technologies" and "familiarity with the climate change topic" received relatively low rankings (respectively mean = 3.2, standard error = 0.28, and mean = 4, standard error = 0.31) indicating that on average participants did not have too much direct experience with AR technologies and had little awareness about the climate change topic.

Figure 6 illustrates the results of the other questionnaire items. As it is possible to notice from the figure, the evaluations were all above neutrality. Through the gallery, participants felt to have learned something new about climate change

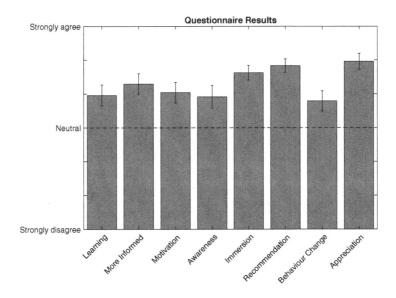

Fig. 6. Mean and standard error of the questionnaire items (evaluated on a 7-point Likert scale).

and its consequences. They reported that the gallery made them more knowledgeable about the showcased topic, motivated them to learn more and improved their awareness about it. Evaluations also indicate a potential for behavioural change that the exhibition could trigger. Results also show that the gallery was welcomed by visitors, in terms of appreciation, engagement and potential for recommendation to other visitors.

Interestingly, high linear correlations were found among the responses to some of the questionnaire items. These were identified by means of a Pearson's correlation test. Table 2 shows the highest among the significant correlations between the questionnaire items. It is worth noticing that high correlations were found between items related to learning aspects and items related to behaviours. This suggests that stimulating knowledge acquisition about climate change and making participants more informed about it via an artistic installation has the potential to rise the public awareness on such a topic. As a consequence, according to the results, this may induce sustainable behaviours in individuals.

Table 2. The highest correlations between questionnaire items, identified with a Pearson's correlation test.

Pair	R	p
Learning-more informed	0.76	<0.001
Learning-motivation	0.79	<0.001
Learning-awareness	0.7	<0.001
Learning-behavioural change	0.6	<0.01
More informed-motivation	0.61	<0.01
More informed-awareness	0.8	<0.001
More informed-behavioural change	0.75	<0.001
Motivation-awareness	0.68	<0.001
Motivation-behavioural change	0.62	<0.01
Awareness-behavioural change	0.84	<0.001

The evaluations illustrated in Fig. 6 and the correlations reported in Table 2 are also reflected in the participants' answers to the open-ended questions. These responses were analyzed using an inductive thematic analysis [3]. The analysis was conducted by generating codes, which were further organized into themes that reflected patterns, as described below.

Enjoyment and Engagement. Five participants commented to have appreciated the experience of exploring Augmented Gallery, and to have felt engaged with it (e.g., participant 9 stated: *"I liked the app because it teaches about climate change."*; participant 23 reported *"I enjoyed being able to see the environments before and after the consequences."*).

AR Medium Appreciation. Four participants appreciated the fact that the AR medium was utilized to convey the messages about sustainability and found this approach original (e.g., participant 17 reported *"It is a different approach on a topic that is usually addressed with other and less interactive tools"*; participant 18 stated *"it is a great app to show how dangerous climate change would affect the earth and the living creatures on it."*).

Increased Awareness. Six participants reported that the exhibition was effective in making them reflect on the climate change issue and about the needs of a sustainable behaviour of mankind. (e.g., participant 2 stated: *"I enjoyed the fact that the app allows people to see what pollution entails and I hope that people put more awareness about it and could adopt more ecological behaviours."*; participant 13 stated *"It was inspiring for me to see how to pass from a normal environment to a changed one and noticing what could remain of it."*; participant 22 reported *"It is a great initiative to represent the future planet if we don't modify our behaviours."*).

4   Discussion and Conclusions

Augmented Gallery differs from most AR applications in that it does not augment objects in a real environment with additional virtual content (e.g., textual annotations or virtual objects that enhance the real objects with contextual information). Rather, it completely substitutes a part of the real environment (typically a wall) with a virtual scene (e.g., a virtual painting). This allows to turn any environment in an art gallery, by simply placing in it the QR codes at the positions where the virtual scenes are intended to be displayed.

Our system was conceived to sensitize visitors towards climate change, with the ultimate goal of triggering sustainable behaviours in them. The results of the evaluation, conducted in ecologically-valid contexts, revealed that visitors' opinions about Augmented Gallery were generally positive. In particular, visitors admitted that attending the gallery increased their awareness on environmental issues and their consequences on the planet and its lifeforms.

Nevertheless, it is important to notice that our system presents technical limitations. We chose the smartphone as a platform for our system given its use much more widespread compared to smart glasses or dedicated AR-headsets. The public is already familiar with the use of smartphones and the distribution and installation of app is trivial. The main drawback of using smartphones is the limited performance of their hardware, which forces the designers to limit the complexity of the AR content displayed in real-time, as well as the scarcity in diversity of input methods, which are limited to touchscreens, cameras and movement sensors.

Overall, it is possible to conclude that Augmented Gallery was successful in evoking awareness among visitors about the climate change and its consequences. Whether or not our artistic creation was actually capable of fostering sustainable behaviours in the visitors was not the object of this study. Therefore, it remains an open question whether Augmented Gallery would have a meaningful impact on visitor's attitudes and behaviours. Nevertheless, we agree with Coen et al. [5]

that there is a lot of potential for social action using AR, in particular to give us a better understanding of our impact on the planet.

In future work, encouraged by the success of the exhibitions reported by visitors, we plan to perform other exhibitions involving Augmented Gallery, to allow audiences to immerse themselves in the challenge of tackling the climate change problem. We also plan to use the same architecture developed for Augmented Gallery, to explore other relevant topics, with the aim of artistically conveying other messages for positive social impact. Via AR-based art it is possible to deliver some incredibly powerful messages, and as a consequence create great awareness and engagement on climate-related communications. It is the hope of the authors that this paper could inspire others to create artistic installations leveraging the AR medium to convey positive messages about the benefits resulting from sustainable behaviours.

References

1. Akkermans, V., et al.: Freesound 2: an improved platform for sharing audio clips. In: Proceedings of the International Society for Music Information Retrieval Conference (2011)
2. Baber, C., et al.: Augmenting museums and art galleries. In: Interact, pp. 439–446 (2001)
3. Braun, V., Clarke, V.: Using thematic analysis in psychology. Qual. Res. Psychol. **3**(2), 77–101 (2006)
4. Chang, K.E., Chang, C.T., Hou, H.T., Sung, Y.T., Chao, H.L., Lee, C.M.: Development and behavioral pattern analysis of a mobile guide system with augmented reality for painting appreciation instruction in an art museum. Comput. Educ. **71**, 185–197 (2014)
5. Coen, S., Drumm, I., Fantinelli, S.: Promoting pro-environmental behaviour through augmented reality and persuasive informational power: a pilot study. Hum. Aff. **29**(3), 339–351 (2019)
6. Coulton, P., Smith, R., Murphy, E., Pucihar, K.Č., Lochrie, M.: Designing mobile augmented reality art applications: addressing the views of the galleries and the artists. In: Proceedings of the 18th International Academic MindTrek Conference: Media Business, Management, Content & Services, pp. 177–182 (2014)
7. tom Dieck, M.C., Jung, T.H., Dieck, D.: Enhancing art gallery visitors' learning experience using wearable augmented reality: generic learning outcomes perspective. Curr. Issues Tour. **21**(7), 2014–2034 (2018)
8. Fogg, B.J.: Persuasive technology: using computers to change what we think and do. Ubiquity **2002**(December), 2 (2002)
9. Geroimenko, V.: Augmented reality technology and art: the analysis and visualization of evolving conceptual models. In: 2012 16th International Conference on Information Visualisation, pp. 445–453. IEEE (2012)
10. Jung, T., tom Dieck, M.C., Lee, H., Chung, N.: Effects of virtual reality and augmented reality on visitor experiences in museum. In: Inversini, A., Schegg, R. (eds.) Information and Communication Technologies in Tourism 2016, pp. 621–635. Springer, Cham (2016). https://doi.org/10.1007/978-3-319-28231-2_45
11. Keil, J., et al.: A digital look at physical museum exhibits: designing personalized stories with handheld augmented reality in museums. In: 2013 Digital Heritage International Congress (DigitalHeritage), vol. 2, pp. 685–688. IEEE (2013)

12. Knowles, B., Blair, L., Walker, S., Coulton, P., Thomas, L., Mullagh, L.: Patterns of persuasion for sustainability. In: Proceedings of the 2014 Conference on Designing Interactive Systems, pp. 1035–1044 (2014)
13. Lanir, J., Wecker, A.J., Kuflik, T., Felberbaum, Y.: Shared mobile displays: an exploratory study of their use in a museum setting. Pers. Ubiquit. Comput. **20**(4), 635–651 (2016). https://doi.org/10.1007/s00779-016-0931-y
14. Mazzanti, D., Zappi, V., Caldwell, D., Brogni, A.: Augmented stage for participatory performances. In: Proceedings of the Conference on New Interfaces for Musical Expression, pp. 29–34 (2014)
15. Pierdicca, R., Frontoni, E., Zingaretti, P., Sturari, M., Clini, P., Quattrini, R.: Advanced interaction with paintings by augmented reality and high resolution visualization: a real case exhibition. In: De Paolis, L.T., Mongelli, A. (eds.) AVR 2015. LNCS, vol. 9254, pp. 38–50. Springer, Cham (2015). https://doi.org/10.1007/978-3-319-22888-4_4
16. Poupyrev, I., et al.: Augmented groove: collaborative jamming in augmented reality. In: ACM SIGGRAPH 2000 Conference Abstracts and Applications, p. 77 (2000)
17. Sallnäs, E.L.: Effects of communication mode on social presence, virtual presence, and performance in collaborative virtual environments. Presence: Teleoper. Virtual Environ. **14**(4), 434–449 (2005)
18. Truax, B.: Soundscape, acoustic communication and environmental sound composition. Contemp. Music Rev. **15**(1–2), 49–65 (1996)
19. Turchet, L., Serafin, S.: Investigating the amplitude of interactive footstep sounds and soundscape reproduction. Appl. Acoust. **74**(4), 566–574 (2013)
20. Tussyadiah, I.P., Jung, T.H., tom Dieck, M.C.: Embodiment of wearable augmented reality technology in tourism experiences. J. Travel Res. **57**(5), 597–611 (2018)
21. Wright, M.: Open sound control: an enabling technology for musical networking. Organ. Sound **10**(3), 193–200 (2005)

Voice Interaction with Artworks via Indoor Localization: A Vocal Museum

Paolo Sernani$^{(\boxtimes)}$, Sergio Vagni, Nicola Falcionelli, Dagmawi Neway Mekuria,
Selene Tomassini, and Aldo Franco Dragoni

Department of Information Engineering, Università Politecnica delle Marche,
Via Brecce Bianche 12, 60131 Ancona, Italy
{p.sernani,a.f.dragoni}@univpm.it
{n.falcionelli,d.n.mekuria,s.tomassini}@pm.univpm.it

Abstract. While the adoption of Information Technology is rapidly
growing in Cultural Heritage with a plethora of possible applications,
there is still the need to offer technology-enhanced museum and exhibition visits without overwhelming or distracting the user from the
artworks. Therefore, this paper presents the Vocal Museum, a system
combining Internet of Things and Artificial Intelligence to offer customized visits to museums and exhibitions. To achieve such goal, the
Vocal Museum is composed of a set of software applications to localize
the user inside the exhibition and communicate with her/him via vocal
or written interactions.

1 Introduction

With the term "Cultural Heritage" (CH) we usually refer to sites, movable and
immovable artifacts, practices, knowledge items, and other things identified as
important and culturally relevant, and thus worthy of conscious conservation
measures [4]. While preserving CH artifacts and artworks, museums and exhibitions are considered an attraction by CH experts as well as by a broader
audience. However, the wideness of the public which might visit a museum or
an exhibition poses important challenges to museums curators, administrators,
and staff, given that visitors differ for their level of expertise, age and general
interests; they might be alone or in group; they might have different interests
on the shown artworks. Such factors make hard for museum curators to catch
the attention of visitors [1]. Moreover, the visitors can be overwhelmed by a
lot of interesting information, but hard to assimilate. Information such as the
biography of a painter or the details about the shown artifacts are essential
in understanding and enjoying the visit. However, such information might also
cause the visitors, especially the youngest, to lose focus, even when summarized
by a human guide [11].

In recent years, Information Technology (IT) has been widely adopted to face
some of the challenges of CH. Digital virtual artifacts are often applied to create

---

D. N. Mekuria—Deceased.

L. T. De Paolis and P. Bourdot (Eds.): AVR 2020, LNCS 12243, pp. 66–78, 2020.
https://doi.org/10.1007/978-3-030-58468-9_5

engaging visits, building Virtual Reality (VR), Augmented Reality (AR) and Mixed Reality (MR) experiences [33]. In addition to make learning enjoyable in CH sites [23], VR, AR, and MR can be used to implement gamified visits: the game elements encourage visitors in moving towards specific points of interest or in exploring additional content [15,20]. Nevertheless, while virtual artifacts are essential in applications to share and visualize through AR the reconstructions of the archeological sites which would be impossible to view [6], they can increase enjoyment at the cost of drifting apart the visitors from the real artworks in a museum. Moreover, audio AR has the potential to encourage participation and interaction in communicating cultural information [5], and to provide plausible 3D experience in virtual environments [7].

Therefore, in this paper, we present an architecture of a system and its implementation, integrating Internet of Things (IoT) for indoor localization and Artificial Intelligence (AI) for chatbots to offer customized visits to museums and exhibitions. The proposed system is based on voice and written interaction, with the aim of supporting the visitors during the exploration of a museum. The system is intended to be personal: the goal is giving the users the chance of asking (and getting) the information they desire and ask for, according to the artwork they are looking at. Moreover, such system is supposed to avoid as much as possible to put digital visual artifacts between the users and the artworks. Thus, we exploit chatbots, i.e. computer programs that interact with users using natural language [30], to build a conversational interface between the visitor and one or more artworks. Through a mobile app, while looking at a specific artwork, the visitor is invited to ask questions and interact via voice or text messages, according to her/his preferences. The system is able to identify the user position inside the museum thanks to an indoor localization component based on the Ultra-WideBand (UWB) radio technology.

Compared to the state of the art about new fruition paradigms of CH, this paper contributes in proposing the integration of mature technologies (indoor localization and chatbots) to build a real system, rather than giving a theoretical contribution. Each user of the system gets the possibility of directly talking about the artworks they are admiring, asking precise information, even continuously if willing to do so. Such personalized service would not be possible with a traditional audio guide or even with a human guide. To this end, the proposed system has the potential to become a stable service that museum curators might be willing to offer, aiming at reaching the broadest audience. The proposed system transforms a museum into a Vocal Museum, i.e. an exhibition the visitor can talk to.

The rest of this paper is organized as follows. Section 2 compares our proposal with the related works about vocal interaction, chatbots and indoor localization in museums and exhibitions. Section 3 presents our system, describing the architecture of each single components and the behaviours which make the system work at runtime. Finally, Sect. 4 draws the conclusions of the presented research and sketches future works.

2 Related Works

The idea of offering voice-based natural interaction with digital tools during guided tours of museums or Cultural Heritage (CH) sites is not new; the suitability of dialogues in cultural tourism has been advocated since the first decade of 2000's [32]. For example, in [25], the authors present the desirable features of tour-guide robots for large-scale exhibitions: the voice interaction is identified as the most natural and user-friendly means of interacting with machines. Following such idea, extensive research has been carried out in exploiting mobile robots as tour guides [31], even if noisy environments and inaccuracy of voice recognition were perceived as potential drawbacks [9]. In parallel, instead of using robots, other works proposed to interact with users using Personal Digital Assistants (PDAs) [2,19]. In fact, this paper starts from the availability of modern handheld devices such as smartphones and tablets, as well as commercial vocal assistants. Hence, this work proposes to exploit such technologies, which are mature enough, instead of expensive mobile robots, as successfully done in Cultural Heritage with Augmented Reality [29].

More recently, voice interaction has been applied to virtualize parts of the visit to a museum or a CH site, including serious games for learning purposes [21], virtual avatars to engage the youngest [34], virtual tours [18], and Virtual Reality applications specifically designed for users with motor disabilities [12]. In fact, virtual elements have been proven useful to increase sentiments such as curiosity and immersion during museum visits, in particular for learning purposes [22]. Nevertheless, the use of virtual elements hides potential issues, such as the risk of presenting virtual artifacts that can decrease interest in actual content [10]. In addition, the research carried out in storytelling with virtual Immersive Museums Environments (IMEs) has been mostly limited to scholarly prose. So far, the research focus has been mostly on the improvements of the technological features, being disconnected from the emotions, evocations and morals which characterize the contemplation of real artifact [24]. Therefore, this work avoids putting virtual artifacts between the visitor and the artworks during the museum tour. Instead, while observing paintings, statues and artworks, the visitor gets the chance to ask information in natural language. The indoor localization via UWB allows getting such information without even specify the correct name of the artworks, exploiting proximity.

However, many factors can negatively impact on the usability of the voice interaction, in particular for the Automatic Speech Recognition (ASR) component needed to understand the input given by the users [27]. In fact, noisy backgrounds, users' age and accent, and even the preference of certain user categories towards texting rather than voice input can undermine visitors' willingness to use the offered voice interaction. To overcome such limitations, as an alternative to voice interaction, the proposed system include the possibility to interact via text messages using a text chatbot included in the system frontend, i.e. the cross-platform mobile app presented in Sect. 3. Other research works highlighted the suitability of chatbots for CH and museums. Schaffer et al. [28] highlights the potential of chatbots, being capable of responding meaningfully to users' input, and they are always available, in contrast to personal tours. In addition, as reported by Gaia et al. [14], chatbots can be applied with the purpose of increasing visitors engagement.

Finally, the proposed system includes a component to perform the indoor localization of the visitor, while she/he moves through the artworks inside the museum. In fact, one of the requirements of the proposed system is understanding the current interest of the visitor using the mobile app. In this way, the system can invite the user to ask questions about specific details of the artwork she/he is contemplating. In the scientific literature, indoor localization inside museums has been achieved in multiple ways [17]. For example, Cliffe et al. [8] uses vision-based recognition to identify artworks and provide audio AR (without voice or text interaction). Alletto et al. [1] also identifies artworks via image recognition, but uses BLE-based indoor tracking to reduce the candidates for the recognition and make user position available to other services. However, the main goal of indoor localization is to provide an enhanced user experience during the visit [26]. To this end, tracking inside museums can provide data to perform behaviour analysis and build personalized visits, as in [16]. While in its current implementation our system uses UWB localization uniquely with the goal of understanding the proximity of the user to a certain artwork, such component has the potential to be used also for behaviour analysis in future developments.

3   A Vocal Museum

We propose a "Vocal Museum" system, i.e. a set of software applications with the following goals:

- provide an interface to the user through which she/he can query the desired information about the museum and its artworks, asking it vocally or in a written chat with a chatbot;
- localize the user inside the museum, in order to understand her/his proximity to artworks and proactively provide the correct information, encouraging her/him to ask questions;
- be reliable and credible during the interactions with the user, generating proper answers with contents related to the artworks shown in the museum.

Obviously, the typical use case for the Vocal Museum system is the visit to a museum or an exhibition. At the entrance, the user is invited to download the museum app, which will act as an interface with the Vocal Museum. Moreover, the staff gives her/him a tag with the instructions to pair it with the mobile app. Thanks to a network of antennas inside the museum, the tag is used to perform the indoor localization of the user, understanding which artwork is the nearest. Such information is sent to a server, which will communicate to the mobile app which artwork is the nearest to the user. Through the mobile app, the user can talk via voice interaction or using a written chat, asking information about the artworks. The mobile app can use the location of the user to proactively invite her/him to ask information about specific artworks.

In the following, we provide a detailed description of the components of the system (Sect. 3.1) as well as of the information flow inside the system, with the interactions among its components (Sect. 3.2).

3.1 System Architecture

To achieve the aforementioned goals, the Vocal Museum system architecture is composed of three components.

Indoor Localization. It is performed thanks to a network of UWB antennas inside the museum, and a wearable tag given to the user at the entrance. The goal of this component is to understand the user's position inside the museum, in order to detect the nearest artwork and convey to the user the proper information.

Mobile Application. It is the interface between the system and user. At the entrance, after the pairing with the wearable UWB tag given to the user, it can be used to start a vocal call or a text chat with the system.

System Server. It is responsible of running three applications for position management, dialog management, and content management, to support the system. Therefore, this component provides to the mobile app the position of the user upon request; it manages the voice-based dialog or the written chat between the user and the system, sending answers to her/his request; it generates the content about the artworks following the user's requests.

Figure 1 shows the distribution of such components between the museum, the user and the cloud hosting the server-side applications. The indoor localization identifies a tag given to the user thanks to a network of antennas distributed inside the museum. The antennas are placed to precisely divide the museum into areas, to detect the tag of the user entering and exiting from such areas. An example of the placement of the antennas and the division into zones is depicted in Figs. 2 and 3, which show the planimetry of the room used to test the system.

Specifically, there are three areas of interaction enclosing the reproduction of three masterpieces: "The Scream" (*L'urlo*) by Munch, "Marilyn Monroe" by Warhol, and "The School of Athens" (*La scuola di Atene*) by Raffaello. Therefore, when the user with the tag enters in the area around one of the masterpiece, such as "The Scream" the mobile app notifies the user that she/he is approaching that artwork and proposes to know more about it, encouraging to ask questions.

The mobile app is downloaded by the user on her/his own handheld device. As an alternative, the museum can offer a tablet with the app pre-installed to the user, as it happens with traditional audio-guides. Figure 4 shows the home page and a written chat about the masterpiece "The School of Athens" in the Vocal Museum mobile app. In the home page of the app, the user is requested to write the id of the wearable UWB tag taken at the entrance. As an alternative, the user can frame with the device camera the QR code on top of the UWB tag, and the app will automatically register the tag id. This process pairs the mobile app with the tag: the app can query the server about its user's position and the server can send notifications to that device.

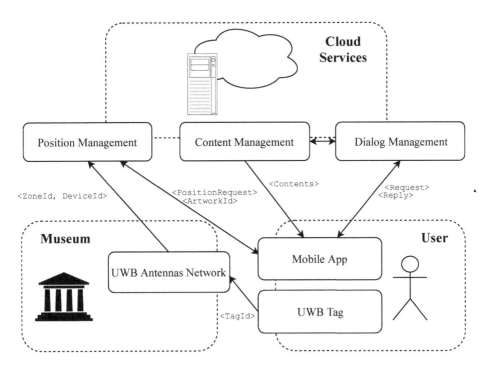

Fig. 1. The components of the Vocal Museum system.

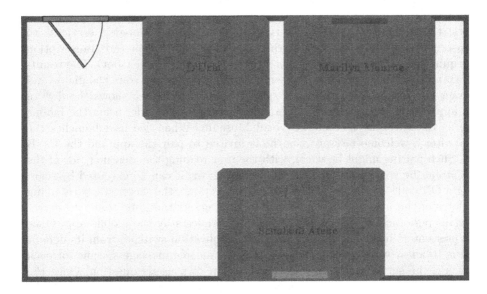

Fig. 2. Example of the division of a room in three areas covered by UWB antennas. The blue color identifies the areas where the mobile app suggests an interaction with the "The Scream" (*L'urlo*), "The School of Athens" (*Scuola di Atene*), and "Marilyn Monroe" artworks. (Color figure online)

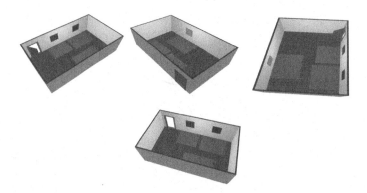

Fig. 3. 3D plan of a room divided into three interaction areas by UWB antennas.

Finally, the core services of the Vocal Museum are the applications running on the server side to track users' position, transcript users' questions, and provide users with contents based on their requests through the mobile app. Concerning the indoor localization, the local server managing the UWB antennas network tracks the wearable UWB tags to update theirs users' positions by sending an http request to the server. Similarly, the mobile app periodically asks the server for an update of the position of the current users, knowing when the user approaches an artwork. More details of such information flows will be given in Subsect. 3.2.

Concerning the interaction with the users and the management of the contents, the mobile app and the server applications use Google's services[1] to transcript user speech to text during the vocal interaction (no transcription is required when the interaction is a written chat with the chatbot). The resulting transcriptions are fed into the server applications to generate the dialog and extract the content available on a specific artwork. Figure 5 shows the flow of the application to manage the interaction on the server side, using the mobile app as the user interface of the Vocal Museum. When the user launches the app, after a welcome message, she/he is invited to pair the app and the UWB tag. Such pairing might be vocal, with the user reading the identifier (id) of the tag; it can be written, typing the id of the tag; or, it can be executed by scanning a QR code on the tag. Once the pairing is done, the server starts receiving updates of the user's position, thanks to the tag. At the same time, the server receives periodical (i.e. in polling) positions requests by the mobile app. Once the user enters inside an artwork area, the application switches from its default status to an artwork-dedicated flow. After a welcome message specific for each artwork, the server waits for the transcription of a user's question. Once the question is received, the server application gets the content to answer, retrieving

---

[1] https://cloud.google.com/speech-to-text/.

Fig. 4. Two pages of the Vocal Museum mobile app: the home page (left) and the written chat with the chatbot (right).

it from the database. In case the question does not match any available content, a default answer is given. As the user leaves the artwork area, a greeting message is presented to the user, and the server application returns in its default status.

3.2   Component Interactions and Implementation

The Vocal Museum runs thanks to the interactions and the information flow between the components presented in Subsect. 3.1. At the system configuration phase, a map specific for each museum or exhibition needs to be created on a local server for the management of the UWB network. Specifically, the virtual area around each artwork has to be defined. In this way, the local server managing the UWB network can update the system server when the state of a UWB tag changes, i.e. when the user enters or exit an area. To perform such task, an http request with the following triple is sent to the server:

$$<id, position, direction>$$

where id is the identifier of the tag, $position$ is an area of the museum, and $direction$ is a parameter to understand if the user is leaving or entering the area. For example, a request encapsulating the following triple

$$<101, school, OUT>$$

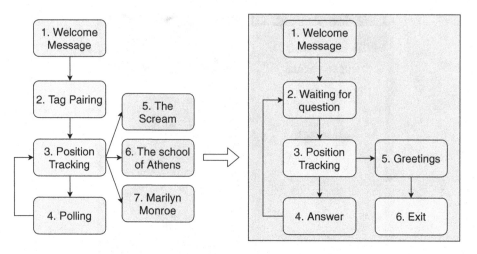

Fig. 5. The server application managing the interaction with the users. The left side shows the application flow when the user is outside the area around an artwork. The right side shows the application when the user is inside the area of an artwork.

indicate that the user with the tag 101 is leaving the area around the artwork "The School of Athens", and, thus, entering an area of the museum with no artworks.

Upon each received request, the application for indoor localization running on the system server updates its in-memory database[2] with the updated position of the user. Hence, using the same database, the server application to manage the interaction with the user is able to read the correct position and provide the proper contents to the mobile app. An in-memory database was preferred to on-disk databases to support a faster response time, as the interaction between the user and the mobile app is in real-time.

The mobile app periodically sends a request of the user's position to the system server, using a polling mechanism. Depending on the user's position, the system server answers with a message: if the user is near an artwork, the back-end will answer with a welcome message specific for that artwork, otherwise it will encourage the user to come closer to an artwork. As the mobile app is the interface between the user and the Vocal Museum, when the user is in an artwork area and makes a question, the app sends to the system server a request with a JSON-formatted message with the question and the id of the tag. The system server replies with the required content or a default answer for the current situation (for example, asking to repeat the question or informing it is not possible to answer). As the user leaves the area, the server replies to the mobile app position request with an artwork-specific greetings message. In addition, the system server is able to manage user questions about artworks in different areas from its current position. For example, the user might want

---

[2] The server database is implemented with Redis: https://redis.io.

to look a large-sized painting from distance, and so, while looking to it, she/he might enter another artwork area. Thus, the server application is able to retrieve information for the other artworks in its database.

The Vocal Museum system was implemented and tested in a laboratory environment[3], deploying the server applications in a local server. The used UWB tags were the Sewio "Tag Piccolino"[4]. The mobile application was developed with Apache Cordova[5]. In fact, doing tests in a laboratory environment, on a local server, represents the main threat to validity of the proposed research. To fully validate the system, tests in a real museum are needed; the deployment of the server applications in cloud would be also useful, in order to test the system scalability with multiple concurrent users.

4   Conclusions

In this paper we presented the Vocal Museum, i.e. a system composed of a set of software applications organized to localize the user inside a museum or an exhibition and communicate with her/him via vocal or written interactions. Exploiting IoT, specifically implementing UWB-based indoor localization, the system is able to understand the proximity of the users to artworks; therefore, the system can proactively encourage the users to ask questions. The services in the system implement chatbots to interact with the users, using a mobile application as the system interface. The vocal interaction is ideal to avoid overlapping virtual artifacts via displays onto artworks, as it happens with Augmented Reality, preventing the danger of distracting the visitor. Moreover, to increase potential users, the mobile application offers the chance of interacting via written chats: the system exploits the same technology of the vocal interaction, and thus keeps the same soundness and reliability of the dialogues even when carried out through written chats.

However, the presented research is in its early-stage and additional work is required to address limitations and improve the proposed system. The system at its current stage of development supports Italian, hence additional languages should be included. In addition to use proximity detected via UWB, the mobile app needs to include a function to frame the artworks with the device camera, in order to recognize it. This feature could be useful for users who want to receive information about an artwork which is not the nearest and their are not able to describe with their own words. Finally, the Vocal Museum system has to be validated in real museums with real, non-IT experts users, assessing its usability via state-of-the-art scales such as the System Usability Scale (SUS) [3] or the Usability Metrics for User Experience (UMUX) [13].

---

[3] Voice interaction demo: https://youtu.be/D7PNjp8UL64
   Chatbot demo: https://youtu.be/m9KaZIj0Rq8.
[4] https://docs.sewio.net/docs/tag-piccolino-5734455.html.
[5] https://cordova.apache.org/.

Acknowledgements. The research presented in this paper has been supported by the project "ChaIn for excellence of reflectiVe societies to exploit dIgital culTural heritAge and museumS" (CIVITAS), funded by Università Politecnica delle Marche.

References

1. Alletto, S., et al.: An indoor location-aware system for an IoT-based smart museum. IEEE Internet Things J. **3**(2), 244–253 (2016). https://doi.org/10.1109/JIOT.2015.2506258
2. Augello, A., et al.: A multimodal interaction guide for pervasive services access. In: IEEE International Conference on Pervasive Service, pp. 250–256 (2007). https://doi.org/10.1109/PERSER.2007.4283923
3. Brooke, J.: SUS-a quick and dirty usability scale. Usability Eval. Ind. **189**(194), 4–7 (1996)
4. Brumann, C.: Cultural heritage. In: Wright, J.D. (ed.) International Encyclopedia of the Social & Behavioral Sciences, 2 edn., pp. 414–419. Elsevier, Oxford (2015). https://doi.org/10.1016/B978-0-08-097086-8.12185-3
5. Bubaris, N.: Sound in museums - museums in sound. Mus. Manag. Curatorsh. **29**(4), 391–402 (2014). https://doi.org/10.1080/09647775.2014.934049
6. Canciani, M., Conigliaro, E., Grasso, M.D., Papalini, P., Saccone, M.: 3D survey and augmented reality for cultural heritage. The case study of the Aurelian Wall at Castra Praetoria in Rome. Int. Arch. Photogram. Remote Sens. Spat. Inf. Sci. **41**, 931–937 (2016)
7. Chatzidimitris, T., Gavalas, D., Michael, D.: SoundPacman: audio augmented reality in location-based games. In: 2016 18th Mediterranean Electrotechnical Conference (MELECON), pp. 1–6 (2016). https://doi.org/10.1109/MELCON.2016.7495414
8. Cliffe, L., Mansell, J., Cormac, J., Greenhalgh, C., Hazzard, A.: The audible artefact: promoting cultural exploration and engagement with audio augmented reality. In: Proceedings of the 14th International Audio Mostly Conference: A Journey in Sound, AM 2019, pp. 176–182. Association for Computing Machinery, New York (2019). https://doi.org/10.1145/3356590.3356617
9. Clodic, A., et al.: Rackham: an interactive robot-guide. In: ROMAN 2006 - The 15th IEEE International Symposium on Robot and Human Interactive Communication, pp. 502–509 (2006). https://doi.org/10.1109/ROMAN.2006.314378
10. Deng, X., Unnava, H.R., Lee, H.: Too true to be good? When virtual reality decreases interest in actual reality. J. Bus. Res. **100**, 561–570 (2019). https://doi.org/10.1016/j.jbusres.2018.11.008
11. Dragoni, A.F., Quattrini, R., Sernani, P., Ruggeri, L.: Real scale augmented reality. A novel paradigm for archaeological heritage fruition. In: Luigini, A. (ed.) EARTH 2018. AISC, vol. 919, pp. 659–670. Springer, Cham (2019). https://doi.org/10.1007/978-3-030-12240-9_68
12. Ferracani, A., Faustino, M., Giannini, G.X., Landucci, L., Del Bimbo, A.: Natural experiences in museums through virtual reality and voice commands. In: Proceedings of the 25th ACM International Conference on Multimedia, MM 2017, pp. 1233–1234 (2017). https://doi.org/10.1145/3123266.3127916
13. Finstad, K.: The usability metric for user experience. Interact. Comput. **22**(5), 323–327 (2010). https://doi.org/10.1016/j.intcom.2010.04.004

14. Gaia, G., Boiano, S., Borda, A.: Engaging museum visitors with AI: the case of chatbots. In: Giannini, T., Bowen, J.P. (eds.) Museums and Digital Culture. SSCC, pp. 309–329. Springer, Cham (2019). https://doi.org/10.1007/978-3-319-97457-6_15
15. Hammady, R., Ma, M., Temple, N.: Augmented reality and gamification in heritage museums. In: Marsh, T., Ma, M., Oliveira, M.F., Baalsrud Hauge, J., Göbel, S. (eds.) JCSG 2016. LNCS, vol. 9894, pp. 181–187. Springer, Cham (2016). https://doi.org/10.1007/978-3-319-45841-0_17
16. Hashemi, S.H., Kamps, J.: Exploiting behavioral user models for point of interest recommendation in smart museums. New Rev. Hypermed. Multimed. **24**(3), 228–261 (2018)
17. Kuflik, T., et al.: Indoor positioning: challenges and solutions for indoor cultural heritage sites. In: Proceedings of the 16th International Conference on Intelligent User Interfaces, IUI 2011, pp. 375–378. ACM (2011). https://doi.org/10.1145/1943403.1943469
18. Lin, H.F., Chen, C.H.: Design and application of augmented reality query-answering system in mobile phone information navigation. Expert Syst. Appl. **42**(2), 810–820 (2015). https://doi.org/10.1016/j.eswa.2014.07.050
19. Mantyjarvi, J., Paternò, F., Salvador, Z., Santoro, C.: Scan and tilt: towards natural interaction for mobile museum guides. In: Proceedings of the 8th Conference on Human-Computer Interaction with Mobile Devices and Services, pp. 191–194. ACM (2006)
20. Mortara, M., Catalano, C.E., Bellotti, F., Fiucci, G., Houry-Panchetti, M., Petridis, P.: Learning cultural heritage by serious games. J. Cult. Heritage **15**(3), 318–325 (2014). https://doi.org/10.1016/j.culher.2013.04.004
21. Neto, J.N., Silva, R., Neto, J.P., Pereira, J.M., Fernandes, J.: Solis'curse - a cultural heritage game using voice interaction with a virtual agent. In: 2011 Third International Conference on Games and Virtual Worlds for Serious Applications, pp. 164–167 (2011). https://doi.org/10.1109/VS-GAMES.2011.31
22. Pallud, J.: Impact of interactive technologies on stimulating learning experiences in a museum. Inf. Manag. **54**(4), 465–478 (2017). https://doi.org/10.1016/j.im.2016.10.004
23. Pendit, U.C., Zaibon, S.B., Bakar, J.A.: Mobile augmented reality for enjoyable informal learning in cultural heritage site. Int. J. Comput. Appl. **92**(14), 19–26 (2014)
24. Perry, S., Roussou, M., Economou, M., Young, H., Pujol, L.: Moving beyond the virtual museum: engaging visitors emotionally. In: 2017 23rd International Conference on Virtual System Multimedia (VSMM), pp. 1–8 (2017). https://doi.org/10.1109/VSMM.2017.8346276
25. Prodanov, P.J., Drygajlo, A., Ramel, G., Meisser, M., Siegwart, R.: Voice enabled interface for interactive tour-guide robots. In: IEEE/RSJ International Conference on Intelligent Robots and Systems, vol. 2, pp. 1332–1337 (2002)
26. Rao, A.S., Sharma, A.V., Narayan, C.S.: A context aware system for an IoT-based smart museum. In: 2017 2nd International Multidisciplinary Conference on Computer and Energy Science (SpliTech), pp. 1–5 (2017)
27. Sahu, P., Dua, M., Kumar, A.: Challenges and issues in adopting speech recognition. In: Agrawal, S.S., Dev, A., Wason, R., Bansal, P. (eds.) Speech and Language Processing for Human-Machine Communications. AISC, vol. 664, pp. 209–215. Springer, Singapore (2018). https://doi.org/10.1007/978-981-10-6626-9_23
28. Schaffer, S., Gustke, O., Oldemeier, J., Reithinger, N.: Towards chatbots in the museum. In: CEUR Workshop Proceedings, vol. 2176 (2018)

29. Sernani, P., Angeloni, R., Dragoni, A.F., Quattrini, R., Clini, P.: Combining image targets and SLAM for AR-based cultural heritage fruition. In: De Paolis, L.T., Bourdot, P. (eds.) AVR 2019. LNCS, vol. 11614, pp. 199–207. Springer, Cham (2019). https://doi.org/10.1007/978-3-030-25999-0_17
30. Shawar, B.A., Atwell, E.: Chatbots: are they really useful? LDV Forum 2007 - Band **22**(1), 29–49 (2007)
31. Shiomi, M., Kanda, T., Ishiguro, H., Hagita, N.: Interactive humanoid robots for a science museum. In: Proceedings of the 1st ACM SIGCHI/SIGART Conference on Human-Robot Interaction, HRI 2006, pp. 305–312 (2006). https://doi.org/10.1145/1121241.1121293
32. Stock, O.: Language-based interfaces and their application for cultural tourism. AI Mag. **22**(1), 85–97 (2001). https://doi.org/10.1609/aimag.v22i1.1546
33. Sylaiou, S., Kasapakis, V., Dzardanova, E., Gavalas, D.: Leveraging mixed reality technologies to enhance museum visitor experiences. In: 2018 International Conference on Intelligent Systems (IS), pp. 595–601 (2018). https://doi.org/10.1109/IS.2018.8710530
34. Traum, D., et al.: Ada and grace: direct interaction with museum visitors. In: Nakano, Y., Neff, M., Paiva, A., Walker, M. (eds.) IVA 2012. LNCS (LNAI), vol. 7502, pp. 245–251. Springer, Heidelberg (2012). https://doi.org/10.1007/978-3-642-33197-8_25

Walk Through a Virtual Museum with Binocular Stereo Effect and Spherical Panorama Views Based on Image Rendering Carried by Tracked Robot

YanXiang Zhang[✉] and Ge Wang

Department of Communication of Science and Technology,
University of Science and Technology of China, Hefei, Anhui, China
petrel@ustc.edu.cn, oga@mail.ustc.edu.cn

Abstract. In order to provide users with a virtual tour which have walk through and binocular stereoscopic experience, the authors propose a method to use the tracked robot carrying a single panoramic camera. Panorama photos of continuous movement are taken by the tracked robot so that the audience can wander freely in the virtual museum. Panoramic photos are captured at the distance calculated according to requirements of stereo vision comfort. The recorded photos are used to make binocular panoramic video. Two adjacent panoramic images are used as stereoscopic pairs so as to realize comfortable stereoscopic vision. Because only one camera is used, not only the amount of data is reduced, but also the occlusion issue is avoided. Videos can be shot at different distances according to the rules of visual comfort so that the users can enlarge the picture and choose an appropriate spacing.

Keywords: Art museum · Spherical panorama · Walking through · Binocular stereo effect

1 Introduction

Nowadays, museums have started to build virtual museum touring system, which allows users to appreciate the exhibits and feel the beauty of history and art even from a long distance. To satisfy the users, virtual museums should meet the following requirements: First, virtual museums should present realistic scenes and comfortable stereoscopic visual effects, so that users can get the best visual experience. Second, when visiting the virtual museum, users should be able to walk and move freely in the virtual space just like in the real museum to achieve the best tour experience. Everyone has different requirements for visual experience of tour. Multi-mode, adjustable and targeted system will be the new trend of virtual panoramic tour in the future. And for the museums, a convenient and simple shooting method would save a lot of money and time. At present, there are generally two ways to realize virtual tour. One is by geometry method for 3D modeling, which can realize strong stereo feeling and directly bring seamless

© Springer Nature Switzerland AG 2020
L. T. De Paolis and P. Bourdot (Eds.): AVR 2020, LNCS 12243, pp. 79–90, 2020.
https://doi.org/10.1007/978-3-030-58468-9_6

walk through experience in the virtual space. Kiourt et al. presented an innovative fully dynamic Web-based virtual museum framework, in which anyone can easily create customised virtual exhibitions, while guaranteeing an engaging experience by relying on modern game engine technologies [10]. But this method needs more technology input and always cannot be as real as the photos [9].

The second method is using panoramic images, which is relatively easy to operate and a direct reflection of real world. However, this method lacks stereo feeling. The current technology can only realize tour jumping between points, not continuous and free roaming of virtual space [1].

In order to realize the virtual tour based on image rendering, Xianghua Ying (2009) [11] used image transformations among images to achieve continuous walk-through between the two adjacent panoramas to realize walk through experience in IBR panoramas. Another attempt by Jang-Hyun Jung (2006) [12] is to generate intermediate panoramic images using panoramic-based image morphing from captured panoramic images.

For image based rendering, there are efforts about optimizing stereo effect and shooting method. Po et al. Presented an approach for 6 DoF panoramic videos from omni-directional stereo (ODS) images using convolutional neural networks (CNNs) to generate panoramic depth maps from ODS images in real-time [18], to further strengthen the stereo effect of the IBR panoramic tour. Digital Route Panoramas [13, 14] are used to archive and visualize street scenes along a route digitally. A rail-track viewer [15] can pre-process the datasets and render key viewpoints on pre-selected paths. Daniel and Ingrid [16] present a method to reconstruct a 4D plenoptic function. Users can move in extensive scope and complex environment. This method can restrict camera motion to a planet eye-height inside the dataset at the same time. Concentric panorama [17] can synthesize realistic scenes, while the viewpoint can move freely within a circular region on a plane.

Dynamic and continuous panorama shooting and viewing method are still worthy of attention in the practical application. Yasushi et al. [2] proposed a TwinCam system, panoramic images taken by both cameras are used as stereoscopic pairs for the left and right eyes, respectively. This simulation of the binocular stereo vision can optimize the depth perception of virtual space compared with system of single panoramic camera, to achieve better stereo feeling [7]. However, it can only realize dynamic shooting and a fixed point, but cannot move freely. And audiences can only get clear view when looking ahead and will see the cameras occlusion each other when turning head. And a huge amount of data is generated by the two cameras.

In this paper, in order to improve the stereo effect of IBR panorama and realize continuous virtual museum tour, the author proposes a moving camera system using a tracked robot carrying a single panoramic camera to take continuous panoramic images of museum. Two adjacent frames are used as stereoscopic pairs to get high-definition and stereoscopic vision. Using the remote control tracked vehicle, continues moving panorama image sequences can be easily recorded. Through the player and the head display device, users can move freely and continuously in the virtual museum space, which improves the sense of freedom and avoids the previous abrupt sense of direct jump between points. The semi-automatic shooting method effectively improves the shooting efficiency and quality. Through this method, occlusion is eliminated and the storage burden is effectively reduced.

According to requirements of vision comfort, the shooting distance can be calculated when the speed of robot is set. The image sequence at different distance can be used for zoom in/out function. Multiple sets of images with different spacing can be chosen by users so as to obtain the stereoscopic effect that suits them so that provide users with a more personalized experience. And the authors suppose that this method can be used in scientific education and popularization, which can show the students around the science and technology venues.

2   System Design and Implementation

In order to allow the users walk freely in the virtual museum, the camera is fixed on the remote-controlled tracked robot, which carries the camera to take pictures in the museum so that can avoid operators appearing in the scene. Because the exhibits in museum are generally static, there is few motion blurs in the image. The author adopts the adjacent two shots as stereo images pair for processing to avoid the occlusion between cameras. Integrated the above two methods, can achieve high definition and stereoscopic visual experience, free and fluent touring experience, and make the shooting process simpler.

2.1   System Design

The automatic camera system is shown in Fig. 1, which is used to take panoramic shots in the museum by remote control. When viewing exhibits in the museum, users' gazing direction is always perpendicular to the walking direction, which provides convenience for the realization of walking tour. As long as the camera lens is fixed in the direction perpendicular to the head, the shooting direction can be ensured to be perpendicular to the movement. The system consists of HMD (Oculus Rift) and a 360° camera (Insta360 One). The base of the machine is driven by a servo motor (RS405CB, Futaba), and the motor is controlled by an Arduino micro controller. The tracked robot can be controlled by remote control handle or mobile phone, and the duty cycle can be adjusted by Arduino to control the speed. The lens aperture of panoramic camera is F2.2 video resolution and frame rate are $5760 \times 2880/30$ fps. The image of each frame is stitched from the images of a double-eye lens, which is stitched into rectangular images by the software of the camera. The adjacent panorama images taken by the camera were taken as stereoscopic pairs. Then the equal-rectangular images of the two frames were projected into the texture of two balls in the virtual space, which were rendered by Unity3D.

Figure 1 shows the shooting system.

Fig. 1. Shooting system. Lens direction of the panoramic camera is perpendicular to the body of the robot.

2.2 Select a Vehicle

To enable the camera to move throughout the space, the vehicle to be used should run as smoothly as possible and can be operated remotely to avoid the photographer from entering the picture. The tracked robot is equipped with an open source Arduino controller and sensor. The duty cycle can be adjusted by Arduino UNO to control the travel speed. The car has a load of 3 kg. The robot car used in the experiment is shown in Fig. 2.

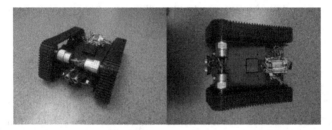

Fig. 2. Tracked robot used in the experiment.

2.3 Select a Panorama Camera

In 2019, Feng et al. propose an end-to-end system that records a scene using a tripod panoramic rig and broadcasts 360° stereo panorama videos in real time. Stereo vision quality is also better preserved by a proposed weighting-based image alignment scheme. However, the big distance between lenses is not suitable for museum application. There are also commercial stereoscopic panoramic cameras available such as Insta 360 Pro 2. However, the distance between cameras lenses are big and there will be unavoidable seams appear due to relatively small space in museum [19].

For a spherical panoramic camera, the larger the distance between the lenses is, the larger the gap visible in the panoramic photo. For the same camera, the nearer the object is, the larger the gap caused by lens distance. During the tour of the museum, people will stand very close to the exhibits to watch them. In order to avoid gaps in the picture stitching, the distance between the lenses of the panoramic camera is required to be as small as possible.

Therefore, Insta 360 one X panoramic camera with fish-eye lens was selected for shooting in the museum, which is showed in Fig. 3. There are two fish-eye lenses on the opposite side, about 27.60 mm apart, which is a relatively small gap. And 5.7K video images with high-definition can be obtained.

The images between the two lenses can be nicely stitched together, and the footage can be stitched together on the accompanying software. An APP on mobile phone can shoot remotely to avoid the operator appearing in the panoramic image.

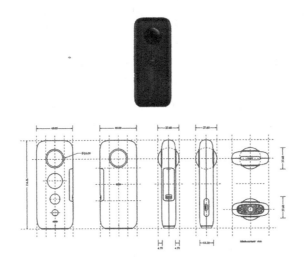

Fig. 3. Panoramic camera used in the experiment and its parameter.

2.4 Method of Automatic Controlling

In order to avoid the heavy work caused by taking spherical panoramic pictures by hand and the operator's appearance, a remotely controlled tracked robot is used. The camera can move in an arbitrary range and distance without restriction, which saves a lot of manpower and material resources and makes the operation easier.

The main control chip of the car is AT Mega328 UNO, and the programming environment is Arduino UNO. The speed of the car is regulated by adjusting duty cycle. The remotely control handle is used to control the direction of travel.

2.5 Determine Shooting Speed and Optimize Visual Experience

When shooting, the distance between the camera and the object also directly affects the stereo effect. In terms of camera height, Tuuli Keskinen et al. [3] found in their research that under different conditions, the most comfortable heights averaged 137–158 cm depending on the condition. The highest still comfortable values were 159–180 cm, and the lowest still comfortable values were 110–142 cm on average. Considering the actual situation, in the museum, the exhibits are usually placed in a lower position to ensure that the audience can see the full view of the front of the exhibits and avoid looking down at the exhibits. Therefore, a relatively lower shooting height is set about 1.2 m.

As for the shooting spacing, since two adjacent panoramic photos will be taken as stereo pairs, in order to produce a good stereo effect, the distance between the two frames should be controlled reasonably first. If the spacing is too large, the stereo effect cannot be formed. If the distance is too small, the number of photos in the data set will be greatly increased.

Stereo effect of human eyes is associated with the interpupillary distance (IPD), adult IPD is around 63 mm, the vast majority of adults have IPDs in the range 50–75 mm, the wider range of 45–80 mm is likely to include (almost) all adults [8]. The setting of the player is similar to human perspective. So, the spacing between two adjacent shots should not be exceed 60 mm, and the smaller the spacing is, the more fluent viewing experience can be realized.

But due to the resolution of the panoramic photo is as high as 5760×2880 pixels, too small spacing can burden the storage. When shooting, the speed of the car will directly affect the spacing of photos. If the spacing of every two frames is set to 1 cm, the speed of the car should be 30/s according to the frame rate of 30 fps, and the speed should be 60 cm/s when the spacing is 2 cm. The rest can be done in the same manner. Travel speed also affects the stereo feeling and comfort. According to Panum's Fusional Area, and the law of human eye parallax, the distance of panoramic image shooting needs to meet the following requirements in order to achieve a good visual experience [4, 6]. When human eyes observe an object, the interpupillary distance is D, and the distance from the object is L. At this time, the angle between the eyes and the object is:

$$\theta = 2 \text{arc} \tan(\frac{D/2}{L}) \tag{1}$$

This angle should meet the following requirements: First, when human eyes are observing nearby objects, there is a distance at which they can see clearly without fatigue. This distance is 25 cm, which is called the apparent distance. At this distance, the angle between the pupil and the object is [4]:

$$2 \text{arc} \tan(\frac{6.5/2}{25}) \approx 12° \tag{2}$$

Otherwise, double shadow will be formed.

Second, when watching an object, the difference of the angle α and β should be less than 1° [5]. As shown in Fig. 4, α is the angle of sight at the nearest point of the object and β is the angle of sight at the farthest point. The difference of two angles shall meet the following requirements:

$$|\alpha - \beta| \leq 1° \tag{3}$$

Exceeding this value can cause visual discomfort.

Assume the distance from the wall to the glass of the display shelf in the museum is T, and the distance from the shelf when shooting is L, it is related:

$$\left| 2 \text{arc} \tan(\frac{D/2}{L}) - 2 \text{arc} \tan(\frac{D/2}{T+L}) \right| \leq 1° \tag{4}$$

The distance from the wall to the glass of the display shelf in the museum is generally 50 cm, when the spacing between panoramic images, which means D = 1 cm, there is an unequal relationship based on formulas (1) and (2):

$$\left| 2\arctan(\frac{1/2}{L}) - 2\arctan(\frac{1/2}{50+L}) \right| \leq 1° \tag{5}$$

When the spacing is 2 cm, there is:

$$\left| 2\arctan(\frac{2/2}{L}) - 2\arctan(\frac{2/2}{50+L}) \right| \leq 1° \tag{6}$$

The shooting distance can be calculated in line with the visual conditions with other shooting spacing (Fig. 4).

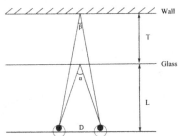

Fig. 4. Schematic diagram of interpupillary distance (which is the spacing when shooting), shooting distance, depth of shelf (the distance between wall and glass) and the angle of sight at the nearest and farthest point of the object.

After calculation, the corresponding shooting speed, shooting distance and magnification range under different shooting spacing are shown in the following table.

Table 1. The corresponding shooting speed, shooting distance and magnifying range under different shooting spacing.

Spacing (cm)	1	2	3	4
Speed (cm/s)	30	60	90	120
Distance (cm)	34.06	54.69	70.98	84.88
Allowable magnification (times)	6.5	3.25	2.16	1.62

When the picture is enlarged, the enlarged focal length is equal to the original focal length times the magnification. As shown in Fig. 5 if the focal length of the camera is f, the observable depth is z, the binocular parallax is d, and the abscissa of the observed object is b, then the relation is [1]:

$$z = \frac{fb}{d} \tag{6}$$

It can be seen that when the parallax increases, the observation depth will decrease. Thus, users can enlarge the image and focus on an object. The two adjacent frames taken in accordance with the above rules are shown in Fig 6.

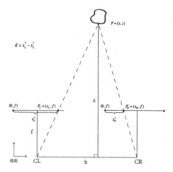

Fig. 5. Diagram of the relationship among focal length, observable depth, binocular parallax and interpupillary distance when looking at an object.

frame n   frame n+1

Fig. 6. Two adjacent frames of spherical panorama video.

2.6 Design of Virtual Tour Player

A tour system is designed, in which users can look around at one point and walk freely in the virtual museum. Users can stand at a fixed point, looking around by moving their mouse. And they can click and drag the mouse to change the situation, like moving in the virtual space.

As for the corner, usually there are no exhibits in the corner of the museum. And the audience usually stands on the opposite side of the wall instead of the corner to watch, so the system is continuous roaming in the straight line, while the corner will be abandoned and directly jump to the roaming of the exhibition frame.

Although the distance between people's eyes is within a fixed range, there are still individual differences in users. And there are also different requirements for stereo effect, which puts forward requirements for the diversity of the tourism system.

Moreover, current panoramic roaming system has only one single viewing mode. Users can only stand at a fixed focal length when visiting the museum. However, for museum exhibits, users often need to focus on one exhibit and watch its details carefully. So, zoom in function is set, and users can choose several different spacing to match their need. The authors use the shooting system to shoot the image of the museum while roaming at different speed and distance according to the data in Table 1, like Fig. 7.

Thus, the images at different speed and distance are used as different binocular stereo image pair sequence. When users want to see the details of an exhibit, the users can zoom in and out the picture to a certain extent through the +/−button to change the view to another sequence at another viewing distance, while ensuring the comfort of stereo vision. Video with different interpupillary distance can cooperate with Oculus head-mounted display. At the beginning of tour, choose the right interpupillary distance mode, so as to meet individual's demand for stereoscopic sense and obtain more personalized using experience.

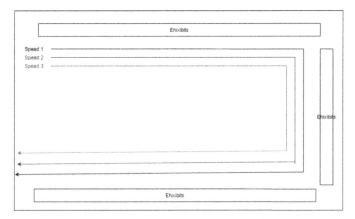

Fig. 7. Screen capture of the system.

3   Feed Back

Six participants are invited to try out the virtual museum, and then asked them about the experience of it. Their basic information is shown in Table 2.

Table 2. Information of the participants

No.	Gender	Age	Occupation
P1	Female	25	Student
P2	Female	25	Student
P3	Female	23	Student
P4	Female	23	Student
P5	Female	25	Student
P6	Male	25	Student

Here are some representative feedbacks:

P6 said: "It is very novel and clear. The feeling of walking is real. However, wearing eyes for a long time may cause people's discomfort and affect the experience."

P3 said: "It's very novel and it's not too vertiginous. It would be better if we could interact with it based on gestures."

P2 said: "The stereoscopic effect of the artwork is great, similar to what you would see in a museum. You can see the artwork from multiple angles."

P4 said: "Unprecedented experience. It's very cool because we can visit the museum. It's also a great help to solve the problem of education equity in poor area."

4   Result

In our virtual tour system, the users can walk freely in the virtual museum due to the use of a moving shooting system. The users can look around with a gyroscope mounted on the head monitor, and move through the virtual scene with joystick, mouse, keyboard or other controllers. During the tour, the users can see stereo panoramic image with high-definition and comfortable experience.

If users want to look at an object carefully, they can zoom in and see the details of the object within a certain range while keeping the eyes comfortable. For the users with different needs for stereo feeling, different picture spacing can be selected to obtain personalized visual experience (Fig. 8).

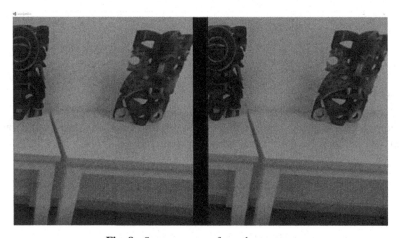

Fig. 8.   Screen capture from the system.

5   Conclusion and Discussion

The authors proposed a panoramic museum tour system using a tracked robot carrying single panoramic camera, which can be applied to capture the scene of virtual museum tour. This system can realize continuous tour in virtual museum and avoid the occlusion between cameras. Also, the amount of data can be greatly reduced. Optional focal length and the function of zooming in and out provided users with brand new personalized experience.

Real museum scenes can be quickly recorded using a remotely controlled robot and camera. Because the floor of the museum is usually very smooth and flat, it is suitable for remote control vehicle walking without any jolting and shaking. Only remote control is needed to allow the mechanical vehicle to walk freely throughout the museum, which greatly saves manpower and material resources. Users can walk continuously and freely in the virtual museum. When using the system, users can choose the appropriate picture spacing, enlarge the picture in the virtual tour, carefully watch the details of an exhibit, and obtain personalized and targeted experience. The authors also propose this method used in science and technology museum so that the visitors can see the science popularization facilities at distance, which can broaden their horizons.

In future work, although remote control shooting can avoid the movement of the operator in the image, it is still difficult to completely eliminate the presence of the operator in general. Tracking sensors can be installed on the tracked vehicle. Since the ground of the museum is usually black or white, the corresponding white or black tape should be applied for the route of the car, which can be fully automated and the operator should not appear in the picture.

Acknowledgments. The work is supported by Ministry of Education (China) Humanities and Social Sciences Research Foundation under Grant No.: 19A10358002.

References

1. Anrui: Study on 3D video comfort enhancement method based on parallax change adjustment. Jilin University (2016). (in Chinese). https://kns.cnki.net/KCMS/detail/detail.aspx?dbcode=CMFD&dbname=CMFD201602&filename=1016083509
2. Ikei, Y., Yem, V., Tashiro, K., Fujie, T., Amemiya, T., Kitazaki, M.: Live stereoscopic 3D image with constant capture direction of 360° cameras for high-quality visual telepresence. In: 2019 IEEE Conference on Virtual Reality and 3D User Interfaces (VR), pp. 431–439. IEEE, March 2019
3. Keskinen, T., et al.: The effect of camera height, actor behavior, and viewer position on the user experience of 360 videos. In: 2019 IEEE Conference on Virtual Reality and 3D User Interfaces (VR), pp. 423–430. IEEE (2019)
4. Zhang, Y., Wang, Z.: Towards visual comfort: disciplines on the scene structure design for VR contents. In: De Paolis, L.T., Bourdot, P. (eds.) AVR 2018. LNCS, vol. 10850, pp. 190–196. Springer, Cham (2018). https://doi.org/10.1007/978-3-319-95270-3_14
5. Wartell, Z., Hodges, L.F., Ribarsky, W.: Characterizing image fusion techniques in stereoscopic HTDs. In: Graphics Interface, pp. 223–232, June 2001
6. Grinberg, V.S., Podnar, G.W., Siegel, M.: Geometry of binocular imaging. In: Stereoscopic Displays and Virtual Reality Systems, vol. 2177, pp. 56–65. International Society for Optics and Photonics, April 1994
7. Allen, B., Hanley, T., Rokers, B., Shawn Green, C.: Visual 3D acuity predicts discomfort in 3D stereoscopic environments. Entertain. Comput. **13**, 1–9 (2016). https://doi.org/10.1016/j.entcom.2016.01.001
8. Dodgson, N.A.: Variation and extrema of human interpupillary distance. In: Stereoscopic Displays and Virtual Reality Systems XI, vol. 5291, pp. 36–46. International Society for Optics and Photonics, May 2004

9. Bastanlar, Y., Grammalidis, N., Zabulis, X., Yilmaz, E., Yardimci, Y., Triantafyllidis, G.: 3D reconstruction for a cultural heritage virtual tour system. Int. Arch. Photogramm. Remote Sens. Spat. Inf. Sci. Beijing **37**, 1023–1028 (2008)

10. Kiourt, C., Koutsoudis, A., Pavlidis, G.: DynaMus: a fully dynamic 3D virtual museum framework. J. Cult. Herit. **22**, 984–991 (2016)

11. Ying, X., Peng, K., Zha, H.: Walkthrough in large environments using concatenated panoramas. In: Proceedings of the 2009 International Conference on Robotics and Biomimetics (ROBIO 2009), pp. 286–291. IEEE Press, Piscataway (2009)

12. Jung, J.-H., Kang, H.-B.: An efficient arbitrary view generation method using panoramic-based image morphing. In: Huang, D.-S., Li, K., Irwin, G.W. (eds.) ICIC 2006, Part I. LNCS, vol. 4113, pp. 1207–1212. Springer, Heidelberg (2006). https://doi.org/10.1007/118 16157_150

13. Zheng, J.Y.: Digital route panoramas. IEEE Multimedia **10**(3), 57–67 (2003)

14. Zheng, J.Y., Zhou, Y., Shi, M.: Scanning and rendering scene tunnels for virtual city traversing. In: Proceedings of the ACM Symposium on Virtual Reality Software and Technology (VRST 2004), pp. 106–113. ACM, New York (2004)

15. Yang, L., Crawfis, R.: Rail-track viewer: an image-based virtual walkthrough system. In: Stürzlinger, W., Müller, S. (eds.) Proceedings of the Workshop on Virtual Environments 2002 (EGVE 2002), p. 37-ff. Eurographics Association, Aire-la-Ville (2002)

16. Aliaga, D.G., Carlbom, I.: Plenoptic stitching: a scalable method for reconstructing 3D interactive walk throughs. In: Proceedings of the 28th Annual Conference on Computer Graphics and Interactive Techniques (SIGGRAPH 2001), pp. 443–450. ACM, New York (2001)

17. Shum, H.-Y., He, L.-W.: Rendering with concentric mosaics. In: Computer Graphics. Annual Conference Series, vol. 33, pp. 299–306 (1999)

18. Lai, P.K., Xie, S., Lang, J., Laqaruère, R.: Realtime panoramic depth maps from omni-directional stereo images for 6 DoF videos in virtual reality. In: 2019 IEEE Conference on Virtual Reality and 3D User Interfaces (VR), pp. 405–412. IEEE, March 2019

19. Panoramic camera usage recording of insta pro2. https://blog.csdn.net/yf160702/article/det ails/101053297. Accessed 23 Sept 2019

The Past Has Ears (PHE): XR Explorations of Acoustic Spaces as Cultural Heritage

Brian F. G. Katz[1](✉)[iD], Damian Murphy[2][iD], and Angelo Farina[3][iD]

[1] Sorbonne Université, CNRS, Institut Jean Le Rond ∂'Alembert,
Lutheries - Acoustique - Musique, Paris, France
brian.katz@sorbonne-universite.fr
[2] Department of Electronic Engineering AudioLab, University of York,
Heslington, York YO10 5DD, UK
damian.murphy@york.ac.uk
[3] Department of Engineering and Architecture, University of Parma,
Via delle Scienze 181/A, 43124 Parma, Italy
angelo.farina@unipr.it
http://www.lam.jussieu.fr/Membres/Katz/

Abstract. Hearing is one of our most pervasive senses. There is no equivalent to closing our eyes, or averting our gaze, for the ears. When we think about great architectural achievements in European history, such as ancient amphitheatres or Gothic cathedrals, their importance is strongly tied to their acoustic environment. The acoustics of a heritage site is an intangible consequence of the space's tangible construction and furnishings. Inspired by the project's namesake (Phé, for the constellation Phoenix), and the relatively recent fires at *Cathédrale de Notre Dame de Paris* and *Teatro La Fenice* opera hall, the PHE project focuses on virtual reconstruction of heritage sites, bringing them back from the ashes. In addressing the intangible acoustic heritage of architectural sites, three main objectives have been identified for this research project: Documentation, Modelling, and Presentation. In parallel, three heritage sites are participating as case studies: Tindari Theatre (IT), Notre-Dame de Paris Cathedral (FR), and The Houses of Parliament (UK). The acoustics of a space is immersive, spatial, and due to the nature of auditory perception egocentric, in contrast to visual perception of an object, which can be observed from "outside". Consequently, presentation methods for communicating acoustic heritage must represent the spatially immersive and listener-centric nature of acoustics. PHE will lead development of a museum grade hardware/software prototype for the presentation of immersive audio experiences adaptable to multiple platforms, from off-site immersive speaker installations, to mobile XR via smartphone applications.

Supported by EU JPI on Cultural Heritage (JPI-CH).

L. T. De Paolis and P. Bourdot (Eds.): AVR 2020, LNCS 12243, pp. 91–98, 2020.
https://doi.org/10.1007/978-3-030-58468-9_7

Keywords: Archaeoacoustics · Digital heritage reconstructions · Audible virtual and augmented reality · Acoustic heritage · Methodology guidelines

1   Introduction

With the recent adoption of UNESCO resolution "The importance of sound in today's world: promoting best practices", complementing the UNESCO Convention for the Safeguarding of the Intangible Cultural Heritage [1,2], we are now entering a new era where the acoustic soundscape of places both existing and historical merit reflection, preservation, and scientific study.

Preserving acoustics of historical buildings and concert halls for the posterity had been the dream of Michael Gerzon back in the seventies [6], and was first made possible by measuring multichannel impulse responses in 2003 [5].

When we think about great architectural achievements in European history, such as ancient amphitheatres or Gothic cathedrals, their importance is strongly tied to their acoustic environment. The acoustics of a heritage site is an intangible consequence of the space's tangible construction and furnishings. It is ephemeral, while also a concrete result of the physical nature of the environment. Through the "Past Has Ears" project (the PHE project[1]), we will explore how via measurements, research, and virtual reconstructions the acoustics of heritage spaces can be documented, reconstructed, and experienced for spaces both existing and in various altered states.

Inspired by the project's namesake (Phé, for the constellation Phoenix), and the relatively recent fires at *Cathédrale de Notre Dame de Paris* (2019) and *Teatro La Fenice* opera hall [20] (1996, *Fenice* also meaning Phoenix), the PHE project focuses on the preservation, conservation, and reconstruction of heritage sites, bringing them back from the ashes for use by researchers, stake holders, cultural institutions, and the general public.

2   Overview

Comprising research teams with experience in acoustic reconstructions and historical research, paired with national heritage monuments of acoustic importance, the consortium will develop a joint methodology for addressing relevant archaeological acoustics issues across Europe with historians of different disciplines. Specialists in tangible/intangible cultural heritage legal issues ensure the viability and longevity of the methodology guidelines. The consortium will prototype next generation exploration tools for presenting digital acoustic reconstructions to scientists and museum visitors alike. Results will be evaluated with associated test heritage sites, created in partnership with stakeholders and experienced content producers. Presentation methods provide first-person *in-situ* or off-site explorations, with the ability to experience various historical periods.

---

[1] https://cvaa.lam.jussieu.fr/doku.php#phenixthe_past_has_ears.

For deteriorated sites, this approach provides access to situations impossible to experience on-site. Additional uses include participative experiences, employing real-time reconstructions for on-site concerts and other events experienced in the heritage acoustics.

Responding to the EU Joint Programming Initiative on Cultural Heritage (JPI-CH) Conservation, Protection and Use joint CFP (2019), PHE addresses the challenges of "Layered conservation", "Sustainable protection and enhancement of values", and "Management of cultural heritage at risk". The project's goal is *developing new methods for presenting acoustic heritage to both researchers and users*, raising awareness and adding value to what is currently intangible heritage. This is achieved through development of a museum grade hardware/software prototype for the presentation of immersive audio experiences adaptable to multiple platforms, from off-site immersive speaker installations, to mobile AA/VR (XR) via smartphone applications.

Three principal objectives have been identified concerning the project: *Documentation*, *Modelling*, and *Presentation*. These research concepts are directed towards three case studies, adjusting to the unique requirements of each site. The overlying goal being the formulation of techniques, tools, and a system prototype that is adaptable to various site conditions and test cases, providing a flexible yet realistic immersive audio rendering of historic states of cultural heritage buildings. It is intended that the results of such a project will facilitate increased acceptance and integration of acoustic aspects within heritage research and communication with the public.

This paper presents an overview of the current project and the principal elements of XR related research. *Modelling* and *Presentation* directly concern XR on the three sites, and are therefor exposed in more detail here. Such research builds on previous results and knowledge previously acquired in the development and use of virtual acoustics and room acoustic simulations.

3   Principal Objectives of the Project

3.1   Documentation: Acoustical, Archaeological, Architectural, and Cultural

Any conservation-restoration process of a heritage site requires gathering documentation, scientific investigations, and a detailed state of repair, which form the basis for the elaboration of a diagnosis and subsequent project. Documentation of acoustics of historic sites is still an emerging notion in various associated fields, with no standards of practice or generally accepted methodologies.

PHE will develop a framework protocol for digital documentation through precise measurements of acoustic states of a site that is sufficient for providing a safeguarded reference in the event of evolution of the site, or in the event of disaster. Like the *Theatro La Fenice* and hopefully for the *Cathédral de Notre Dame de Paris*, such heritage sites can emerge from the flames of disaster with their acoustics preserved, being an integral part of their historic value. An open public database will be constructed consisting of descriptions, associated acoustic property characterisations and measurements, and *in-situ* recordings when possible to foster an accepted reference for discussion and exchange among researchers across Europe in the different domains. Such a database shall improve the quality of historical acoustic simulations, but providing much needed data on acoustic and physical properties of materials rarely used today in modern constructions, and therefore poorly documented.

3.2   Modelling: From Evidence to Auralisation, Layered History Modelling and Simulations

Physical and digital reconstruction methods have been used in acoustics for decades. However, it is only relatively recently that evolutions in computational technologies have opened the doors to improved quality and resolution of acoustic modelling for large-scale spaces where acoustics is crucial and spaces are increasingly complicated. Recent efforts in calibration techniques have shown that properly simulated spaces can be perceptually comparable to actual on-site spatial recordings [16,17]. Once created, these models are modified to explore alternative states, testing acoustic conditions under various architectural or decorative configurations, source and listener positions, use contexts, etc. As a tool, acoustic simulations provide a new and powerful resource for historical studies, providing researchers a sensorial presentation of heretofore-textural descriptions [8,11,15].

The "transparent" nature of acoustics provides ideal conditions for studying the layered nature of history within architectural sites. With a geometrically accurate 3D model, incorporating acoustic properties of materials and construction, accurate predictions are made of the evolution in the acoustics as a function of changes in different material's history. Changes occurring through the introduction, modification, or removal of significant elements as well as degradation over time or major catastrophes are incorporated based on accurate documentation and informed extrapolation through archaeological evidence. Changes in use are examined, focusing on the evolution of a site in relation to the evolution of culture and customs over time and the associated actions of our predecessors to adjust their acoustic environment to accommodate their needs.

As evidenced by prior works [12,13,18,19], there are varieties of methods available to carry out such simulations. Such variety of choice implies an equal variety in modelling parameters and results. With the aim of providing common research environments in acoustic heritage, it is necessary to work towards a uniform model definition methodology, independent of the tools employed, while providing an assessment of different approaches available.

An evaluation of current state-of-the-art and under development modelling methods will be carried out, examining for example ray-tracing, digital wave-guides, image-source method, finite-difference time domain (FDTD), and stochastic processing approaches which have all been shown to hold hold some promise which each exhibit certain limitations. The quality of resulting simulations are evaluated regarding authenticity from metric analysis perspectives and human perception perspectives, as listening to digital reconstructions is often more meaningful as a means to study acoustic heritage and to communicate its cultural nature, raising awareness for non-specialists [9,14].

3.3   Presentation/Use of Heritage Acoustics

The acoustics of a space is immersive, spatial, and due to the nature of auditory perception egocentric (first-person reference frame, individual), in contrast to visual perception of an object, which can be observed from "outside" (*e.g.* bird's eye view), or where the observation position does not seriously affect the information conveyed. Consequently, presentation methods for communicating acoustic heritage must represent the spatially immersive and listener-centric nature of acoustics. "Auralization" is the sound equivalent of visualization for the results of modelling techniques. The auditory presentation of accurate acoustical numerical models, through auralization over headphones or speaker arrays, allows users to experience spatial acoustic properties of a site as if present [3,4,7,10,16].

Due to the intangible nature of acoustics, and reactive nature of room acoustics, in that it does not "sound" on its own, requiring a sound source to be heard, the choice of sound material, and its presentation, have significant impacts on information transmission to users when attempting to provide a relevant and meaningful experience. Choice of source material are highly pertinent in raising awareness and integrating acoustic heritage in its cultural and societal context. The connection of heritage sites to their surroundings, through soundscape analysis and reconstruction, provides further means for communicating the temporal and cultural context, raising awareness of heritage's importance as a whole.

Different means for presenting acoustic heritage have been employed in recent years, with each production often being limited to the presentation system employed. While developments for off-site presentation have been more prevalent, *in-situ* rendering of immersive acoustic heritage has not advanced beyond the traditional "audio-guide", with its associated limitations. PHE will lead development of a museum grade hardware/software prototype for the presentation of immersive audio experiences adaptable to multiple platforms, from off-site immersive speaker installations, to mobile XR via smartphone applications.

On-site XR presentation will focus primarily on spatial audio rendering, using hear-through headphones. This direction allows for the actual visual state of a heritage site to be combined with a spatially coherent immersive auditory scene. Platform agnostic spatial audio formats (e.g. Higher-Order Ambisonics) will be used to minimize the impact of rendering in multiple user scenarios. Tracking will be integrated in the headphone device while a comparable smartphone application may use the orientation sensors available and standard headphones for a lower-quality but still immersive experience. Off-site presentation will focus on the use of speaker-array installations, which can be combined with image projection, for multiple users or off-the-shelf VR headsets.

Various degrees of interaction are possible, depending on the presentation platform. In addition to the ability to move about in the space, the user will be able to adjust their time-window perspective through history, experiencing the layered history. Focus can be applied to different elements or event. Further interaction with the acoustics of the virtual space is also possible, given available computing power, allowing the user for example to experience their own voice on stage in the former theatre in front of a full audience.

4 Cultural Heritage Site Case Studies

The project explores how through measurements, research, and finally virtual reconstructions the acoustics of heritage spaces can be documented, reconstructed, and experienced. Spanning a variety of heritage site conditions, three case studies with prominent heritage sites where *acoustics* plays a major role will be used to examine how to address the conservation, protection, and use of spaces both *past* and *present*. The case study sites represent public sites of importance in the form of an ancient Greek theatre (far from its original condition), a Gothic Cathedral (in the midst of recovering from a serious catastrophe, inaccessible to the public for some years), and the House of Commons (limited accessibility to the public, of significant cultural and political importance, and a key site for future preservation).

Notre-Dame de Paris: As soon as it was built at the end of the XIIth c., the Gothic cathedral of Notre-Dame de Paris became the emblematic place of musical creation in Europe. For more than 850 years, Notre-Dame de Paris has been the sounding box for the city's sacred music. Built to amplify the sacred word spoken or sung, the Cathedral is a multiform sound space where the clamor of the pilgrims circulating in the ambulatory and the chanting of the services protected by the choir's enclosure, the soloist singing the mass and the humming of the low masses in the radiant chapels, used to coexist until today, when before the fire, the call to silence for noisy visitors, the sound of the masses, the bursts of sound from the great organs and the concerts alternated.

House of Commons: This work builds upon the *Listening to the Commons* project, where the goal was to develop a first-stage acoustic model of pre-1834 UK House of Commons Chamber and the roof-void above, where women, who were otherwise excluded from this space, gathered to access and engage with political debate via listening through a ventilator. Measured acoustic data has also been gathered from the current House of Commons Chamber, and other historic sites in the UK comparable in design and period to the pre-1834 Chamber. The Commons chamber itself houses of one of the world's first parliamentary democracies.

Theater of Tindari: This ancient building erected at the end of the IVth BC, was renovated, and transformed during the Roman period, then abandoned during the Late antique period. Research on the possible use of the space will help understand its fate until the XXth c. With a capacity of $\approx$3000, it was used continuously until the Roman imperial age before undergoing substantial modifications, accommodating gladiatorial and animal combat. Today, it hosts musical and theatrical events.

5 Conclusion

The transparent and ephemeral nature of acoustics facilitates understanding of temporalities of acoustic heritage, whereby layers of cultural meaning and temporal history of materials and constructions are analysed by researchers, conveyed to interested users and the community as a whole. Combining methodical and generalized documentation procedures with validated digital modelling and simulation methods to ensure both physical and historic authenticity, the development and use of new digital tools and methods focusing on the emerging impact of auditory-VR/AR will foster new understandings and interpretations of sites and associated events. In proposing a temporally layered presentation, previous, present, and future interpretations are updated according to results of current and future historical research and discoveries.

Acknowledgements. Funding has been provided by the JPI-CH project PHE.

References

1. The importance of sound in today's world: promoting best practices. Technical report Resolution 39 C/49, UNESCO (2017). https://unesdoc.unesco.org/ark:/48223/pf0000259172
2. Convention for the safeguarding of the intangible cultural heritage. Technical report, UNESCO (2018). https://ich.unesco.org/en/convention
3. Capra, A., Binelli, M., Marmiroli, D., Martignon, P., Farina, A.: Correlation between subjective descriptors and objective parameters of theatres and auditoria acoustics simulated with binaural sound systems. In: International Congress Sound and Vibration, pp. 1–8 (2006)
4. Farina, A.: Acoustic quality of theatres: correlations between experimental measures and subjective evaluations. Appl. Acoust. **62**(8), 889–916 (2001). https://doi.org/10.1016/S0003-682X(00)00082-7
5. Farina, A., Ayalon, R.: Recording concert hall acoustics for posterity. In: Audio Engineering Society Conference Volume Multichannel Audio, The New Reality, June 2003. http://www.aes.org/e-lib/browse.cfm?elib=12277
6. Gerzon, M.A.: Recording concert hall acoustics for posterity. J. Audio Eng. Soc. **23**(7), 569–571 (1975). http://www.aes.org/e-lib/browse.cfm?elib=2669
7. Harriet, S., Murphy, D.T.: Auralisation of an urban soundscape. Acta Acustica United Acustica **101**(4), 798–810 (2015). https://doi.org/10.3813/AAA.918874
8. Katz, B.F.G., Mervant-Roux, M.M.: Comment entendre le passé? Quelques leçons d'une collaboration de recherche entre acousticiens et spécialistes d'études théâtrales. Revue Sciences/Lettres SI: L'Écho du théâtre (6), 1–14 (2019). https://doi.org/10.4000/rsl.1645. English title: How to hear the past? Some lessons from a collaborative research between acousticians and theatre studies specialists

9. Lovedee-Turner, M., Murphy, D.: Application of machine learning for the spatial analysis of binaural room impulse responses. Appl. Sci. **8**(1), 105 (2018). https://doi.org/10.3390/app8010105
10. Binelli, M., Pinardi, D., Nili, T., Farina, A.: Individualized HRTF for playing VR videos with Ambisonics spatial audio on HMDs. In: Audio Engineering Society Conference Volume AVAR, pp. 1–10 (2018)
11. Murphy, D., Shelley, S., Foteinou, A., Brereton, J., Daffern, H.: Acoustic heritage and audio creativity: the creative application of sound in the representation, understanding and experience of past environments. Internet Archaeol. **44** (2017). https://doi.org/10.11141/ia.44.12
12. Murphy, D.: Spatial audio measurement, modeling and composition. Leonardo **39**(5), 464–466 (2006). https://doi.org/10.1162/leon.2006.39.5.464
13. Noisternig, M., Katz, B., Siltanen, S., Savioja, L.: Framework for real-time auralization in architectural acoustics. Acta Acustica United Acustica **94**, 1000–1015 (2008). https://doi.org/10.3813/AAA.918116
14. Postma, B.N., Demontis, H., Katz, B.F.: Subjective evaluation of dynamic voice directivity for auralizations. Acta Acustica United Acustica **103**, 181–184 (2017). https://doi.org/10.3813/AAA.919045
15. Postma, B.N., Dubouilh, S., Katz, B.F.: An archeoacoustic study of the history of the Palais du Trocadero (1878–1937). J. Acoust. Soc. Am. SI: Room Acoust. Model. Auralization 2810–2821 (2019). https://doi.org/10.1121/1.5095882
16. Postma, B.N., Katz, B.F.: Perceptive and objective evaluation of calibrated room acoustic simulation auralizations. J. Acoust. Soc. Am. **140**(6), 4326–4337 (2016). https://doi.org/10.1121/1.4971422
17. Postma, B.N., Katz, B.F.G.: Creation and calibration method of acoustical models for historic virtual reality auralizations. Virtual Reality **19**(3), 161–180 (2015). https://doi.org/10.1007/s10055-015-0275-3
18. Southern, A., Murphy, D.T., Savioja, L.: Boundary absorption approximation in the spatial high-frequency extrapolation method for parametric room impulse response synthesis. J. Acoust. Soc. Am. **145**(4), 2770–2782 (2019). https://doi.org/10.1121/1.5096162
19. Stevens, F., Murphy, D.T., Savioja, L., Välimäki, V.: Modeling sparsely reflecting outdoor acoustic scenes using the waveguide web. IEEE/ACM Trans. Audio Speech Lang. Process. **25**(8), 1566–1578 (2017)
20. Tronchin, L., Farina, A.: Acoustics of the former Teatro-la Fenice-in Venice. J. Audio Eng. Soc. **45**(12), 1051–1062 (1997). http://www.aes.org/e-lib/browse.cfm?elib=7834

Applications in Medicine

Virtual Reality to Stimulate Cognitive Behavior of Alzheimer's and Dementia Patients

Daniela De Luca[✉] and Francesca Maria Ugliotti

DISEG Department, Politecnico di Torino, Corso Duca degli Abruzzi 24, 10129 Turin, Italy
{daniela.deluca,francesca.ugliotti}@polito.it

Abstract. Seniority and Alzheimer's and dementia's diseases lead to progressive cognitive impairment. The exploitation of Virtual Reality is investigated to test innovative entertainment and therapeutic activities that can provide new stimuli and interests for patients. The game approach activates mechanisms able to train memory and energize the mind through visuospatial and sound inputs. A full-immersive application has been developed to allow the patient to perform this kind of experience at home for daily training, becoming short therapeutic cycles, thanks to the affordability, the transportability and the flexibility of the infrastructure put in place. The cognitive path foresees successive levels of interaction, alternating relaxing and inspiring settings and exercises. It can improve the quality of life by learning to manage and monitor actions and feelings. In this way, these kind of experience can generate positive benefits not only for those who show fragility, but also for their families in addition to a tool to support health workers for diagnostics and training.

Keywords: Alzheimer's disease · Serious game · Cognitive exercises

1 Introduction

Nowadays, Virtual Reality (VR) is being extended to several sectors including healthcare and medicine. The main areas of application in these fields concern: training for nurses and caregivers, diagnostics and prevention, and physical and psychophysical rehabilitation [1]. Through the reproduction of virtual models, it is possible to simulate specific processes and scenarios in a realistic way focusing on cause and effect factors. An efficient VR system is able to offer a truthful three-dimensional rendering of human body parts or an avatar that can interact with situations and objects to achieve different objectives depending on the subjects involved. Thanks to technological evolution, the healthcare sector can also innovate towards a forefront healthcare system [2]. The contribution focuses on the creation of virtual reality environments and exercises for patients who are in certain medical conditions. Virtual reality is used to treat a wide variety of medical pathologies, becoming excellent tools to support traditional therapeutic processes. Over the years, several successful applications have been developed for the treatment of phobias, stress, anxiety and post-stroke rehabilitation [3]. The possibility to customize the scenes and activities, to make them more engaging, and to adapt the therapy according to the feedback of patients on performance are some of the advantages of

© Springer Nature Switzerland AG 2020
L. T. De Paolis and P. Bourdot (Eds.): AVR 2020, LNCS 12243, pp. 101–113, 2020.
https://doi.org/10.1007/978-3-030-58468-9_8

experimenting with new visualization method. According to statistics, in Italy, there are more than 600.000 people with Alzheimer disease, equal to 4% of the population over 65. It is expected that in 2050 the over 65 s will represent 34% of the population, making the country one of the most affected. This condition is often accompanied by dementia. According to the scientific community around the world, the case of dementia will tend to increase dramatically, bringing about 152 million people with dementia to 2050 [4]. The loss of cognitive functions such as thinking logically, remembering events of the present and the loss of behavioral skills are the main causes that hinder daily activities. The traditional exercises are usually focused on the simulation of correct daily habits, consequences of addictions and to learn about their prevention and treatment, to develop physical and cognitive exercises for rehabilitation, as well as to create simulations for the treatment of cognitive behaviors and special situations. The use of VR represents an opportunity to innovate the current tools and to enhance particular treatments related to human psychological, motor and cognitive functions [5]. The VR instruments on the market are so advanced and adaptable to every event that they can be professionalized and specialized. Cognitive training based on digital tasks and exercises can be a good solution to involve participants in structured mental activities and improve their cognitive functions, especially if the motivational and playful aspect is emphasized. The serious game presented in this article aims to stimulate emotions and the memory of Alzheimer patients, evaluating the most effective way of interaction.

2 Methodological Approach

2.1 Research Background

The objective of the study is to test the use of virtual reality for relaxation and cognitive stimulation of patients. The specific contribution is part of a wider research that aims to investigate the conditions that can make the experimentation effective in terms of: pathology, patient target (i.e. age, gender, social background), self-sufficiency (i.e. independent, caregiver-assisted or doctor-guided experience), level of immersivity (full-immersive, semi-immersive) and place where to carry out the experience (i.e. patient's home, dedicated rooms in the hospital or nursing home). From the matrix of combinations that is generated our research is currently directed towards diseases leading to cognitive impairment experimenting different technological systems depending on the context of use. Specifically, it was considered to experience semi-immersive experiences in hospital-healthcare environments, while totally immersive in a domestic environment. This choice can be traced back to the hardware devices to be used. Actually high-performance graphic calculation projection and tracking systems are deployed to obtain a three-dimensional experience with the possibility to focus both on the digital image and on the real objects, images, smells, that surround the user. If the advantage lies in being able to extend the experience to group of users, this mode of immersion is connoted by tools of large dimensions and high costs. Meanwhile the instrumentation for an immersive virtual experience is more limited, easily transportable and affordable, therefore it is easier to install at home. It is necessary to equip the patient with a head-mounted device, sensors for tracking human movement and recognition of the real environment, fast conversion systems to transfer real inputs within the virtual environment. The level of interaction control and the sensation of involvement are incomparable, although wearing the device may not be suitable for all patients.

2.2 Comparison Among Technologies: Virtual Wall and HTC Vive

In order to assess which technological solutions currently available on the market can be used to achieve the objectives identified in the previous paragraph, a workshop was organized with professionals from different backgrounds, including doctors and nurses. This was an opportunity for experimentation, evaluation and participatory design of virtual reality applications. Among the solutions examined are stereoscopic wall projection system and viewers.

Virtual Wall

Through a semi-immersive system such as the *Virtual Wall*, it is exploit the potential of different tools that generate a virtual environment. It is part of a larger system called *Cave*, using only one screen with projector and two cameras to make the virtual room transportable. The advantage of these technologies is the possibility of using a high precision stereoscopic holographic projector that transmits the three-dimensional model to a screen. The user perceives the three-dimensionality through 3D glasses equipped with reflective markets. With infrared cameras connected to the workstation, the tracking signal is transmitted. The higher the signal accuracy, the greater the user tracking in the surrounding space. By using only two chambers, a fairly large movement area can be covered without signal dispersion. If the environmental and user conditions are unfavorable, the addition of more rooms positioned at the end of the room make the movement more fluid. The problem with this system is the reflective surfaces and the amount of permeable light. If the room is neutral in colors and light, the more the system makes the environment immersive.

HTC Vive

Systems such as HTC Vive or Oculus Rift, are certainly cheap and easy to use. Since the equipment to make the experience immersive is simple and unsophisticated. What affects most in these types of tools is the PC graphics card, because it requires an NVIDIA GeForce GTX 1060. Also in this case the two bases for detecting the user's position present; 360° play area tracking coverage, wireless syncing and fits standard threaded mounting point. The headset is equipped with infrared cameras to communicate the movements with the two bases and render the virtual setting with modest frames. In addition, a knob is provided to adjust the focal distance and sharpen the images. Through a regulation system it adapts to every type of user. Finally, it can be integrated with other Virtual Reality systems that monitor limb movements such as overalls or gloves. The feeling that the two systems release is of a total immersion in real time, thanks to an easier use of the controllers. They are currently used for motor rehabilitation in hospital and at home, simulation of surgical interventions, training for doctors. If used for a long time during the day they can generate discomfort such as headaches and dizziness. The new systems have tried to reduce this problems with customizable lenses and using ergonomic helmets for wearing eyeglasses. The cost of this equipment is around 1000/600 €. Figure 1 shows the technical specifications of the two equipment considered.

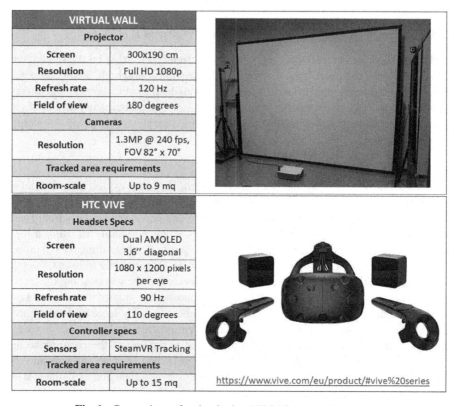

Fig. 1. Comparison of technologies: HTC Vive and Virtual Wall.

2.3 Immersive Application for Patients' Relaxation and Cognitive Stimulation

In relation to the scenario outlined, an immersive VR application has been implemented for Alzheimer's and dementia patients. These degenerative diseases are characterized by a gradual loss of memory and a deterioration of cognitive functions which, in the most acute phases, can compromise normal daily activities. The goal is to offer an entertainment experience with multi-sensory stimuli useful to reactivate and train the mind of older people through a gamification approach. Many studies have been carried out in recent years in this field, focused on the preservation of residual skills and executive functions through the reproduction of everyday contexts and actions. A walk in the park [6], the search for products on the shelves of a supermarket [7], the execution of a recipe [8], are some activities that require the implementation of choices and strategies (Figs. 2 and 3). Considering the age of the target group, the activities are designed to take place at home assisted by a caregiver.

Fig. 2. Forest experience Source: https://youtu.be/cMnia8KprIE

Fig. 3. Virtual supermarket experience. Source: https://www.alzheimer-riese.it/~alzheim3/contri buti-dal-mondo/annunci/4413-un-gioco-di-realta-virtuale-per-la-stimolazione-cerebrale-puo-ril evare-lmci-che-spesso-precede-lalzheimer

The application provides a path with gradual levels of complexity in order to test different behaviour and abilities. It is divided in three activities: (i) exploration of relaxing environment, (ii) basic memory exercises, and (iii) advanced memory exercises. The interaction with the patient is also progressive: from an almost passive stage of exploration to tasks that involve observation and recognition of forms, objects, colours and actions to be carried out in sequence.

Development of the Virtual Environment Through Gaming Platforms

There are different development platforms for Virtual Reality applications. Some of them require a high level of knowledge in terms of programming. In addition to the skills of the developers, it is useful to take into account for the purposes described in the contribution, the graphic detail that can be obtained with these platforms. The software that today meets the requirements described above is Unity 3D, inside it it is possible to generate three-dimensional environments with a high realism thanks to the rendering by frame of the light on the set materials.

The virtual environment is create by importing the elements, developed with specific software for 3D modeling. In particular, the interoperable format with the platform used for the virtual environment is fbx. This format reduces the meshes of the object and maintaining the element hierarchy after we have assigned the materials.

Once inserted the objects in Unity that make up the virtual model, it is useful to set the properties of the materials, lights and realism effects such as wind oscillation in the objects and sounds and animations. Among the advantages that this software offers, we find the possibility to import animated 3D objects, developing a Rigidbody with all the nodes. This skeleton that is created, however, cannot be modified directly on Unity but it is necessary to act on the starting software. For these reasons, Unity maintains an internal interface to create animations on an object from scratch, controlling the different nodes through scripts. Figure 4 highlights the management of animations through scripts.

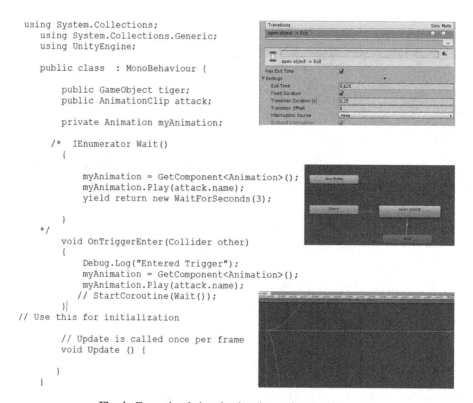

Fig. 4. Example of virtual animation and control by script

Furthermore, the reading of the movements created within the software are more fluid and realistic. The other advantage of the Unity platform, is the import of free packages that the different VR platform developers make available to facilitate interactions via the viewer controllers used. In fact in our case, both for HTC Vive and Oculus Rift, the appropriate packages have been downloaded. To implement the interactions, specific scripts have been studied for each action that recall the basic functions present within the package. In this way, by inserting the actions to the virtual scene and connecting the desired headsets in the setting properties of the VR supports, the executable can generate. This file is independent of the Unity project and can be use in any workstation that supports the minimum requirements required by headsets.

The creation of the virtual scene is quite simple and the hierarchy of the elements is easy to find thanks to the control panels that the Unity project preserves. In fact, through the "Console" bar, the program warns the developer if during the association of the script with the object it is correct or if the code has gaps. The intuitiveness of the software and the online guide that supports developers in the implementation of the code makes the choice of software successful and scalable to every need.

First Level Activity: Exploration of Relaxing Environment
Like in reality, space design plays a key role in delivering positive experiences for Alzheimer patients, virtual environments can also contribute. In fact, peaceful and comfortable locations can help to reduce agitation and anxiety making users feel good and improving their mood. To achieve this goal, it is important to create scenes in which the colors, light, and sounds are well calibrated in order to return feeling of relaxation. The quality of the setting can engage and delight the user, stimulating reactions and reaction and memories and encouraging communication. As the next level activities require greater interaction and concentration by the patient, the acclimatisation phase is essential to establish an optimal psychophysical condition. In order to test the user's preference according to the specific perception, two settings have been created: a multisensory room

Fig. 5. First level activity. Exploration of relaxing environment. Source: images from the Carvajal's Master Thesis [9]

[9] and a natural landscape. As visible in Fig. 5, natural elements and animals are used, recalling familiar landscapes and pleasant personal sensations associated with them.

Second Level Activity: Basic Memory Exercises

The second stage provides for the active involvement of the patient. To execute the *Train your memory by colour, forms and number* exercise it is necessary to become familiar with the joysticks, memorizing the correct buttons to take actions. The activity session is organized by three tasks [9] as illustrated in Fig. 6.

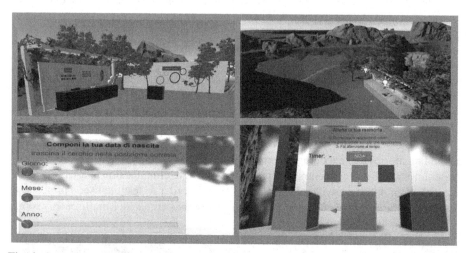

Fig. 6. Second level activity: Train your memory by colour, forms and number. Source: images from the Carvajal's Master Thesis [9]

Task 1: Color Sequence Recomposition

A sequence of three cubes with different colours is presented to the patient. After observing it, the objects disappear and it is requested to restore the correct order by clicking on them. If the sequence is right, a new sequence to be memorized with a higher number of cubes is displayed to continue the game. If it is not correct, the activity stops and must be restored. The introduction of a timer help the patient to be more stimulated in reaching the goal in the shortest possible time. This activates a competition with oneself, encouraging users to continue playing the game to achieve better results. Each cube contains sub-objects that are used for the construction of the interaction. A script manage and recalls the object's colors and the relative order.

Task 2: Important and Current Dates Composition

The task concerns the possibility of composing dates, such as birthday, year of marriage, children's birth, current date, in a virtual way. Through editable sliders, the user can select the day, month and year by simply dragging the cursor on the corresponding button. The management of number is effective in keeping the brain active in remembering personal data and keeping in touch with everyday life. The caregiver can ask to remember other dates or even memorize new ones, training the mind in an alternative mode.

Task 3: Puzzle Composition

The last exercise concerns the creation of a virtual puzzle. There are several choices. The pictures are linked to images that stimulate the memory. For example, a map of the city divided into districts is proposed. The pieces have been reproduced through three-dimensional shapes in brilliant colours so that they are pleasing to the visual senses of Alzheimer's patients. They must be placed on a background that presents the same colour scheme. Puzzles are designed to give a sense of satisfaction to patients when they complete the picture. Each piece is controlled by elements and a script to read the position on the table and associate it with the correct orientation once near the map. This type of exercise in addition to helping the mind can increase the motor functions of the limbs, as if it were a small physiotherapy session led by the controller.

Third Level Activity: Advanced Memory Exercises

Currently there are several applications related to the possibility of cooking in Virtual Reality. An example is *CyberCook*. It allows users to create recipes from all over the world using real-time virtual ingredients. It allows to learn how to create a variety of international dishes, providing indications for each step of the recipe, up to the cooking. Through a series of techniques and virtual tools, users can execute the recipe by listening to the instructions inside the viewer. The more ingredients are inserted into the pan in the correct way, the expert chef accumulates points to advance the level and unlock more and more complex recipes [10].

Another application with pedagogical function is *Mes crêpes Lactel* presented during the Laval Virtual fair. In this case the user activates a real journey: from the virtual visit of the production plants to the search on the shelves of the virtual kitchen for the useful ingredients to complete the recipe. The peculiarity of this application is the combination of cooking and the teaching function, making the production processes known to the public, such as observing the chemical molecules during the milk preservation process [11].

Thanks Virtual Reality, the users can actively learn the information and through specific tasks involving perception/action, the transfer of knowledge and behavior acquired in a virtual world into the real world can be promoted [12]. According to some studies, excellent results can be obtained, evaluating first the same actions done in real life and then repeating them in virtual. In fact, by associating a global score for assisted autonomy, the patient can obtain modest but significant benefits (15.4% from the virtual, 11.3% from the real condition), reaching scores of 90.8% through Virtual Reality applications and the 94.4% replicating them in reality [13].

By exploiting these potentials, the developed *Train your mind by cooking* application in Fig. 7 can become a useful support for Alzheimer's patients, not only to train the mind but above all to restore the correct functionality to the objects that will be used in everyday life. In this case, combining the game with the passion for cooking, each action is controlled and managed through Virtual Reality. It become a valid support creating safe environments where the patient can make mistakes without impacting on real life. Another objective that this activity wants to highlight is the possibility of transferring virtual actions into everyday life, becoming a valid support for the patient's autonomy. The activities are divided into different steps.

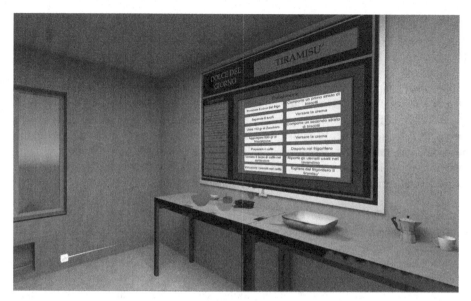

Fig. 7. Third level activity: train your memory by cooking.

Task 1: Choose the Recipe of the Day

Using a virtual button, the patient with the operator will activate the list of ingredients on the blackboard and read the activity.

Task 2: Execute the Recipe

The user must perform the previously read action and memorize the correct movement. If the activity is not carried out adequately with respect the indications, the ingredient button will not change color and the users cannot continue with the recipe. In this way, movements and actions can be controlled by giving the right value to the object. During the learning process, the user always has the opportunity to read the instructions to strengthen the correct answer, and reduce the production of errors.

Task 3: Interaction with Animations

The game is made even more interactive by activating animations. For example, it is possible turn on the stove and hear the sound of the coffee maker. In this phase, other senses are also activated, such as sound and perception of the action in a concrete way. This is thanks to a detailed modeling of the context and animations. Realism is fundamental in educating the patient in the correct use of objects and in the sense of danger. In fact, if during the execution of the recipe, the patient forget to turn off the stove or close the water tap, a second button activate an audio alarm so the patient know that something is not working properly. The study of interactions is basic and does not require great skills to facilitate the use of this system even for those who are not familiar with technologies. In fact, simple actions, such as activating/deactivating the buttons or touching and opening/closing objects are associated with a single button on the joystick. All the actions that the user can carry out have a visual or audio correspondence which facilitates interactivity and can guide in the correct execution.

3   Results and Discussion

The application has been realized in an experimental way with the specific objective of formulating an easy to manage experience to allow patients to carry it out at home. Although there is no doubt that the non-immersion mode is the simplest to deliver, the aim is to test whether total immersion can amplify the effectiveness. From a technical point of view, the use of low-cost functional environments such as HTC Vive and Oculus Rift makes it possible to easily distribute the application on a larger scale. The transportability of the system allows to amplify the results achieved in the hospital thanks to the family environment and the actions carried out in the daily life of one's own home. Currently the application has been submitted to about thirty people without disease in a dedicated workshop to evaluate its functionality. Participants' satisfaction is mainly influenced by the correct correspondence between actions and movements. The more the VR system used is correctly calibrated the more the interaction is in real time reducing response times. While it was tested on a limited sample of patients on a voluntary basis. Considering the age of the patients, it emerges that, despite the interest in testing virtual environment, the support of an operator or caregiver available to learn how to use the devices is necessary. On the other hand, the game experience can be configured as a good support to entrust to the caregiver who assists the patient at home. Since the game is divided into several levels, it is possible to calibrate the activities and differentiate the sessions. For example, immersion in a virtual setting is indicated to offer the patient a distraction and calm him/her down, while the exercises are used to stimulate him/her when he/she is more calm. The more exercises are implemented, the more options are available. This new type of treatment has led to the definition of new sensations thanks to the continuous implementation of the virtual environment. In fact, working on realism, the user feels no sense of disorientation. In particular with regard to the recipe, which requires the performance of real-life actions, the main advantage of the training is the error-free learning mode. The user is directed to take alternative measures to solve the problem or respond to inputs from external agents, based on his psychophysical condition. The best way to act on cognitive presence is to formulate very specific questions and requests to the user. In this way the patient always has the awareness of what he/she will do. Verifying the cognitive presence of patients undergoing these types of exercises using virtual reality is essential to ensure progress and improvements in their mental abilities, as well as to determine changes and improvements in the design of applications based on the type of dementia. To implement the effectiveness of this new methodology, evaluation tools called Pool Activity Level (PAL) can be used [15]. These systems help to measure mental and physical progress, and assess cognitive and behavioral independence in the face of unexplored situations. The purpose of the PAL instrument is to allow caregivers to involve people with dementia in meaningful activities, provide information about the individual's strengths and abilities, and ensure that activities are appropriate. It consists of four levels: planned, exploratory, sensory and reflex. Evaluation systems such as the PAL introduce new mechanisms between the patient and the therapist. In fact, to test the effectiveness of the treatment, the therapist needs tools to evaluate the user's history. In this way, the personalization of the treatment can lead to detailing the activities based on the preferences indicated through PAL questionnaires. By working mainly on the exploratory activity, the patient is helped in carrying out common activities in family environments, for example, reproducing his home in which to do the activities in virtual. This facilitates the concentration and the final development of the exercise. This triggers a mechanism such that the sensory stimuli amplify the movements and help the mind to remember thanks to the emotions that the three-dimensional setting arouses.

4 Conclusion and Next Development

Many studies are ongoing to determine whether the Virtual Reality could be used as an alternative method that alleviate the course of diseases such as Alzheimer and dementia [14]. Initial findings reveal that the patient is attracted to the game approach which allows to carry out the activity with greater motivation and interest. The unique ability of Virtual Reality to transport you elsewhere can be used to simulate increasingly realistic actions and processes. For certain pathologies VR environments can be seen as tools able to develop new mechanisms between patient, caregiver and medical staff, strengthening traditional treatment systems. If the exercises can be studied and calibrated according to the clinical needs of the patients, at the same time the research tries to understand how to make the experiences more and more customized, so as to provide experiences that can evoke moments of their personal, family, and working life. The Virtual Reality application developed and the experience as a whole will be further refined according to the feedback received in order to carry out a real trial considering a well-defined sample target of patients. Tomorrow's therapist will therefore no longer need real environments but will activate virtual travel that will help people overcome their fears and mental deficits. Furthermore, among future developments, Virtual Reality can also be used as a diagnostic tool in the case of Alzheimer's and dementia patients, helping doctors to prevent and constantly monitor the course of the disease. In the coming years, the Virtual Reality will be used to improve the accuracy and effectiveness of current procedures and the capabilities of the human being, both as a caregiver and as a patient.

Acknowledgements. The authors would like to thank the La Casa nel Parco CANP Project for the support to develop this research. Our work continues to study how the introduction of technologies can improve the quality of space and patients' lives. Special thanks to Ricardo Carvajal, Riccardo Levante and Francesco Alotto for contributing to the realization of the application.

References

1. Sik Lányi, C.: Virtual reality in healthcare. In: Ichalkaranje, N., Ichalkaranje, A., Jain, L. (eds.) Intelligent Paradigms for Assistive and Preventive Healthcare. Studies in Computational Intelligence, vol 19, pp. 88–116. Springer, Heidelberg (2006)
2. Riva, G.: Virtual reality for health care: the status of research. CyberPsychol. Behav. **5**(3), 219–225 (2002)
3. Robert, P.H., et al.: Recommendations for the use of serious games in people with Alzheimer's disease, related disorders and frailty. Front. Aging Neurosci. 6 (2014). Article 54
4. Alzheimer's Disease International (ADI): World Alzheimer Report 2018 The state of the art of dementia research: New frontiers (2018). https://www.alz.co.uk/research/WorldAlzheim erReport2018.pdf. Accessed 11 Feb 2020

5. Buss, B.: Virtual reality training system for patients with dementia. Master Thesis, ETH Zurich, pp. 1–83 (2009). https://doi.org/10.3929/ethz-a-005899172

6. Moyle, W., Jones, C., Sung, B., Dwan, T.: Alzheimer's Australia Victoria The Virtual Forest project: Impact on engagement, happiness, behaviours & mood states of people with dementia. Griffith University (2016)

7. Zygouris, S., et al.: Can a virtual reality cognitive training application fulfill a dual role? Using the virtual supermarket cognitive training application as a screening tool for mild cognitive impairment. J. Alzheimer's Dis. **44**(4) (2015). https://doi.org/10.3233/jad-141260

8. Steam. https://store.steampowered.com/app/857180/The_Cooking_Game_VR/. Accessed 26 Feb 2020

9. Carvajal, R.: Virtual Reality in Treatments for Alzheimer's patients. Master Thesis, Politecnico di Torino, Torino (2019)

10. X-TECH BLOG. http://x-tech.am/lets-start-to-cook-virtual-reality-cooking-lessons/. Accessed 26 Feb 2020

11. HE SPREADER. http://ghcfrancaise.blogspot.com/2017/04/unusual-lactel-embarks-on-virtual.html. Accessed 26 Feb 2020

12. Howland, J.L., Jonassen, D., Marra, R.M.: Goal of technology integrations: meaningful learning. In: Howland, J.L., Jonassen, D.H., Marra, R.M. (eds.) Meaningful Learning with Technology, 4th edn., vol. 1, pp. 1–9. Pearson, Boston (2012)

13. Foloppe, D.A., Richard, P., Yamaguchi, T., Etcharry-Bouyx, F., Allain, F.: The potential of virtual reality-based training to enhance the functional autonomy of Alzheimer's disease patients in cooking activities: a single case study. Neuropsychological Rehabil. **28**(5), 709–733 (2018). https://doi.org/10.1080/09602011.2015.1094394

14. Rizzo, A.A., Kim, G.J.: A SWOT analysis of the field of VR rehabilitation and therapy presence Teleoper. Virtual Environ. **14**, 119–146 (2005)

15. Dudzinski, E.: Using the Pool Activity Level instrument to support meaningful activity for a person with dementia: a case study. Br. J. Occup. Ther. **79**(2), 65–68 (2016). https://doi.org/10.1177/0308022615600182

Dynamic Cutting of a Meshless Model for Interactive Surgery Simulation

Vincent Magnoux⬤ and Benoît Ozell$^{(\boxtimes)}$⬤

Polytechnique Montréal, Montréal, Canada
`benoit.ozell@polymtl.ca`

Abstract. Virtual reality has become a viable tool for training surgeons for specific operations. In order to be useful, such a simulation need to be as realistic as possible so that a user can believe what they experience and act upon the virtual objects. We focus on simulating surgical operations that require cutting virtual organs. They offer a particular set of challenges with respect to simulation stability, performance, robustness and immersion.

We propose to use a fully continuous movement representation and collision detection scheme between cutting tool and other simulated objects to improve the robustness of the simulation and avoid breaking immersion with errors in topology changes. We also describe a new way to attach the surface of a simulated object to its underlying physical model, consistently while it is being cut. This feature helps maintain immersion by keeping the visual aspect of the object coherent with its physical behavior and by allowing correct transmission of actions from the user on the object.

Our tests show that the proposed tool movement representation properly generates continuous cuts in simulated models, even as they move and deform. It also allows cutting when a moving model comes into contact with a motionless tool, and to model a curved or deforming tool without additional effort. Our surface mapping method results in a visual model that closely follows the movement and deformation of the physical model after it has been cut.

Keywords: Surgery simulation · Virtual reality · Cutting simulation · Physically-based simulation · Meshless methods

1 Introduction

Surgery simulation technology using virtual reality has become a useful and practical tool for learning specific operations like lung tumor removal [33], aneurysm clipping [2] and many others [20]. As with all virtual environments, an important aim for these simulations is to create a world in which the user can feel immersion and presence as much as possible. This sensation may come from how the world is perceived by the user's senses, such as vision, hearing and touch, and from how the world reacts to the user's actions. The research presented in this paper

© Springer Nature Switzerland AG 2020
L. T. De Paolis and P. Bourdot (Eds.): AVR 2020, LNCS 12243, pp. 114–130, 2020.
https://doi.org/10.1007/978-3-030-58468-9_9

focuses on the latter aspect, more specifically on how virtual objects like organs are modified through cutting actions from the user during a surgical operation.

There has been a lot of progress in cutting simulation, both on the physical and the visual aspects, yet there remain open challenges to improve the realism of this interaction. Our goals are to develop a tool representation that increases the *robustness* of the simulation during a cutting action and to maintain *coherence* between the visual surface and the underlying physical model at the same time. Together, these objectives will improve simulation interactivity by providing a more accurate representation of hand movement, avoiding breaks in immersion in a straightforward way and ensuring a realistic reaction of soft tissue to user action.

On the one hand, we improve the robustness by ensuring that any part of a simulated object traversed by a cutting tool will indeed be cut. This means that no geometric element will be missed due to the discrete nature of the simulation or to the movement and deformation of either the object or cutting tool.

On the other hand, we preserve coherence between the visual and physical models by elaborating a set of criteria that determine how the surface mesh moves with the physical model and how it can transmit forces to it.

1.1 Background and Related Work

Soft body simulations that allow cutting may be classified according to the physical simulation method, which may either be mesh-based or meshless. A thorough review of the various cutting methods may be found in [35]. Mesh-based cutting involves removing and recreating elements along the tool trajectory [5,6,11,12,28,34], while meshless methods rely on updating the connection or visibility between the particles that form the physical object [13,17,25,26,31]. For both simulation categories, cutting requires modeling the trajectory of the tool as well as finding the intersection of the tool with the object along that trajectory. At the lowest level, this intersection is often computed as the contact between edges or between triangles and points of either model.

Tool Representation. Most simulations represent the cutting part of the tool as a one-dimensional edge composed either of a single segment [9,21,23] or multiple ones [6,32]. The area between the position of the cutting edge during the previous frame and its position during the current frame is considered the *swept area* [32]. It may be approximated by a plane [9,21,23] or be triangulated to obtain a more closely fitting cutting surface [10,13,15,24,31].

One major drawback of this approximation is that it does not capture well the movement of the cutting edge when it does not lie in the same plane between two frames. This may cause some contact detection to be missed, eventually resulting in erroneous modifications in the modeled object surface. [21] propose to use a continuous representation of the cutting edge, which partially offsets this problem by providing a more realistic approximation of the edge movement. However, it still fails to take into account the movement and deformation of the object being cut.

There are however approaches that go in a different direction. A single point with an orientation may be used to represent the tool [4, 30]. Together, the position and orientation of the point define a plane which can be used to compute level sets at every frame, which in turn determine where different material points are with respect to the tool. In other cases, some represent the tool with a volume and check for an instantaneous (discrete) intersection between the tool volume and the object volume [1, 28]. In a similar way, [11] uses as a cutting surface the intersection of the tool volume with the object, represented with voxels – resulting in an approximate cut. Finally, rather than using a well-defined geometric shape, the tool volume may simply be sampled with a set of points [26].

Surface Mapping. In general, simulations may either use an implicit or explicit surface representation to draw an object on the screen. However, implicit representations usually require a lot of computing power and are thus not well suited for an interactive simulation [16, 22]. Some manage to perform volume- and point-based rendering in real time on parts of a model using surface splatting [17, 37] or, more recently, ray casting on the entire object [30].

Explicit surface representations must be somehow attached, or *mapped*, to the physical object model so that they can properly move according to the results of the physical simulation and continue to transmit interaction forces.

For mesh-based physical models, the trivial case consists in using the boundary faces of volume elements to display the surface [5]. However, the resolution of the surface is thus directly tied to that of the physical model. A separate representation allows to display the object in much greater detail than it is possible to physically simulate it.

With mesh-based physical models, this mapping between the surface mesh and physical object is done by selecting to which volume element a surface vertex belongs and computing its barycentric or trilinear coordinates within that element [6, 11, 12, 14, 28, 29, 34]. When the element is displaced or deformed, the new vertex position is computed using the mapping coordinates in the new element configuration.

With meshless models, the mapping is done by selecting a set of appropriate particles and computing a set of weights for each of them relative to the vertex. Instead of weights calculated through barycentric or trilinear coordinates – since there is no geometrically set element – a moving least squares (MLS) scheme is often used [13, 15, 17, 26, 31, 36]. Other weighted mappings are also possible, based on how the displacement field is sampled in the physical simulation [8, 18, 25].

1.2   Contributions

This paper describes the following contributions:

- A fully continuous cutting interaction between a tool and a surface that includes detecting the cut primitives and modifying the surface mesh in consequence. Both the tool and the object may be deforming during that interaction.

– A small set of criteria that allow mapping the surface on its underlying volume model to maintain visual coherence.

Section 2 describes the details of these contributions, while Sect. 3 demonstrates their utility through a set of examples.

2   Method

2.1   Tool Representation and Collision Detection

For the purpose of cutting, the interacting part of the tool is represented by a series of points joined by straight line segments, collectively called the *cutting edge*. The only interaction on which we will focus in this paper is for cutting, without exchanging forces between the tool and other simulated objects. The cutting edge is considered ideal, in the sense that it has no volume, cuts as soon as it comes in contact with a simulated object and does not generate any force on it. In addition to the cutting tool, the term *edge* will refer to the primitives used for detecting intersections. For the surface, they are the lines between surface vertices that form triangles and for the underlying physical object, they are the links between integration points and particles that form its topology.

The object itself is deformed and cut using the method described in [3] and [19]. For the purpose of topology modifications, the object is entirely composed of edges, as defined above. Cutting only occurs when edges are intersected, not when a point enters a triangle on the surface. Furthermore, we only mention cutting the object's surface, but everything discussed in this section applies in an identical way to cutting the edges that define its volume.

As the tool is displaced from one frame to the next, each of its edges form a skew quadrilateral with the four points being the two ends of the edge at the first frame and the two ends at the second frame, as shown in Fig. 1. The set of 3-dimensional quads form the surface swept by the blade during the frame. When detecting collisions, the deformed object's surface is similarly only considered as a set of edges that move through space between animation frames. The detection is made between each pair of edges that belong to the separate objects, according to the continuous collision algorithm described in [27].

We assume each point of the blade moves in a straight line during a frame. This approximation remains accurate as long as the displacement between frames is relatively short, which is the case when animating the simulation at a rate of 60 frames per second, leaving less than 17 ms per frame.

This operation is more complex than with an explicitly-triangulated swept surface since it requires continuous edge-edge collision tests rather than just a series of discrete triangle-edge tests. However, there are several situations where it provides a correct solution, in contrast to a discrete detection scheme.

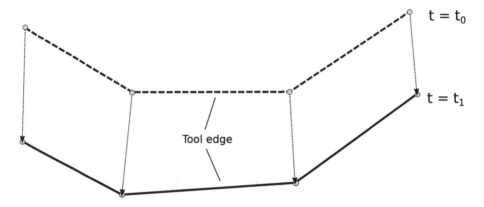

Fig. 1. The area swept by the cutting tool is only described in terms of the position of its edge at the previous frame (t_0) and its position at the current frame (t_1).

Situation 1. The continuous method allows for a completely gap-less detection of cut edges, which is especially useful when both objects are moving between frames. For example, an edge from the deformed object could move across an entire swept area quadrilateral during a frame time, leaving it undetected when using a discrete scheme. Figure 2 illustrates such a situation in two dimensions. The cutting tool is displayed as a wedge in this diagram, but only the tip has any physical presence in a 2D setting. Its movement traces a line – rather than a swept area in 3D – which can be used for detecting intersections with surface triangles.

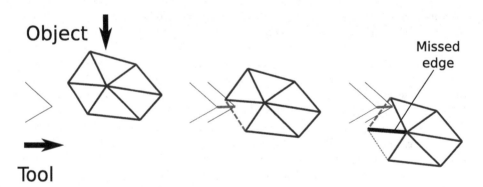

Fig. 2. Example of *Situation 1*, in 2D, where a collision detection scheme that is continuous only with the tool movement would fail to detect a certain triangle edge. The large arrows indicate the direction of movement of the tool and object. The red line between tool positions represents the space swept by it between frames (Color figure online).

Situation 2. That method also avoids detecting cuts in places where a surface edge enters the swept area *after* the blade has passed, as in Fig. 3. In that case, the tip of the cutting tool was always outside the object, but the line that connects the current position to the previous one still intersects some edges in the object at its current position.

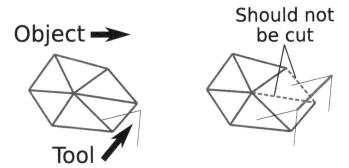

Fig. 3. Example of *Situation 2*, where the line spanned by the tip of the cutting tool intersects two of the objects edges at the end of the frame, even though the tool was outside the object at every point in time between the two frames. The large arrows indicate the direction of movement of the tool and object. The red line between tool positions represents the space swept by it between frames (Color figure online).

Situation 3. Another case where this description is essential is when the blade is not moving but the deforming object is, whether under gravity or elastic forces. In such a case, the blade does not sweep any area, but the object must still be cut, as shown in Fig. 4.

Fig. 4. Example of *Situation 3*, where a simulated object moves downward onto a motionless cutting tool. The tool's edge does not sweep any area, but must still be able to cut the object.

When the tool is moving, the continuous method also provides a slightly more accurate approximation of the swept area as well as a more accurate point of contact, both in space and in time, since it is not flattened by using triangles.

Since the tool may also cut while not moving, we must take particular care with defining some quantities. For example, we might want to know on which side of the cutting edge lie each pair of vertices. In our method, the new normal on the surface is entirely determined by the position of each intersection – the trajectory of the cutting tool relative to the object. This avoids relying on the normal of a swept surface that does not exist when the tool is motionless.

One point worth mentioning is that with the movement representation described above, the cutting tool itself can be deformed during the simulation without the need to handle that case differently.

2.2   Surface Mapping and Remapping

To ensure that the surface remain coherent with the movement of the physical simulated object and thus provide a proper interface with other virtual objects and with the user, we establish a set of constraints that determine how each surface vertex moves with the physical object model. These criteria are tailored to the deformation and cutting method of [19], where the particles are embedded in a regular background integration grid; however, they can be applied almost directly to any method that maps a triangulated surface on a set of particles.

Since the displacement of a material point inside the object is determined by interpolating the displacement of neighboring particles using shape functions computed with an MLS scheme, a natural solution is to use the same scheme for surface vertices. The set of particles that determine the position of a point will be called the *mapping* of that point in the remainder of this paper.

The main challenge with this method consists in choosing the right particles on which to map a vertex. This choice does not simply depends on the distance between the vertex and particles, because we need to take into account the initial topology of the object as well as the cuts introduced with the tool. We may however choose that criterion as a starting point for the set of constraints, since it is how it would be done for a convex object that does not contain any cut.

It should be mentioned that when determining where to map a given vertex, only the rest configuration of the object is considered. While intersections are detected in the current (deformed) configuration, their location in the object at rest can be determined in a straightforward way: since they always occur on edges, between two points, they can be fully described by a proportion along the vector connecting the two points. For simplicity, we consider that proportion to always be the same, whether in the rest or deformed configuration.

To avoid mapping a vertex to particles that belong to physically separate parts of the object – while still being geometrically close – we first decide to select particles that are in the neighborhood of a single integration point. This guarantees that they will all move in a locally coherent way. The mapping problem is thus reduced to finding a single most suitable integration point for each vertex of the surface mesh. This approach is sound also because the integration elements are more closely related to the geometry of the object – they distribute its volume and mass to the particles. They are all at least partially inside the object, whereas particles may lie slightly outside the surface of the object as described in [3].

When the object contains a cut, or simply a concave portion, the integration point nearest to a certain vertex may actually be in another part of the object (see Fig. 5). To avoid any such wrong mapping, we add as a criterion that the integration point on which a vertex is mapped must lie below the plane defined by the vertex and its normal.

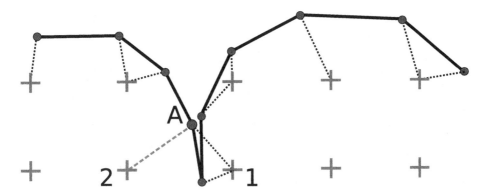

Fig. 5. Illustration in 2D of a situation where the nearest integration point to a certain vertex would not be the best mapping. Integration points are displayed as red crosses and vertices as blue circles, with dotted lines indicating the nearest integration point. Vertex A has integration point 1 as its closest, which lies across another surface boundary. We would rather choose an integration point that is *not* separated by another part of the surface, such as point 2, connected to the thicker green line (Color figure online).

There are however many cases where the plane test by itself is not sufficient to determine the right mapping point. For example, in Fig. 6, when the cutting tool passes between a certain vertex and the integration point on which it is mapped, using only the criteria mentioned earlier, we would try to map the vertex to the same integration point. We therefore associate with the vertex an additional plane below which the mapped integration point must also be, whenever a new cut is introduced into the object near that vertex.

The final criterion we need to define allows to take *all* introduced cuts into account – rather than just the most recent one – without specifying an arbitrarily large number of cutting planes. For each vertex, we only choose as potential mapping targets integration points which are connected to a set of particles *similar* to that of neighboring vertices. In other words, we need to consider not just the integration point, but the set of particles on which vertices are mapped. For an integration point to be considered valid, it has to have at least one particle in common with every vertex that form a triangle with the unmapped vertex. This also ensures that vertices that are close to each other will be mapped to integration points that are also close to each other, keeping the displacement of the surface locally coherent.

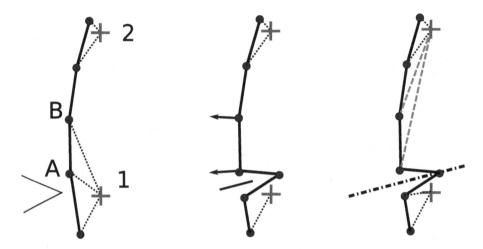

Fig. 6. Illustration of the need for an additional constraint plane when finding a good mapping. *Left:* A cutting tool approaches from the left, below vertex A. *Middle:* The introduced cut has caused vertices A and B to lose their previous mapping. Their initial normal is indicated. Using only that normal would cause them to be mapped on the integration point 1, from which they were just unmapped. *Right:* The introduced cutting plane causes vertices A and B to be mapped to point 2.

In summary, when choosing a new integration point to which a vertex will be mapped, that point must be

- connected to some of the same particles on which neighboring vertices are already mapped;
- below the plane tangent to the surface at that vertex;
- below an additional plane defined when a cut was introduced.

From the integration points that match all these criteria, the one closest to the vertex under consideration is chosen.

2.3   Dynamic Simulation

Whenever a part of the object is intersected by the cutting tool, all affected vertices must find a new mapping. We define in the next paragraphs which surface vertices to remap after an interaction with the cutting tool.

When a surface edge is cut, two vertices are added: they must be mapped. The endpoints of the (now cut) edge must be remapped, and receive an additional plane corresponding to the surface normal of the cut (see Fig. 6, right). There is also the case where the blade intersects the segment between a vertex and the integration point on which it is mapped. In that case, the vertex has to be remapped and be associated with an additional plane. That new plane passes through the cut point and has the vertex-integration point line as a normal, as if that line were just another surface edge.

Adjustments to the mapping also need to be made when the underlying physical model is cut. A modified connectivity between particles and integration points changes the eligibility of affected integration points in certain cases, so any vertex that is mapped to these points needs to be remapped. For example, two integration points that share a certain particle may become separated and no longer be considered as neighbors, affecting how nearby vertices must be mapped.

When the mapping of a vertex changes, its position at the next frame may change slightly, even if the object is not moving. Using a fully continuous collision detection scheme prevents any missed surface edge.

Animation Loop. The order in which the main steps of the simulation are carried out is important to obtain a consistent interaction between the dynamic tool and the object. An animation step in our current implementation consists of four operations:

1. Process user input. This only consists in moving the cutting tool to its new position, as determined by a haptic device, for example.
2. Detect collisions. These collisions are currently only for cutting.
3. Perform topology changes, based on the intersections detected in the previous step. This results in updated data structures describing the object – physical model, surface and mapping between the two.
4. Solve the dynamic system. This system incorporates internal elastic forces, gravity and external forces. This step also updates the surface vertex and integration point positions according to the new particle positions given by the system solution, as described in [3,19].

In such a scenario, input by the user is considered to occur during the displacement of surface positions, even if it is only processed after. Any movement from the user that happens during the animation step will have an effect based on the *next* surface and object position.

3   Results

The applicability of our method is demonstrated through an implementation using the SOFA framework [7]. We show examples of various situations described in the previous section where it is useful, both on simple geometries and on organ models. The proper functioning of the surface mapping criteria is apparent is some of these scenes, but is most visible in the accompanying video.

The most obvious advantage of having a fully continuous collision detection scheme, is that we can still properly detect tool-object intersections when the blade is static and the object is moving. This can occur for example under the action of gravity or elastic forces. This capability contrasts with the usual method where only the cutting edge is considered to be moving from one frame to the next. Figure 7 shows three different frames of a simulation where a circular cylinder is falling on a simple straight cutting edge. Even if the edge does not sweep any area, the object can still be cut. This example also shows how the surface position remains consistent with the position of the object. Surface vertex positions are entirely dependent on the position of the underlying physical model, not shown in this picture.

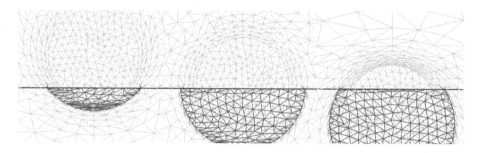

Fig. 7. A circular cylinder is moving downward and being cut by a horizontal edge that remains in the same place. The surface of the cylinder (including the newly-generated part) properly follows the movement of the underlying physical model.

As a comparison, Fig. 8 shows a similar scene, this time where the circular cylinder is static and the cutting edge is moving upward. One can see that the resulting cut surface is very similar to that of Fig. 7. The surface generation method remains identical; the only difference is the sequence and speed at which triangle edges are intersected.

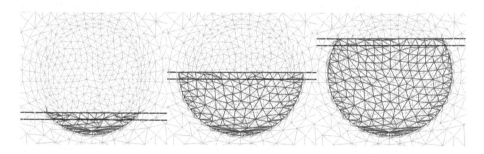

Fig. 8. A horizontal cutting edge moves upward in an fixed circular cylinder and cuts it.

Another major advantage of the fully continuous motion modeling is that the cutting edge will never miss a triangle edge because of their movement between frames – barring any numerical error. This can occur in many situations, especially when the blade movement is almost parallel to a surface edge, or when it undergoes a twisting motion relative to the surface. Figure 9 displays such a situation, where a curved blade is rotating while advancing and cuts a surface edge that is almost parallel to its local motion.

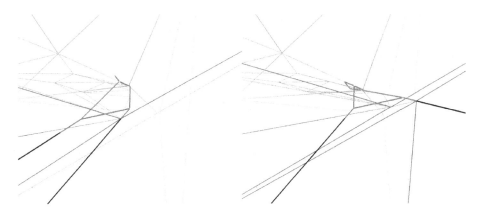

Fig. 9. Cutting edge (in black) that is curved and that twists as it moves forward.

In a surgery simulation, most simulated objects are more complex than those shown so far. Our proposed tool representation and surface mapping methodology are not affected by the complexity of the model being cut, in theory. The difficulty lies mostly in how to manage the cuts that are detected. Once the surface and physical model are cut, the mapping can proceed as with any other model. Figure 10 presents a brain hemisphere being cut by a slightly curved blade. This model has many grooves and folds that the blade enters and leaves simultaneously or at different times. This gives rise to situations where the cutting edge traverses several separate parts of the model in a given frame. Our method handles these multiple fronts merging and splitting as the blade moves forward the same way as it does a single front.

Figure 11 shows that a single object may be cut multiple times with the same tool. In the first image, the cut surface appears to be slightly curved, because the scene was animated during the cutting operation and the liver was slowly tilting

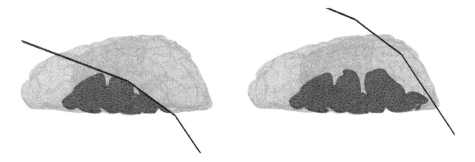

Fig. 10. Cutting a more complex model that may appear in a surgical simulation scenario. The cutting tool is able to deal with the numerous folds present in a human brain.

down as the blade went through it. Figure 11 also shows that the displacement of the surface remains consistent with the cuts introduced by the tool.

Figure 12 offers a more detailed perspective on how surface vertices are mapped on the underlying physical model. On the cut surface, it shows that each mapped vertex is linked to an integration point on its own side of the cut. That point is generally the closest that fits all mapping criteria, taking the new cut into account.

Limitations. The correctness of mapping a surface based on the criteria described in Sect. 2 depends greatly on the relative size of the surface mesh

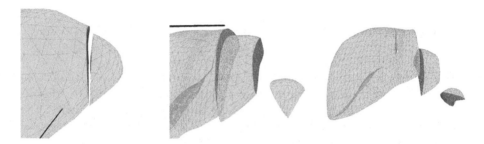

Fig. 11. Illustration of a series of cuts in the same object. A slight curve is noticeable in the first cut and is caused by the movement of the liver under the effect of gravity while the cut was performed.

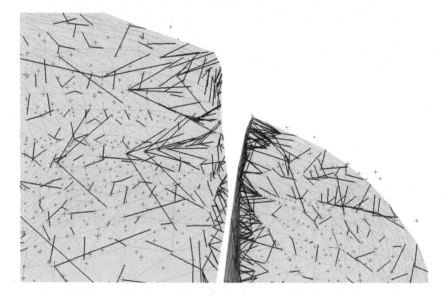

Fig. 12. A view of the liver cut scenario that displays the integration points (red crosses) and highlights to which point each vertex is mapped (blue lines). Each vertex is properly mapped to a point on its own side of the cut (Color figure online).

and that of the physical model on which it is mapped. The surface mesh *must* be at least as dense as the integration point grid. Otherwise, it will not be possible to find a point near a vertex that is somewhat close to every triangle formed by that vertex.

A related issue is that of the smallest possible cut in a model. While it is possible to create and display a surface with an arbitrary level of detail, it is not possible to cut these details away from the rest of the simulated object if there are not enough integration elements under them. If a sufficiently small part of the surface is separated from the rest of the object, it will not be possible to map it to the underlying physical model. With the scheme used for this research for distributing particles and integration points, the thinnest part of an object that can be fully separated from the rest and still be properly mapped is about the width of two integration elements.

4   Conclusion and Future Work

We have described and demonstrated the use of a dynamic tool representation that allows to interactively cut a deforming object in a variety of situations: with a static, moving or deforming tool on a static, moving or deforming surface. We have also described a method to successfully map the cut surface of the object on its underlying cut physical model, itself based on a set of particles and a background mesh.

Together, these two methods lead to a more robust and coherent simulation, improving the immersion and interactivity of the virtual environment in a surgical setting. This work forms a component that will become part of an existing simulation system.

That system displays a surgical scene on a 3D screen, offering sufficient visual immersion for accomplishing tasks on the relatively small work area of the surgery site. It is also equipped with a haptic device that provides a virtual surgical tool as the single means through which the user can interact with the scene. Using that system will enable us to make our method available for testing by surgeons and will be the subject of future research.

Acknowlegement. This work is funded by the Natural Sciences and Engineering Research Council (NSERC) under grant 501444-16, in collaboration with OSSimTech.

References

1. Agus, M., Giachetti, A., Gobbetti, E., Zanetti, G., Zorcolo, A.: Real-time haptic and visual simulation of bone dissection. Presence: Teleoper. Virtual Environ. **12**(1), 110–122 (2003). https://doi.org/10.1162/105474603763835378
2. Alaraj, A., et al.: Virtual reality cerebral aneurysm clipping simulation with real-time haptic feedback. Neurosurgery, 1 (2015). https://doi.org/10.1227/NEU.0000000000000583

3. Brunet, J.N., Magnoux, V., Ozell, B., Cotin, S.: Corotated meshless implicit dynamics for deformable bodies. In: International Conferences in Central Europe on Computer Graphics, Visualization and Computer Vision, pp. 91–100. Pilsen, Czech Republic, May 2019. https://doi.org/10.24132/CSRN.2019.2901.1.11

4. Cheng, Q., Liu, P.X., Lai, P., Xu, S., Zou, Y.: A novel haptic interactive approach to simulation of surgery cutting based on mesh and meshless models. J. Healthcare Eng. **2018**, 1–16 (2018). https://doi.org/10.1155/2018/9204949

5. Cotin, S., Delingette, H., Ayache, N.: A hybrid elastic model for real-time cutting, deformations, and force feedback for surgery training and simulation. Vis. Comput. **16**(8), 437–452 (2000). https://doi.org/10.1007/PL00007215

6. Dick, C., Georgii, J., Westermann, R.: A hexahedral multigrid approach for simulating cuts in deformable objects. IEEE Trans. Visual. Comput. Graph. **17**(11), 1663–1675 (2011). https://doi.org/10.1109/TVCG.2010.268

7. Faure, F., et al.: Sofa: a multi-model framework for interactive physical simulation. In: Soft Tissue Biomechanical Modeling for Computer Assisted Surgery, pp. 283–321. Springer, Heidelberg (2012). https://doi.org/10.1007/8415_2012_125

8. Faure, F., Gilles, B., Bousquet, G., Pai, D.K.: Sparse meshless models of complex deformable solids. In: ACM SIGGRAPH 2011 Papers. pp. 73:1–73:10. SIGGRAPH 2011, ACM, New York, NY, USA (2011). https://doi.org/10.1145/1964921.1964968

9. Gutiérrez, L.F., Ramos, F.: XFEM framework for cutting soft tissue including topological changes in a surgery simulation. In: Proceedings of the International Conference on Computer Graphics Theory and Applications, pp. 275–283. Angers, France, January 2010. https://doi.org/10.5220/0002836402750283

10. Holgate, N., Joldes, G.R., Miller, K.: Efficient visibility criterion for discontinuities discretised by triangular surface meshes. Eng. Anal. Boundary Elements **58**, 1–6 (2015). https://doi.org/10.1016/j.enganabound.2015.02.014

11. Jeřábková, L., Bousquet, G., Barbier, S., Faure, F., Allard, J.: Volumetric modeling and interactive cutting of deformable bodies. Progress Biophys. Molecular Biol. **103**(2–3), 217–224 (2010). https://doi.org/10.1016/j.pbiomolbio.2010.09.012

12. Jia, S.-Y., Pan, Z.-K., Wang, G.-D., Zhang, W.-Z., Yu, X.-K.: Stable real-time surgical cutting simulation of deformable objects embedded with arbitrary triangular meshes. J. Comput. Sci. Technol. **32**(6), 1198–1213 (2017). https://doi.org/10.1007/s11390-017-1794-z

13. Jung, H., Lee, D.Y.: Real-time cutting simulation of meshless deformable object using dynamic bounding volume hierarchy. Comput. Animat. Virt. Worlds **23**(5), 489–501 (2012). https://doi.org/10.1002/cav.1485

14. Kim, Y., et al.: Deformable mesh simulation for virtual laparoscopic cholecystectomy training. Vis. Comput. **31**(4), 485–495 (2014). https://doi.org/10.1007/s00371-014-0944-3

15. Li, S., Zhao, Q., Wang, S., Hao, A., Qin, H.: Interactive deformation and cutting simulation directly using patient-specific volumetric images. Comput. Animat. Virt. Worlds **25**(2), 155–169 (2014). https://doi.org/10.1002/cav.1543

16. Li, Y., et al.: Surface embedding narrow volume reconstruction from unorganized points. Comput. Vis. Image Understand. **121**, 100–107 (2014). https://doi.org/10.1016/j.cviu.2014.02.002

17. Luo, J., Xu, S., Jiang, S.: A novel hybrid rendering approach to soft tissue cutting in surgical simulation. In: 2015 8th International Conference on Biomedical Engineering and Informatics (BMEI), pp. 270–274, October 2015. https://doi.org/10.1109/BMEI.2015.7401514

18. Luo, R., Xu, W., Wang, H., Zhou, K., Yang, Y.: Physics-based quadratic deformation using elastic weighting. IEEE Trans. Visual. Comput. Graph. **24**(12), 3188–3199 (2018). https://doi.org/10.1109/TVCG.2017.2783335

19. Magnoux, V., Ozell, B.: Real-time visual and physical cutting of a meshless model deformed on a background grid. Comput. Animat. Virt. Worlds, e1929 (2014). https://doi.org/10.1002/cav.1929

20. Malukhin, K., Ehmann, K.: Mathematical modeling and virtual reality simulation of surgical tool interactions with soft tissue: a review and prospective. J. Eng. Sci. Med. Diagnost. Therapy **1**(2), 020802 (2018). https://doi.org/10.1115/1.4039417

21. Mor, A.B., Kanade, T.: Modifying soft tissue models: progressive cutting with minimal new element creation. In: Delp, S.L., DiGoia, A.M., Jaramaz, B. (eds.) Medical Image Computing and Computer-Assisted Intervention - MICCAI 2000, pp. 598–607. Lecture Notes in Computer Science, Springer, Heidelberg (Oct 2000). https://doi.org/10.1007/978-3-540-40899-4_61

22. Müller, M., Keiser, R., Nealen, A., Pauly, M., Gross, M., Alexa, M.: Point based animation of elastic, plastic and melting objects. In: Proceedings of the 2004 ACM SIGGRAPH/Eurographics Symposium on Computer Animation, pp. 141–151. SCA 2004, Eurographics Association, Aire-la-Ville, Switzerland (2004). https://doi.org/10.1145/1028523.1028542

23. Nakao, M., Minato, K., Kume, N., Mori, S.i., Tomita, S.: Vertex-preserving cutting of elastic objects. In: 2008 IEEE Virtual Reality Conference, pp. 277–278, March 2008. https://doi.org/10.1109/VR.2008.4480799

24. Nienhuys, H.W.: Cutting in deformable objects. Utrecht University Repository (2003). http://dspace.library.uu.nl/handle/1874/882

25. Pan, J., Yan, S., Qin, H., Hao, A.: Real-time dissection of organs via hybrid coupling of geometric metaballs and physics-centric mesh-free method. Vis. Comput. **34**(1), 105–116 (2016). https://doi.org/10.1007/s00371-016-1317-x

26. Peng, Y., Li, Q., Yan, Y., Wang, Q.: Real-time deformation and cutting simulation of cornea using point based method. Multimedia Tools Appl. **78**(2), 2251–2268 (2018). https://doi.org/10.1007/s11042-018-6343-4

27. Provot, X.: Collision and self-collision handling in cloth model dedicated to design garments. In: Thalmann, D., van de Panne, M. (eds.) Computer Animation and Simulation 1997. pp. 177–189. Eurographics, Springer, Vienna (1997). https://doi.org/10.1007/978-3-7091-6874-5_13

28. Qian, K., Jiang, T., Wang, M., Yang, X., Zhang, J.: Energized soft tissue dissection in surgery simulation. Comput. Animat. Virt. Worlds **27**(3–4), 280–289 (2016). https://doi.org/10.1002/cav.1691

29. Seiler, M., Steinemann, D., Spillmann, J., Harders, M.: Robust interactive cutting based on an adaptive octree simulation mesh. The Visual Computer **27**(6–8), 519–529 (2011). https://doi.org/10.1007/s00371-011-0561-3

30. Shi, W., Liu, P.X., Zheng, M.: Cutting procedures with improved visual effects and haptic interaction for surgical simulation systems. Comput. Methods Prog. Biomed. **184**, 105270 (2020). https://doi.org/10.1016/j.cmpb.2019.105270

31. Si, W., Lu, J., Liao, X., Wang, Q.: Towards interactive progressive cutting of deformable bodies via phyxel-associated surface mesh approach for virtual surgery. IEEE Access **6**, 32286–32299 (2018). https://doi.org/10.1109/ACCESS.2018.2845901

32. Steinemann, D., Otaduy, M.A., Gross, M.: Splitting meshless deforming objects with explicit surface tracking. Graph. Models **71**(6), 209–220 (2009). https://doi.org/10.1016/j.gmod.2008.12.004

33. Tai, Y., et al.: Development of haptic-enabled virtual reality simulator for video-assisted thoracoscopic right upper lobectomy. In: 2018 IEEE International Conference on Systems, Man, and Cybernetics (SMC), pp. 3010–3015. IEEE, Miyazaki, Japan, October 2018. https://doi.org/10.1109/SMC.2018.00511

34. Wu, J., Westermann, R., Dick, C.: Real-time haptic cutting of high-resolution soft tissues. In: Studies in Health Technology and Informatics (Proceedings of the Medicine Meets Virtual Reality 2014) vol. 196, pp. 469–475 (2014). https://doi.org/10.3233/978-1-61499-375-9-469

35. Wu, J., Westermann, R., Dick, C.: A survey of physically based simulation of cuts in deformable bodies. In: Computer Graphics Forum, vol. 34, pp. 161–187. Wiley Online Library (2015). http://onlinelibrary.wiley.com/doi/10.1111/cgf.12528/full

36. Zerbato, D., Fiorini, P.: A unified representation to interact with simulated deformable objects in virtual environments. In: 2016 IEEE International Conference on Robotics and Automation (ICRA), pp. 2710–2717, May 2016. https://doi.org/10.1109/ICRA.2016.7487432

37. Zou, Y., Liu, P.X., Wu, D., Yang, X., Xu, S.: Point primitives based virtual surgery system. IEEE Access **7**, 46306–46316 (2019). https://doi.org/10.1109/ACCESS.2019.2909061

Virtually Alone

How Facilitated Aloneness Affect Self-study in IVE

Naoko Hayashida[1]([⊠]) [iD], Hideaki Kuzuoka[2] [iD], and Kenji Suzuki[3] [iD]

[1] Fujitsu Laboratories Ltd., Kawasaki, Japan
`hayashida.naoko@fujitsu.com`
[2] The University of Tokyo, Tokyo, Japan
`kuzuoka@cyber.t.u-tokyo.ac.jp`
[3] University of Tsukuba, Tsukuba, Japan
`kenji@ieee.org`

Abstract. For most learners, appropriate learning climates within spaces selected for self-study (e.g., libraries) are helpful in sustaining self-regulated learning efforts. In order to provide learners with appropriate self-study spaces, we examined an immersive virtual environment (IVE) for English phonemes acquisition practice. Social settings of a learning environment sometimes yield positive effects, but sometimes not. To assess the influences of social interactivity against learner's effort towards his/her persistent skill development, we have conducted exploratory studies.

In this paper, we examined self-regulated learning in IVEs that provided little social interactivity. We compared two "alone" environments: a literally solo space and a shared space devoid of communication capability. Participants in the shared space with a silent other recorded quite better scores compared to those in the solo space at the beginning of the experimental tasks.

Keywords: Virtual Reality · Intrinsic motivation · Self-regulation · Aloneness · Self-study · English phonemes acquisition practice system

1 Introduction

For most learners, appropriate learning climates within spaces selected for self-study (e.g., libraries, fitness spaces) are helpful in sustaining self-regulated learning efforts. In real-life self-study taking place in libraries, learning environments seem to provide an appropriate learning climate either in closed spaces or open study areas [1]. Social environments in a learning space sometimes yield positive effects [2], but sometimes they negatively impact psychological safety while also posing challenging learning behaviors [3, 4]. In order to provide appropriate climates for learners—even within a computer-based practice scenario, and even without other learners existing in real, physical places—we have been examining an immersive virtual environment (IVE) for self-regulated learning. In this work, we present an IVE for English-as-a-second-language (ESL) learning, specifically in the area of phonemes acquisition practice.

© Springer Nature Switzerland AG 2020
L. T. De Paolis and P. Bourdot (Eds.): AVR 2020, LNCS 12243, pp. 131–146, 2020.
https://doi.org/10.1007/978-3-030-58468-9_10

To assess the influence of other learner(s) being present in space against learning behaviors towards the continuous skill development of a self-study learner, we have conducted several exploratory studies. In this paper, our basic research question was:

RQ: How does another learner being present with little social interactivity in an IVE affect learning climates, and in turn, self-regulated learning behaviors?

We predict that learners who are in a shared space with a silent other will experience different aloneness (social deprivation) with those in a solo space. The presence of a silent other will result in the perception of a certain degree of relatedness. The inherent sense of a peer with whom one has a minimal social link will, in turn, momentarily increase intrinsic motivation [5]. However, perceived aloneness could negatively impact persistent self-regulated effort [6].

We present the laboratory experiment results pertaining to how the two "alone" environment types (i.e., a literally solo space and a shared space devoid of communication capability) each affect self-regulated learning. As a result, participants in the shared space with a silent other saw better initial learning achievements. Through this study, we had lessons learned that the shared place with a silent other sometimes seems not to be the same place with the literally solo space for a self-study learner.

2 Background

2.1 State of the Art

The social environment in a real physical classroom has been evaluated, particularly from the aspect of the teacher [7]. Compared with classrooms, real-life self-study taking place in libraries seems to provide a different climate either in closed spaces or open study areas [1]. This implies that whether a self-study learner is or is not in the same physical place with other learners may affect his/her learning behaviors.

The factors contained in the appropriate climates while providing challenging learner's efforts [3] will depend on the IVE. Culbertson et al. showed that a 3D environment populated by both human- and computer-controlled characters has successfully created socially situated language learning experiences [8]. Meng-Yun et al. showed that a facilitated tradeoff for a virtual classroom between learning experiences and social interactivity affects learning outcomes [9]. We also assume that social interactivity is an important research factor, and there is a tradeoff between appropriate learning climates for self-study learners and social interactivity. In other words, we assume that an IVE full of friendly peers may be comfortable environment, but it may also hinder his/her challenging learning behaviors.

2.2 Phonemes Acquisition Practice

In this paper, we developed an IVE for ESL, particularly for phoneme-acquisition practice. Being able to recognize English sounds is a fundamental skill for decoding words [10]. Even though this skill fosters baseline English literacy, moreover instructors and students are aware of its importance, we have assumed that many ESL classes lack sufficient practice opportunities. One of the reasons is because these kinds of practices for skill acquisitions, in general, require several thousands of hours. Thus, we have been trying to realize a phonemes acquisition practice in VE, and moreover, appropriate learning climates fostering self-regulated learners' persistent learning efforts.

3 Related Works

3.1 Importance of Self-regulation and Effect of Aloneness

The completion rate for the most massive open online courses (MOOCs) was reported at below 13% [11]. The increased use of computers as online learning tools has led to the creation of computer-based practice systems oriented towards self-study; however, persistent self-regulated learning has not necessarily been achieved under the current online learning scenario.

The factors discriminating between completers of online learning courses and dropouts from them were investigated [12, 13]. Lee et al. showed that persistent students had higher levels of self-regulation skills [14].

Self-regulation, which is a deliberate, conscious effort, explained as self-control, has various models [15, 16]. One key aspect of whether people can exert self-regulation is related to cognitive resources. When a person has a suitable environment that is well-matched with his/her cognitive resources, he/she will persevere through the challenges of performing self-regulated behaviors and thus exhibit a favorable learning result.

An environment being presented with other people in which learning and self-regulation are taking place affects an individual's cognitive resources in several ways. Loneliness, for example, is most likely to lead to severe ego-depletion and self-regulation depletion [6, 17].

However, not all aloneness leads to loneliness. And whether aloneness is appropriate for a particular individual is affected by his/her ideal position on the individualism versus collectivism spectrum [18], or his/her ability to control environmental issues, such as audible noise [19]. Ideally, people will autonomously select their environments, balancing the we-mode for collaborative work with the me-mode for solo work [20].

Thus, our research group has been examining an IVE providing demanded appropriate climates. In this paper, we focused on the desired degree of aloneness for self-regulated learning.

3.2 Design Issues with Climates Perception of Learners in IVEs

In real-life self-study taking place in libraries, half of the learners seem to prefer climates in closed spaces [1]. To construct an IVE providing the desired degree of aloneness for self-regulated learning, similar to those preferably taking place in real physical spaces with silent other learners, we controlled the following three design aspects about users' perception.

Immersive Embodiment
Embodiment [21] (experience of being in the location of a body that you see) is experienced through a learner's embodied virtual body (i.e., avatar). Thus, the viewpoint, size,

and head-movement synchrony of avatars were investigated to design an appropriate immersion environment [22, 23]. For example, people felt a greater embodiment when they saw a virtual body from a first-person viewpoint compared with a third-person one [22].

In addition, given the awareness of climates of IVEs, we believe that movement synchrony will be an important embodiment factor because users show their desire to approach or avoid others in the context of intentional relationship regulation using the various movements of their heads and body parts [24].

To facilitate the required experiences of presence (an immersive feeling of being there) and embodiment, we developed an IVE implementing an ego-centric viewpoint and an avatar that reflected a user in terms of size and movement, including the head movements of the user's physical body.

Silent But Co-present Other

The human consciousness system detects physiological or social pain through interoceptive feeling [25]. Several past studies have shown that people who are immersed in IVEs are still perceptive, not only of physiological pain but also of stress [26] or social pain with particular sensitivity to explicit social exclusion [27]. In a public speaking task [26], a group presenting in front of a virtual audience showed significantly higher stress levels, and they confirmed that their stress response was derived from the presence of the virtual audience and not merely from the virtual apparatus.

We think the co-presence [28] (an immersive feeling of being somewhere together) with silent other learners affect facilitated aloneness in IVEs. Since VR experiences, in general, have been influenced by characteristics of a head-mounted display (HMD) in particular its narrow field of view, we had set up a priming procedure induced co-present feeling with a silent another learner in this study.

Minimal Social Link

A bottom line framework for the autonomous regulation of goal-directed behavior was explained by human motivation theory, particularly self-determination theory (SDT) [5]. SDT explained that intrinsic motivation (the motivation to work hard on tasks for their own sake) could be promoted or thwarted according to the degree of fulfillment of basic psychological needs of autonomy, competence, and relatedness. Various studies have confirmed intrinsic motivation is associated with better learning.

Walton et al. showed that the activation or inhibition of goal pursuit could occur relatively strongly when people see their peers having minimal social links while tackling or completing a task [2]. People's mental construal of others' significance and association with their own goals also impacted goal pursuit behaviors with regard to persistence and performance [29].

The inherent sense of a peer with whom one has a minimal social link will, in turn, momentarily increase intrinsic motivation. To invoke minimal social link with a silent other learner, we designed the priming procedure conducted in pre-session in this study. In the pre-session, the peer was not directly introduced to a participant in face-to-face, but the existence of the peer was introduced using the learner's avatar.

4 System

4.1 System Implementation

Each participant wore an HMD, through which the learner could observe the IVE and his/her own body from a first-person perspective.

We employed a standalone HMD[1] to allow participants a full range of natural motion. The HMD has six-degrees-of-freedom (DoF) cameras and three DoF wireless handheld controller device. Participants' real-world movements were reflected in their avatars' motions via these sensors. The display is 2560×1440 resolution providing a $110°$ field of view.

The IVE system was developed with a 3D game engine, named Unity[2]. The 3D objects facilitated to the VR space, e.g., avatar and room, were fbx format. For the avatar object, the fbx file includes not only textures and meshes but also a human skeleton. We aligned the human skeleton's design with Unity's common avatar format. Thus, participants' real-world movements acquired with the HMD-specific Software Development Kit (SDK)[3] were easily reflected in the avatar's motions in Unity.

4.2 VR Setup

Figure 1 introduces an overview of the system. Specifically, the IVE is designed for phonemes acquisition practice. We used a voice recognition device (VRD)[4] and its web API[5] to measure a learner's recorded phoneme scores (RPS; see measures section) and showed those to the learner as feedback of his/her learning progress.

In the IVE, there was a whiteboard on the front wall that simulated a real classroom and the following three personal user interfaces (UIs) geared towards enabling constructive learning for phoneme acquisition through self-feedback. The UI used to control the system was displayed as buttons or a scroll bar in the IVE, and participants used the UIs by using a handheld controller device.

After participants pushed the results button on the desktop board (UI2), the recorded phoneme scores corresponding to the English text displayed on the whiteboard were plotted as a line graph on the desktop board (UI2). Each dot of the line graph on UI2 is plotted the RPS of each phoneme item. A lookup table (UI3) explaining how to pronounce each phoneme was displayed to the participants' left. Recently pronounced and recorded data was displayed on the overhead board (UI1). These recorded data were synchronized with recent activity every five seconds and scrolled up automatically. Participants were able to scroll through the entire list of recorded words by using a scroll bar if needed.

The general use case is as follows (numbers in the parentheses and user interface numbers (i.e., UI1, UI2, UI3) correspond with those shown in Fig. 1(d)). After an English

---

[1] Lenovo Mirage Solo with Daydream, https://www.lenovo.com/jp/ja/vr-smartdevices/augmented-reality/lenovo-mirage-solo/Mirage-Solo/p/ZZIRZRHVR01.

[2] Unity 3D, https://unity.com/.

[3] Google VR SDK for Unity, https://developers.google.com/vr/develop/unity/get-started-android.

[4] Google Home, https://store.google.com/us/product/google_home_speaker?hl=en-US.

[5] Dialogflow, https://dialogflow.com/.

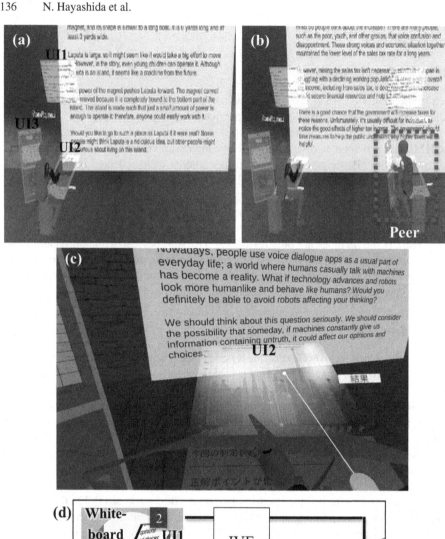

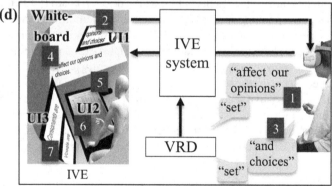

Fig. 1. VR setup - 3rd person perspective view of the solo condition (a) and the silent other condition (b); 1st person perspective view (c); system use case (each number is used for explanation of general use case) (d)

text is displayed on the whiteboard in the IVE (in this case, '... affect our opinions and choices.'), a learner launches the VRD using a wake-up phrase and starts to read the text. By recognizing the short silence after the learner's voices, for example, "affect our opinions," the VRD responses with the word "set" (1) and the IVE system shows the recognized phrase in the UI1 (2). Then, the learner continues to read the text "and choices" (3, 4). The learner can check his/her RPSs by pressing a button on the UI2 (5) and a displaying line graph (6). To figure out which phonemes need further practice, the learner sees the UI3 (7).

5   Experiment

5.1   Participants

Table 1 shows the demographic characteristics of the subsamples. They were recruited through the monitor recruitment agency. All participants had a pre-intermediate English skill level. Participants were assigned to one of two conditions of subject design (i.e., the solo or the silent other condition) using a participant list ordered by major English tests' scores[6,7]. This list was created prior to the experiment to ensure that both condition groups had participants with roughly the same English skills.

Table 1. Demographic characteristics of subsamples.

Characteristic	Solo	Silent other
N	10	10
Age		
Mean	32.7	32.4
Range	21–54	21–60
English test score		
Mean	595.5	588.5
Range	450–695	445–700
Gender	M 50%/F 50%	M 50%/F 50%

Note: M = Male, F = Female. English test score here was aligned using a major Listening & Reading Test score (See footnote 6).

5.2   Design and Procedures

There were two conditions, namely, the solo and the silent other condition. In the solo condition, a participant's avatar situated him/her alone in the VR space. In the silent other

---

[6] TOEIC Listening & Reading Test, https://www.iibc-global.org/english/toeic/test/lr/about.html.
[7] EIKEN, https://www.eiken.or.jp/eiken/en/grades/.

condition, participants' avatars situated them with the avatar of a peer. In this study, the peer avatar was controlled by a confederate who posed as another participant.

At the beginning of the experiment, all participants were informed that the purpose of the experiment was to test and improve a novel, self-regulated English learning system using VR. And at the same time, before starting pre-session, they were introduced to the VR system from the third-person perspective. This priming manipulation was intended to lay the foundation for invoking the appropriate sensations of aloneness for each condition as described in 'silent but co-present other' section and 'minimal social link' section. For the silent other condition, participants saw the VR space in which two avatars were located and were informed that the left-side avatar would be used as their own while the right-side avatar would be used by another participant who was physically located in another laboratory room. For the solo condition, participants saw the VR space where one avatar was located and was informed that that avatar would be used as their own. Participants' avatars were located on the left side, and the geometric locations in the VR space were the same for both conditions, as shown in Fig. 1(a), (b).

The duration of the experiment's tasks was approximately sixty minutes, less twenty minutes of pre-session, and ten minutes of post-session. During the pre-session, procedures were explained, participants signed consent forms, they learned how to use the IVE, including learning how to use the lookup tables, and after that, they started training to improve their pronunciation using the system.

During the post-session, the participants filled out questionnaires.

5.3 Task

The experimental tasks consisted of a total of nine text reading sessions for each participant. To assess the overall learning achievement through the experiment's components, the last English text (session eight of the nine) was identical to the first (session zero). Given that each reading session was limited to a duration of six minutes, the English texts displayed on the whiteboard in the VR space automatically changed after that six minutes had passed.

Participants were told that this system was aimed at promoting self-regulated learning so they could feel free to follow how they would most naturally learn English using the system. Even though the displayed text changed automatically after every pre-determined time slot, natural use included taking short breaks at any point between task beginning and task end. It was not limited to after participants finished reading each English text.

5.4 Materials

The English texts displayed on the whiteboard in the VR space automatically changed after that six minutes had passed. Each text contained between 150 and 180 words because it was assumed that a person of pre-intermediate English skill would be able to read that volume of words at his/her own pace within three minutes, roughly half of the task's time slot.

The pieces of text included were essentially comprised only of A1–B1 words as classified by the Common European Framework of Reference for Languages (CEFR)

[30]. This was done in an attempt to facilitate easy reading and comprehension for people at the pre-intermediate English skill level. Articles were varied; we included news items, fairy tales, etc.

The English text used for practicing how to use the IVE was made in the same manner but a different English text from those for the experiment session.

The lookup tables explain forty-two phonemes (the top table explains twenty-four consonants, and the bottom one explains eighteen vowels).

As mentioned in the task section, how the IVE would be used was varied.

5.5 Measures

Intrinsic Motivation

According to SDT, intrinsic motivation can sustain learner's effort over time and facilitate greater learning. We asked participants' intrinsic motivation at the post-session right after the experiment tasks. As a measure of intrinsic motivation based on SDT, we used an Intrinsic Motivation Inventory (IMI) [31]. IMI comprised a forty-five item questionnaire consisting of six sub-scales (i.e., interest/enjoyment, perceived competence, effort/importance, pressure/tension, perceived choice, value/usefulness, and relatedness). All items were measured on a seven-point Likert-type scale ranging from one = "not at all true" to seven = "very true." For the solo condition, we did not ask about relatedness, because there was no other person mentioned.

Psychological Response to Learning Climate

To discuss RQ, particularly the psychological factors that are positively affected by learning climates, we asked how the learning experiences were in the IVE, as shown in Table 2. All items were measured on a six-point Likert-type scale ranging from one = "do not at all feel so" to six = "feel very much so."

Table 2. Questions on psychological responses in IVE.

Question number	Question "learning in the virtual environment (VE) was"
LE1_EJY	Enjoyable
LE2_ATN	Attention-getting
LE3_RLX	Relaxing
LE4_ALN	Aloneness-exerted

Self-regulated Learning Efforts

In this study, we did not measure learners' basic English skill acquisition for listening or speaking. Instead of that, to estimate how a learning climate foster participants' effort towards self-regulated phoneme acquisition, we calculated *each session's recorded phoneme ratio by a user over voice recognition system as a **recorded phoneme score***

(RPS) for each phoneme item of forty-two-phoneme. For example, if a unique word occurrence in a Session-X's text including the phoneme 'w' was registered as four (i.e. 'would', 'between', 'one', 'requires'), the situation observed as "User Alice's RPS for the phoneme 'w' was 50 for a Session-X" means that Alice recorded two words included in the registered list in the Session-X over the system. The reasons why the rest of the registered words not being recorded would not be affected by only the leaning climate but also the situation, such as a voice recognition environment. However, we think the RPS can be a measure that is being reflected in a participant's self-regulated learning efforts. To discuss RQ, particularly the learning climate causing the persistent self-regulated learning effort, we used the RPS of nine text reading sessions.

5.6 Results

Statistical analyses were conducted using statistics software[8], considering a significance level of $p < 0.05$ (two-tailed). Each test effect size was estimated using r. Not only for questionnaire responses but also for RPSs, we showed quartiles in figures. In a figure showing boxplots, an outlier was shown as a small circle.

Intrinsic Motivation

Figure 2 shows the intrinsic motivation expressed by participants in the solo condition and the silent other condition. Each IMI subscale had no significant difference between the two conditions on Mann-Whitney test.

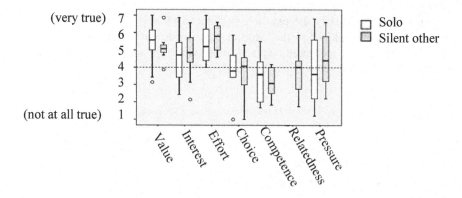

Fig. 2. Intrinsic motivation by condition.

Psychological Response to Learning Climate

Figure 3 shows the psychological responses expressed by participants in the solo condition and the silent other condition. Each item had no significant difference between the two conditions on Mann-Whitney test.

---

[8] IBM SPSS Version 21.

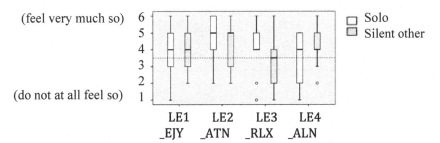

Fig. 3. Psychological responses by condition.

Self-regulated Learning Efforts

Figure 4 shows the violin plots displaying the distribution of RPSs for each session by the condition. Participants in the silent other condition recorded quite better scores than those in solo spaces at the beginning of the experimental tasks. At the beginning sessions, in particular session zero and session one, the differences were significant on Mann-Whitney test (session 0: $p = 0.00 < 0.05$, session 1: $p = 0.00 < 0.05$). In session four, participants in the silent other condition recorded low scores than those in solo condition, Mann-Whitney test ($p = 0.00 < 0.05$).

For the rest of the experimental tasks, the RPSs of participants in the silent other condition did not show a statistically significant difference with those in the solo condition. Moreover, their effect sizes declined (session 0–8: $r = 0.24, 0.12, 0.05, 0.06, 0.12, 0.02, 0.03, 0.04, 0.03$).

6   Discussion

To check how participants accomplished their self-regulated learning differently in the two solitary environments, we used the same English text at session zero (the first time) and session eight (the second time). During the first attempt, participants in the silent other condition recorded significantly higher scores for RPSs than participants in the solo condition. However, the second-time attempt results were statistically not significantly different for the two conditions. Since the effect size of each session in the second half was relatively small than those in the first half, the differences derived from the conditions might be limited to the time period starting his/her learning in the place. It implies that IVE designers should sometimes take into account the influences of silent another learner in an environment.

Our next question will be: Would these solitary environments effectively and persistently increase self-regulated learning efforts in a wild setting? For solo space, there were no extrinsic factors in the IVE. Thus, solo-space participants' learning curves throughout the experimental tasks were improved by their self-regulated efforts. We think that if a learner in the wild would visit a similar space autonomously, his/her self-regulated learning efforts may be continuously elevated. For the silent other condition, we think that this solitary environment did not foster learning climates in the same way as solo space did, which may have caused negative effects in long-term participants' self-regulated learning. The participants of the silent other condition stayed practically at the same

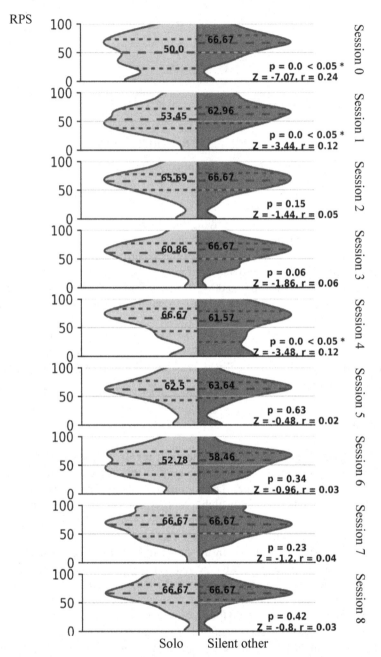

Fig. 4. Violin plots displaying the distribution of RPSs for each session by condition; Each curve is smoothed by a kernel density estimator function. The lower, middle, and upper dashed lines represent the first quartile, median, and third quartile, respectively. The number above the middle line also indicates a median. A statistical test result for each session is shown on each right corner.

level after about an hour of learning as compared to participants in solo spaces who improved 16.67 points of the median value.

The descriptive differences of the following IMI subscales may help to assume what kinds of learners' perceptions potentially related to long-term intrinsic motivational learning effort are associated with solitary IVEs.

Pressure and Effort. We assume that the peer pressure exerted by a silent other would itself cause the silent other condition learner's own effort felt to be greater than those felt by a literally solo learner. Moreover, if a learner with a silent other made extra efforts than the usual solo learner, it would affect an individual's cognitive resources [16]. Thus it may have caused negative effects in long-term participants' self-regulated learning.

Perceived Competence. In this study, the presence of a silent other seemed, at least, not to ease learners' potential feelings of incompetence.

In order to design an IVE for self-regulated learning, we should take into account the potential negative effects of peer-pressure, moreover, how the environment fosters learners' own useful perceptions of their own ability to meet the challenges of self-regulated learning.

7 Limitations and Future Works

Justifications and Data Distribution. We used nonparametric tests as statistical tests not only for questionnaire responses but also for RPSs. This was because these data did not follow a normal distribution. We consider phoneme-acquisition practices, especially for ESL learners include several levels of difficulties. Thus, RPSs might include several types of tendencies. In this study, the sample size of each condition is not enough to avoid type II errors (false negatives). In other words, the results did not show any statistical differences in this study were still not sure whether there are differences or not. Thus, we did not describe the descriptive differences in the results section but only in the discussion section.

Measures. In this study, we did not measure learners' basic English skill acquisition for listening or speaking. Although we think an RPS can be a measure that is being reflected with a participant's self-regulated learning efforts. We also think we should measure how a learning climate affects participants' skill development (e.g., a listening skill) to evaluate how this system effective as the place of self-study. However, skill development, in general, requires both of several thousand hours and lasting learners' self-regulated learning efforts. Thus, in the current preliminary stage of our research, learners' self-regulated learning efforts would be a reasonable measure to examine how a learning climate affects participants' learning behaviors. In future work, we should show whether, and if so, how RPSs correlate with a stage of a learner's skill.

Time Allocations. In this study, the English texts displayed on the whiteboard in the IVE automatically changed after that six minutes had passed. And the activities during the time period until the next English text appeared on the whiteboard after he/she finished reading of the current text were totally up to him/her. It was aimed at having the time of additional intrinsic motivational practices or taking short breaks. Through this study, we think this time allocation may also have a role to avoid a rash practice and keep his/her own's pace reading.

Tasks. To avoid an experiment result affected by a task (e.g., difficulties of the task), the use of a simple task is a preferable way in general. In other papers, we also used a simple task. On the other hand, we think that desirable learning climates in the place depend on types of leaning, hence in our exploratory studies, we have tried to construct both of an IVE and its learning climates along with the purpose of realizing phonemes acquisition practice in VE.

Future Works. Through this study, we had lessons learned that shared place with silent another learner sometimes seems not to be the same place with literally solo space for a self-regulated learner. As the interesting thing, regarding how a learning climate where a self-regulated learner surrounded by other peer learners having communication capabilities could lead to positive learning efforts, our other preliminary study using same IVE setting [32] showed that the not-aloneness-exerted IVE surrounded by other peer learners was not necessarily better than the solo environment. On the other hand, the learning climate exerted from the other peer learners in the preliminary study seems to have a good influence on intrinsic motivational factors, in particular, perceived competence. Moreover, through a seven-days-long experiment in a wild setting, we observed a designed VE in which others' efforts were made tangible by exaggerating their learning activities rather than the co-present classmates themselves [33]. In the designed VE, participants among other learners showed longer learning durations and better learning achievements than those in the solo learner setting.

Thus, the next question will not be simple suchlike "to be, or not to be virtually alone." We think the next research question towards realizing an appropriate IVE for self-regulated learning will be an IVE design balances shared space and solitary space by incorporating the strengths of both solitary environments as well as peer effects.

8   Conclusion

In this paper, we showed the laboratory experiment results pertaining to how the two "alone" environment types (i.e., a literally solo space and a shared space devoid of communication capability) each affect self-regulated learning. Participants in shared spaces with a silent other recorded better scores compared to those in solo spaces at the beginning of the experimental tasks. However, since self-regulated learning in solitary IVEs may be negatively influenced by a learner's potential perception of his/her own incompetence, in future research, an IVE for long-term self-paced learning should utilize further·positive peer effects.

Acknowledgments. We wish to thank the anonymous reviewers and all those who participated in this project for their useful comments and help.

References

1. Oliveira, S.M.: Space preference at James White Library: what students really want. J. Acad. Librariansh. **42**, 355–367 (2016). https://doi.org/10.1016/j.acalib.2016.05.009
2. Walton, G.M., Cohen, G.L., Cwir, D., Spencer, S.J.: Mere belonging: the power of social connections. J. Pers. Soc. Psychol. **102**, 513 (2012)
3. Dadds, M.: The feeling of thinking in professional self-study. Educ. Action Res. **1**, 287–303 (1993)
4. Porges, S.W.: The Polyvagal Theory: Neurophysiological Foundations of Emotions, Attachment, Communication, and Self-regulation. W. W. Norton, New York (2011)
5. Deci, E.L., Ryan, R.M.: The "what" and "why" of goal pursuits: human needs and the self-determination of behavior. Psychol. Inq. **11**, 227–268 (2000). https://doi.org/10.1207/S15327965PLI1104_01
6. Cacioppo, J.T., Patrick, W.: Loneliness: Human Nature and the Need for Social Connection. Norton, New York (2008)
7. Patrick, H., Ryan, A.M., Kaplan, A.: Early adolescents' perceptions of the classroom social environment, motivational beliefs, and engagement. J. Educ. Psychol. **99**, 83–98 (2007). https://doi.org/10.1037/0022-0663.99.1.83
8. Culbertson, G., Wang, S., Jung, M., Andersen, E.: Social situational language learning through an online 3D game. In: Proceedings of the 2016 CHI Conference on Human Factors in Computing Systems, pp. 957–968. ACM, New York (2016). https://doi.org/10.1145/2858036.2858514
9. Meng-Yun, L., Ching Ying, S., Hao-Chuan, W., Wen-Chieh, L.: Virtual classmates: embodying historical learners messages as learning companions in a VR classroom through comment mapping. In: 2019 IEEE Conference on Virtual Reality and 3D User Interfaces (VR), Osaka. IEEE (2019)
10. Kazanina, N., Bowers, J.S., Idsardi, W.: Phonemes: lexical access and beyond. Psychon. Bull. Rev. **25**(2), 560–585 (2017). https://doi.org/10.3758/s13423-017-1362-0
11. Onah, D.F., Sinclair, J., Boyatt, R.: Dropout rates of massive open online courses: behavioural patterns. In: Proceedings of EDULEARN 2014, pp. 5825–5834 (2014)
12. Halawa, S., Greene, D., Mitchell, J.: Dropout prediction in MOOCs using learner activity features. In: Proceedings of the Second European MOOC Stakeholder Summit, vol. 37, pp. 58–65 (2014)
13. Lee, Y., Choi, J.: A review of online course dropout research: implications for practice and future research. Educ. Technol. Res. Dev. **59**, 593–618 (2011). https://doi.org/10.1007/s11423-010-9177-y
14. Lee, Y., Choi, J., Kim, T.: Discriminating factors between completers of and dropouts from online learning courses. Br. J. Educ. Technol. **44**, 328–337 (2013)
15. Bandura, A.: Social cognitive theory of self-regulation. Organ. Behav. Hum. Decis. Process. **50**, 248–287 (1991)
16. Baumeister, R.F., Heatherton, T.F., Tice, D.M.: Losing Control: How and Why People Fail at Self-regulation. Academic Press, Cambridge (1994)
17. Baumeister, R.F., Bratslavsky, E., Muraven, M., Tice, D.M.: Ego depletion: is the active self a limited resource? J. Pers. Soc. Psychol. **74**, 1252–1265 (1998). https://doi.org/10.1037/0022-3514.74.5.1252
18. Heu, L.C., van Zomeren, M., Hansen, N.: Lonely alone or lonely together? A cultural-psychological examination of individualism-collectivism and loneliness in five European countries. Pers. Soc. Psychol. Bull. **45**, 780–793 (2019). https://doi.org/10.1177/0146167218796793
19. Evans, G.W., Johnson, D.: Stress and open-office noise. J. Appl. Psychol. **85**, 779 (2000)

20. Congdon, C., Flynn, D., Redman, M.: Balancing "We" and "Me": The Best Collabora-tive Spaces Also Support Solitude (2014). https://hbr.org/2014/10/balancing-we-and-me-the-best-collaborative-spaces-also-support-solitude

21. Biocca, F.: The cyborg's dilemma: progressive embodiment in virtual environments. J. Comput.-Mediated Commun. 3 (1997). https://doi.org/10.1111/j.1083-6101.1997.tb00070.x

22. Romano, D., Llobera, J., Blanke, O.: Size and viewpoint of an embodied virtual body affect the processing of painful stimuli. J. Pain 17, 350–358 (2016). https://doi.org/10.1016/j.jpain.2015.11.005

23. Slater, M., Spanlang, B., Sanchez-Vives, M.V., Blanke, O.: First person experience of body transfer in virtual reality. PLoS ONE 5, e10564 (2010)

24. Hayashida, N., Suzuki, K., Kuzuoka, H.: Quantifying social behaviors affecting interpersonal relationships in a collaborative virtual environment. In: "Theory Transfers? Social Theory & CSCW Research," a Workshop of CSCW 2017 (2017)

25. Craig, A.D.: How Do You Feel?: An Interoceptive Moment with Your Neurobiological Self. Princeton University Press, Princeton (2014)

26. Kothgassner, O.D., et al.: Salivary cortisol and cardiovascular reactivity to a public speaking task in a virtual and real-life environment. Comput. Hum. Behav. 62, 124–135 (2016). https://doi.org/10.1016/j.chb.2016.03.081

27. Kassner, M.P., Wesselmann, E.D., Law, A.T., Williams, K.D.: Virtually ostracized: studying ostracism in immersive virtual environments. Cyberpsychol. Behav. Soc. Netw. 15, 399–403 (2012)

28. Kilteni, K., Groten, R., Slater, M.: The sense of embodiment in virtual reality. Presence Teleoperators Virtual Environ. 21, 373–387 (2012)

29. Shah, J.: Automatic for the people: how representations of significant others implicitly affect goal pursuit. J. Pers. Soc. Psychol. 84, 661–681 (2003). https://doi.org/10.1037/0022-3514.84.4.661

30. Council of Europe, Council for Cultural Co-operation, Education Committee, Modern Languages Division: Common European Framework of Reference for Languages: Learning, Teaching, Assessment. Cambridge University Press, Cambridge (2001)

31. The Center for Self-Determination Theory (CSDT): Intrinsic Motivation Inventory (IMI). https://selfdeterminationtheory.org/intrinsic-motivation-inventory/

32. Hayashida, N., Kuzuoka, H., Suzuki, K.: Beyond learning alone – how other learners affect self-study in IVE. In: "Social VR," a Workshop of CHI 2020 (2020)

33. Imada, S., Hayashida, N., Kuzuoka, H., Suzuki, K., Oki, M.: Making others' efforts tangible. In: Stephanidis, C., Antona, M. (eds.) HCII 2020. CCIS, vol. 1225, pp. 239–247. Springer, Cham (2020). https://doi.org/10.1007/978-3-030-50729-9_34

XR-Based Mindfulness and Art Therapy: Facing the Psychological Impact of Covid-19 Emergency

Carola Gatto[1(✉)], Giovanni D'Errico[2], Fabiana Nuccetelli[3], Valerio De Luca[2], Giovanna Ilenia Paladini[2], and Lucio Tommaso De Paolis[2]

[1] Department of Cultural Heritage, University of Salento, Lecce, Italy
carola.gatto@unisalento.it
[2] Department of Engineering for Innovation, University of Salento, Lecce, Italy
{giovanni.derrico,valerio.deluca,ilenia.paladini,
lucio.depaolis}@unisalento.it
[3] Centro Medex, Medicina di Eccellenza, Squinzano, Lecce, Italy
fabiana.nuccetelli88@gmail.com

Abstract. The latest events related to the spread of the Covid-19 virus have seen the rise of new social needs in countries like Italy, especially regarding the most vulnerable individuals. The emergency highlighted the insufficiency of some traditional methods of psychological support for that part of the population concretely facing the risk of social isolation. This research aims to discuss an innovative methodology that, by exploiting information and communication technologies (ICT) resources, combines the need to protect the vulnerable population with the need to prevent their social isolation, by intervening on the psychological well-being of users most at risk. In particular, we want to evaluate the feasibility of a Cross Reality (XR) project that combines the technologies of Virtual, Mixed and Augmented Reality with the most consolidated therapeutic methods of Mindfulness and Art Therapy.

Keywords: Cross Reality · Virtual reality · Mindfulness · Art Therapy · Covid-19 · e-Health · Psychological support · Biofeedback

1 Introduction

During the quarantine due to the COVID-19 pandemic emergency, because of the lockdown measures adopted in each country, people living in clinical contexts, in precarious conditions, in restriction of freedom, or with disabilities have been particularly at risk, not only for general vulnerability to the virus, but also because of the total isolation with the world outside. Prolonged periods of isolation could have serious effects on the mental health of older people taking into account that they have less likely to be digitally included [1].

In the United Nation (UN) report, titled "Policy Brief: The Impact of COVID-19 on older persons" is written *"COVID-19 exacerbates global economic inequalities and*

© Springer Nature Switzerland AG 2020
L. T. De Paolis and P. Bourdot (Eds.): AVR 2020, LNCS 12243, pp. 147–155, 2020.
https://doi.org/10.1007/978-3-030-58468-9_11

exposes existing inequalities that affect older persons, especially older women and older persons with disabilities. This includes inadequate access to essential goods and basic services, limited social protection services, and widespread age discrimination. It is critical that responses to this crisis specifically identify and prioritize older persons, who may be at particular risk of being left behind or excluded, during the pandemic response and recovery phases."

Indeed, if on the one hand these measures were aimed at safeguarding overloaded health systems and protecting people at risk such as the elderly from contagion, it is also true that separation from family members and the network of informal relationships can have worrying consequences for this population.

Among the risks for those persons the United Nation has identified both short- and long-term policy and programmatic responses managed across four key priorities for action; the one we are focusing on is the so called "Strengthen social inclusion and solidarity during physical distancing". Regarding this priority axis, it has been said that, even if physical distancing is crucial, it needs to be accompanied by social support measures and targeted care for older persons, including by increasing their access to digital technologies. Social isolation is not only a risk in emergency: loneliness among young, middle-aged, and older adults is a serious public health concern of our time because of its strong connection with cardiovascular, autoimmune, neurocognitive, and mental health problems [2]. This topic has been discussed from the beginning of the COVID-19 emergency by the scientific community: specialists agree that the impact of the isolation had demonstrated the lack of means able to guarantee psychological support to the weakest category, in particular for the older people.

Starting from these considerations we decided to focus our research on the potential of information and communication technology as new media for reducing isolation and negative feeling in situation not only of emergency, how actually COVID-19 is, but also in normal life for those categories that need this kind of help. It is important to consider that, with the advent of the new reforms, "digital healthcare" (e-health) is destined to assume an increasingly important role in the world of healthcare. Among all the technologies that make up e-health, Cross Reality (XR), a technology that allows the generation of immersive, interactive and collaborative virtual environments, can represent a decisive paradigm of innovation both in an emergency period and in normal life.

This draft aims to provide a preliminary study of the exploitation of VR in the field of e-health, focusing on therapeutic and meditative environments for the mental well-being of those people who live in isolation. Therefore, we analyse a brief background and related works on VR technologies that experiment with Art Therapy and Mindfulness for the stress reduction, emotional wellness, meditative and therapeutic applications.

Then we pass to introduce our idea that aimed to design a platform for specific Mindfulness and Art Therapy session by means of collaborative virtual environments.

2   Mindfulness and Art Therapy as Theoretical Base for Innovative Psychological Procedures

In this draft we do not discuss the validity of the scientific results in the field of Mindfulness and Art Therapy, both proven by ten-year studies. Rather, we want to highlight how it is increasingly necessary to develop a system that, exploiting the potential offered by digital technologies, creates a new approach that reinforces these same practices, making them much more accessible.

Art Therapy is built upon the idea that art is the most accessible form of communication for human experience, since it makes use of visual symbols and images [3]. There are many schools of Art Therapy [4], mostly based on an approach called "depth-psychology", that comes from the studies of the founders of modern depth psychology, Carl Gustav Jung, along with Alfred Adler and Sigmund Freud [5]. Depth psychology explores *"the hidden or deeper parts of human experience by seeing things in depth rather than taking them apart"* [6], and involves a deep inquiry into the symbolic meaning of things, such as symbols or complex images. This approach is already oriented to analyse the human being by means of figures and images, such as in the exploration of dreams, complexes, and archetypes. All of these reasons provide the theoretical connection between depth psychology and museums. Indeed, museums display the *"commonalities among human situations, emotions, difficulties and achievements as expressed in aesthetic form"* [7]. Gathering in a non-medical setting, surrounded by artworks and objects, away from the austerity of the hospital, the stigma of the mental health clinic, medical devices and white coats, makes people feel that they are in a more hospitable and friendly environment, which can lead to inspiration. Therefore, the museum can serve as a therapeutic environment that can foster Art Therapy [8].

Art Therapy practice in museum has become increasingly popular for the well-being of vulnerable individuals, seen as active members of a social context. This practice was born in Canada in 1996 as part of a project aimed to provide assistance to cancer patients by helping them, through the museum path, to visually express their experience on different levels. The program was developed at the McMichael Canadian Art Collection in partnership with the Toronto-Sunnybrook Regional Cancer Centre-Bayview Support Network [9]. From that moment, numerous experiments followed, arriving in 2018, also in Canada, to talk about the possibility of allowing doctors to "prescribe" guided visits to museums for patients with chronic disorders and depression as an effective therapy.

In the study conducted in 2014 by the Research Centre for Museum Studies of the Leicester University titled "How museum impact health and well-being" [10], clearly shows how museums are able to respond to public health needs, using their collections to improve people's health and well-being, to contribute positively to the objectives of public health. The aim was precisely to keep elderly people physically and socially active, intervening on the emotional well-being of the target. Age is not the only factor considered for the identification of the target, but also these studies are aimed to subjects affected by depression, cognitive decline, social isolation, poverty, disability, increasing fragility and vulnerability to injury.

The excellent results of this project lead us to hypothesize that this kind of target may be equally responsive for our experimentation project.

However, it should be noted that the traditional method has some significant issues in term of accessibility: not all of people to whom the therapy is addressed have the possibility of moving outside. This is why the technological contribution could be significant in order to establish a new good practice in those places where people live, without the possibility of going out safely. Certainly, we encourage the physical presence of the visitor at the museum, for all of the targeted public, when this can happen in totally safety, but we also want to design a solution addressed to an audience that is not able to move independently.

Therefore, XR technology can be inserted within this context as a useful tool to restore the sense of presence where physical presence is not possible due to contingencies linked to the individual.

On the other hand, Mindfulness-based interventions are claimed as effective tool for stress reduction and more generally, mindfulness practice can achieve a wide range of benefits on psychophysical well-being [11]. In the definition given by Kabat-Zinn [12], Mindfulness is that process capable of bringing a certain quality of attention to the experience present moment by moment and in a non-judgmental way. This self-regulation of attention refers to the non-elaborative awareness of mental events, that is, thoughts, feelings and sensations, as they arise [13]. The interest in clinical and cognitive psychology for the benefits that Mindfulness-based Interventions (MBI) offer compared to a whole series of problems related to stress (anxiety, depression, chronic pain) [11, 14–16] has grown enormously. Among these interventions, Mindfulness-based Stress Reduction (MBSR) [11] constitutes a well-established program for the promotion of psychophysical well-being and represents the practice that most of all has the merit of having introduced mindfulness into modern Western therapeutic practices.

In recent years the interest in computer-supported Mindfulness interventions has grown exponentially, justifying the presence on the stores of a wide range of mobile apps to support the practice and a certain attention by the scientific community on the generated benefits [17]. Among these interventions, a prominent place occupies the use of Virtual Reality (VR) whose support for the Mindfulness experience rests on a fundamental peculiarity offered by this technology: the sense of presence. Through VR the user is faced with immersive virtual stimuli capable of inducing the sensation of actually being within the virtual world [18].

In the next paragraph we analyse some of the most significative studies about the potential of XR technology, with a focus on VR experience in the field of psychological well-being.

3 XR Application for Mindfulness and Art Therapy: Where We Are?

Nowadays it is more common to talk about Cross Reality (XR), defined as a larger set of technologies that includes Augmented Reality (AR), which improves the experience of the real environment by superimposing "synthetic" virtual elements above physical environment, Mixed Reality (MR) in which virtual elements overlap reality in a conscious way of spaces and surfaces, and Virtual Reality, a total computer-generated world. The best definition has been given by Paradiso-Landay/Coleman in 2009 [19], which connotes the XR as a subset of Mixed Reality, composed of a portion of reality (coming from a network of sensors/actuators) and a part of virtuality (coming from shared online virtual worlds).

In this paragraph we are going to discuss how XR technologies can provide to mental stimulation, a connection to autobiographical memory through reminiscence and enhanced quality of life (QoL).

The potentials of Art therapy in XR has been studied mostly as new creative medium for clinical procedures [20]. Artistic expression in VR can actually figure as an innovative medium which opens to new possibilities of digital art, extending beyond classical expressive art medium. Creation in VR includes options such as three-dimensional painting, immersive creative experience, dynamic scaling, and embodied expression. This practice is based on the idea that the creative process of art facilitates reparation and recovery and is a form of non-verbal communication of thought and feelings [21].

An interesting study is provided in [22], where a bio-responsive virtual reality experience explores visual forms of entrainment through amorphous nature-inspired phenomena that evolves and reacts in real time thanks to physiological feedback. In this case the project aims to design a multi-user scenario where the biofeedback of one user alters di the visual representation of the second user in virtual space, by means of interactive images that can create a digital art installation.

In literature it is possible to find significant experiences in the field of virtual museum, defined as a *"digital entity that draws on the characteristics of a museum, in order to complement, enhance, or augment the museum experience through personalization, interactivity and richness of content"* [23]. The virtual museum in some case can be similar to the concept of Virtual Tour, in which the user can move into the virtual space thanks to different available tasks. Most of the biggest museums has a virtual tour available on Internet, and, especially after the lockdown period, ever more institutions have felt the need to publish their virtual museum as new media for showing their exhibition. The forced temporary closure of museums during the lockdown suddenly brought to the fore the digital communication with the public. We witnessed a wave of virtual tours, published on the museums' websites and disseminated via their social media accounts [24]. There are new studies in which some virtual tours have been compared: in "Evaluating Museum Virtual Tours: The Case Study" [25] for example, the virtual tour of sixteen Italian museums is studied by using a combination of two multi-criteria decision-making theories.

All of the studies analysed so far meet only partially our research needs, as long as our aim is not to create a new media of artistic expression [20, 21], neither to "communicate" the museum in a period in which this is not accessible (i.e. because of the lockdown) [23, 24]. So far, we have tried to highlight the contact points between the Art Therapy as well-being practice, the museum as place and collection, and XR technologies as new tools.

Regarding the exploitation of XR in Mindfulness practice, many studies explored the potential of XR-based practice for the psychological well-being, showing encouraging results as well as highlighting new issues that are interesting to explore [26, 27].

The use of virtual environment can reduce the wandering of the mind in the form of distracting thoughts (mind wandering), because the subject's attention is drawn to specific virtual elements, promoting an experiential focus on the present moment. A distinction is useful between those systems that follow a non-adaptive paradigm in the delivery of the Mindfulness experience and those in which the user's psychophysiological state is crucial to the evolution of the experience (this is the case that involves the use of biofeedback and neurofeedback sensors discussed in detail later).

Some projects exploit VR in order to immerse the user in natural scenarios [28], in accordance with the so-called Attention Restoration Theory (ART) and with design principles focused on Biophilia. These demonstrate a close link between immersion in natural environments and intrinsically restorative properties of attention and indirectly influencing the quality of awareness practice. In this research field it has been proved how a nature-inspired virtual environment can have some restorative or relaxing properties and that such these effects can translate into deeper mindfulness sessions.

By limiting the distractions of the real world, increasing the sense of presence and offering people a stimulating and suitable place for practice, virtual reality can actually be seen as a solution to extend accessibility also to mindfulness practice.

Among the advantages of a VR mindfulness system is mentioned also the possibility to provide beginners with real-time feedback, especially thanks to the use of neuro and biofeedback [29]. In literature has been noted the increasing of the number of serious games as effective tools in AR\VR Exposure Therapy for the treatment of phobias, anxiety or hyperactivity disorders [30].

Gamification paradigms are motivation tools that allow to improve the effectiveness of the VR Mindfulness practice, both for specific activities, such as Mindfulness Based Stress Reduction (MBSR), Dialectical Behavioural Therapy (DBT), Acceptance and Commitment Therapy (ACT), and for more general activities, such as the training of the mindfulness skills. It is clear how the use of motivational design is fundamental for a good virtual mindfulness experience [31, 32].

4   Proposal

The project aims to raise the quality of life level of vulnerable and digitally isolated subjects, in particular the elder people hospitalized in assistance centres, that don't have the opportunity to go out for meeting other people or visiting other places. Indeed, this target is facing situations of social isolation not only in times of emergency, such as the lockdown due to COVID-19, but in everyday life. This project aims to experiment an alternative, innovative and effective psychological assistance tool, that can effectively contribute to the cases of social exclusion. To achieve this main goal, we intend to decline the proposal into the following specific objectives:

- Emotional involvement of the user for reducing stress and inducing pleasant-relaxing emotional states, by means of guided Mindfulness sessions;
- Cognitive abilities stimulation of the user, such as memory, attention and learning, by means of Art Therapy sessions;
- Gamification module extension, as a tool to keep interest and constancy in practice;
- Possibility of single as well as multi-user session; in this second case each experience can be shared with other users of the medical centre or with family members, in order to increase opportunities for socialization (Collaborative Virtual Environment - CVE);
- Analysis of the quality of life level by surveys and tests before and after the execution of the protocol;
- Monitoring through specific sensors the progress of physiological responses to the proposed activities (biofeedback).

In summary, by means of virtual reality headsets equipped with controllers for interaction, such as the Oculus Go, we aim to provide a participatory and collaborative platform for guided Mindfulness session and Art Therapy experience. Furthermore, biofeedback systems will be used in order to obtain immediate and continuous information on physiological responses such as heart rate, galvanic skin feedback, temperature or blood pressure. We intend to use sensors as a non-invasive tool for monitoring, collection, and real-time analysis of the psychophysical state of the patients involved in the experience, helping therapists and patients to maximize the results of the sessions.

5   Conclusions

In this paper we discuss an innovative methodology that combines the need to protect the vulnerable population, with the need to prevent their social isolation (elderly in particular) by intervening on the psychological well-being thanks to an innovative solution that exploit Cross Reality technology. In particular, we evaluated the feasibility of a proposal that combines the technologies of the collaborative virtual environments with the consolidated therapeutic methods of Mindfulness and Art Therapy.

Over the next months we will design the proposal exposed in this paper in a more specific way, thanks to a multidisciplinary team that includes psychologist, Mindfulness therapist, expert of Art Therapy, engineers and manager of an assisted-living facility, that we assume as experimentation case.

Contribution. The author Carola Gatto wrote Sect. 1 "Introduction" and all the Art Therapy contributions in Sect. 2 "Mindfulness & Art Therapy as theoretical base for innovative psychological procedures" and in Sect. 3 "XR application for mindfulness and art therapy: where we are?".

She took part to the elaboration of Proposal and Conclusions with the other authors.

References

1. United Nation Report, Policy Brief: The Impact of COVID-19 on older persons (2020)
2. Gerst-Emerson, K., Jayawardhana, J.: Loneliness as a public health issue: the impact of loneliness on health care utilization among older adults. Am. J. Public Health **105**, 1013–1019 (2015)
3. Ford-Martin, P.: Art Therapy. Gale Encyclopedia of Psychology, 2nd edn., pp. 48–49. Gale Group, New York (2011)
4. Song, M., Tadeo, T., Sandor, I., Ulas, S., DiPaola, S.: BioFlockVR: exploring visual entrainment through amorphous nature phenomena in bio-responsive multi-immersant VR interactives. In: Proceedings of the 2nd International Conference on Image and Graphics Processing (ICIGP 2019), pp. 150–154. Association for Computing Machinery, New York (2019)
5. Ellenberger, H.F.: Discovery of the Unconscious: The History and Evolution of Dynamic Psychiatry. Fontana Press, London (1970)
6. Bright, B.: On Depth Psychology: It's Meaning and Magic. Depth Insights (2019)
7. Salom, A.: The therapeutic potentials of a museum visit. Int. J. Transpersonal Stud. **27**, 98–103 (2008)
8. Ioannides, E.: Museums as therapeutic environments and the contribution of art therapy. Museum Int. **68**(3–4), 98–109 (2016)

9. Deane, K., Carman, M., Fitch, M.: The cancer journey: bridging art therapy and museum education. Can. Oncol. Nurs. J. **10**(4), 140–146 (2000)
10. Dodd, J., Jones, C.R.: Mind, Body, Spirit: How Museums Impact Health and Wellbeing (2014)
11. Grossman, P., Niemann, L., Schmidt, S., Walach, H.: Mindfulness-based stress reduction and health benefits: a meta-analysis. J. Psychosom. Res. **57**(1), 35–43 (2004)
12. Kabat-Zinn, J.: Mindfulness-based interventions in context: past, present, and future. Clin. Psychol. Sci. Pract. **10**(2), 144–156 (2003)
13. Bishop, S.R., et al.: Mindfulness: a proposed operational definition. Clin. Psychol. Sci. Pract. **11**(3), 230–241 (2004)
14. Chiesa, A., Serretti, A.: Mindfulness-based stress reduction for stress management in healthy people: a review and meta-analysis. J. Altern. Complement. Med. **15**(5), 593–600 (2009)
15. Brown, K.W., Ryan, R.M., Creswell, J.D.: Mindfulness: theoretical foundations and evidence for its salutary effects. Psychol. Inq. (2007)
16. Chiesa, A., Serretti, A.: Mindfulness based cognitive therapy for psychiatric disorders: a systematic review and meta-analysis. Psychiatry Res. **187**(3), 441–453 (2011)
17. Bostock, S., Crosswell, A.D., Prather, A.A., Steptoe, A.: Mindfulness on-the-go: effects of a mindfulness meditation app on work stress and well-being. J. Occup. Health Psychol. **24**, 127–138 (2019)
18. Sanchez-Vives, M.V., Slater, M.: From presence to consciousness through virtual reality. Nat. Rev. Neurosci. **6**, 332–366 (2005)
19. Paradiso, J.A., James, A.L.: Guest editors' introduction: cross reality environments. IEEE Pervasive Comput. **8**, 3 (2009)
20. Hacmun, I., Regev, D., Salomon, R.: The principles of art therapy in virtual reality. Front Psychol. **9**, 2082 (2018)
21. Malchiodi, C.A.: Handbook of Art Therapy, 2nd ed. Guilford Press (2012)
22. Song, M., Ulas, S., Tadeo, T., Dipaola, S., Sandor, I.: BioFlockVR: exploring visual entrainment through amorphous nature phenomena in bio-responsive multi-immersant VR interactives (2019)
23. V-Must Homepage. http://www.v-must.net. Accessed 15 May 2020
24. ICOM Report: Museums, Museum Professionals and COVID-19 (2020)
25. Kabassi, K., Amelio, A., Komianos, V., Oikonomou, K.: Evaluating museum virtual tours: the case study of Italy. Information **10**, 351 (2019)
26. Navarro-Haro, M.V., López-del-Hoyo, Y., Campos, D., Linehan, M.M., Hoffman, H.G., García-Palacios, A., et al.: Meditation experts try virtual reality mindfulness: a pilot study evaluation of the feasibility and acceptability of virtual reality to facilitate mindfulness practice in people attending a Mindfulness conference. PLoS ONE **12**(11), e0187777 (2017)
27. Navarro-Haro, M.V., et al.: The use of virtual reality to facilitate mindfulness skills training in dialectical behavioral therapy for borderline personality disorder: a case study. Front. Psychol. **7**, 1573 (2016)
28. Costa, Mark R., Bergen-Cico, D., Grant, T., Herrero, R., Navarro, J., Razza, R., Wang, Q.: Nature inspired scenes for guided mindfulness training: presence, perceived restorativeness and meditation depth. In: Schmorrow, D.D., Fidopiastis, C.M. (eds.) HCII 2019. LNCS (LNAI), vol. 11580, pp. 517–532. Springer, Cham (2019). https://doi.org/10.1007/978-3-030-22419-6_37
29. Shaw, C., Gromala, D., Fleming, S.A.: The meditation chamber: enacting autonomic senses. Proc. of ENACTIVE **7**, 405–408 (2007)
30. Barba, M.C., et al.: BRAVO: a gaming environment for the treatment of ADHD. In: De Paolis, L.T., Bourdot, P. (eds.) AVR 2019. LNCS, vol. 11613, pp. 394–407. Springer, Cham (2019). https://doi.org/10.1007/978-3-030-25965-5_30

31. Van Rooij, M., Lobel, A., Harris, O., Smit, N., Granic, I.: DEEP: a biofeedback virtual reality game for children at-risk for anxiety. In: Proceedings of the 2016 CHI Conference Extended Abstracts on Human Factors in Computing Systems, pp. 1989–1997. ACM (2016)

32. Kanth, R.K., Lingelbach, K., Bui, M., Vukelić, M.: MindTrain: how to train your mind with interactive technologies. In: ACM International Conference Proceeding Series, pp. 643–647 (2019)

33. Prpa, M., Cochrane, K., Riecke, B.E.: Hacking alternatives in 21st century: designing a bio-responsive virtual environment for stress reduction. In: Serino, S., Matic, A., Giakoumis, D., Lopez, G., Cipresso, P. (eds.) MindCare 2015. CCIS, vol. 604, pp. 34–39. Springer, Cham (2016). https://doi.org/10.1007/978-3-319-32270-4_4

Vestibular Damage Assessment and Therapy Using Virtual Reality

A. Adjindji[1], C. Kuo[1(✉)], G. Mikal[2], L. R. Harris[1], and M. Jenkin[1]

[1] Centre for Vision Research, York University, Toronto, Canada
adamzis@my.yorku.ca, cyk@cse.yorku.ca, harris@yorku.ca,
jenkin@eecs.yorku.ca
[2] Physiomobility Health Group, Toronto, Canada
gmikal@physiomobility.ca

Abstract. Vestibular damage can be very debilitating, requiring ongoing assessment and rehabilitation to return sufferers to normal function. The process of rehabilitation can require an extended period of therapy during which patients engage in repetitive and often boring tasks to recover as much normal vestibular function as possible. Making these tasks more engaging while at the same time obtaining quantitative participation data in these tasks is critical for a positive patient outcome. Here we describe the conversion of vestibular therapy tasks into virtual reality and technology that enables their deployment in both directly- and remotely-supervised vestibular rehabilitation. This infrastructure is currently being evaluated in tests within a clinical setting.

Keywords: Virtual reality · Vestibular rehabilitation · Vestibular assessment

1 Introduction

Vestibular impairment can occur as a consequence of a stroke [5,12,14], concussion [1] or other head trauma [9]. Dizziness and related vestibular-like issues can also occur with no obvious physiological cause, especially in the elderly [10]. Vestibular impairment can be extremely debilitating, and if severe, can impair normal daily activities. One of the most critical functional behaviours supporting quality of life is mobility, and falls are one of the biggest threats to older adults' safety and mobility. One-third of older adults in Canada will fall at least once each year and one-quarter will experience a fall-related injury [16]. Dizziness and low vestibular functioning is an important contributor to this problem, and yet, methods of assessing progress in vestibular therapy rely largely on self-reporting.

Various rehabilitation therapies have been proposed to help restore normal vestibular function (see [6,7]) and are generally recommended in order to enable

The financial support of the CFREF VISTA project is gratefully acknowledged. The authors would like to thank Yaser Kerachian for his support throughout the project.

© Springer Nature Switzerland AG 2020
L. T. De Paolis and P. Bourdot (Eds.): AVR 2020, LNCS 12243, pp. 156–164, 2020.
https://doi.org/10.1007/978-3-030-58468-9_12

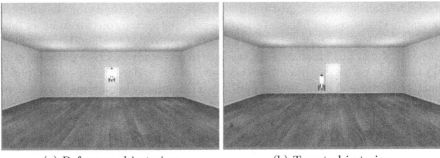

(a) Reference object view   (b) Target object view

Fig. 1. The Find Target task. The patient first fixates the reference object (a), and then once this object is selected, must move their viewpoint to fixate on the target object (b). The possible locations of the target object are defined by the clinician and are set to exercise the patient's head motion and thus their vestibular system.

such individuals to return to their normal daily lives [17]. Many of the required therapies involve repetitive exercises that encourage adaptation to the underlying damage to the vestibular system. Monitoring such exercises, and in particular, ensuring that patients perform such exercises between visits to therapists is thus critical to improving patient outcome. Lack of adherence to these assigned exercise regimes usually comes down to two reasons: patient anxiety from lack of guidance or boredom from repetitiveness of exercises [13]. Gamification of therapeutic exercises can alleviate boredom by providing guided and personalized treatment progression from the safety and comfort of a patient's home [11,15], but even here, monitoring and refining of assigned exercises is critical to the outcome of the patient's recovery.

Here we describe an infrastructure enabling vestibular stimulation exercises that can be carried out either under direct supervision within a clinical setting or between clinical visits at the patient's home. The same virtual reality infrastructure can be used as a vestibular function assessment tool. The system described here utilizes commodity virtual reality hardware (the Lenovo Daydream Mirage Solo) and software tools (Unity) integrated with a cloud-based system providing control of rehabilitation tasks and their settings as well as data collection from individual patient sessions. Although testing to date has concentrated on supervised clinical testing with a trained physiotherapist in attendance, the long term goal is be develop a system that can be used by patients under remote supervision.

2   Exercise Treatments

In order to enable patients' engagement in vestibular exercises at home, many tasks are designed to be straightforward and utilize material that is readily available. For example, a task might require a patient to fixate playing cards that have been secured to the walls of a patient's home and then to make head motions that cause the patient to move their head so that it is directed at different cards. Recognizing the need to transfer existing vestibular exercises and also recognizing the limits of commodity virtual reality hardware, we concentrated initially on two exercises that require the patient to produce head motions in a controlled manner. In particular, as the commodity head mounted display used in this study lacks eye tracking, only tasks that rely on head motion have been evaluated to date. The pen-and-paper version of traditional exercises are performed using household items (e.g., a deck of playing cards and painter's tape to mount these cards on a wall) and the task is made more challenging as the patient recovers. For example, as the patient progresses the distance to the wall is changed, more complex wall textures are used, and the subject may conduct the experiments while sitting on an exercise ball. Here we concentrate on two such exercises, one in which the patient must search the visual space to find a target and one in which the patient must move their head to choose between two different targets. We refer to these exercises as *Find Target* and *Choose Target* which are described below.

For both the exercises described below, a given treatment consists of a sequence of localization tasks with a common theme (Choose Target or Find Target). These exercises consist of a sequence of steps with similar simulated room sizes and visual complexity. Specific parameters that can be set for a given step in a trial include:

- **Room type:** Simulated rooms can either be small or large and can be either "unstructured" or "textured." Unstructured rooms are bare with just a door, walls, floor and ceiling. Textured rooms are decorated. Larger rooms allow for larger head rotations and are thus more suitable for advanced patients. Visual complexity of the background adds to the difficulty of directing the head towards the target.
- **Number of trials:** The number of trials that appear during the step. As patients progress, more trials are added.
- **Trial timeout:** The maximum duration of a trial in a given step. If the patient does not complete a trial correctly within this time then the trial is counted as having failed and the next trial begins.
- **Monocular/binocular presentation:** Clinicians have the option of presenting targets in only the left or right eye, if desired.
- **Target population:** The collection of targets that will be used in a given trial. Smaller scale targets are used for more advanced patients with mild hypofunction, and larger targets are used for those with more severe hypofunction.
- **Target space:** In Find Target, choose the direction of the target object relative to the reference object (horizontally, vertically, or diagonally displaced.) For Choose Target, choose where a target object and a distractor object are relative to one another (horizontally, vertically, and diagonally displaced).

2.1   Find Target

The Find Target exercise is a head movement exercise treatment in which a patient moves their head from a neutral position indicated by the reference

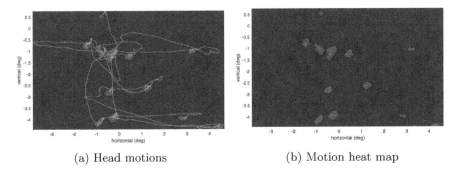

(a) Head motions   (b) Motion heat map

Fig. 2. Tracked head orientation during the find target task. In (a) multiple trials are shown, each with a track that begins approximately at (0,0) and moves to the orientation of the target to be found. (b) shows a heat map of the dwell time at each head orientations over multiple trials.

object to point towards a location indicated by a target object (see Fig. 1). In the pen-and-paper exercise, target objects can be represented by playing cards or pieces of paper with writing either held in the clinician's hand or taped to a wall. The target may be horizontally, vertically, or diagonally displaced relative to the neutral head position, depending on the type of hypofunction and treatment goals. When the patient is comfortable repeating this activity for 1–2 min, the task can be made more complex. For example, the object can be placed against a visually complex background, such as patterned wallpaper or a dynamic background such as a television screen. Patients progress from a seated position, to seated on a stability ball, to standing, to standing on soft surfaces or on one leg.

The virtual reality version of this task is illustrated in Fig. 1. Here the user is placed in a virtual environment and the reference target (a 3d placeholder) is rendered directly in front of the patient. The patient fixates on the reference object and presses a button using a wand when the reference object is fixated. At this point, the reference object is replaced by a target object at some displacement relative to the reference object. The patient then moves their head around the space until the target is fixated and their head is pointing to the target and then presses a button using the wand to indicate that they have localized the target.

The pen-and-paper and the virtual reality-based version of this task perform the same basic treatment. The clinician identifies particular horizontal and vertical offsets from a "straight ahead" direction. The target object is placed in some direction that will cause the patient to move their head in a particular manner. In the pen and paper version of this task, the object might be playing cards taped to the wall. The card locations are fixed and patient performance is not recorded unless they are supervised directly. The virtual environment version provides the opportunity to personalize the environment and choose the objects to be displayed. The virtual reality version of the task also provides considerable

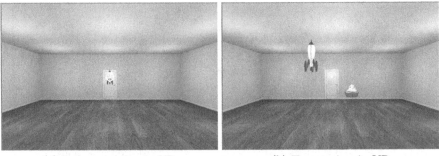

| (a) Reference view in VR | (b) Target view in VR |

Fig. 3. The choose target task. The patient first fixates on the reference object (a), and then once this object is selected, they must move their viewpoint to choose the target object (b). A distractor object is also presented in the virtual space. The possible locations of the target object are defined by the clinician and are set to exercise the patient's head motion and thus their vestibular system in specific ways.

information about the actions of the patient. Quantitative information about time taken, velocity of the patient's head motion, etc. are recorded. One critical advantage of the VR-based solution is that quantitative data concerning head motion is recorded "automatically" as a consequence of the VR nature of the rendering. For example, for the find target task, head directions can be recovered and a heat map of head orientation dwell times can also be recovered (Fig. 2).

2.2 Choose Target

Choose Target adds a second target to the Find Target task described above (Fig. 3). Adding another target allows a patient to practice moving their eyes and head between the two. Ideally, the additional target is placed just inside their periphery so they can move their focus between the two such that only a single target is clear at any given time. These objects can be separated horizontally, vertically or diagonally relative to one another.

These target exercises allow for one target to be placed directly in front of the patient, and the other, for example, to appear over their left shoulder or over their right shoulder, all at eye level. While seated the patient looks from one target to another. Only one of the two targets is the same as the reference target which is the one that must be looked at. The other target is a distractor. As the displacement between the two targets is increased the patient must make larger and larger head motions to bring the correct target into view. The controlled direction of separation between the two test targets forces the patient to make head motions in the desired directions when performing the task. As with the Find Target exercise, once the patient is sufficiently comfortable carrying out the exercise seated and with the targets against a neutral background, they may progress to gradually more complex backgrounds, or to standing on one or both feet, or seated on a stability ball.

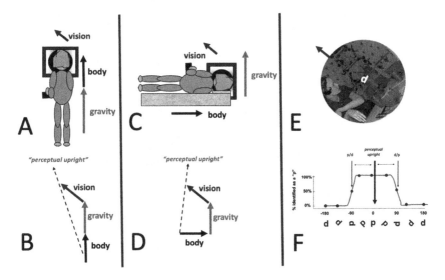

Fig. 4. The OCHART test. Observers view a screen arranged so that nothing outside the circular display (E) is visible either when upright (A) or lying on one side (C). The display (E) shows a highly polarized scene with a clear upright. Superimposed on this image is the probe character (p/d) and the participant's task is to simply respond as to whether the character looks more like a "p" or a "d". By plotting the percentage of time, one interpretation is chosen (F), and the points of ambiguity can be determined. The perceptual upright is defined as being midway between these orientations.

3 Measuring Vestibular Function

A final step in providing personalized VR-based vestibular treatment is a mechanism to quantify the current state of vestibular information processing. In 2006, Dyde, Jenkin and Harris [4] developed a quantitative measure for estimating the relative importance of the main factors that determine the perceptual upright using visual probes presented to an observer while they were in different body positions. By separating upward sensation signaled by the bodily, gravity and visual cues, we were able to quantify their individual contributions. This tool, known as OCHART (the Oriented CHAracter Recognition Test), has proven successful in estimating a subject's perceptual upright and the relative contributions of vision, gravity and the body to that estimate (e.g., [2,3,8]). The OCHART test uses a character – the identity of which depends on its orientation. The perceptual upright is defined as the orientation of that character at which it is most unambiguously identified. To find this orientation, the points of greatest ambiguity are found (at which the character is equally likely to be identified as either interpretation) from which the orientation of least ambiguity can be deduced (Fig. 4).

The perceptual upright can be modeled as the sum of three vectors corresponding to the orientation signaled by visual cues, gravity cues and the internal

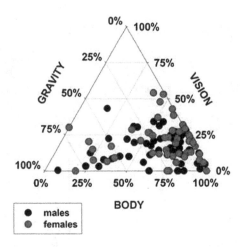

Fig. 5. The relative contribution of vision, gravity and the body in a large group of neuro-typical participants.

representation of the body [4]. By testing in at least two body orientations, (e.g., upright and on one's side, Figs. 4 A and C) the relative lengths of the vectors corresponding to the contributions of the vision, gravity and the body can be calculated using simple geometry. The direction of the perceptual upright can be modeled as the sum of three vectors corresponding to the directions of upright signaled by the visual display, gravity, and the orientation of the body (B and D) from which the relative lengths of the vectors can be calculated, corresponding to the relative contributions of body, gravity and visual cues to upright. Figure 5 shows the relative contributions of visual, bodily and gravity cues for a large sample of neuro-typical participants. The diagram is a ternary plot in which the percentage contribution of each source of information is plotted on each of the axes. This is possible because the contributions are relative to each other and therefore sum to 100%. What can be seen is that the data cluster in the bottom right corner of the diagram indicates the typical contributions of vision (around 20–25%), gravity (10–20%) and the body (>50%) to the perceptual upright. Note that even in this normal population there are some outliers with high contributions of vision or gravity cues (>50%).

4   Managing Users and Treatments

As modern HMDs like the Lenovo Mirage Solo incorporate an integrated computer with WIFI access, it is useful to exploit this capability in order to control treatment plans on individual devices. Patients register a given HMD with a web-based server and clinicians manage their patients and their patients' treatments using a web application. The front end of the application was created using the Angular web application framework and the Angular Material component library. The back end server exchanges and stores data to and from the

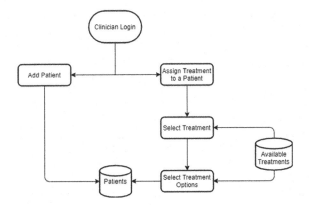

Fig. 6. This is a diagram detailing the intended workflow of a clinician using the treatment management web application.

front end and HMDs. It was implemented using Node.js, written in TypeScript with the Express.js framework, and uses MonogoDB as the database.

Clinicians provide treatments to patients following the workflow illustrated in Fig. 6. A calendar view provides a convenient mechanism for clinicians to view upcoming treatments, to customize treatments for specific patients, and to review patient performance.

5 Ongoing Work

The technical infrastructure described here is currently being used in a clinical setting to explore the acceptance of the approach by patient populations and to better understand how clinicians might best deploy the technology both in a directly supervised mode as well as remotely. This final case being of particular interest given the ongoing global pandemic and the interest in being able to provide remote treatment for populations not in close proximity to a treatment centre. As part of this process, we are exploring the development of additional treatment mechanisms including treatments that rely on eye tracking capabilities of the HMD. (A number of manufacturers provide such functionality.) We are also porting the technology from the Lenovo/Daydream platform to the Oculus platform given the lack of ongoing support for Daydream in the commodity market. As the HMD infrastructure leverages standard tools, such as Unity for rendering, and standard networking tools for interaction, this process is relatively straightforward.

References

1. Alsaheen, B.A., et al.: Vestibular rehabilitation for dizziness and balance disorders after concussion. J. Neurol. Phys. Therapy **34**, 93–97 (2010)

2. Barnett-Cowan, M., Dyde, R.T., Fox, S.H., Moro, E., Hutchison, W.D., Harris, L.R.: Multisensory determinants of orientation perception in parkinson's disease. Neuroscience **167**, 1138–1150 (2010)

3. Dearing, R., Harris, L.R.: The contribution of different parts of the visual field to the perception of upright. Vis. Res. **51**, 2207–2215 (2011)

4. Dyde, R.T., Jenkin, M., Harris, L.R.: The subjective visual vertical and the perceptual upright. Exp. Brain Res. **173**, 612–622 (2006)

5. Glasauer, S., Dieterich, M., Brandt, T.: Neuronal network based mathematical modelling of perceived verticality in acute unilateral vestibular lesions - from nerve to thalamus and cortex. J. Neurosci. **265**, 101–112 (2018)

6. Hall, C.D., et al.: Vestibular rehabilitation for peripheral vestibular hypofunction: an evidence-based clinical practice guideline: from the american physical therapy association neurology section. J. Neurologic Phys. Therapy **40**, 124 (2016)

7. Han, B.I., Song, H.S., Kim, J.S.: Vestibular rehabilitation therapy: review of indications, mechanisms, and key exercises. J. Clin. Neurol. **7**, 184–196 (2011)

8. Harris, L.R., Jenkin, M.: The effect of blur on the perception of up. Optometry Vis. Sci. **91**, 103–110 (2014)

9. Herishanu, Y.O.: Abnormal cancellation of the vestibuloocular reflex (vor) after mild head and or neck trauma. Neuro-Ophthalmol. **12**, 237–240 (1992)

10. Hobeika, C.P.: Equilibrium and balance in the elderly. Ear, Nose Throat J. **78**, 558–566 (1999)

11. Holden, M.K., Dyar, T.: Virtual environment training: a new tool for neurorehabilitation. Neurol. Report **26**(2), 62–71 (2002)

12. Karnath, H.O., Broetz, D.: Understanding and treating 'pusher syndrome'. Phys. Ther. **83**, 1119–1125 (2003)

13. Khan, O., Ahmed, I., Cottingham, J., Rahhal, M., Arvanitis, T.N., Elliott, M.T.: Timing and correction of stepping movements with a virtual reality avatar. PLoS ONE **15**(2), e0229641 (2020). https://dx.plos.org/10.1371/journal.pone.0229641

14. Saj, A., Honore, J., Bernati, T., Coello, Y., Rousseaux, M.: Subjective visual vertical in pitch and roll in right hemispheric stroke. Stroke **36**, 588–591 (2005)

15. Saposnik, G., Levin, M.: Virtual reality in stroke rehabilitation. Stroke **42**(5), 1380–1386 (2011)

16. Statistics Canada: Senior's Falls in Canada: Second Report (2014). http://www.phac-aspc.gc.ca/seniors-aines/publications/public/injury-blessure/seniors_falls-chutes_aines/index-eng.php

17. Telian, S.A., Shepard, N.T.: Update on vestibular rehabilitation therapy. Otolaryngol. Clin. North America **29**, 359–371 (1996)

The Feasibility of Augmented Reality as a Support Tool for Motor Rehabilitation

Isidro III Butaslac[1]([✉]) [iD], Alessandro Luchetti[2] [iD], Edoardo Parolin[2] [iD],
Yuichiro Fujimoto[1] [iD], Masayuki Kanbara[1], Mariolino De Cecco[2] [iD],
and Hirokazu Kato[1] [iD]

[1] Nara Institute of Science and Technology, Nara, Japan
{isidro.butaslac.hw2,yfujimoto,kanbara}@is.naist.jp
[2] University of Trento, Trento, Italy
{alessandro.luchetti,mariolino.dececco}@unitn.it
edoardo.parolin@studenti.unitn.it

Abstract. The aim of this work is to facilitate the application of Augmented Reality (AR) in rehabilitative clinics to support the therapist by providing real-time AR visualizations. The feasibility of AR as a support tool in rehabilitation is explored by developing a prototype that would meet the demand of the therapists during their evaluations. In this work, a prototype which consists of two parts has been developed; one for chair training and another for walking training. Different combinations of AR technologies and concepts that would best serve the therapist's needs in the rehabilitation and training setting are discussed. After the development phase, a qualitative user research was done through demonstrations and interviews to validate the effectiveness and feasibility. The overall feedback from the participating therapists was positive, confirming the potential of this work to be extended to everyday clinical use.

Keywords: Augmented reality · HoloLens · Rehabilitation · Data visualizations

1 Introduction

According to the World Health Organization, the Global Burden of Disease Study presents that 74% of the years lived with disability worldwide are related to health conditions that can be mitigated with the support of rehabilitation. Today, the number of health conditions associated with severe disability rates has reached 183 million [13]. The resources needed for addressing rehabilitation needs out-measures accessibility, resulting to inadequacies to these services. To cope with these demands, education and training of therapists that had just finished schooling may find their knowledge and expertise to be lacking in the actual field [1]. This is mainly due to the differences between the scope of the theoretical knowledge in the literature about rehabilitation concepts and their application in clinical practice. Developing the "Clinical Eye" would take years and years of

© Springer Nature Switzerland AG 2020
L. T. De Paolis and P. Bourdot (Eds.): AVR 2020, LNCS 12243, pp. 165–173, 2020.
https://doi.org/10.1007/978-3-030-58468-9_13

practicing the profession, so novice therapists would have difficulties in making complicated clinical decisions and evaluations. As a solution to this problem, this work proposes AR as a support tool used by therapists for motor rehabilitation. The introduction of this technology may be more useful for therapists with less experience, but could also prove to be a great support to veteran therapists by speeding up the evaluation process or showing a more detailed patient data.

The question now arises: how can AR be used as a support tool for these therapists? Simply put, AR is the technique of integrating computer graphics into the user's view of the real world. By providing relevant data as virtual objects, AR has the potential to improve a user's understanding of the scene. The reason is that virtual objects can display information which the user cannot detect with just his own senses [4]. This is an example of what Brooks calls "Intelligence Amplification (IA): using the computer as a tool to make a task easier for a human to perform" [5], or in this case to make the patient factors and variables during rehabilitation easier to understand.

New technologies on rehabilitation can provide more possibilities for recovery or improvements on the clinical process. Nevertheless, the lack of knowledge by clinicians regarding technological advances and apprehensions related to the role of technology in the rehabilitation scene leads them wanting to stick to the standard practices [7]. In this work, a prototype that is designed specifically for the use of therapists on motor rehabilitation has been developed. The feasibility of this prototype as a support tool is also discussed by assessing the prototype based on the New Technology Evaluation by Jones et al., specifically looking at the clinical applicability, financial, marketability and safety factors aspect of the system [8].

2   Related Work

AR in the medical field is already a thoroughly researched area. For example, AR technology can be used to give surgeons "X-ray vision" to allow them to see the insides of the patient. To name a few of the classic literature in this area, State et al. shows in real-time 3D ultrasound visualization of a fetus. This creates the illusion of viewing inside the womb of an expecting mother, with the doctor wearing the HMD feeling like using a "3D stethoscope" [9]. Another example of a work demonstrated by State et al. is on the operation of biopsy of the breast through an ultrasound-guided needle [10].

In the field of motor rehabilitation or patient evaluation, the surface electromyography (sEMG) can be considered one of the most significant biological signals used to track muscle performance. Aung et al. developed an AR system which took advantage of four sEMG signals while the patient is doing different kinds of exercises. With their system, they help the therapist map and monitor the muscle strength in real time to better understand the mannerisms of the patient while performing the task [2,3].

Another project called AUSILIA (Assisted Unit for Simulating Independent LIving Activities), focuses on promoting the autonomy of elderly people or people with pathologies. The AUSILIA system is an apartment-wide project that allows the individual to be tracked and supported by fully sensorizing the whole area. In this way, the doctor is able to monitor and evaluate the patient remotely, visualizing all important data such as interactions with the environment or physiological parameters of the patient through the use of a non-real time Augmented Virtuality system [6].

From the AUSILIA project follows the work of Stocco et al. where he introduced AR to the rehabilitative setting with the goal of improving the quality of the medical services provided. He presented a way to augment the therapist's clinical eye with data such as skeletons, applied force visualizations, and an overview status of the patient [11]. This work extends from where Stocco has left off, such as providing situated visualizations using real-time data stream from different kinds of sensors and realizing its feasibility to actual rehabilitation scenarios. Examples of the sensors and visualizations used will be described in the following sections.

3   Research Overview

In this paper, the following research questions are answered:

Q1. With the current limitations of AR, is it feasible to use as support for therapists in rehabilitation?

Q2. What combination of AR technology/concepts are best for observing and analyzing rehabilitation?

The research methodology used in this work is of a qualitative approach. First we ask our collaborators, the therapists, about their opinions on which training scenario would most benefit additional visual information. In the course of this work, two types of scenarios were selected and analysed; one concerning chair training and the other for walking training. To be able to make a good prototype suit their requirements, these three questions are used as guidelines for development:

1. What kind of data would be helpful for this training?
2. How should these data be visualized?
3. Which device is best for these kinds of data visualizations?

After answering these three questions, AR applications based on the conditions of the training for rehabilitation have been developed. Once development was completed, demonstrations to the hospitals have been scheduled and each clinical staff have the chance to try out the AR technologies that we have offered. After the demonstrations, feedback from these medical experts on the nature and extent of the usability of AR applications applied to specific training scenarios were collected through interviews. Building up from these comments, an improved version of the prototype is realized, as seen in the prototype making cycle of Fig. 1.

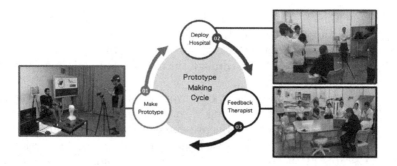

Fig. 1. The prototype making cycle to answer the requirements of the therapists.

4   Prototype Development

A prototype consisting of two parts has been developed, one for chair training and another for walking training. The chair training was chosen because the Sit-to-stand, or the STS movement, is a standard practice in rehabilitation that helps the therapist determine the functional level of a person. The walking training was determined because gait rehabilitation is very much in demand in the vicinity of our area, with the number of patients steadily increasing. In this section, the prototype developed is described by answering the three guidelines listed in the previous section. Deployment of prototype and gathering of feedback were realized with the help of two hospitals in Japan, namely Kyoto University Hospital and Takanohara Central Hospital.

4.1   Presented Data

The types of data that were found most helpful for the two training are for example: force distribution on the chair, force distribution of the foot provided by a sensorized sole, and 3D position of body joints as shown in Fig. 2. During training, the therapist want to see how much pressure the patient is exerting on certain parts of the chair or of the foot, which is important since they do not want patients to overexert muscles during rehabilitation. Another important point is tracking the joints of the patient. From the joints position data, the angles in which the patient bends his joints can be derived. This is helpful for the therapist because proper posture and form is necessary when dealing with precise rehabilitation. The data of these joint positions over time are recorded so that the path trajectory of the patient can be traced. Furthermore, EMG sensors were added to measure the muscle activities of the patient indicating if proper form is being followed. Lastly, sensors for heart rate and body temperature were included to measure the physiological parameters of the patient whether or not the training has become too intense.

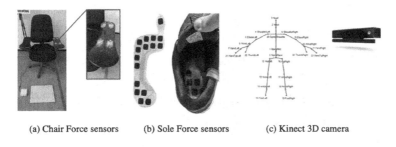

(a) Chair Force sensors   (b) Sole Force sensors   (c) Kinect 3D camera

Fig. 2. Some examples of sensors used for data acquisition.

4.2   Visualization Method

One fundamental idea in making good AR applications is situated visualization, which means "visualizing relevant virtual data directly in the context of the physical site" [12]. This just means the angle visualizations have been placed just beside the corresponding joints of the real patient, and graphs are rendered in the location of the chair area where the force is exerted. The system was designed to be as intuitive as possible, such as colors of the skeleton changing when angles reach certain thresholds, signaling danger warnings (sound feedback warning were also added). As situated visualizations also suffer from the problem of data overload, toggling on/off visualizations functionality has been added. For the therapist to understand the whole picture of the entire training session, the visualizations seen in Fig. 3 were realized. The head and feet path trajectories enabled the therapist to see data of the patient's patterns, and visualize comparisons against previous training data to ascertain patient improvements overtime. Values for speed at which the patient is moving, heart rate, and body temperature is shown beside him for the therapist to easily monitor the proper pacing of the training. A graph that changes from 0 to 100% shows the muscle activity representing the amount of strain the patient is exerting at that located muscle. A vertical guideline is also added as a visualization showing whether the patient is maintaining proper posture in the duration of the training. Lastly, sole visualization anchored to the foot of the patient were shown to view how the patient is distributing his weight under his feet, using a color scale from green to red corresponding increasing force.

4.3   Device

In answering the third question of which device best fits the proposed data visualizations, OST-HMDs (e.g. HoloLens) and handheld devices (e.g. tablet with ARCore capabilities) were explored. In general, there is no big difference between them as both cases allow the viewing of the surrounding environment with the proper virtual contents. However, impressions regarding the HoloLens had more impact on the medical staff as it provided a more immersive AR experience. Another reason is that the tracking capabilities of the tablet is limited, making

Fig. 3. Visualization methods and concepts that was used for the prototype.

it difficult to place spatial anchors. This requires the tablet to always have the marker in its camera view, rendering the AR visualizations to sometimes appear shaking and unstable. Lastly, as handheld devices make the hands of the therapists unavailable to do anything else, its becomes difficult to guide and correct the patient in training. For this reason, the HoloLens was chosen as this device can be simply equipped in the head, leaving the hands free to assist the patient.

5   Discussion

Q1. With the current limitations of AR, is it feasible to use as support for therapists in rehabilitation? To determine the feasibility of the prototypes made as a support tool for motor rehabilitation, the clinical application and relevance, financial feasibility, and safety of the system are investigated by discussing some of the guidelines prepared by the New Technology Committee described by Jones et al. [8].

The feedback from the therapists about the system during the two demonstrations were positive, with the additional comment that the potential for this kind of technology to be used in the clinical setting is very exciting. It was discussed in the Related Works section how supplementing more information about the patient to the therapist can help them better understand and assess the current situation, thus making them capable of providing a more informed evaluation. Providing in-situ visualization data to therapists proves to be a valuable asset when they are in the process of conducting rehabilitation and training. A total of 25 therapists from two different hospitals who say they want to use our system is evidence enough that this kind of technology is beneficial for medical professionals working on rehabilitation.

The cost for the development of the chair force sensors was really cheap because these components have been built from scratch using local electronic components. For the EMG, heart rate and body temperature sensors, it is easy to integrate into our scalable system as hospitals already possess these kinds of sensors. Sadly, the price for the sole pressure matrix is hard to estimate as it was a prototype system built by an Italian company called 221e. The market price for the Kinect camera is around $150, which is relatively cheap when thinking about the capabilities that it can do. The expensive part of the system is the HoloLens, which costs $3000. The HoloLens is vital in providing good AR visualizations that are properly registered into the patient's body, however, another alternative to show these AR visualizations is with a tablet having ARCore capabilities. Although spatial mapping and registering of virtual objects does not have high accuracy in the tablet version, it can still be a viable option when the price is of top concern.

Most of the sensors used in this system are approved for safety as these are already sold publicly in the market with safety warranties. The only part of our system that poses safety concerns is the part we developed ourselves from scratch, which is the force chair sensors. Safety concerns such as loose wirings from the electrical components that were soldered, or wooden material that was used as casing for these sensors may be unstable and not very suitable for actual use of patient with a serious disability. In future developments we will improve our system to be accident-proof when used by disabled people, but for now, our system works perfectly fine for doing demonstrations.

Q2. What combination of AR technology/concepts are best for observing/analyzing rehabilitation? The first concept to discuss is the possibility of toggling on and off the visualizations as seen in Fig. 4a. To avoid visual clutter, the therapist has the freedom to make visible only the visualizations he wants to see and hide the rest. This is an important point because data overload can be a serious problem; where AR visualizations would, instead of aiding, hinder the understanding of the therapist. To make this process easy to use, especially to people who are new to this kind of technology, the smartphone was used as a means of interface control as a substitute for the HoloLens air tap and bloom hand gestures.

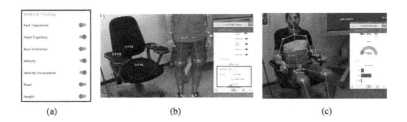

Fig. 4. Interface for toggling on/off visualizations (a), choosing the type of visualizations (b) and visualizing gauges and charts in smartphone compared to AR (c).

Another concept is the importance of data presentation that facilitates easier understanding. As seen in Fig. 4c, the therapist is presented with the option to also view the stream of data in the form of gauges and charts in the smartphone, aside from viewing it as AR visualizations. The comment from therapists is that situated visualizations are better because it gives an overall picture, which would aid better understanding compared to the figures found in the smartphone.

Finally, the last concept to discuss is the capability of the therapist to choose the types of visualizations and to have some degree of control over where to place these visualizations. In Fig. 4b, the therapist is given complete freedom to choose what type of visual representations he wants to see; for example seeing text only, graphs, or arrows. One person may understand better using one type of visualization, but another person may not. In this case, the ability to choose is of importance. Another point is choosing the location of where to visualize these virtual objects. For example, the sole visualization located beneath or beside as seen in Fig. 5a and 5b is much easier to understand when the patient is doing the action of walking, as these visualizations provide directional cues to where the foot is pointing. Therapists however, prefer the billboard type visualization seen in Fig. 5c the patient is stationary and they are the one going around and surveying the patient. This is because the billboard type visualization always faces the sole representation towards the camera/therapist view, maximizing visibility.

(a)   (b)   (c)

Fig. 5. Example on different ways to situate sole visualization: (a) Beneath, (b) Beside, and (c) Billboard type of visualizations.

6   Conclusions and Future Work

This work has described the initial steps in introducing the use of AR visualizations to supplement the understanding of therapists and guide them with their observations and evaluations during rehabilitation and training. With the medical knowledge and support from therapists, prototypes have been developed and presented to two hospitals in Japan. Demonstrations have shown them the possibilities of AR technology and how it can help them in their profession. The data the therapists need during rehabilitation have been investigated, the effective visualization types of these data have been explored, and the device most suitable to show these visualizations has been determined. Some technological limitations about AR have been discussed, but positive feedback from therapists have shown that it is feasible to use AR as a support tool. Concepts of AR visualizations that benefit the therapists are discussed, such as the ability to toggle on/off the visualizations and the methods in which these visualizations are presented. This gives the therapists the ability to control what types of visualizations they prefer or where they want these visualizations to be situated.

The communication network of the system was designed to be scalable, so for future work it is possible to add as many sensors as the therapists want. Furthermore, conducting an objective user study is necessary to measure the effectiveness of AR visualizations in helping the therapists give better evaluations during and after rehabilitation with real patients.

Acknowledgements. This research was supported by the Japan Science and Technology Agency as part of the Japan-Taiwan Collaborative Research Program.

References

1. Atun-Einy, O., Kafri, M.: Implementation of motor learning principles in physical therapy practice: survey of physical therapists' perceptions and reported implementation. Physiotherapy Theory Pract. **35**, 1–12 (2018)
2. Aung, Y., Al-Jumaily, A.: Augmented reality based illusion system with biofeedback. In: 2nd Middle East Conference on Biomedical Engineering, pp. 265–268, February 2014
3. Aung, Y., Al-Jumaily, A.: Augmented reality-based rehabio system for shoulder rehabilitation. Int. J. Mechatron. Automat. **4**, 52–62 (2014)
4. Azuma, R.T.: A survey of augmented reality. Presence: Teleoper. Virt. Environ. **6**, 355–385 (1997)
5. Brooks, F.P.: The computer scientist as toolsmith ii. Commun. ACM **39**, 61–68 (1996)
6. Cecco, M., et al.: Augmented reality to enhance the clinician's observation during assessment of daily living activities. In: Augmented Reality, Virtual Reality, and Computer Graphics, pp. 3–21, June 2017
7. Gaggioli, A., Keshner, E., Weiss, P., Riva, G.: Advanced technologies in rehabilitation. IOS Press - Studies in Health Technology and Informatics, January 2009
8. Jones, M., Mueller, J., Morris, J.: Advanced technologies in stroke rehabilitation and recovery. Topics Stroke Rehabilit. **17**, 323–327 (2010)
9. State, A., et al.: Case study: observing a volume rendered fetus within a pregnant patient. In: Proceedings IEEE Visualization 1994. vol. 18, pp. 364–368 (1994)
10. State, A., et al.: Technologies for augmented reality systems: realizing ultrasound-guided needle biopsies. In: Proceedings of the 23rd Annual Conference on Computer Graphics and Interactive Techniques, pp. 439–446, August 1996
11. Stocco, M., et al.: Augmented reality to enhance the clinical eye: the improvement of adl evaluation by mean of a sensors based observation. In: Virtual Reality and Augmented Reality, pp. 291–296, October 2019
12. White, S., Feiner, S.: Sitelens: situated visualization techniques for urban site visits. In: Proceedings of the 27th International Conference on Human Factors in Computing Systems, pp. 1117–1120, April 2009
13. World Health Organization: The need to scale up rehabilitation. https://www.who.int/disabilities/care/Need-to-scale-up-rehab-July2018.pdf?ua=1. Accessed 10 Jan 2020

Parametric Design for Online User Customization of 3D Printed Assistive Technology for Rheumatic Diseases

Alessia Romani$^{(\boxtimes)}$ (iD) and Marinella Levi (iD)

Department of Chemistry, Materials and Chemical Engineering "Giulio Natta",
Politecnico di Milano, Piazza Leonardo da Vinci 32, Milan, Italy
alessia.romani@polimi.it

Abstract. New spaces for the co-creation of Assistive devices have been increasing according to the current lack in specific products for everyday user needs satisfaction. Moreover, Open Innovation is gradually increasing the user role in product development thanks to new digital technologies spread. Nevertheless, the knowledge and the affordance of this bottom-up solutions is still limited amongst the potential users.

The aim of this work is to show and investigate one application of the Virtual Reality related to Assistive Technology customization, as well as the customization process for the user. Starting from a Co-design approach, variables for customization were detected on specifically co-created products for users with rheumatic diseases. By means of specific 3D modeling tools and an online platform, an Open Source online configurator was then developed for the customization of these products. In this way, customized STL files of the objects can be downloaded and created by using low cost Additive Manufacturing technologies. Consequently, affordable Assistive products for specific needs can be easily spread, increasing the users quality of life.

Keywords: Parametric design · Customization · Assistive design

1 Introduction

Assistive products focused on rehabilitation and medical treatments can be generally provided by following the guidelines and indications provided by the hospital institution or the professional figures involved in a specific therapy. Therefore, their purchase is quite easy. Because of the stigma related to their use for their pronounced medical aesthetics and a partial user need satisfaction, abandonment rates for this kind of product is considerably high [1].

In addition, another assistive products category could be individuated. More in detail, these kinds of tools are employed mostly during users everyday activities, and they specifically fulfill patient's needs, according to their disease. Even though they are less known from the users than the previous ones, their use is a valuable solution for improving the quality of life [2].

© Springer Nature Switzerland AG 2020
L. T. De Paolis and P. Bourdot (Eds.): AVR 2020, LNCS 12243, pp. 174–182, 2020.
https://doi.org/10.1007/978-3-030-58468-9_14

Thanks to the spreading of Open Innovation and Co-creation phenomena [3], some projects related to assistive tools co-design have been developed. Consequently, the user is assuming an even more centered role in defining his own needs, and digital technologies (e.g. low cost Additive Manufacturing) are the most suitable media for this aim [4, 5]. Nevertheless, the resulting assistive products are not enough affordable for the users at the moment. Their knowledge amongst the potential users is not well-established, consequently the purchase of this kind of assistive products is complex. Moreover, only certain tools can be customized considering the specific user needs, resulting in less suitable solutions. For these reasons, the use of Virtual Reality (VR) environments and the Open Source approach can be a promising way [2, 6].

In this paper, a VR environment application for customizing assistive design products for users affected by rheumatic diseases is introduced and explained. Specifically, the present work is part of "Noi Non Ci Fermiamo" (NNCF) project related to assistive products co-design considering rheumatic diseases impact on specific daily needs. Starting from the workflow and the tools used during the project, an online configurator for the users was developed by using a parametric design definition uploaded on a specific customization platform. In this way, Open Source customizable assistive products can be purchased directly from the user. Main results about this VR application and the resulting customization processes are then described, including the main implications. At the moment, this work can be considered one of the first methods for involving the user, and increasing the effectiveness and affordability of the assistive products, reducing also their abandonment rates.

2 Methods

2.1 Workflow

This work has been performed in the 3D Printing and Materials Laboratory +LAB of the Department of Chemistry, Materials and Chemical Engineering "Giulio Natta", Politecnico di Milano, Italy.

Nine users affected by rheumatic diseases and two occupational therapists participated to the project together with the design team during the brief definition, concept generation and product development phases. The steps were useful for defining the assistive products to be designed during the project, starting from unsatisfied real user needs in everyday activities. These products were obtained by using a strongly Co-design oriented approach that actively involved the selected users through the whole design process as co-designers [7]. As a consequence, the same products were used as a starting point for the current experimentation.

During the product development, variables (or parameters) that should be considered for the customization of each product were identified with the co-designers' feedback. In this way, the customization work was limited only to parameters and pieces with a tangible benefit from the customization itself, avoiding issues related to a large variety of customization parameters for the users [8].

Then, the parametric definitions for the customizable pieces were obtained by considering the chosen parameters. For each of them, the lower and the upper limit of the value variation was set considering the overall product shape, the physical prototypes tested from the co-designers, their feedback and the specific product usage scenario. Moreover, anthropometric studies [9] were also taken into account for a better value definition.

Further modifications to the definitions were performed for integrating and improving the user experience related to the online customization through the configurator (i.e. selection of the piece to visualize). Finally, clear instructions for the final user were generate by testing the products assembly, and the configurators have been spread online for the users.

2.2 Tools

During the project, different software have been used according to the different design needs. Firstly, 3D modeling software were adopted through the design phase of the assistive products: concepts and non-customizable pieces were made with Solidworks (Dassault Sistèmes, France) and Creo Parametric (Parametric Technology Corporation, US) CAD systems. For customizable pieces, Rhinoceros (Robert McNeel and Associates, US) and Grasshopper (GH) plugin for Rhinoceros (Robert McNeel and Associates, US) were the main tools adopted.

Shapediver online platform for Grasshopper definitions and Shapediver Materials Add-On (Shapediver, Austria) were adopted for managing the Online User Customization of the assistive products. The resulting 3D interfaces were then inserted in "+Ability" website together with the non-customizable parts models and assembly instructions in order to be accessible from the users for the physical realization.

Gcode files for 3D printed trials were created by using Cura (Ultimaker B. V., Holland) or Slic3r PE 1.41.3 open source slicing software (Prusa Research, Czech Republic). Subsequently, Delta 2040 (Wasp S.r.l., Italy) or Prusa i3 MK3S FDM 3D printers (Prusa Research, Czech Republic) were used for the 3D printed parts. According to the specific technical requirements, they were primarily made with PLA, PETG or TPU (90 Shore A) filaments or, alternatively, by casting silicone with mid Shore A values in 3D printed PLA molds.

3   Results and Discussion

3.1   Online User Customization Configurator

Parameters Selection. Similarly to the product development in NNCF project, the user customization configurator development started with a Co-design phase during the first usability tests. In this case, its purpose was firstly to identify the parts of each product that should be customized from the final user. Then, the most important parameters for the customization were detected for the resulting parts.

Secondly, parameters range variation had to be defined considering not only the specific co-designer need, but also taking in consideration the whole usage scenario. For this reason, tests with different 3D printed prototypes have been performed, as well as anthropometric guides have been considered. An overview on the selected customizable pieces and customization parameters for each product is visible in Table 1.

Table 1. Variables for the user customization for each product of NNCF project

Product	Customizable parts	Parameters for user
Le Micheline (Handles for Cutlery)	External Grip Internal Core	Product height, width Handle Outline Cutlery to handle
Angie's Brush (Hair Washing Brush)	Handle Mold Internal Core	Handle height, width, outline Surface grip presence
Daisy (Bottle Opener)	External Holder Inserts for plastic bottle caps	Insert types, Product height Holder width and outline
Pinzamisù (Credit Cards Pliers)	Main Body	Product dimensions Handle width Grabbing angle variation
Pinzamigiù (Credit Cards Pliers)	External Grip Internal Core	Product dimensions Handle width
L'Hook (Safety Belt Grabbing Tool)	Handle Handle Fixing components	Handle width Internal core diameter
Scarpe Diem (Telescopic Shoehorn)	Handle	Handle height, width, outline
Manola (Objects Pick-up Tool)	Handle	Handle width, outline

Product Customization Settings. Consequently, 3D models were generated by creating the GH definition starting from the above-mentioned parameters. Each of them was set by using the proper components combination. Number Slider and Value List components were the most used ones in case of numerical variation, such as dimensions.

For more complex variations (i.e. outline or shape-related features), a combination of Value List, Evaluate and Cull Pattern components was adopted. More in detail, the different outlines were previously created through a specific definition into the GH canvas. For each of them, a consequential integer number has been defined in the Value List component. Contemporarily, the outlines have been linked to the Cull Pattern component, which in turn is linked to the Evaluate one. By defining a repeating true/false pattern with If-then conditional expressions, it is possible to choose only a specific outline by changing the Value List selection. Therefore, outline customization would be possible by choosing from a list of different preset shapes made in accordance with the starting co-designers' feedback.

The If-then conditional inserted in the GH definition was set as it follows:

```
If(x=N, true, false)
```

where x is the variable, and N is the consequential integer number of a specific outlines in the Value List. A GH definition example for shape customization from three different outline alternatives is shown in Fig. 1.

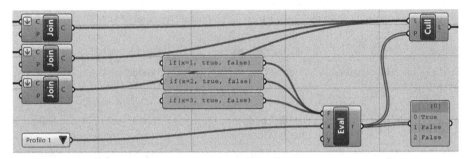

Fig. 1. GH definition example for shape customization through Value List (Profilo 1 component) from three different outline alternatives (Join components)

Configurator Settings. After the parametric 3D model definition, configurator settings should be defined for an easy customization process for the user. In this case, settings were defined both in the GH definition and in the ShapeDiver online platform website [10]. This is due to the fact that interface issues were mainly related to the online platform settings, while the parts visualization and download managing had to be previously defined in the GH definition.

For this reason, the parametric 3D model was affected not only by the product definition and its customization possibility, but also by the interaction between the user and the configurator itself. Consequently, the If-then conditional approach was also adopted for the visualization of two or more parts of from an assembly (Table 1). In fact, the user should clearly understand which part is going to be modified during the customization for a better experience. Thanks to the If-then conditional, he could define on his own the parts to be shown during the configuration process. Further modifications were made for including STL download settings, and they were set in the definition thanks to the Shapediver Material Add-On specifically provided from Shapediver.

As an example, the GH definition of Daisy bottle opener for the online user customization through the configurator is visible in Fig. 2. The 3D model construction for each customizable piece is linked with the User Customization variables. Then, the outputs are linked with the STL File exporting settings for the download and with the configurator visualization settings.

Finally, the interface settings of the online configurator were performed on the platform website. It has been possible to set the visualization of the user variables, as well as the 3D model visualization in the virtual environment. Its interface is visible in Fig. 3.

Discussion. Considering the configurator developing, added-value has been generated from the starting Co-design phase focused on parameters individuation. However, the designer should sort the co-designers' output in order to avoid Mass Confusion issues related to a high number of detected variables.

In addition, the selected parameters for the GH definition development were primarily related to the geometry of the 3D model itself. Other kinds of variables for customization such as colors, materials or finishing were considered differently, since their managing was not completely controllable during the creation of the GH definition. In fact, colors selection could be possible by adding a Value List component in the GH canvas, but

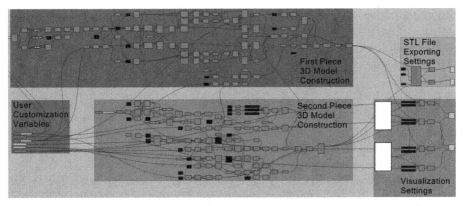

Fig. 2. GH definition organization of Daisy bottle opener 3D model for the online user customization

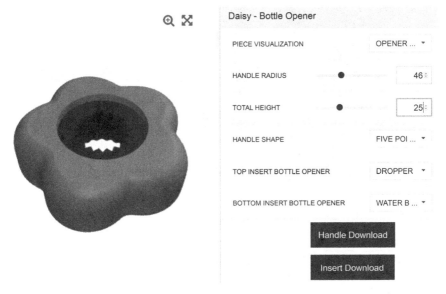

Fig. 3. Online User Configurator interface for Daisy Bottle Opener Product

it would not generate a real constraint on the GH definition. Moreover, the STL file cannot be affected by the color choice. As a consequence, this parameter was set as a free choice for the user, that would decide it after the STL file generation. Since standard performances of the final product should always be guaranteed, materials and finishing variables were not free for the user, but they were strictly defined from the instructions provided on the +Ability website.

Even though If-then conditionals allowed to better define the configuration process, they were adopted maximum twice in a single GH definition. This is mainly due to the amount of milliseconds that each real-time modify on the parameters requires for being updated, depending on the components in the GH definition. Consequently, an excessive utilization of the IF-then conditional combination could generate remarkable delays in real-time modification during the configurator use, affecting negatively its performances and also the whole user experience.

3.2 Online User Customization

The online user configurators and the related customizable assistive products were subsequently inserted in the +Ability website [11] together with the non-customizable parts (STL files) and the assembly instructions.

Some variants of Daisy Bottle Opener product can be seen in Fig. 4. They were obtained by using the online user configuration and 3D printing the resulting STL files according to the related instructions.

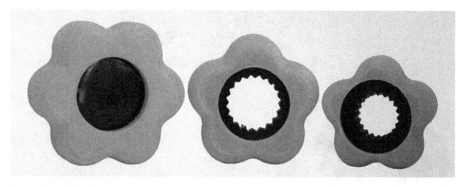

Fig. 4. Daisy Bottle Opener Product Variants obtained by the STL files customized with the online user configurator

In this way, NNCF project is accessible for the users, and the 3D models could be freely purchased. Through a Creative Common Open Source license, the files can be customized and downloaded for being 3D printed and assembled, and the only costs for the users will be linked to the parts production and buy components purchase.

The online user customization process can be summarized in Fig. 5. Firstly, the user has to identify his need and, consequently, the most suitable NNCF product available for the customization from +Ability website. Accordingly, he should take some simple measurements for the customization (i.e. palm of the hand), or refer to everyday object measures (i.e. jars or bottles). So, the user can customize his own product from the online configurator, and the 3D model will be updated in real-time thanks to the VR environment. When the user is satisfied, the customized STL files of the 3D model can be downloaded by clicking the proper button into the environment. From the website, the user should also download the non-customizable STL files of the selected product and the corresponding assembly instructions.

By this point, STL files can be used for 3D printing the product independently or by means of a 3D printing service. Finally, the final product can be easily assembled directly by the user according to the instructions.

Fig. 5. Customization workflow of the user configurator system (from user need to its satisfaction): references measuring, user online customization of the product, download of the STL files and instructions, STL 3D printing, assembly with the required buy parts from the instructions

Discussion. Through the development of the online configurator explained before, specific user needs can be promptly satisfied. In fact, users can purchase a customized product in an easier way than using traditional channels. Moreover, the purchase can be done "on demand", which means only when the product is needed. So, this VR application can give a solution to the lack of customized and easily accessible assistive products.

The Open Source distribution of the customizable products through the online user configurator brings the advantages and disadvantages of the Open Innovation and Co-creation practices. Consequently, its use is encouraged and spread by the Creative Commons License, even if some expedients should be considered for safeguarding the authorship of the design products and configurator work.

4 Conclusions and Perspectives

To sum up, an online VR configurator starting from user needs has been developed for spreading Open Source customizable assistive products to be produced via low cost additive manufacturing technologies. Moreover, its developing process and the user customization procedure have been furtherly explained and discussed.

Finally, some other aspects need a deeper investigation. This VR based configurator could be adopted also for customizing other assistive products focused on different kinds of diseases, and further work could be done for various everyday needs. Other kinds of variables for customization could also be implemented, especially considering the tactile an senso-aesthetic properties of the products. In addition, an exhaustive analysis from an economical point of view could be performed. To close, VR allowed the affordability of specific customized assistive products from the users, creating a virtuous connection between people and technology for an increased quality of life.

Acknowledgments. This work is part of NNCF (Noi Non Ci Fermiamo) project developed at +LAB 3D printing Lab (Politecnico di Milano) in collaboration with Roche S.p.A. The authors would like to thank the Italian rheumatic diseases patients associations ANMAR, APMARR and ALOMAR, the users, the occupational therapists and the design team involved in the project. They also gratefully acknowledge the support of Shapediver online service during the User Configurator development.

References

1. Sugawara, A.T., Ramos, V.D., Alfieri, F.M., Battistella, L.R.: Abandonment of assistive products: assessing abandonment levels and factors that impact on it. Disabil. Rehabil.: Assist. Technol. **13**, 716–723 (2018)
2. Buehler, E., et al.: Sharing is caring: assistive technology designs on thingiverse. In: CHI 2015: Proceedings of the 33rd Annual ACM Conference on Human Factors in Computing Systems, Seoul, pp. 525–534 (2015)
3. Rayna, T., Striukova, L.: Open innovation 2.0: is co-creation the ultimate challenge? Int. J. Technol. Manag. **69**, 38–53 (2015)
4. Ostuzzi, F., Rognoli, V., Saldien, J., Levi, M.: +TUO project: low cost 3D printers as helpful tool for small communities with rheumatic diseases. Rapid Prototyp. J. **21**, 491–505 (2015)
5. Chen, X., Kim, J., Mankoff, J., Grossman, T., Coros, S., Hudson, S.E.: Reprise: a design tool for specifying, generating, and customizing 3D printable adaptations on everyday objects. In: UIST 2016: Proceedings of the 29th Annual Symposium on User Interface Software and Technology, Tokyo, pp. 118–124 (2018)
6. Rayna, T., Striukova, L., Darlington, J.: Co-creation and user innovation: the role of online 3D printing platforms. J. Eng. Technol. Manag. - JET-M **37**, 90–102 (2015)
7. Romani, A.: Over 5/95: Stampa 3D e Modellazione Parametrica per la Personalizzazione di Prodotti d'Uso Quotidiano. Master Degree Thesis in Design & Engineering. Politecnico di Milano (2018)
8. Piller, F., Schubert, P., Koch, M., Moeslein, K.: Overcoming mass confusion: collaborative customer co-design in online communities. J. Comput.-Mediat. Commun. **10**(4) (2005). https://doi.org/10.1111/j.1083-6101.2005.tb00271.x
9. Dreyfuss, H., Powell, A.: Designing for People. Allworth, New York (2003)
10. Shapediver. https://www.shapediver.com/. Accessed 24 Feb 2020
11. +Ability. http://piuability.it/. Accessed 24 Feb 2020

Applications in Education

Augmented Reality to Increase Interaction and Participation: A Case Study of Undergraduate Students in Mathematics Class

Roberto Capone[1](✉) and Mario Lepore[2](✉)

[1] Dip. Matematica, University of Salerno, Fisciano, SA, Italy
`rcapone@unisa.it`
[2] Consorzio di Ricerca Sistemi ad Agenti CORISA, University of Salerno, Fisciano, SA, Italy
`marlep@corisa.it, marlepore@unisa.it`

Abstract. This work focuses on the Augmented Reality trying to improve students' interaction and participation in the educational dialogue, preventing the drop out, tested with university mathematics courses. Students often have difficulties on some topics related to the transition between different representations, within the same representations and language, for example when dealing with the study of two-variable functions, but also about the exact differential forms and the identification of the domain to integrate a function of several variables. These difficulties lead to a decrease in interaction and participation, and sometimes to dropping out of the course. Augmented Reality has been used to overcome some of these difficulties, also with the use of some technological tools (3D glasses, computers, tablets) and innovative methodologies. In order to evaluate the impact of this approach on students' interaction and participation, an experimentation with an e-learning platform based on Augmented Reality was carried out evaluating some affective and interaction parameters, computed through a Fuzzy Cognitive Map.

Keywords: Augmented Reality · Mathematics Education · Fuzzy Cognitive Map

1 Introduction

One of the difficulties in learning mathematics arises due to the impossibility of conceptualization based on meanings referring to a concrete reality. On the one hand, in fact, every mathematical concept uses representations, because there are no "objects" to exhibit, that is, conceptualization needs to go through representative registers; on the other hand, the management of representations is difficult because of the lack of concrete objects to relate the representations themselves, both in terms of their production and in terms of transformations. These difficulties are found not only in students beginning in mathematics, as recent research in Mathematics Education shows. [12, 18, 35] but some difficulties continue to be encountered in secondary school students and are also found

© Springer Nature Switzerland AG 2020
L. T. De Paolis and P. Bourdot (Eds.): AVR 2020, LNCS 12243, pp. 185–204, 2020.
https://doi.org/10.1007/978-3-030-58468-9_15

in students attending the first year of science degree courses. In fact, some students who enroll in a scientific faculty not only do not have strong mathematical skills but do not always have a "good relationship" with the subject; some have difficulties in approaching the study both to the intrinsic difficulties of mathematics as epistemological obstacles [7], misconceptions strengthened by inadequate teaching practices in the first cycle [35] and in upper secondary school (Functions, [40]; Infinity, [2]; Limits [3] and to difficulties in mathematics [42]. Moreover, in addition to difficulties related to epistemological and didactic obstacles in mathematics, many researches have shown difficulties related to different uses of language such as, for example, the relationship between verbal and formal language [19]. Other difficulties are due to linguistic specificities of the mathematical text [6, 12], the use of different systems of semiotic representation [18] and gestures, the formulation of problem texts and the relationship between the contexts and the questions proposed [42].

Referring to the university courses of calculus, it is not rare that many students, due to these difficulties, participate a little at a time less and less in the educational dialogue, interact little by little with their colleagues and, in some cases, drop out of the course, even shortly after the beginning. This phenomenon, called drop-out, is increasingly common among students who are not involved and motivated enough by the learning experience. For these reasons, a university course should not be reduced to the simple delivery of learning content, but should support students throughout their learning experience, leading them to successfully achieve the objectives of the course. So, a blended online teaching using an e-learning platform and in-class format can encourage students to experiment by themselves with an instrumental genesis linked to a proposed activity, using a specific tool (artifact) and the e-learning platform to carry out a given task. The authors have already experimented, in cohorts prior to the current one, didactic paths with new methodologies, such as blended teaching supported by flipped learning [5] or innovative methodologies such as Just in Time Teaching and Peer-Led Team Learning [8]. In both cases, an e-learning platform was used to support the teaching. Although the above researches show an improvement of mathematical competences in the students and an increased motivation to study the discipline, the learning platform did not always show to be adaptive, in the sense that it did not provide each student with the contents, feedback, suggestions and experience adapted to his or her learning status. [5, 9]. In this work, some benefits of using an e-learning platform that also supports Augmented Reality and the use of some technological tools (3D glasses, computers, tablets) and innovative methodologies are described. This is an adaptive e-learning system, realized in part within the research project "Moliere", based on the use of Fuzzy Cognitive Maps for the identification of the current status of the student. The status represents the student's current situation, mainly in both participation and interaction. The status is identified by analyzing the student's behavior and interactions with the system. The aim of the system is to keep a high level of participation and interaction for all students. This work focuses mainly on helping university students in Calculus, trying to overcome the obstacles related to the passage between different representations, within the same representations and language. We have focused mainly on difficulties related to the study of the functions of several variables but also related to the study of the exact differential forms and the correct identification of the domain to integrate a function of several variables. We found in Augmented Reality (AR) a useful tool to overcome some of these difficulties, observing also how the use of some technological tools (3D glasses, computer, tablet) and innovative methodologies seems to bring the student nearer to mathematics developing good motivational and affective attitude. The system has been evaluated with an experiment involving university students applying a comparative evaluation technique to measure the improvement of the students' level of participation and interaction using an e-learning platform based on augmented reality.

In the following, we will describe, in Sect. 2, the background knowledge, making reference to the importance of the study of functions in two variables for students in the STEM area, interaction and participation as two important components of the teaching-learning process, the use of cognitive fuzzy maps [26] as a model of systemic structure to analyze the critical success factors of a learning management system [33] taking into account the related works that our research refers to; in Sect. 3, the use of AR for the study of the functions in two variables analyzing the implementation of the application and giving the technological details of the framework where it is inserted; in Sect. 4, an educational experiment with proposed context, sample and tests; finally, in Sect. 5, the conclusions of the experimentation.

2 Related Works

In this section, the background of this research is described. The section is divided into four subsections: in Subsect. 2.1, the two educational variables carried out in this work are described, i.e. students' participation and interaction during the educational activities, both in presence and in online modes; in Subsect. 2.2, the fuzzy cognitive map is analyzed as a tool to describe and model complex systems/environments in a symbolic way highlighting events, processes and states; in Subsect. 2.3, refers to the importance of using different representations to achieve a mathematical concept; in Subsect. 2.4, describes some studies that have been pioneering this research and that have been used to reconstruct a learning environment based on Augmented Reality.

One of the difficulties in learning mathematics arises due to the impossibility of conceptualization based on meanings referring to a concrete reality. On the one hand, in fact, every mathematical.

2.1 Participation and Interaction in Learning

Here interaction and participation in the literature framework and the meaning they take on in this research are described.

Participation refers to the action of taking part in activities and projects, the act of sharing in the activities of a group. The process of participation fosters mutual learning. Collaboration is a useful tool used within participatory culture as a desired educational outcome [16]. Participation is also linked to the individual's emotional issues.

Interaction refers to the cognitive and perceptive relationship between students and learning materials that produce meaning for students, such as reading paper or digital texts, observing or listening to the media, or searching for information [25]. Participation and interaction are fundamental to engage students both in-presence and in online courses. Strategic management of these core components consists of the analysis, decisions, and course of action that an organization or individual that operates programs or classes needs to create and sustain to ensure the quality of learning.

According to some studies [23, 37], Interaction and Participation are related to improving student performance.

According to studies from Indiana University [22], it is possible to highlight how to counteract a low level of interaction. The following are some of the factors that, according to these studies, affect students' interaction and participation in educational dialogue. The presence of the teacher in discussions can facilitate learning and clarify any questions of learners (Instructor participation in class discussion). Attention to discussion, therefore, especially in the conceptualizing, is very important in learning processes. For example, in mathematics, it is justified every time the constitution of a mathematician is involved, from the outside (real world mathematization) or from the inside of Mathematics (theory of functions).

The approach to discussion is understood as an attempt to provide a set of tools for analysis and planning by the experienced teacher without reducing the responsibility of the pupils. This Vygotskijan process refers to interactions between subjects (teachers and pupils) who play different roles that must be preserved and valued both in the teaching-learning activity [9]. Also, Sarder [34] supports the importance of Establish an online presence, i.e. the importance of the teacher's presence to stimulate and facilitate learning by intervening when the learner needs it.

An important aspect is to encourage, within a teaching community (also virtual) peer learning by creating working groups or encouraging the free aggregation of students in working groups through Team-based learning methods [28]. The importance of peer education, as a driving force and propulsion to encourage students' participation in educational dialogue, can be found in Piaget's theory [31], where it is argued that peer interaction in learning is useful in the processes of intellectual construction and that this is enhanced by the sharing of language, the immediate communication and the need for friendship. Vygotsky [41] also emphasizes that peer communication allows for the internalization of cognitive processes implicit in interactions and provides new patterns that influence individual thinking, with emphasis on the proximal development zone.

Research carried out by M. Samir Abou El-Seoud [21] has shown that the positive actions on interaction and participation are:

- Add a variety of tasks and ways of thinking, i.e. giving the student the opportunity to find different solutions to a given problem can be helpful in terms of motivation.
- Use examples to demonstrate a concept: Using practical examples it is easier for learners to learn concepts.
- Clarity of explanation: Clarify concepts that are unclear and provide clarification.
- Providing support: support the learner within the platform.

Finally, from the studies carried out by MD B. Sarder [34] highlighted the actions that have the greatest impact on participation. In addition to the already mentioned importance of the teacher's presence that can facilitate learning by intervening when the learner needs (Establish an online presence) it is important to take into account the different learning styles of the students and therefore encourage a multitude of tools (a video, a pdf, a ppt) from which the student can choose (Personalized learning). Also, for Sarder it is very important that students feel part of a community and therefore the teacher should promote collaboration between learners (Establish a sense of community). Research has suggested that making efforts to establish a sense of community within an online course is an effective way to engage students. "Community, in the online sense, can be defined as an environment which is enabled through the interaction and collaboration of its members using various technology and mixed media methods." Interaction is the essential building block of any community. If members of a community are not able to interact in some form or fashion, then it does not exist [34].

The teacher must also be aware of students' fear and anxiety because this anxiety can impact negatively on their participation and motivation (Reassure students).

In this work, parameters related to Interaction and Participation, and their causal relationships, have been identified and analyzed through a Fuzzy Cognitive Map in order to describe the state of the student during the course.

2.2 Fuzzy Cognitive Map

A Fuzzy Cognitive Map (FCM), as introduced by Kosko [26], is a symbolic representation based on a fuzzy graph useful for representing causal relationships. It can be used to describe complex systems/environments in a symbolic way, highlighting events, processes and states. An FCM consists of an interconnection of nodes through weighted edges: a node of the graph is called concept and an edge is called weight. The edge allows for implementing a causal relationship between two concepts, and the weight represents the strength of the influence of the relationship, described with a fuzzy linguistic term (e.g., low, high, very high, etc.). Basically, a Fuzzy Cognitive Map is developed by integrating existing experience and knowledge related to a system. This can be achieved by using a group of experts to describe the structure and behavior of the system under different conditions. With FCM it is usually easy to find which factor needs to be changed and, being dynamic modeling tools, the resolution of the system representation can be increased by applying further mapping.

Participation refers to the action of taking part in activities and projects, the act of sharing in the activities of a group. The process of participation fosters mutual learning. Collaboration is a useful tool used within participatory culture as a desired educational outcome [14]. Participation is also linked to the individual's emotional issues.

An FCM can be formalized through a 4-tuple (N, W, A, f), where:

1. $N = \{N_1, N_2, ..., N_n\}$ is the set of n concepts which are represented by the nodes of the graph;
2. W: $(N_i, N_j) \rightarrow w_{i,j}$ is a function (N × N → [−1, 1]) which associates the weight $w_{i,j}$ to the edge between the pair of concepts (N_i, N_j);
3. A: $N_i \rightarrow A_i$ is the activation function which associates to each concept N_i a sequence of activation values, one for each time instant t: $\forall t$, $A_i(t) \in [0,1]$ is the activation value of the concept N_i at time t.
4. $A(0) \in [0,1]$ n is the initial activation vector containing the initial values of all the concepts; $A(t) \in [0,1]$ n is the state vector at a certain time instant t.

5. f: R → [0,1] is a transformation function with a recursive relation t ≥ 0 between A(t + 1) and A(t):

$$\forall i \in \{1, \ldots, n\}, A(t+1) = f\left(\sum_{\substack{i=1 \\ j \neq i}}^{n} w_{ji} A_j(t)\right) \tag{1}$$

Different types of functions can be used as f (x), such as the sigmoid function, the bivalent function or the linear function. FCM can be used to make a what-if inference, starting from a given initial activation vector A(0), to understand what will happen next to the modeled system/environment.

In this work, we use an FCM to understand what happens to some variable representing the learner's status (e.g., her interaction and participation) considering for the activation vector, a sequence of known values regarding her activities in the e-learning platform (e.g., quiz scores, time spent on contents, etc.).

2.3   An Approach to Representation of 3D Function in Two Variables

Here In this subsection, the importance of the study of the two-variable functions for students in the STEM area is described, also considering the international literature on the theme.

The study of two variable functions is very important for real world applications. It is related to the acquisition and enhancement of visual-spatial skills which is of fundamental importance to recognize and understand objects in the physical world, especially for students of mathematics, physics, engineering, architecture. As Chen and Chi said [11], from an engineering point of view, the training needed to build the spatial ability of students will help them to easily transfer three-dimensional objects into their two-dimensional projections. For engineering students this ability has many applications, such as designing and sometimes constructing spatial models, interpreting diagrams, describing and accurately interpreting the geometric properties of mechanical objects. The terms visual and spatial skills include five components: spatial perception, spatial visualization, mental rotation, spatial relations and spatial orientation [24]. Regarding the acquisition of these skills, the improvement of the levels of participation and interaction can affect the overcoming of certain difficulties.

In fact, studies carried out in Mathematics Education [40] show that students have difficulty in choosing and using appropriate representations in calculus. Robert and Boschet [32] have remarked that the most successful students have always been those who have been able to use a variety of approaches in a flexible way: symbolic, numerical, visual. Dreyfus and Eisenberg [17] reported students' unwillingness to use visual concepts in mathematical analysis. They provide examples where visual representations would solve some problems in an almost trivial way, but students refrain from using them because the preference developed over the years is for a numerical, symbolic approach. Nevertheless, research shows that visual images can provide crucial insights. However, it can sometimes be difficult for students to connect global representation to a sequential deductive form of thought.

Already in 1993, Tall provides some remedies for teaching-learning calculus, including using active learning, getting to the formalization of concepts through an informal way, using computer graphics, computer programming, symbol manipulators [41]: the potentialities of Augmented Reality were not yet thought out.

2.4 Augmented Reality in Mathematics Education

In this subsection, the literature review on augmented reality is described.

The topic of AR, for its interdisciplinarity, involves researchers from different areas: Computer scientists, pedagogists, experts in mathematics teaching, sociologists and cognitivist psychologists. Recently there has been an attempt to give a systematic representation of the existing literature [29], from which it can be inferred a growing interest in research related to the various applications of AR ranging from Continuous professional development to Innovative training approach, from Teacher training to student training and extended to many fields.

Many positive aspects of AR in teaching have been highlighted by experts in cognitive and socio-cultural theories. In fact, the focus on action, found in many studies in recent years, especially in the areas of neuroscience, enactivity and simplexity, has highlighted the recursive relationship between action and knowledge, and between action and perception [4, 31] and the role of technologies in these processes [36]. Since in the educational field the relationship between experience and conceptualization is at the basis of learning processes, it becomes central to understand how the presence of digital artifacts impacts on the process of educational mediation, modifying both the artifacts and the awareness that users have of them.

The digital technology has changed the way we operate and conceptualize human activity. On the one hand, the distance between the subject's work on the artifact and the artifact's intervention on the world increases. The operator acts on the basis of data that she obtains from screens and indicators. The mediation between the screen and the manipulation on the world is carried out by the artifact that becomes a boundary object between subject and world [27, 38]. At the same time, it creates real metaphors with which it describes processes, which it can often neither experience nor directly control, and conceptualizes paths [30].

Studies related to AR are part of Human Computer Interaction (HCI) that studies the design and use of computer technology, focused on the interfaces between people (users) and computers. Researchers in the field of HCI observe the ways in which humans interact with computers and design technologies that let humans interact with computers in novel ways. As a field of research, human-computer interaction is situated at the intersection of computer science, behavioral sciences, design, media studies, and several other fields of study.

In the area of Mathematics Education, recently studies [1] have highlighted how visual-kinesthetic activities can help students to experience the multiple levels of sophistication and develop the multiple meanings of covariational reasoning [39]. Quintero and his working team present an augmented reality application in order to promote spatial visualization in Calculus courses for engineering students; in their experience, technology has come to transform the perception of what is possible in the teaching of mathematics, and consequently, the traditional approach of learning mathematics cannot remain unchanged. Coimbra and her team also highlight augmented reality since it can encourage motivation, comprehension and a higher involvement with the contents to be learned. Thus, it may increase the use of information and the access to knowledge, improving digital and info-inclusion.

The intention to include the AR could help to motivate students to learn mathematics, and this could also improve students' interest in this science. However, the main aim we seek in our projects is to focus on the educational benefits of providing useful knowledge with a new sense of accessibility for a learning experience. This perspective suggests a new role for technological means in the learning process. Several authors have produced appropriate frameworks to study the educational benefits of teaching involving the use of technological resources. Our perspective shares the concept of digital technology acting as a mediator between the user and mathematical knowledge. The purpose of the interaction between user and technology should favor a cooperation that promotes a thinking process affecting learning. Technology should act as a kind of cognitive partner for the learner, enhancing mathematical understanding. Our perspective on digital technology takes into account the knowledge that the mathematics education now organizes in cognitive and socio-cultural theories.

3   E-Learning System Prototype

The proposed approach to improve the level of participation and interaction of a student through augmented reality was implemented in a prototype of e-learning system, currently under development at CORISA, in the context of the "MOLIERE" research project. One of the objectives of this project is the adoption of a motivational approach to learning by creating an engaging experience for the student, in order to reduce student dropout during the course [14]. The conceptual architecture, as depicted in Fig. 1, was designed to create an adaptive e-learning environment to offer a personalized experience to students. The prototype platform is based on a series of open source solutions. The Web infrastructure is developed using the Model-View-Controller (MVC) model implemented using Play 2.7 (www.playframework.com), Akka (https://akka.io) and Java. The analysis process for the generation of the student's situation through FCM was implemented using the JFCM library (https://jfcm.megadix.it), based on Java. The collection of data, their storage and their treatment are carried out through traditional techniques based on semantics, as described in previous works [10, 13].

The architecture was organized tiered subsystems; from top to bottom we have: i) Presentation module; ii) Recommendation module; iii) Learning Management System iv) Status identification; v) Behavioral tracker; vi) Data management system; vii) Data fusion and storage. The Presentation module is the subsystem that deals with the display of information to system users according to the models and principles of Situation Awareness and Goal-Directed Task Analysis [20]. The Recommendation module aims at producing and forwarding adaptive and personalized feedback, both in batch and in real-time, useful for maintaining adequate levels of interaction and participation in

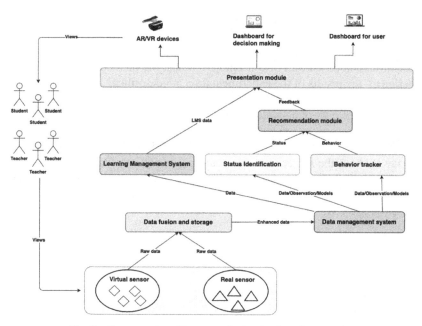

Fig. 1. Conceptual architecture of adaptive learning system.

order to limit the phenomenon of learner drop-out of the course. The generation of feedback in batches, at a predetermined frequency, for example weekly, involves the use of data from the Status Identification and Behavior tracker modules. Feedback can be generated automatically or through teacher supervision. For the generation of real-time feedback, the data is provided in a continuous flow to the Recommendation module for an analysis on the fly; however, these data are also stored in the system for subsequent long-term analyzes [14, 15]. The Status identification contains the Fuzzy Cognitive Map (FCM) used to identify the current status in terms of participation and interaction. The Behavior Tracker subsystem acquires data, observations and models that are examined and processed in order to produce useful knowledge to derive user behavior on the platform. In particular, it is useful for extracting some behavioral models to identify students at risk of dropping out. The Learning Management System (LMS) includes the necessary modules for the classic services of an e-learning system such as Course Management, User Management, Blog, Forum, Chat etc. The Data fusion and storage level deals with acquiring the raw data provided by the sensors, analyzing and integrating them. Such processed data are transferred, after being enriched to the Data management system. Such subsystem includes relational databases and triple stores capable of storing data and models used by (LMS), Status identification and Behavior Tracker. Real and virtual sensors are necessary to record the student's interactions with the system and to monitor her facial expressions during the use of the system, useful for identifying her status.

4   AR Experience Evaluation

The experimentation is described in this section. Specifically, an approach to learner's status identification based on Fuzzy Cognitive Maps, the methodology for evaluating the experiment, the results of the experimentation are described. The aim of the experimentation is to verify whether the use of an augmented reality application, developed within the prototype e-learning platform considered, is useful for increasing the level of participation and interaction of students in university mathematics courses, contrasting the phenomenon of dropout. A student with a high level of these indices is more motivated in the study of the subject and this could positively influence any improvements in skills. In this way, we could understand if the use of augmented reality improves the student's state, measured above all on the basis of participation and interaction levels, assessed through FCM.

4.1   An Approach to Learner's Status Identification Based on Fuzzy Cognitive Maps

In this This section describes the learner's status identification technique, based on a Fuzzy Cognitive Map (FCM), that was defined and implemented in the learning system. The objective of the FCM is to consider all the effects that the variables identified in the model have on the interaction and participation of the learner, which are the two high-level concepts representing the current status of the learner. Specifically, the proposed map is represented in Fig. 2. The FCM has been defined by a team of five experts of the Research Project "MOLIERE". Each expert proposed his FCM to identify the causal relationships and the weights existing between the concepts starting from a critical analysis of the literature about participation and interaction. The weights are represented by seven linguistic terms: no impact = 0.00, very low = 0.165, low = 0.335, medium = 0.50, almost high = 0.665, high = 0.835, very high = 1.00. Then, we aggregate the different maps proposed by the experts to obtain one FCM. When some differences arise between the relationships and weights proposed by the experts, we asked them to discuss these differences and try to find an agreement, until they achieve a sufficient degree of consensus.

The inputs of the FCM are the values of the variables described below. The parameters related to interaction are:

- Time spent on content and interactive content interaction: time spent on teaching material and level of interaction with interactive elements.
- Time spent on quiz and scores: time spent and score on the quizzes taken.

The parameters related to participation are:

- Happiness and Peacefulness: parameters related to personal emotions, intrinsic to the learner.
- Interest, Curiosity and Enthusiasm: conscious emotions related to the cognitive mental state of the learner.

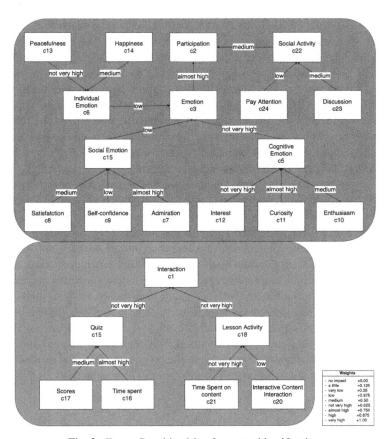

Fig. 2. Fuzzy Cognitive Map for status identification.

- Satisfaction, Self-confidence and Admiration: parameters related to self-awareness and self-evaluation towards others and by others.
- Discussion and pay attention: parameters related to the level of discussion and attention shown by students during the social interaction phases.

Figure 2 shows the interaction and participation map, with links to the concepts obtained from the parameters considered.

Each of the input parameters listed above is transformed into an activation value of the corresponding concept in the FCM. When a value of these variables' changes (due to the actions performed by the student), the other concepts of the FCM are influenced by the causal relationships between them. This will entail a change in the student's current state in terms of new participation and interaction values calculated by applying the function in Eq. 1. In particular, we use the linear function as a transformation function f:

$$A(t+1) = \alpha \sum_{\substack{i=1 \\ j \neq i}}^{n} w_{ji} A_j \qquad (2)$$

The weights on the edges of the FCM have 9 values, in the range [0.0, 1.0], each one with an associated linguistic term, as depicted in Fig. 2. The concepts described below are of higher level; they are calculated starting from the variation of the input concepts. The Lesson Activity concept is influenced by the concepts Time Spent on Content and Interactive Content Interaction, measured within the system through the use of counters. While the concept Quiz Activity is influenced by the concepts Time Spent on Quiz and Scores, these also measured internally by the system. The root of this sub-map is the most important concept, namely Interaction which takes into account the level of interaction of the student with the system. Emotions play a crucial role in the learning process. Positive emotions can increase students' interest in learning, increase classroom involvement and motivate students. On the other hand, negative emotions have an unfavorable influence on students and can distract their learning. To represent this concept we use Emotions, composed of the three types of emotions: Individual, Cognitive and Social. Happiness and Peacefulness influence the concept of individual emotion. Satisfaction, Self-Confidence and Admiration influence the Cognitive Emotion concept. Social Emotion is influenced by Satisfaction, Self-Confidence and Admiration. Emotions are potential indicators of the quality of the student's learning process. They can be detected through Sentiment Analysis which involves the study of physiological signals through facial recognition systems. The concept of Social Activity is linked to community activities and represents the interaction activities between learners. This concept is composed of: discussion and pay attention. This concept allows you to understand how motivated and interested the learner is in the proposed topic. The root concept of this sub-map is Participation, influenced by emotions and social activity.

4.2 Method

To carry out the experiment, a scenario is identified according to the requirements of the MOLIERE project. This scenario is simulated with the adaptive learning system. The participants in the simulation are students from two math classes in engineering and environmental science. The scenario foresees the use of the didactic material (pdf, video) for the two variable functions related to the calculus II course and the possibility to carry out the related assignments. The goal shared by the students is to support and pass the final quiz on this topic in order to access the next one. The participants in the experimentation use the system that simulates the above-mentioned scenario, allowing the system to acquire the necessary parameters to evaluate through FCM the student's status, expressed in terms of participation and interaction, i.e.:

– time spent studying the proposed content;
– time spent on assignments and scores obtained;
– level of interaction with the interactive elements presented on the interface;
– emotions (individual, cognitive and social, detected through Sentiment Analysis);
– social activities (level of discussion and attention).

The students were divided into two equal groups, both numerically and in terms of their basic skills. The first group (control group) interacted with the platform without using augmented reality; the second group (experimental group) interacted on the platform using augmented reality.

This scenario is proposed to test the impact of augmented reality on the student's state.

In Fig. 3, a screenshot of the dashboard used by the students in the first group (without augmented reality) is shown.

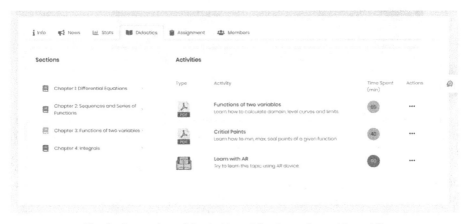

Fig. 3. Screenshot of the dashboard for the student without AR.

In particular, the first group has only textual and audiovisual material of the lessons available; the assignments must be made in the forms of the web pages of the platform. On the other hand, the second group can access an augmented reality content section to observe the graphic objects by studying them from different perspectives, interacting with the screen, for example by zooming, rotating and using the interactive elements on the interface. It is also possible for them to perform augmented reality assignments. In Fig. 4, a screenshot of augmented reality used by the second group is shown.

In both ways, students receive real-time feedback on their progress. The feedback slideshow changes according to the device on which it is displayed, in case augmented reality is used the feedback is presented in the form of animation. As an example, at the end of the quiz in the two-variable functions chapter, feedback is generated suggesting the next action the student should perform, based on the score obtained:

- score 0/5, the student is guided through the repetition of the chapter using simpler content, with the teacher's support;
- score 1/5 and 2/5, the student is encouraged to do more using additional material and using the forums for any doubts;
- score 3/5 and 4/5, the student receives positive feedback and is encouraged to compare with other colleagues;
- score 5/5, the student, having achieved excellent results, receives positive feedback to reinforce them.

Fig. 4. Screenshot of the AR app for the student.

In Fig. 5a, the feedback sent to the students in case of score on the final 0/5 test presented on the platform is shown; in Fig. 5b the same feedback is shown but rendered on the augmented reality application.

Emotions and social activities are established through sentimental analysis on the video streaming of the webcams filming the students, carried out by the specific module of the platform. The data provided by the system for the different parameters of interest, are analyzed through FCM execution to create the student's state; by comparing the states of the participants it will be possible to understand if the use of augmented reality is useful to increase their degree of interaction and participation.

The users who participated in the evaluation were chosen arbitrarily; the sample was taken inside the University of Salerno, in the courses of Engineering and Environmental Sciences with the participants all external to the MOLIERE project. Cochran's formula was used to calculate the sample size:

$$n_0 = \frac{Z^2 pq}{e^2} \tag{3}$$

Where:

- e is the desired level of precision (i.e. the margin of error);
- p is the (estimated) proportion of the population which has the attribute in question;
- q is $1 - p$;
- the z-value is found in a Z table. It is s the abscissa of the normal curve that cuts off an area α at the tails ($1 - \alpha$ equals the desired confidence level, e.g., 95%);
- n_0 is the sample size.

In our experimentation the chosen parameters were: {$Z = 1.96$; $p = 0.85$; $e = 0.15$}. From the application of the formula with these parameters, a sample size of 22 participants emerged, which were equally divided into a group of 11 students who have used the platform without augmented reality and a group 11 students who have used the augmented reality app.

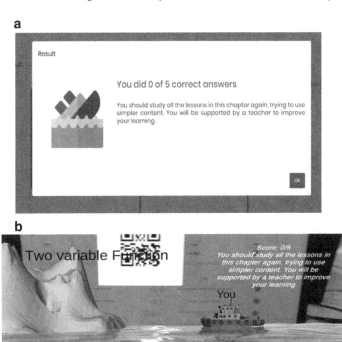

Fig. 5. a. Feedback sent by the system in the event that the final test obtains a 0/5 score on the platform. b. Feedback sent by the system in the event that the final test obtains a 0/5 score in AR app.

To measure the correlation between the statistical variables analyzed, Pearson's correlation index was used, which, in accordance with Cauchy Schwarz's inequality, has a value between $[-1; +1]$; where $+1$ corresponds to the perfect positive linear correlation, 0 corresponds to an absence of linear correlation and -1 corresponds to the perfect negative linear correlation.

4.3   Results and Discussion

In this subsection, the quantitative results of the experimentation conducted are shown. To verify if the obtained results are statistically significant, we performed an ANOVA test, comparing two groups: No AR Group (students who have used the platform without augmented reality) and AR Group (students who have used the augmented reality app). We obtained the following results for the F-test statistics, considering a significance level $\alpha = 0.05$:

- Considering the level of interaction, F-critic $= 8.09$ e p-value $= 7.43$;
- Considering the level of participation, F-critic $= 9.7$ e p-value $= 7.95$.

Consequently, the tests demonstrate that the results are statistically significant. The results obtained are schematized through Figs. 6a and 6b.

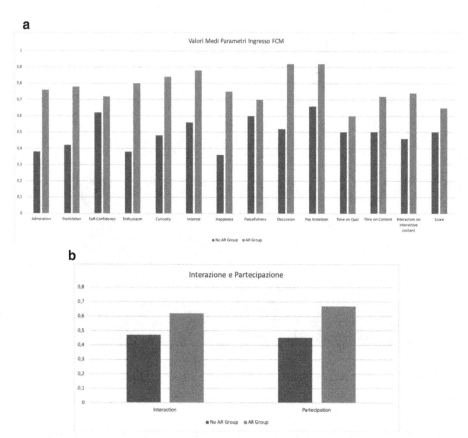

Fig. 6. a. Results of the evaluation: average values of FCM input parameters for the two groups. b. Results of the evaluation: average values of interaction and participation for the two groups. (Color figure online)

Figure 6a shows the average input values for the FCM concepts, listed in Sect. 2.3; while, the average levels of interaction and participation calculated through the execution of the FCM are shown in Fig. 6b. In the two charts, the comparison between the two groups of students into which the sample was divided is reported: part of the "No AR Group" (represented in blue), students who have not used the augmented reality application, while in the "AR Group" (shown in orange) there are students who have used the augmented reality application.

Analyzing the results obtained and reported in Fig. 6a and Fig. 6b, it can be observed that, on all the input parameters considered, there is an increase for students who have used augmented reality. Furthermore, if the two groups are compared, there is an increase for those who have used the augmented reality application of 22% for the level of participation and 15% for the level of interaction. Among the factors that have contributed most to the increase in the values of interaction and participation, there are:

- the possibility of interacting with three-dimensional didactic materials made available;
- receiving adaptive feedback rendered as animations.

In this regard, in Fig. 7, an evidently enthusiastic student is shown, intent on displaying in AR the feedback obtained at the end of the last summary quiz on two-variable functions.

Fig. 7. Facial expression of a student, intent on visualizing the adaptive feedback received in augmented reality at the end of the quiz.

From the experimentation conducted it seems that augmented reality offered the opportunity for students to be able to tackle the course topics, in a more immersive and interactive way, thus improving their status, as assessed through the interaction parameters and participation. Augmented reality seems to be the right compromise between formal approach, informal approach and epistemic curiosity. In fact, by analyzing the average values of some input parameters (pay attention, curiosity, interest, and time on quiz), Fig. 6a, the student seems to be more concentrated in the study. During the experimental phase, the teacher stood aside as an observer. This made it possible to intervene on a methodological level by favoring the negotiation of meanings, their sharing and stabilization. In fact, the reformulation of already proposed concepts and clearer and more complete information emerged in order to reorganize the discussion in the classroom.

From the more specific point of view of the acquisition of skills, it seems that the score obtained by the students on the tests is directly related to the level of interaction, i.e. the higher the level of interaction and the higher the score obtained on the tests. This parameter was measured through the Pearson correlation index whose value is $\rho = 0.8$. On the other hand, there seems to be no correlation between the level of student participation and the assessment obtained on the tests (Pearson correlation index $\rho = -0.05$).

Ultimately, the use of augmented reality seems to have affected the improvement of participation and interaction parameters as well as the achievement of some specific learning objectives specific to the discipline. Furthermore, the use of the eLearning platform, integrated with augmented reality, seems to have brought some more riotous students closer to the study of mathematics, as can be seen from the parameters Curiosity, Admiration and Happiness, shown in Fig. 6a.

5   Conclusion

In this paper, we examined a case study in which first year students from universities attending the engineering and environmental sciences course approached the study of some topics with augmented reality. Our research focused mainly on one aspect: whether the use of augmented reality supported by an innovative teaching methodology could improve the student's state in terms of interaction and participation. The research is based on the fact that an improvement in interaction and participation can generate good motivational and emotional dispositions. The data analysis was quantitative and exploited the potential of Fuzzy Cognitive Maps. This was constructed using expert based methods to describe the state of the student in terms of interaction and participation according to the parameters of interest identified such as emotions, social activities and actions carried out through the didactic contents. The protocols submitted to the students had as their object the functions in two variables, because it is a transversal theme to all the other themes of the course of Calculus II, mainly related to the difficulties that the student encounters in the passage from one representation to another and in the management of different registers of representation of the same mathematical object, a well-known research topic in Mathematics Education.

The experiment showed that for the students who used augmented reality the levels of interaction and participation had an average increase of 15% and 22% respectively compared to the control group. From the analysis of the parameters it seems that some students overcame some difficulties linked to epistemological obstacles and faced the study of the proposed topics with greater serenity, due to the overcoming of the obstacles linked to the passage between different representations or within the same representations. The use of the augmented reality platform also seems to have allowed students to learn more adaptive and linked to their own personal style. Further developments of this experimentation will focus on the research of the correlation between the improvement of mathematical skills and the increase of interaction and participation levels.

Acknowledgements. This research was supported in part by the Italian Ministry of Economic Development (MISE) under the Project "MOLIERE (MOtivational Learning and Interactive Education Revolution)" – PON I&C 2014-2020. The authors would like to thank Italdata S.p.A, the CORISA and the DISA-MIS of the University of Salerno who participated in the project, for the interesting discussions and suggestions.

References

1. Aldon, G., Raffin, C.: Mathematics learning and augmented reality in a virtual school. In: Augmented Reality in Educational Settings, pp. 123–146. Brill Sense (2019)
2. Arrigo, G., D'Amore, B.: Lo vedo ma non ci credo. Ostacoli epistemologici e didattici al processo di comprensione di un teorema di George Cantor che coinvolge l'infinito attuale. L'insegnamento della matematica e delle scienze integrate **22B**(5), 465–494 (1999)
3. Bagni, G.T.: Limite e visualizzazione: una ricerca sperimentale. L'insegnamento della matematica e delle scienze integrate **22B**(4), 333–372 (1999)
4. Berthoz, A.: La décision Odile Jacob (2003)

5. Branchetti, L., Capone, R., Tortoriello, F.S.: Un'esperienza didattica half-flipped in un ambiente di apprendimento SCALE-UP. Annali online della Didattica e della Formazione Docente **9**(14), 355–371 (2018)
6. Branchetti, L., Viale, M.: Tra italiano e matematica: il ruolo della formulazione sintattica nella comprensione del testo matematico. In: Ostinelli, M. (ed.) La didattica dell'italiano. Problemi e prospettive. Dipartimento formazione e apprendimento, Scuola universitaria professionale della Svizzera italiana, Locarno (2015)
7. Brousseau, G.: Théorie des situations didactiques. La Pensée Sauvage, Grenoble (1998)
8. Capone, R.: Just-in-time teaching and peer-led team learning in mathematics education using social platform with undergraduate students. Int. J. Math. Educ. Sci. Technol. 1–19 (2020, printing)
9. Capone, R., Del Regno, F., Tortoriello, F.: E-teaching in mathematics education: the teacher's role in online discussion. J. e-Learn. Knowl. Soc. **14**(3), 41–51 (2018)
10. Chang, M., D'Aniello, G., Gaeta, M., Orciuoli, F., Sampson, D., Simonelli, C.: Building ontology-driven tutoring models for intelligent tutoring systems using data mining. IEEE Access **8**, 48151–48162 (2020). Art. no. 9031710
11. Chen, Y.C., Chi, H.L., Hung, W.H., Kang, S.C.: Use of tangible and augmented reality models in engineering graphics courses. J. Prof. Issues Eng. Educ. Pract. **137**(4), 267–276 (2011)
12. D'Amore, B.: Lingua, Matematica e Didattica. La matematica e la sua didattica. **1**, 28–47 (2000)
13. D'Aniello, G., Gaeta, A., Gaeta, M., Tomasiello, S., Self-regulated learning with approximate reasoning and situation awareness. J. Ambient Intell. Humaniz. Comput. **9**(1), 151–164 (2018)
14. D'Aniello, G., De Falco, M., Gaeta, M., Lepore, M.: A situation-aware learning system based on fuzzy cognitive maps to increase learner motivation and engagement. In: 2020 IEEE International Conference on Fuzzy Systems, FUZZ-IEEE 2020, Glasgow, UK (2020)
15. D'Aniello, G., De Falco, M., Gaeta, M., Lepore, M.: Feedback generation using Fuzzy Cognitive Maps to reduce dropout in situation-aware e-Learning systems. In: 2020 IEEE International Conference on Cognitive and Computational Aspects of Situation Management, CogSIMA 2020, Victoria, BC, Canada (2020)
16. Domínguez, R.G.: Participatory learning. In: Seel, N.M. (ed.) Encyclopedia of the Sciences of Learning. Springer, Boston (2012). https://doi.org/10.1007/978-1-4419-1428-6
17. Dreyfus, T., Eisenberg, T.: On visual versus analytical thinking in mathematics. In: Proceedings of PME 10, London, pp. 152–158 (1986)
18. Duval, R.: Registres de Répresentations sémiotiques et Fonctionnement cognitif de la Pensée. Annales de didactique et de sciences cognitives **5**, 37–65 (1993)
19. Ferrari, P.L.: Tecnologia informatica e sistemi di rappresentazione nell'insegna-mento universitario della matematica. Convegno UMI (2003)
20. Endsley, M.: Designing for Situation Awareness: An Approach to User-Centered Design. CRC Press, Boca Raton (2016)
21. El-Seoud, M.S.A., Ghenghesh, P., Seddiek, N., Nosseir, A., Taj-Eddin, I.A., El-Khouly, M.M.: E-Learning and motivation effects on Egyptian higher education. In: 2013 International Conference on Interactive Collaborative Learning (ICL), pp. 689–695. IEEE, September 2013
22. Gopalan, V., Zulkifi, A.N., Abubakar, J.A.A.: A study of students' motivation using the AR science textbook. In: AIP Conference Proceedings, vol. 1761, no. 1, pp. 27–35 (2016)
23. Harandi, S.R.: Effects of e-learning on students' motivation. Proc.-Soc. Behavi. Sci. **181**, 423–430 (2015)
24. Kaufmann, H., Steinbügl, K., Dünser, A., Glück, J.: General training of spatial abilities by geometry education in augmented reality. Ann. Rev. CyberTher. Telemed.: Decade VR **3**, 65–76 (2005)

25. Kyei-Blankson, L. (ed.): Handbook of Research on Strategic Management of Interaction, Presence, and Participation in Online Courses. IGI Global, Hershey (2015)
26. Kosco, B.: Fuzzy cognitive maps. Int. J. Man Mach. Stud. **24**, 65–75 (1986)
27. Latour, B.: On actor-network theory. A few clarifications plus more than a few complications. Soziale Welt **47**, 369–381 (1996)
28. Michaelsen, L.K., Watson, W.E., Cragin, J.P., Fink, L.D.: Team-based learning: a potential solution to the problems of large classes. Exchange: Organiz. Behav. Teach. J. **7**(4), 18–33 (1982)
29. Miranda, S., Marzano, A.: The augmented reality in the professional development: a systematic map. Form@ re-Open Journal per la formazione in rete **19**(3), 207–220 (2019)
30. Piaget, J.: The stages of the intellectual development of the child. Bull. Menninger Clin. **26**(3), 120 (1962)
31. Rivoltella, P.C.: Neurodidattica. Insegnare al cervello che apprende. Raffaello Cortina (2012)
32. Robert, A., Boschet, F.: L'acquisition des débuts de l'analyse sur R dans un section ordinaire de DEUG première année, Cahier de didactique des mathématiques 18–1, IREM, Paris VII (1984)
33. Salmeron, J.L.: Augmented fuzzy cognitive maps for modelling LMS critical success factors. Knowl.-Based Syst. **22**(4), 53–59 (2009)
34. Sarder, B.: Improving student engagement in online courses. In: Proceedings of the 2014 Annual Conference on ASEE (2014)
35. Sbaragli, S., Santi, G.: Teacher's choices as the cause of misconceptions in the learning of the concept of angle. Int. J. Stud. Math. Educ. **4**, 1–41 (2011)
36. Simondon, G.: Technical mentality. Parrhesia **7**(1), 17–27 (2009)
37. Stanford-Bowers, D.E.: Persistence in online classes: a study of perceptions among community college stakeholder. J. Online Learn. Teach. **4**(1), 37–50 (2008)
38. Star, S., Griesemer, J.R.: Institutional ecology. 'Translations' and boundary objects: amateurs and professionals in Berkeley's Museum of Vertebrate Zoology. Soc. Stud. Sci. **19**, 387–420 (1989)
39. Swidan, O., Schacht, F., Sabena, C., Fried, M., El-Sana, J., Arzarello, F.: Engaging students in covariational reasoning within an augmented reality environment. In: Augmented Reality in Educational Settings, pp. 147–167. Brill Sense (2019)
40. Tall, D., Vinner, S.: Concept images and concept definition in mathematics with particular reference to limits and continuity. Educ. Stud. Math. **12**, 151–169 (1981)
41. Vygotsky, L.: Interaction between learning and development. Read. Dev. Child. **23**(3), 34–41 (1978)
42. Zan, R.: Difficoltà in matematica: osservare, interpretare, intervenire. Springer, Milano (2007). https://doi.org/10.1007/978-88-470-0584-6

A Content Creation Tool for AR/VR Applications in Education: The ScoolAR Framework

Maria Paola Puggioni[1], Emanuele Frontoni[1], Marina Paolanti[1(✉)],
Roberto Pierdicca[2], Eva Savina Malinverni[2], and Michele Sasso[3]

[1] Dipartimento di Ingegneria dell'Informazione,
Università Politecnica delle Marche, Ancona, Italy
`m.puggioni@pm.univpm.it,`
`{e.frontoni,m.paolanti}@univpm.it`
[2] Dipartimento di Ingegneria Civile Edile e dell'Architettura,
Università Politecnica delle Marche, Ancona, Italy
`{r.pierdicca,e.s.malinverni}@univpm.it`
[3] Ubisive s.r.l., Ancona, Italy
`michele.sasso@ubisive.it`

Abstract. Nowadays, in education environments, new societal challenges and opportunities induce teachers to use new methods to improve the quality of learning. For this purpose, technology has proved to be a helpful aid in education, since it allows to ease the teaching methods, increasing the performances by introducing affordable and reliable means to convey digital contents. Studies revealed that Augmented Reality (AR) and Virtual Reality (VR) have a great potential to help two kinds of users: on one side the students, improving their knowledge and skills; on the other teachers, widening their teaching methods. In fact, the relation between AR/VR and education makes the teaching and learning experience more efficient and stimulating. Notwithstanding, a platform specifically designed does not exist for an agile creation of AR/VR contents, even for not skilled programmers. There is thus the necessity of developing new tools to enable users to become, easily, producers of such experiences. The aim of this paper is to introduce a novel framework, named ScoolAR, specifically designed to allow teachers to create tailor-made didactic proposals involving the students in the training action, thus bringing more involvement and contents awareness, managed in the realization of AR and VR applications and declined within the disciplinary topics.

Keywords: Augmented Reality · Virtual Reality · Education · Learning · Framework

1 Introduction

Nowadays, there are many fields of application and development of Augmented Reality (AR) and Virtual Reality (VR) [6,9]. The school, albeit in more discreet

L. T. De Paolis and P. Bourdot (Eds.): AVR 2020, LNCS 12243, pp. 205–219, 2020.
https://doi.org/10.1007/978-3-030-58468-9_16

ways and with slower times than in other sectors, is opening up to these new technologies [7]. Such technologies find fertile ground in their use because of their appeal to a young audience, such as students, who are already familiar with devices that offer applications for AR and VR [14,16], especially in the video game sector. This familiarity constitutes one of the elements of strength that allows an easier introduction of the new digital methodologies in the didactic field [1]. All young people know the features of a smartphone, they know how to download apps, how to search and manage content in internet. However, the so-called digital natives [19] need to be educated in the use of AR and VR technologies to prevent them from being identified only as a game tool for its own sake. Besides, it is essential the contribution of the teacher who, mediating the contents and methods of approach and use of the devices, makes these tools effective and functional to the learning path, through a correct valorisation and a real strengthening of the intrinsic and extrinsic characteristics which has been mentioned. The figure of the teacher then determines the level of training and the correct and complete transmission of knowledge through the use of different teaching/learning methods. Another element to take into consideration concerns not only the levels of learning and the active involvement of students, but also the correct use of the contents they transmit through disciplinary knowledge [18]. In fact, immersive technology risks overloading students with information and decreasing the ability to correctly process data [12]. The intervention of the teacher who plans and organizes the didactic action is fundamental, carrying out the necessary maieutic function in the learning process. Lessons supported by AR and VR applications shall be, therefore, planned and structured in order to not lead to stereotypes, since they could be misleading for the students, who are used to different learning dynamics that are created within the classes.

Given the above, the aim of this paper is to introduce a novel framework, named ScoolAR, specifically designed to enable teachers and students in creating tailor-made contents and didactic proposals. The present research work follows a previous study [10] in which the benefits of using AR and VR applications has been proved, highlighting the necessity to facilitate the development of multimedia experience even by non-expert programmers. After demonstrating the potential of such technologies with a real user test, emerged the need to provide students and teachers with an editor platform for autonomously developing AR and VR applications. Interested readers can find the full research results in [17]. It is well known, in fact, that a bottleneck which prevents the diffusion of such technologies for learning purposes is the lack of easy editing applications. For this purpose, ScoolAR has been developed to overcome such limitation, enabling an autonomous content creation process and thus bringing more involvement and awareness in the realization of AR and VR applications. The synergy between traditional didactic actions and technological innovation allows to obtain better results both in terms of knowledge and skills, especially in the experiences in which the disciplines interface in a transversal way. Supported by the results achieved so far and from the data collected in terms of improved knowledge and students' satisfaction (in synergy with a traditional activity of knowledge transmission), the validity of ScoolAR framework is shown, together with its main concept and design.

2   Related Works

Applications based on AR and VR can help students to improve their knowledge and skills. In fact, the link between AR/VR and education makes the teaching experience more efficient and engaging [9]. Using these technologies, students not only learn better, but learning processes to reach a more accurate knowledge [4]. In this regard, the work conducted by Gargalakos and others [11] has shown that the technology has significantly improved learning outcomes by increasing the ability to attract students and their willingness to communicate and share their experiences, their provision in the use of new technologies and acquisition of knowledge, while having fun and experiencing new realities. However, according to [2] there are challenges and disadvantages in using AR/VR as an educational tool in most classes of the world. In 2009, Dunleavy, Dede and Mitchell designed Alien Contact!, a mobile augmented reality (MAR) game that focuses on teaching mathematics, language arts and scientific literacy to middle and high school students. Students can interview virtual characters, collect digital objects and solve scientific, mathematical and linguistic problems to answer the question and find out why the aliens have landed on earth. The results obtained from the study documented the high involvement of students in the various case studies [8]. In 2009, Ardito and others [3] presented a MAR game called Explore! with the aim of supporting the exploration of middle school students towards archaeological sites in Italy. From the study of the results, it was shown that the students had fun playing with Explore! but for learning, there were no significant differences. The authors in [13] proposed an educational application called EnredaMadrid to make it easier for students to learn history using mobile devices based on geolocation and AR technology. The evaluation was carried out through a questionnaire and the results showed that AR certainly contributes to making learning better and more enjoyable. The virtual application, Google Expeditions[1] allows to take part of several virtual visits to the most evocative locations around the world but also in the depths of the oceans and in the space. It is a product purposely designed for classroom work. A VR tour, produced with a mobile phone and a Google Cardboard headset, requires 360° viewing so that the participant overall observes the scene they are viewing. The Vatican app[2] is an application that provides tours and information about the Vatican in Rome. Students can enter each room with High Definition pictures. This application is only available for 360 views and not Google Cardboard. Cave Automatic Virtual Environments (CAVE) [4] is a tool supporting immersive VR approach where the user is in a room where all the walls and the floor are projection screens and the user can wear 3D glasses where he can move around freely in the projected world. CAVE environments are still rather expensive and is particularly used in cultural heritage education [15].

---

[1] https://edu.google.com/products/vr-ar/expeditions/?modal_active=none.
[2] http://w2.vatican.va/.

3   Materials and Methods

Prior to describe the ScoolAR framework, for the sake of completeness, a brief overview of the users' test is given. As well, to facilitate the reader in understanding the potentials of the developed framework, a brief description of the applications used for this tests is reported.

The AR and VR apps contained within the SmartMarca[3] project have been the support for the didactic action undertaken within the school programs developed during the year, in order to test the contribution of digital technology in the learning process of the students. The AR apps concern the guided reading of two paintings preserved in exhibition structures in the territory of Fermo, in the Marche region. The first concerns the painting "Adorazione dei pastori" of P.P. Rubens preserved in the Palazzo dei Priori in Fermo, the second concerns the painting "Paesaggio" by O. Licini kept inside the artist's house-museum in Monte Vidon Corrado (Fig. 1).

Fig. 1. AR applications: left "Adorazione dei Pastori" by P.P. Rubens, right "Paesaggio" by O. Licini

The VR app allows a 360° view of the reconstruction of the Roman Theater of Falerone. All the apps allow the reading of the works through tags that, illustrating the fundamental elements, propose a more accurate view of the details and

---

[3] http://www.marcafermana.it/it/SmartMarca/.

the entire work. The SmartMarca project is mainly aimed at a public of tourists, but in the drafting of the texts of the app, edited by the teacher (Fig. 2), it was also thought to a didactic use that allows to start a first proposal of knowledge of the artist, the work or the monument in its essential elements.

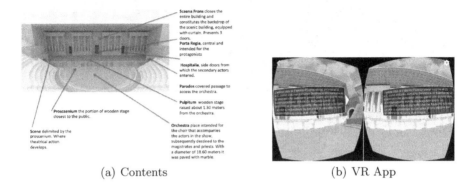

(a) Contents   (b) VR App

Fig. 2. Teaching content developed by the teacher inserted in the tags of the Smart-Marca application and related to the theater of Falerone.

In general, art and architecture lend themselves to an empathetic cognitive approach because they are based mainly on the image, shapes and colors, thus favoring a direct knowledge through the view that results according to Classen "... the most important of the senses and the sense more closely linked to reason" [5].

The protagonists of the methodological analysis are the students of the Course of Surveyors (now C.A.T. Construction Environment Territory) of the ITET Carducci Galilei of Fermo. The students were invited to read the works in different ways: with or without the teacher's explanation, with or without the use of the app. The combination of the different readings was then completed with an online verification, prepared by the teacher, on Socrative[4] an application that allows to carry out checks and collect results, data and statistics related to the learning of the students. The analysis of the collected data has led to the following conclusions:

– The combination of the frontal lesson with the use of the app is the best learning method in terms of motivation and knowledge of the contents.
– During the teaching/learning action the apps proved to be a useful compendium of theoretical and practical knowledge.
– The use of the devices involves a greater level of attention and involvement of the students in the proposed activities.

A further verification phase was carried out to compare the two AR and VR technologies and verify their best correspondence both in terms of teaching and

---

[4] https://socrative.com.

use. For this purpose, the SmartMarca application was used for VR with the 360°
view of the Piazza del Popolo di Fermo (Fig. 3), for AR with the "Adorazione
dei pastori" of P.P. Rubens.

Fig. 3. Students test the use of Virtual Reality applied to the 360° view of the "Piazza
del Popolo" in Fermo, collected with 360° camera.

In this case, the data (Fig. 4) were collected through a questionnaire formu-
lated through the Google Docs application, to which the students had access in
real time, at the end of the test and through a QR code.

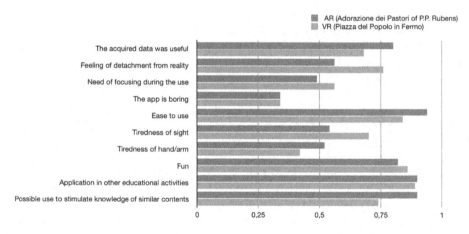

Fig. 4. Comparative histogram of the answers to the questions in the online questionnaire about the comparison between AR and VR.

The following conclusions have been deduced:

- Virtual Reality is the medium most known and used by young people, thanks
  to its diffusion in the video game sector and despite creating greater detach-
  ment from reality and straining the eyes with the use of the viewer.
- Augmented Reality, a lesser known tool, encourages greater contact with the
  surrounding reality and stimulates better involvement in the comprehension
  of the proposed text.

The results gathered from the research carried out so far validate the potential of the AR and VR applications in the didactic field, as a support tool and compendium of the training action. For the teacher, the development of the content of the app, its use within the training course offered to the students and the following verification has constituted an interesting methodological study. In fact, in tracing the founding points of the subject matter, to carry out the insertion in the various tags, the teacher has identified the so-called minimum disciplinary objectives necessary for the students to develop the skills and knowledge that can be spent in a transversal way. Characteristics to be developed emerge such as those concerning the long-term verification of the knowledge acquired by students, the possibility of creating similar methodological situations declined on the different topics and on the different disciplines, the involvement of students in the realization of the training path to create a participatory teaching. To this end, the development of the ScoolAR project is an excellent training ground for continuing to study new scenarios for the shared use of the resources offered by AR and VR.

4 Description of ScoolAR Framework

As stated, based on the tests conducted on AR and VR experiences, the necessity of developing new tools has increased to enable users to become producers of contents of AR/VR experiences, because a platform specifically designed does not exist yet for an agile creation, even for not skilled programmers.

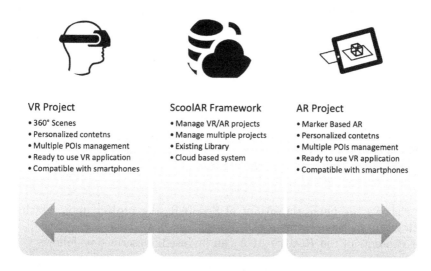

VR Project
- 360° Scenes
- Personalized contetns
- Multiple POIs management
- Ready to use VR application
- Compatible with smartphones

ScoolAR Framework
- Manage VR/AR projects
- Manage multiple projects
- Existing Library
- Cloud based system

AR Project
- Marker Based AR
- Personalized contetns
- Multiple POIs management
- Ready to use VR application
- Compatible with smartphones

Fig. 5. General overview of ScoolAR; the schema demonstrates the modularity of the framework which enables a multi-scale and multi-app development.

The aim of this section is to describe the educational ScoolAR application, a platform for the creation of educational contents (a brief overview of the developed framework is reported in Fig. 5).

Fig. 6. Screenshot of the ScoolAR homepage.

The intent is to propose a cooperative platform between teachers and students, which allows the use of innovative technologies (AR and VR) to stimulate student learning. After the log-in, the user will be able to access a series of sections that will give the opportunity to continue the projects started, create new projects or consult the catalog of available content. The main objectives of the educational platform are:

- Provide a user-friendly platform for creating educational content.
- Use of innovative technologies to stimulate learning.
- Create a cooperative platform between teachers and students.
- Drivers for the digitization of the territory.
- Platform for selling partners' digital content.

Figure 6 shows the home screenshot of ScoolAR, the project upon which our research group has concentrated the efforts.

The contents of the *HOMEPAGE* can be briefly described as follows:

- *New project:* Opens a new work area for AR or VR projects.
- *Buy contents:* Access the "Catalog" section containing shared or purchasable content.
- *Saved projects:* list of projects saved by the user.
- *From the catalog:* User projects from the catalog.

Fig. 7. Screenshot of the catalog.

- *Charge project:* Upload projects previously exported and modified by third parties.

In the *CATALOG*, the contents shared by other users and purchasable projects will be available.

- *Navigation bar:* The icons redirect the user to the user page, dashboard, catalog (Fig. 7), shopping cart and favorites.
- *Project catalog:* Windows show a preview of the contents with basic information and action buttons.
- *Filters:* To facilitate searching for projects of interest, completing the research area by name.

Clicking on the "Preview content" action button, the page related to the selected project is opened. This will allow users to find more information and to view the contents.

The contents of the *PROJECT PREVIEW* section, of which an example is showed in Fig. 8, are:

- *Content preview:* includes a series of useful information (Content Type, Subjects, Topics, Recommended Age, Available Languages, Related Projects, Last Update, Author); in addition to a brief description and images of the content.
- *Similar content:* automatically recommended based on the characteristics of the content displayed.
- *Action keys:* can be placed in the shopping cart or added to favorites.

Fig. 8. Screenshot of the "Project preview".

4.1   AR Project

When opening a new AR project, the user will be asked to upload a target image, i.e. the image object of the project that the application will have to recognize. Feedback will be immediately provided on the resolution of the uploaded image but above all on its recognizability. Once the image is approved, it will be possible to add tags. All elements on the work area will be editable via Drag-and-drop. Selecting *Add Tag* in the right section will open a panel with the tool for selecting the Tag area. Once the instrument has been selected, the image will appear in semi-transparency, thus helping the selection. Once the area is selected, the *tag navigation bar* will appear at the bottom, which will contain all the selected areas, giving the user the possibility to easily navigate between them. In case of selection not sufficiently recognizable by the application, a negative feedback will be provided which will force the user to reselect the tag area.

Adding information content to the right panel, a containment window will appear automatically. All contents, including the window, will be editable via Drag-And-Drop. A dialog box will help the user addressing it to an *Instructions* page. Once the project is completed, the user can save it on his dashboard and/or export it for the application. An example of a completed project is showed in Fig. 9.

4.2   VR Project

When creating a new VR project, the user will be asked to upload a 360° image, in order to start working. Feedback on the resolution of the uploaded image will be immediately provided. Once the image has been approved, it will be possible

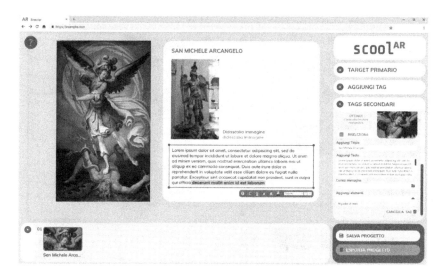

Fig. 9. Screenshot of a new completed AR project.

to add elements, Waypoints and Hotspots. Waypoints allow to navigate from one image to another; Hotspots to insert windows with informational contents. By adding a Waipoint, the associated icon will appear on the work area that will allow the passage from one 360° image to another. On the right panel will be present all the Waypoints created. In the active Waypoint section, it will be possible to select the image to be associated, via drop-down menu if previously loaded, or load another. All the 360° images loaded will be visible at the bottom on the 360° *image bar*.

Adding a Hotspot, the associated icon will appear on the work area that will allow consultation of the contents inserted. Once added, as for AR projects, a series of elements will appear to be added to the contents window of the hotspot. By filling in any section, a containing window can be created which can be modified using Drag-and-Drop. Once the work is finished, the project can be saved on the user dashboard and/or exported. An example of a completed project is showed in Fig. 10.

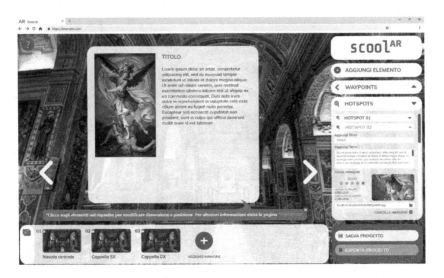

Fig. 10. Screenshot of a new completed VR project.

5   Discussion and Conclusion

For evaluating the framework performances, preliminary tests have been conducted with teachers of the same higher school. In particular, we proposed a comparison between existing development platforms (namely Unity3D for VR and Unity Vuforia Plug-in for AR). From the very beginning of the test, it emerged a clear difficulty on developing AR/VR contents autonomously by the teachers, which obviously didn't have programming skills. Using ScoolAR instead, teachers were able to create AR/VR projects by their own. Unity3D is actually the only platform which permits the development of AR/VR experiences within the same environment[5]. Albeit it is a powerful tool, its interface is very complex; for instance, developing VR experiences requires programming skills for allowing the end-user to interact with 360° scenes. As well, the development of AR experiences is entrusted on the use of Vuforia (a plug-in based on marker-based AR) which presents a more easy-to-use development pipeline but it is not designed for non-experts. In the following, a comparison between the two frameworks (Unity and ScoolAR) is reported Table 1, highlighting the benefits of our approach.

To summarise, the proposed ScoolAR framework enables users to become producers of contents of AR/VR experiences; it tackles the challenging issue of facilitating the use of new media in the education environment. In fact, up to now, there no exists a platform specifically designed for an agile creation of AR/VR applications. We can affirm that the proposed framework revealed to be a promising solution. The intent is to propose a cooperative platform between teachers and students, which allows the use of innovative technologies (AR and VR) to stimulate student learning. Students use a platform that makes them

---

[5] https://www.oreilly.com/ideas/.

Table 1. Comparative analysis between Unity 3D and our framework

Feature	Unity3D	ScoolAR
Time spent for developing AR app	5 h	1 h
Time spent for developing VR app	N/A	1 h
Manage multiple projects	No	Yes
Easy to use interface	No	Yes
Programming skills required	Yes	No
3D Environment	Yes	No

more autonomous and aware of the contents, managed in the realization of AR and VR projects within the disciplinary topics. The main novelties introduced by our framework are the creation of an all in one solution for the creation of AR/VR applications, the autonomous content creation thanks to the easy and friendly interface (aimed for not expert programmers) and the deploying of ready to use AR/VR applications suitable for different devices.

As a final remark, it is fair to say that, in its current version, this framework is not multi-language (only Italian language is supported). Moreover, it is designed to become a commercial tool, in which costs are related to the purchase of existing projects and on annual fees, depending to the hosting platform, hence to the dimension of the content that the user should manage. Though this framework has been developed for the education domain, it can be foreseen, in the future, that other domains like tourism or gaming can benefit from it.

Even the benefits of AR/VR in the educational context deserve few comments. The introduction of new AR and VR technologies can help teachers in their task of learning new topics, increasing the ability to attract and involve more and more students. Tests were conducted on two classes of adolescents for which the different teaching approaches served as a method of evaluating the effectiveness of the use of these technologies for the educational process. However, despite technology is capable of transmitting "disposable" information, it does not stimulate the students' self-elaboration, which still remains entrusted to the role of teacher. The only way to facilitate the introduction of new media in the education domain is to enable non-expert users to create by multimedia contents autonomously, and ScoolAR paves the way in this direction. In our future work, we are planning to evaluate, with specific learning paths, the benefits for learning at different levels. Moreover, it will be interesting to expand the platform to other fields beyond Cultural Heritage, as there are several disciplines that could be taught with the support of AR/VR applications.

References

1. Akçayır, M., Akçayır, G.: Advantages and challenges associated with augmented reality for education: a systematic review of the literature. Educ. Res. Rev. **20**, 1–11 (2017)

2. Ardiny, H., Khanmirza, E.: The role of AR and VR technologies in education developments: opportunities and challenges. In: 2018 6th RSI International Conference on Robotics and Mechatronics (IcRoM), pp. 482–487. IEEE (2018)

3. Ardito, C., Buono, P., Costabile, M.F., Lanzilotti, R., Piccinno, A.: Enabling interactive exploration of cultural heritage: an experience of designing systems for mobile devices. Knowl. Technol. Policy **22**(1), 79–86 (2009). https://doi.org/10.1007/s12130-009-9079-7

4. Christou, C.: Virtual reality in education. In: Affective, Interactive and Cognitive Methods for E-Learning Design: Creating an Optimal Education Experience, pp. 228–243. IGI Global (2010)

5. Classen, C.: Foundations for an anthropology of the senses. Int. Soc. Sci. J. **49**(153), 401–412 (1997)

6. Crosier, J.K., Cobb, S., Wilson, J.R.: Key lessons for the design and integration of virtual environments in secondary science. Comput. Educ. **38**(1–3), 77–94 (2002)

7. Dede, C.: Emerging technologies and distributed learning in higher education. In: Higher Education in an Era of Digital Competition: Choices and Challenges. Atwood, New York (2000)

8. Dunleavy, M., Dede, C., Mitchell, R.: Affordances and limitations of immersive participatory augmented reality simulations for teaching and learning. J. Sci. Educ. Technol. **18**(1), 7–22 (2009). https://doi.org/10.1007/s10956-008-9119-1

9. El Sayed, N.A., Zayed, H.H., Sharawy, M.I.: ARSC: augmented reality student card. In: 2010 International Computer Engineering Conference (ICENCO), pp. 113–120. IEEE (2010)

10. Frontoni, E., Paolanti, M., Puggioni, M., Pierdicca, R., Sasso, M.: Measuring and assessing augmented reality potential for educational purposes: SmartMarca project. In: De Paolis, L.T., Bourdot, P. (eds.) AVR 2019. LNCS, vol. 11614, pp. 319–334. Springer, Cham (2019). https://doi.org/10.1007/978-3-030-25999-0_28

11. Gargalakos, M., Giallouri, E., Lazoudis, A., Sotiriou, S., Bogner, F.X.: Assessing the impact of technology-enhanced field trips in science centers and museums. Adv. Sci. Lett. **4**(11–12), 3332–3341 (2011)

12. Makransky, G., Terkildsen, T.S., Mayer, R.E.: Adding immersive virtual reality to a science lab simulation causes more presence but less learning. Learn. Instr. **60**, 225–236 (2017)

13. Martín, S., Díaz, G., Cáceres, M., Gago, D., Gibert, M.: A mobile augmented reality Gymkhana for improving technological skills and history learning: outcomes and some determining factors. In: E-Learn: World Conference on E-Learning in Corporate, Government, Healthcare, and Higher Education, pp. 260–265. Association for the Advancement of Computing in Education (AACE) (2012)

14. Naspetti, S., Pierdicca, R., Mandolesi, S., Paolanti, M., Frontoni, E., Zanoli, R.: Automatic analysis of eye-tracking data for augmented reality applications: a prospective outlook. In: De Paolis, L.T., Mongelli, A. (eds.) AVR 2016. LNCS, vol. 9769, pp. 217–230. Springer, Cham (2016). https://doi.org/10.1007/978-3-319-40651-0_17

15. Ott, M., Pozzi, F.: ICT and cultural heritage education: which added value? In: Lytras, M.D., Carroll, J.M., Damiani, E., Tennyson, R.D. (eds.) WSKS 2008. LNCS (LNAI), vol. 5288, pp. 131–138. Springer, Heidelberg (2008). https://doi.org/10.1007/978-3-540-87781-3_15

16. Pierdicca, R., Frontoni, E., Pollini, R., Trani, M., Verdini, L.: The use of augmented reality glasses for the application in industry 4.0. In: De Paolis, L.T., Bourdot, P., Mongelli, A. (eds.) AVR 2017. LNCS, vol. 10324, pp. 389–401. Springer, Cham (2017). https://doi.org/10.1007/978-3-319-60922-5_30

17. Pierdicca, R., Frontoni, E., Puggioni, M.P., Malinverni, E.S., Paolanti, M.: Evaluating augmented and virtual reality in education through a user-centered comparative study: SmartMarca project. In: Virtual and Augmented Reality in Education, Art, and Museums, pp. 229–261. IGI Global (2020)
18. Pierdicca, R., Paolanti, M., Frontoni, E.: eTourism: ICT and its role for tourism management. J. Hosp. Tour. Technol. **10**(1), 90–106 (2019)
19. Prensky, M.: Digital natives, digital immigrants part 1. Horizon **9**(5), 1–6 (2001)

A Framework for Educational and Training Immersive Virtual Reality Experiences

David Checa[1](✉), Carola Gatto[3], Doriana Cisternino[2], Lucio Tommaso De Paolis[2], and Andres Bustillo[1]

[1] Departamento Ingeniería Informática, Universidad de Burgos, Burgos, Spain
{dcheca,abustillo}@ubu.es
[2] Department of Engineering for Innovation, University of Salento, Lecce, Italy
{doriana.cisternino,lucio.depaolis}@unisalento.it
[3] Department of Cultural Heritage, University of Salento, Lecce, Italy
carola.gatto@unisalento.it

Abstract. The fast development and progressive price reduction of Virtual Reality (VR) technologies promotes their implementation in areas beyond gaming. This makes it increasingly applied in other areas such as the development of educational or training applications. However, the development of these applications from scratch can involve a very high time and research investment. To solve this limitation, this paper presents an immersive virtual reality framework that simplifies the development of applications and allows researchers to focus on the design of the educational or training experience, once the framework already solve the main technical issues of the VR environment's development. This Virtual Reality framework is based in Unreal Engine, therefore compatible with most virtual reality helmets on the market. The framework includes tools for all the required tasks to create virtual reality experiences: movement of the player, interactions with the scenario and objects and the creation of scene objectives among others. To validate its suitability, two cultural heritage environments have been used, in which it has been applied to create two educational experiences.

Keywords: Virtual reality · Framework · Education · Cultural heritage

1 Introduction

For many years the literature referred to virtual reality as those using a computer screen and interaction controlled by the mouse. This opens countless new possibilities, but user immersion was very low, although this virtual environments increase student receptivity and learning rates [1]. In later years, novel virtual reality environments such as CAVEs were introduced, but they were very expensive solutions [2, 3]. It was only in recent years that virtual reality became more widespread. Both in hardware, with new and more economical Head Mounted Displays (HMD), and in software, with the development and widespread of Virtual Reality Environments (VREs) such as Unity™ or Unreal Engine 4™. These factors have led to the fast spread of immersive virtual reality technology in

© Springer Nature Switzerland AG 2020
L. T. De Paolis and P. Bourdot (Eds.): AVR 2020, LNCS 12243, pp. 220–228, 2020.
https://doi.org/10.1007/978-3-030-58468-9_17

recent years, and not only in the gaming market. The potential of this technology makes it increasingly used in the fields of education and training [4]. The use of immersive virtual reality for education or training point to a substantial improvement in the interest in learning in these environments, as well as can facilitate the understanding of complex concepts [5] and reduce misconceptions [6]. This makes evident the need to create new virtual reality environments for learning or training. It is also evident that the creation of these Virtual Reality Environments (VREs) is a time-consuming activity. For that reason, some studies use VREs environments are based on pre-created applications. If we choose to create our own VREs we can divide them according to their characteristics into: Explorative Interaction, Explorative, Interactive Experience and Passive Experience [4]. Explorative interactions are those experiences that allow the user to explore and interact freely with the VRE. A more restricted solution is the explorative experience, which allows free exploration, although no direct interaction with the virtual environment. The interactive experiences allow user interaction with the environment, but no free movement through it. Finally, the most limited solution is the passive experience, in which user interactivity and movement are limited. That is why most of the literature in education uses passive experiences with low immersion devices such as cardboards. This is because they are cheaper, easier to create and improve student satisfaction, but they fail to achieve significant learning and skill improvements [4]. However, interactive virtual reality experiences are currently the most appropriate because of their good balance between cost, current technology development, immersion and interactivity. This framework focuses on the creation of interactivity and explorative experiences as being the most effective, although it can also create experiences of all the other described types. The design of these experiences and the principles followed in their design have been identified from the literature and from the experience of creating VREs before. Figure 1 illustrate the principles followed for the design immersive virtual reality experiences. The first stage is a pre-design phase, we must carry out an analysis in two areas: a first one in which we must identify the requirements of the application and choose the best technology and type of experience for it. In order to create an immersive virtual environment that represents an archaeological site as it was in the past, it is necessary to conduct a requirement analysis in advance. This analysis primarily identifies the learning outcomes, considering the specific features of the context. This methodology allows us to build the basis of the narration that we want to provide.

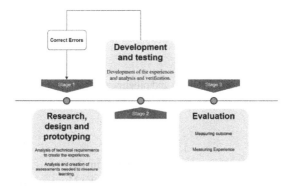

Fig. 1. Principles followed for the design immersive virtual reality experiences.

The second stage focuses on the development of the experience. The more detailed the previous phase, the fewer errors will appear in this phase of development. It is also important not to forget that we must take into account that there are four key objectives in the creation of virtual reality environments, interaction, immersion, user involvement and, to a lesser extent, photorealism [7]. Finally, the third stage consist of the evaluation of the user performance. The evaluation should take four different elements into account: 1) the key factors to be evaluated; 2) the way they are evaluated; 3) the number of individuals testing the serious game; and 4) the existence or otherwise of a reference group.

This research is focused on the Development and Testing stage. Developing a virtual reality application requires a multidisciplinary team. This framework is created for developers, with or without experience, to create virtual reality applications quicker and more efficiently. The framework simplifies the game development process with functions and services that are pre-programmed and allow reuse it effectively. This fact allows developers to focus their time on designing the experience and not waste time dealing and struggling with the development itself. Finally, to demonstrate the capabilities of this framework, it has been used for developing the experience of two study cases related to cultural heritage.

2 Framework Development

The framework has been designed inside Unreal Engine™. Unreal Engine™ stands out in two things: its high capacity to create photorealistic environments and the ease of use. Also, its visual scripting system, the blueprint editor, allow to create complex experiences without knowledge of coding. The framework is divided into four main parts: Player, Scene, Utilities and Metrics. A diagram of the pipeline for the creation of experiences and the framework implementation can be seen in Fig. 2.

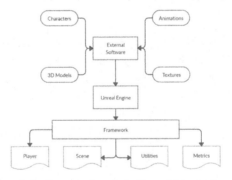

Fig. 2. Diagram of the framework and pipeline of the creation of experiences

2.1 Player

In this section we refer to all the options available in the framework for the user of the virtual reality experience. The framework utilizes the Unreal Engine camera rig for rendering and tracking the HMD and its controllers. In a VR room setup, the player can walk in the limited space, but if the user wants to go further, he can use teleportation. The framework teleportation is through two personalized techniques; parabolic teleportation and direct movement:

The object manipulation is the foundation for Virtual Reality immersion [8]. It enables players to interact with the elements present in the scene precisely. The framework can be adapted to a wide variety of controllers thanks to its function mapping, although it is currently optimized for Oculus controllers and Vive controllers. The representation can be in the form of controllers (Changes automatically depending on the HMD used) or with realistic hands, which can additionally have a watch/display that will serve us as UI for the user.

2.2 Scene

The development of educational or training applications may involve gamification through task or objectives for the player. With this framework different types of tasks can be implemented in form of an evaluation manager. The user can see which task has to be completed to accomplish the experience. These functions are controlled from the task manager that handles the creation and loading of the instructions. The framework also includes a queuing system for the task actions. By default, the system loads the next task after the current task is completed. With this evaluation manager, the student can track and record his own evolution during the experience. The evaluation manager can be used on the hand watch or can be placed on panels within the experience for greater usability as shown in Fig. 3. These panels, as well as the watch, can also hold more scene information, such as a map. This map can be 2D or 3D, which can significantly help in the compression of the spaces.

Fig. 3. Panels showing information from the evaluation manager and maps in watch and fixed panel versions.

2.3 Utilities

This section includes other utilities developed in the framework that are useful in the creation of this type of experiences. One of the most important is the one referred to the scene transfer, which allows the user to autonomously change between levels without losing his overall progress. Also, a load menu that can be of contextual type located in the level or deploy it in your own hand and select the destination level from there.

Another tool developed is the gaze view events, which allows to create actions on objects that are activated when the user looks directly at them. These are very useful in passive experiences typical of cardboard devices for trigger events. Gaze view events can also be used in any experience to show information when the user is looking at an object for example.

Finally, in these experiences it is also important that people who are not immersed in virtual reality can adequately observe the participant's performance. Therefore, we have created the spectator view tool. It serves as viewpoint for a second person watching the active player in the VR experience from the monitor.

2.4 Metrics

One of the weaknesses of many studies using virtual reality for education is the evaluation phase [6]. Having data collected during the process becomes indispensable in the creation of this type of experience today. Also, the analysis of extracted data and importing of feedback into the game in real time can be very useful. For this purpose, a Blueprint type plugin has been integrated in this framework. It has been coded in in C++, with generated Blueprint modules to collect the data we want to extract from the game. The advantage of this plugin is that it works internally using UDP, which reduces the latency of data transmission. The architecture of the metrics in the framework will consist of the following parts (Fig. 4):

- UE4 Plugin: the architecture of the UE4 plugin, implemented in C++, has two parts.

    - Sender module: it must collect the game data and broadcast it to the local network using the UDP multicast protocol.
    - Receiver module: it will oversee receiving data from sources external to the game/environment for use within the EU4 environment.

- External data receiver: It receives the data emitted by the data sender module of the UE4 plugin. It is an external part of the plugin. It must be in the same subnet as the plugin's sender for optimal communication.
- External data sender: element external to the plugin that sends data. It has a defined IP, a port and a message size. It will send data via UDP, and the receiver module will oversee listening to this data.
- Parameterizable Python script. The input parameters will be the IP and the port of the Plugin's data sender module and the message size. Internally, it will be possible to perform the required tasks according to the objective: transmit to an external network via TCP (more secure communication), store the data in a database (i.e. SQL), process the data....

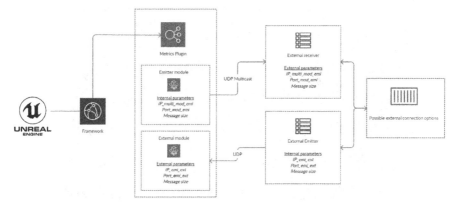

Fig. 4. Architecture of the metrics in the framework

3   Case Studies

This framework has been implemented in two case studies for validation. The aim of those implementations is to demonstrate its capabilities in the field of creating immersive virtual reality experiences focused on cultural heritage.

3.1   The Charterhouse of Miraflores, Burgos, Spain

The Charterhouse of Miraflores is not far from the city of Burgos. It was built at the end of the 15th century in a culture that had discovered the "New World" almost at the same time and was beginning to expand the dominance of Catholic monarchs throughout much of Latin America. The building belongs to a very important moment in the history of Western Europe and is characterized by its excellent artistic quality. It is a monumental funeral composition that perpetuates the memory of Isabella's parents.

There are two reasons for this choice. The first is the importance of this building for the artistic and historical identity of the city, since it has been of great importance in the history of the Kingdom of Castile and Leon. The second is its beauty, cultural fusion and the visual clarity of this monument. Being created for real-time environments makes it very easy to integrate into Virtual Reality platforms. An educational experience has been designed based on a series of tasks in collaboration with historians that allow users to discover the temple at their own pace and learn the most relevant data about it. To facilitate this issue, several information points were placed in the VR-environment that respond to the user's gaze, as Fig. 5 shows. If they are not looked at, the information points remain folded with; Then, when the user looks directly at those points, they expand revealing the text-based information. The framework integrates also functions such as the 2D/3D map and the evaluation manager that the user can consult in his hand watch.

3.2   Vaste Church, Salento, Italy

Fondo Giuliano [9] is an archaeological area located a few miles to the north of Vaste, near Poggiardo (Lecce, Italy). The excavations have brought to light three churches as

Fig. 5. Example of an information point to display text, images or sound.

can be seen in Fig. 6. The first phase (second half of the 4th century), second phase (second half of the 6th century) and third phase (9th century). The challenge is to help users to understand the chronological sequence of these ancient buildings through a virtual reality experience. The goal is to build a virtual environment in order to make students aware about:

Fig. 6. Blueprint of the excavations of the three phases [10], and VR experience.

- Complexity of archaeological stratigraphy: the "travel" is in time, between more phases;
- Architectural evolution through the centuries, in terms of construction techniques and styles;
- Uses and customs of the people, deducible from the archaeological data.

The contents that we need in order to achieve these goals are absolutely to be found in the archaeological scientific bibliography, referring to the studies conducted by the experts and working in constant synergy with them. Another fundamental aspect is to understand for each real context the index of "archaeological visibility": in Vaste site we do not have any kind to structures standing, but only perimeter traces of the holy buildings, from which archaeologists have deduced the architectural complexity of the ancient constructions. This leads us to adopt an immense virtual environment as the most suitable solution, since we have to de-sign and model the whole buildings in order to show how they were at that age. It was also very important to refer to photo and surveys in bibliography, as well as to the multimedia products previously created (3D models, 2D drawings, reconstruction, videos etc.). This material has been used as starting point, and the 3D models [11] in particular have been upgraded and "refreshed" by means of new development tools, and also adapted in order to answer to our learning goals.

Through integration into the framework, an experience has been created that allows users to explore the environment in all three different phases. The first challenge in this integration into the framework is to adapt the preexisting models. These models are highly realistic and have been created by relying on specific bibliography and historical studies conducted by Department of Cultural Heritage of the University of Salento [12]. To improve the understanding of the different environments, a context menu allows the user to quickly switch from one phase to another. In addition, a 2D and 3D map is available to better understand the change in architecture as can be seen in Fig. 6. Elements such as a torch have also been added so that the user can explore the dark areas inside the church. This experience will be expanded in the future and more extensive testing will be done with students to validate their educational competence.

4   Expected Results and Further Work

The present work is the result of the work of a multidisciplinary team, which has made possible the creation of a framework oriented towards the creation of educational and training experiences. This flexibility in the development of immersive virtual reality experiences gives a great versatility. Furthermore, as it is integrated in Unreal Engine, and thanks to its visual code editor, it opens even more the range of potential users who can apply it in their research.

The framework has been implemented in two case studies related to cultural heritage. The following steps go through evaluation of the user performance and measure outcome. The effort in the creation of the metrics of this framework is focused on being able to extract results in the final validation with students. This is one of the weaknesses that have been constantly detected in the validations of educational experiences of virtual reality and that we intend to change with the application of this framework. Future work will focus on validating the framework with its integration into other types of experiences.

Acknowledgments. This work was partially supported by the GruaRV project (Reference Number INVESTUN/18/0002) of the Consejeria de Empleo of the Junta de Castilla y León (Spain) and we gratefully acknowledge the support of NVIDIA Corporation with the donation of the Titan Xp GPU used for this research. The author Carola Gatto wrote Sect. 3.2, entitled "Vaste Church, Salento, Italy".

References

1. Chen, S., Pan, Z., Zhang, M., Shen, H.: A case study of user immersion-based systematic design for serious heritage games. Multimed. Tools Appl. **62**, 633–658 (2013). https://doi.org/10.1007/s11042-011-0864-4
2. Bustillo, A., Alaguero, M., Miguel, I., Saiz, J.M., Iglesias, L.S.: A flexible platform for the creation of 3D semi-immersive environments to teach Cultural Heritage. Digit. Appl. Archaeol. Cult. Herit. **2**, 248–259 (2015). https://doi.org/10.1016/j.daach.2015.11.002
3. Paolis, L.T.: Walking in a virtual town to understand and learning about the life in the middle ages. In: Murgante, B., et al. (eds.) ICCSA 2013. LNCS, vol. 7971, pp. 632–645. Springer, Heidelberg (2013). https://doi.org/10.1007/978-3-642-39637-3_50
4. Checa, D., Bustillo, A.: A review of immersive virtual reality serious games to enhance learning and training. Multimed. Tools Appl. **79**, 5501–5527 (2019). https://doi.org/10.1007/s11042-019-08348-9
5. Checa, D., Bustillo, A.: Advantages and limits of virtual reality in learning processes: Briviesca in the fifteenth century. Virtual Reality **24**(1), 151–161 (2019). https://doi.org/10.1007/s10055-019-00389-7
6. Mikropoulos, T.A., Natsis, A.: Educational virtual environments: a ten-year review of empirical research (1999–2009). Comput. Educ. **56**, 769–780 (2011). https://doi.org/10.1016/j.compedu.2010.10.020
7. Roussos, M., Johnson, A., Moher, T., Leigh, J., Vasilakis, C., Barnes, C.: Learning and building together in an immersive virtual world. Presence Teleoper. Virtual Environ. (1999). https://doi.org/10.1162/105474699566215
8. De Paolis, L.T., De Luca, V.: The impact of the input interface in a virtual environment: the Vive controller and the Myo armband. Virtual Reality (2019). https://doi.org/10.1007/s10055-019-00409-6
9. D'Andria, F., Mastronuzzi, G., Melissano, V.: La chiesa e la necropoli paleocristiana di Vaste nel Salento. Riv. di Archeol. Cris. **LXXXII**, 231–322 (2006)
10. Mastronuzzi, G.: Vaste e Poggiardo. Il patrimonio culturale e ambientale. Maglie (2015)
11. La chiesa di fondo Giuliano a Vaste. http://itlab.ibam.cnr.it/index.php/vaste/
12. Cisternino, D., Gatto, C., De Paolis, L.T.: Augmented Reality for the enhancement of Apulian archaeological areas. In: De Paolis, L.T., Bourdot, P. (eds.) AVR 2018. LNCS, vol. 10851, pp. 370–382. Springer, Cham (2018). https://doi.org/10.1007/978-3-319-95282-6_27

Applications in Industry

Augmented Reality Smart Glasses in the Workplace: Safety and Security in the Fourth Industrial Revolution Era

Roberto Pierdicca[1](✉), Mariorosario Prist[2], Andrea Monteriù[2],
Emanuele Frontoni[2], Filippo Ciarapica[3], Maurizio Bevilacqua[3],
and Giovanni Mazzuto[3]

[1] Department of Civil Engineering, Building and Architecture,
Università Politecnica delle Marche, Via Brecce Bianche 12, 60131 Ancona, Italy
`r.pierdicca@staff.univpm.it`
[2] Department of Information Engineering, Università Politecnica delle Marche,
Via Brecce Bianche 12, 60131 Ancona, Italy
[3] Department of Industrial Engineering and Mathematical Science,
Università Politecnica delle Marche, Via Brecce Bianche 12, 60131 Ancona, Italy

Abstract. Industry 4.0 is reinventing the way in which production is performed. Based on its eight pillars, I4.0 environments are adopting digital solutions in order to make production smart. One of these is the concept of augmented operator, which can act with the aid of digital tools to facilitate daily work. Augmented Reality can represent the turnkey. In this light, the aim of this research is to present a case study of a "security and safety" application through the use of AR smart glasses, tested in a real scenario. For our experiments, Vuzix Blade smart glasses have been tested in combination with a cloud-based architecture connected with an oil-extractor plant. The goal is to develop an AR application that allows to assist the operator during the working process. In particular, it acts as a guide system for the operator who wears glasses, provides remote support (remote operator) and, from a security point of view, sends real-time alerts in dangerous situations. The application has been validated after a number of practical tests carried out by specialised technicians who normally perform the work.

Keywords: Augmented Reality · Glasses · Industry 4.0 · Training on the job · Human-computer interaction

1 Introduction

Augmented reality (AR) is a technology that we can define as "immersive", which aims to make the boundary between the real world and the virtual world less clear, creating a feeling of immersion between elements deriving from different and heterogeneous areas [9]. AR does not replace the real environment but takes advantages of it by generating new points of interaction between the environment and the user, enriching or rather "augmenting" the link between the

© Springer Nature Switzerland AG 2020
L. T. De Paolis and P. Bourdot (Eds.): AVR 2020, LNCS 12243, pp. 231–247, 2020.
https://doi.org/10.1007/978-3-030-58468-9_18

senses and the phenomenon being observed [3]. It adds to the existing objects, digital layers generated by a computer (such as images, information or instructions) that overlap the real world and with which a user can interact and can use for his own purposes. In practice, users point their devices, which can be smartphones or tablets, interactive fixed screens or projectors, wearable devices, towards a particular image. The acquired input is processed by a system that allows to create a 2D or 3D projection with which the user can interact [1]. Despite AR is still considered an emerging technology, it has proved to be a valuable solution for several purposes: cultural heritage [4], environmental monitoring [11], medicine [5] and is one of the emerging technologies involved in the novel industry environments. Today, it has reached a degree of maturity that make it ready for being used within the production environments. From a conceptual point of view, it is possible to bring immersive technologies back to the broader set of the actual fourth industrial revolution (*Industry 4.0*). These technologies are designed to make the parts of the business more integrated and, more extensively, to efficiently connect the business with the outside world. Some expected effects from the application of new technologies in the business environment are: increase in productivity, increase in employment, optimisation of business processes, increase in flexibility, greater efficacy towards consumers [12].

Industry 4.0 has different cases concerning AR application in the field of industrial automation [8]. Very important has become the virtual simulation. In fact, this is one of the most used techniques in the manufacturing sector since it allows to evaluate the complexity of the systems, also modifying configurations during the work, simulating changes in operating strategies and verifying their effects at an organisational level. Through simulation, times and costs of product development can be significantly reduced, favouring the integration of skills and knowledge coming from different processes and avoiding the repetition of errors, thus facilitating the optimisation of the production cycle.

The new generation AR devices can be used for the prevention of individual, collective and environmental risk. They can support operators in real time during both ordinary and maintenance work, detecting potential health and safety risks for workers linked to the presence of incompatible physical fields and environmental contamination or to incorrect or dangerous positions between workers and work equipment. Moreover, where possible, they can replace humans in high-risk activities. In addition, thanks to these technologies, it is possible to emulate virtual work environments, in particular the most hostile or particularly complex ones, where risks for workers are known and often recurring reason for accident. They can promote a more "realistic" training both in its provision and in the results of assessing the adequacy for particular categories of workers. Therefore, it is believed that AR tools constitute an important added value to safeguard the health and protection of workers' safety. According to their use, the development of dedicated platforms requires studies oriented towards diversified work scenarios, from the manufacturing and process industry to that of services, for which the investments for their application are widely justified, also taking into account functional characteristics and compatibility with existing systems. Moreover, according to [8], before to develop an architecture of a security system, it is necessary to take into account the definition of security requirements.

Albeit AR technology has reached a high degree of maturity to be used though handheld devices [2], the same cannot be said talking about head-worn displays (also called Head Mounted Displays (HMD)). Wearable devices are defined as small electronic devices made up of one or more sensors with computational capacity [13]. They can be worn in different parts of the body, such as the head, arms, feet and can store a great deal of information, from the simplest to the most complex. Smart glasses are among the most used wearable devices, in fact they allow the user not to take his eyes off what he is doing by superimposing information directly on the real environment and minimising the possibility of error. Moreover, despite the existing technological limitations, "smart glasses" may become an everyday workplace tool in the foreseeable future, since they entails a fundamental advantage: workers can perform tasks hands-free while viewing real-time.

In this context, the aim of this research is to present a case study of a "security and safety" application through the use of AR smart glasses, tested in a real scenario. For our experiments, Vuzix Blade smart glasses have been tested in combination with a cloud-based architecture connected with an oil-extractor plant. The goal is to develop an AR application that allows to assist the operator during the working process. In particular, it acts as a guide system for the operator who wears glasses, provides remote support (remote operator) and, from a security point of view, sends real-time alerts in dangerous situations. The application has been validated after a number of practical tests carried out by specialised technicians who normally perform the work. The main contribution of this work lies on the implementation of a real-world application which, paired with a cloud-based system, can provide real-time functionalities to assist the operator during his/her work; beside this, as the machinery is constantly monitored for controlling the operating condition, the AR based solution is specifically designed to be compliant with safety regulations, which are not, in nowadays scenario, entrusted on digital solutions.

The remainder of this paper is organised as follows. Section 2 is an overview of the existing approach of augmented reality applied in industry, focusing on security and safety applications. Section 3 details the methodology used to develop the proposed solution. Section 4 reports the results obtained from the developed tests. Conclusions and future researches to increase the performances of the implemented architecture, are discussed in Sect. 5.

2   Related Works

Although the majority of literature studies regarding the AR application for industrial environment mainly refer to maintenance tasks [10], there exist interesting works focused on AR applications for security and safety in industrial environments.

For security and safety tasks, the interesting work of Vignali *et al.* [17] proposes an augmented reality application to increase the safety of operators in a food industry. The authors consider a hot-break juice extractor that separates seeds and peel, obtaining juice from fruits and vegetables. The maintenance task of the AR application is to forecast the cleaning of the porous sieves and their substitution that needs to be done every 12 h during the functioning. To verify the performance of the AR application, experimental tests have been performed in a real environment.

The research of Tatic [15] proposes an AR application for mobile devices to safeguard health and safety and the safe execution of tasks in a technological process, following virtual instructions in the workplace. The AR system is used to impart safety and work instructions to workers while carrying out the activities. In this regard, a client-server architecture has been created to project the relevant instructions on the screen of the mobile device and to keep track of all the phases performed by the worker. As an example, the application has been designed for certain tasks in electro-energy industrial plants.

The same author in another research [16] presents a system based on augmented reality technologies in order to reduce risk factors at work, the error rate and prevent accidents. The system implemented on mobile devices aims to project augmented reality instructions directly on the work. A worker is guided step by step by the system through the processing and safety procedures that must be performed. Considering the professional training of the workers and their work experience, the system is customised according to the skills of the workers. The authors proposed a case study by experimentally implementing the AR application as an education and safety system at work during the processing in a universal lathe of the Ugljevik thermal power plant in Bosnia and Herzegovina.

The study conducted by Talmaki *et al.* [14] has the aim to present the research conducted in collaboration by the University of Michigan and the largest electricity and gas service company in the area on the use of real-time kinematic GPS, combining with geospatial databases of underground utilities to design a new AR technology for the purpose to predict possible collisions between excavator and utility. From geospatial data available and superimposed in the workspace of an excavator through georeferenced augmented reality, they create 3D models of buried utilities so that the operator and the spotter have visual information on the position and the type of utility that exists in the near of the excavator. This preliminary research describes the first results obtained in the experimental phase.

In [7], the authors demonstrate the concept of "mobile Augmented Reality" (MAR) to improve the performance of building damage and the evaluation of safety *in-situ*. The study concerns the implementation of AR techniques when natural disasters occur. They create a mobile AR application that overlays various types of virtual reference or pre-disaster information on real post-disaster buildings data. The framework consists of four complexity levels and for each of these, the types of data, the required processing stages, the implementation of the AR and the use for damage assessment are described. They offer mAR prototypes for both internal and external purposes. Finally, to validate the proposed approach for assessing the damage and safety of the building, they conduct a user evaluation.

In [6], the authors put in evidence that the use of smart glasses for AR application, has a relevant importance for safety and health of human in industrial environments. They explain how this kind of device can help workers during the normal processing operations, protecting them in real time from dangerous situations, leaving some freedom of movement. Taking into account this study, also our approach uses smart glasses as device to implement AR application for security and safety in industrial environment, allowing to the operator to continuously frame what he is working on.

3   System Architecture

In this section is highlighted a preliminary description of the blocks composing the system architecture (depicted in Fig. 1), which are namely:

- Real plant (RP);
- Physical Sensor Network (PSN) at the plant level;
- Blackbox (BB);
- Distributed Cloud storage & Computing module (CM);
- Notification System (NS);
- AR Device (ARD).

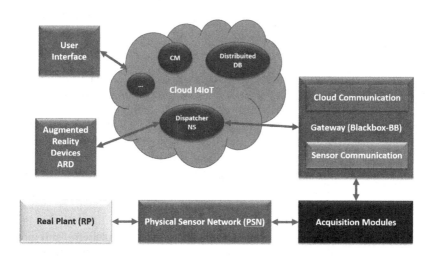

Fig. 1. Block Diagram of the system architecture.

An effective management of health and safety in the workplace starts from a preventive and accurate analysis, assessment and subsequent management of risks, which are related to the machine requirements, work equipment, plant or product, as well as behavioral factors. In this context, it is important to have a real scenario RP from which to extract risk specifications and to test the effectiveness of AR support and the alert notifications. The second step is to gather plant state variables using the PSN composed by acquisition modules and transducers. The BB, a dedicated embedded pc in which runs a custom software service, is used from one hand to receive data from acquisition module at PSN level, and from other to send data to the Cloud module after being configured via Auth2 authorization. The CM module is based on I4IoT, Advanced Cloud Solution for Industry 4.0, developed by Syncode Scarl, which provides a modular data acquisition core and a modular industrial communication protocols interface. The CM module includes features and functions, data storage, data management, analysis, simulation and visualization. The NS, instead, is fully-managed real-time messaging service allowing to send and receive messages between Cloud and ARD module in order to support the operator in maintenance tasks and to receive alert notifications. The NS is a new module developed and integrated into the I4Iot cloud service with the aim to create real-time communication between the players in the system and reducing any delays that could occur in a classic push-pull notification system. The management of the timing of sending alerts to operators is very important in order to prevent dangerous situations. It is worth to note that the architecture does not perform direct control actions on the real plant and it allows to perform monitoring tasks which can be used at the supervision level or for the decision support systems. In the rest of this section, we describe the notification cloud dispatcher and the real plant highlighting the main characteristics, but without a detailed description of their implementation.

3.1 Cloud and Real-Time Communication

The notifications dispatcher is the main module of this project in order to support the ARD to receive alert messages. The paradigm that is used to meet this specification is the Publish/Subscribe, or an architecture that meets the asynchronous and low coupling communication requirements between the communicating parts, required by the distributed systems (See Fig. 2). Publishers are actors who publish data and subscribers are other actors who subscribe to receive information published by publishers. Subscribers can express interest in a certain type of event and, whenever a Publisher publishes such event, the system will deliver it to all interested Subscribers.

This mechanism is based on the presence of an intermediate system, a Dispatcher, which receives the events (produced by the Publishers) and notifies them to the Subscriber, who act as event consumers. The Dispatcher in the Cloud Module is the node itself. Once the BB creates a connection with a Cloud node, it automatically becomes a Publisher. Instead, the ARD connecting to the node can choose what to subscribe to:

- All data in real-time;
- data from a specific analysis performed by the cloud node. To allow this, the services designated to the Cloud nodes are also considered Publishers.

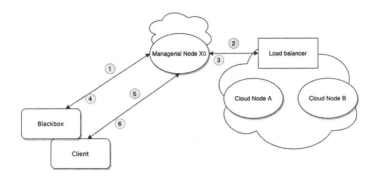

Fig. 2. Cloud real-time response and communication protocol.

In order to manage and customize the warning messages sent to the AR glasses, an ad hoc user interface has been developed that allows to create the notification rules following the occurrence of particular events. In detail, it is possible to insert both single rules in which only one variable of interest is selected and associates with a mathematical operator, such as "if the pressure V7 is greater than x bar then fire..", and mixed rules with multiple variables and conditions.

3.2 Pilot Case

The Cloud and AR architecture has been tested on a prototype plant designed by the Department of Industrial Engineering and Mathematical Sciences of Polytechnic University of Marche (Italy) in order to study the two-phase ejectors for the oil industry. In Fig. 3 is highlighted a section of real plant where is possible to see the high number of pipes and tank for the accumulation of fluid under pressure. The petroleum extraction can be done in two different ways, depending on the pressure of the subsoil: if it is sufficient, the raw material receives an upward thrust that it rises to the surface without any external action. Pressure pushes the oil inside the pipes to reach the oil well independently. In other cases, however, the pressure in the subsoil it is not enough to bring oil up and this requires the installation of additional pumps in order to convey the oil upwards and to provide the necessary thrust to let it come out to the surface. In this context, the plant described has been built to provide a valid alternative to the additional pumps, recreating the same effect through the join of an ejector with the pressure generated by an adjacent still active oil well. So, taking advantage of the ejector's potential and the pressure given by the engine fluid (See Fig. 4), a depression can be created to suck not only air, but any fluid, for example petroleum from a well where the pressure is no longer sufficient for a natural leak.

Fig. 3. Pilot case. A real plant section.

3.3   Risks Management

In a general context, in the Italian jurisdiction, the risks for the operator when using pressure equipment are managed by INAIL[1], the National Institute for Insurance against Accidents at Work, a public non-profit entity safeguarding workers against physical injuries and occupational diseases, and can be summarized as risk of:

- Explosion;
- toxic gas leakage;
- crushing.

Industrial pressure equipment, used for the containment or conversion of substances, and their components are subject to aging phenomena which, over time, can affect the safety levels of the entire plant as they increase the risk of loss of containment and reduce the performance of the entire system. Aging manifests itself as a general form of component degradation, which is associated not only with service time but with its condition and how it changes over time. The most common mechanisms by which equipment deteriorates represent a significant percentage of failures and component replacements. The knowledge of the "cause-effect" relationships, of the "boundary conditions-propagation speed", of

---

[1] https://www.inail.it/cs/internet/home.html.

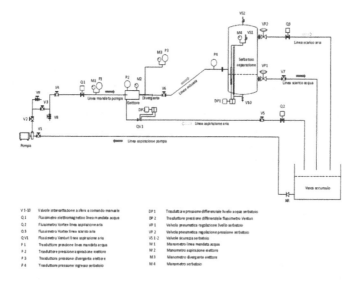

Fig. 4. Technical schema of the Plant used as pilot case for the experiment.

the "identification-measurement" and of the prevention measures are useful in order to monitor the equipment deterioration, to implement safe management and to reduce the operators risks.

Pressure Plant Anomalies. In the current configuration, as highlighted in Fig. 4, the smallest pump provides to the system a maximum pressure of 5.5 bar. The 780-L vertical tank/separator is tested and equipped with a 10 bar safety valve (*VS1*). The parts of the plant made with PVC pipe eventually connected with glued fittings can withstand pressures up to 6 bar but, as a precaution, it has been chosen to assume 4 bar as maximum pressure limit considering that a part of the plant is made of glued methacrylate.

The plant areas subject to risk issues are:

- The piping section starting from the ejector and ending to the tank, considering that the mixing section and the pressure recovery diverter, downstream of the ejector, are composed of methacrylate with glues pipes;
- the water level indication and measurement unit in the tank is partly made of methacrylate;
- the air intake line from the ejector to the valve V5.

Pressure Plant Operator Risks. The improvements in support of security can be summarized in:

- The entire plant section from the ejector to the two pneumatic valves (VP1 and VP2) should be placed under control and safety devices, as well as the air intake line;

- for the presence of the shut-off valve V6, (usually kept open), it is necessary to consider two separate zones and, for each of them, a safety pressure switch should be installed;
- Each pressure switch should intervene to interrupt the pump supply with a manual reset after having verified and eliminated the anomaly causes;
- It would be useful to provide each pressure switch with an alarm device, both visual and audible, configured to a value slightly lower than the maximum value of the block to avoid unexpected and unnecessary process interruptions.

In detail the principal criticalities, which are under control and supervised by system notification of AR device, are:

- **Anomaly 1** is due to an obstruction of the air intake line or closure of the V5 shut-off valve. In this case, a high vacuum condition could be created inside the ejector until its explosion. The alert message is "Alert!! High vacuum ejector. Explosion risk.".
- **Anomaly 2** Anomaly 2 is due to an obstruction of the ejector outlet line, or to the closing of the V6 shut-off valve, with the possibility of ejector malfunction, flooding of the air suction line and pump cavitation. The alert message is "Alert!! Pump cavitation. Explosion risk.".
- **Anomaly 3** is due to an obstruction of the water outlet duct from the tank, or to the closing of the shut-off valve V7. It causes uncontrolled growth of the liquid level inside the vertical separator with the possibility of ejector malfunction, flooding of the air suction line and pump cavitation. The alert message is "Alert!! High liquid level. Flooding risk.".
- **Anomaly 4** is due to an obstruction of the air outlet duct from the vertical separator. This would lead to an overpressure inside the vertical separator and, consequently, air leakage in the water discharge line at pressures higher than those tolerated by the pipeline. The alert message is "Alert!! Overpressure in vertical separator. Explosion risk.".
- **Anomaly 5** is due to an obstruction of the water inlet duct from the water tank to the pump, or to the closing of the V1 shut-off valve causing the pump cavitation. The alert message is "Alert!! Pump cavitation. High pressure air leakage risk.".

3.4   Smart Glasses Application

As stated in the introduction section, the purpose of this project is to test the effectiveness of Smart Glasses based AR application for "safety and security". The application has been thus designed to assist the operator in all the steps of the maintenance work of the pipes.

Hardware Components. After appropriate research among the available models [10], the devices chosen are Vuzix Blade[2], which have the following hardware

---

[2] https://www.vuzix.com/products/blade-smart-glasses.

features: full colour see through display with 8 MPix camera, Quad Core ARM CPU, gesture touch pad and voice recognition, support both Wi-Fi and Bluetooth connectivity. The operating system is based on Android 4.0, the battery ends up to 2 h. A more self-explanatory sight of the smart devices can be found in Fig. 5

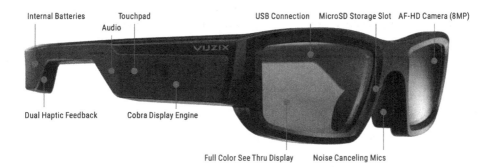

Fig. 5. Snapshot of the Vusix Blade smart devices (https://vuzix-website.s3.amazon aws.com/files/Content/pdfs/vuzix-blade-smart-glasses-d04.pdf)

3.5 Software Components

The application was developed within Unity 3D, exploiting Vuforia SDK for the implementation of the AR experience. The main reason is that Unity allows the development of multi-platform applications, with the possibility to directly build the APK application, suitable for the AR glasses. As such, it is designed for managing Vuforia SDK, which represents one of the most advanced solutions for the development of AR applications for mobile devices. The development can be performed as standard Android mobile app, so that it has been possible to include features like touch interaction for the touch controlled, notifications and direct connection via internet.

3.6 Application Workflow

The development of the application followed a strict pipeline, designed in a close cooperation with the INAIL experts, in order to be compliant with the requirements reported in the previous sections. More in deep, the application fulfils the following actions:

1. **training**: in specific focus points of the pipe plant, markers have been placed in order to indicate the workers which action is needed.
2. **alerting**: the application, in communication with the cloud-based architecture, displays notifications when an emergency risk occur.
3. **remote operator**: the application enables the user to visually communicate with the control station, in order to receive in real time the assistance in case of emergency.

4   Results and Discussion

The application has been validated after a number of practical tests carried out by specialized technicians who normally work in this kind of plants. Even if tests were conducted within the University Polytechnic of Marche labs, settings perfectly reproduce a real working environment. We also worked with the technicians during all phases of the application development, as well as to improve usability and build an application that meets the real needs of end users. As stated in the previous Subsect. 3.6, the application performs three main tasks that are depicted in the following.

4.1   Training Task

The first task is to guide the operator through sequential instructions to be made during the working activity; in particular:

- INSTRUCTIONS FOR REPLACING THE PNEUMATIC VALVE SEALS in case of leakage
  1. Make sure the system is switched off;
  2. Disconnect the valve supply;
  3. Close the compressed air supply knob to the valve;
  4. Close the electrovalve upstream shut-off valve;
  5. Close the electrovalve downstream shut-off valve;
  6. Secure the electrovalve by positioning the appropriate support underneath it;
  7. Unscrew the six bolts on the right using a number 22 wrench;
  8. Unscrew the six bolts on the left using a number 22 wrench
  9. Replace the two worn seals with the new ones making sure they have a 5 cm internal diameter and a 10 cm external diameter;
  10. Tighten bolts;
  11. Open the electrovalve upstream and downstream shut-off valves;
  12. Open the compressed air supply knob to the valve;
  13. Connect the valve power supply.
- INSTRUCTIONS FOR REPLACING A WORN-OUT PIPELINE
  1. Make sure the system is switched off;
  2. Close the upstream shut-off valve of the pipeline to be replaced;
  3. Close the downstream shut-off valve of the pipeline to be replaced
  4. Secure the pipeline to be replaced by positioning the appropriate support underneath it;
  5. **If flages are present**, unscrew the pipeline upstream and downstream flages;
  6. Replace the pipeline section;
  7. Screw the flages upstream and downstream of the pipeline
  8. Open the upstream and downstream shut-off valves of the pipeline to be replaced
  9. **If flages are not present**, cut the pipe section to be replaced;

10. Glue two fittings on the new pipe section
11. Wait for 10 min;
12. Glue the new pipe section, with the fittings, to the system pipes;
13. Wait at least one hour before restarting the system.

To recall the aforementioned instructions, visual markers have been placed on specific locations of the pipes. In order to deliver the instructions, we though two ways to train the worker: i) providing overlaid virtual labels and ii) visualize a written manual in pdf format. The user, to switch to the next instruction, just simply have to swipe with the right hand on the side tough bar, built-in the smart glasses. The running application is depicted in Figs. 6 and 7.

4.2 Alerting Task

The second functionality of the application is the visualisation of notifications. This function exploits the standard notification system of Android based apps. The innovation in this case lies in that of the smart glasses are in communication with the cloud system prior described. Once the cloud based architecture discloses a potential risk for the operator, e.g. pressure or temperature thresholds overcoming, the device visualises the notification. This way, there is not the need for any further action by the operator. The alerting task is real time and guides the user to the right place where the risk occurred An example of real time notification is showed in Fig. 8.

4.3 Remote Operator Task

Lastly, the system has been developed in order to fulfil the remote operation function. In practice, the operator, in case of necessity, is enabled to communicate

Fig. 6. Example of training on the job. In this case, the step three of the procedure is showed.

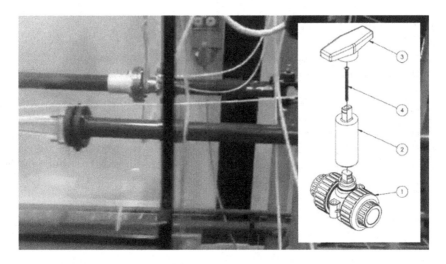

Fig. 7. Example of training on the job. In this case, the picture of assembling instruction is showed.

in real time with a remotely connected colleague, which can interact with the operator who is conducting an inspection. In case of necessity, as reported in the example (see Fig. 9), the operator open a call with a fixed workstation, where a colleague can deliver real time instruction, seeing exactly what the operator is facing with in the working environment.

The application with the functionalities describes so far, has been tested inside the laboratories, with the machinery in working conditions. It has been developed in a close cooperation with safety and security experts, operators and developers in order to be compliant with a real-world scenario. However, the application is still in a validation phase, and further usability test are required in order to assess its potential for security. Some remarks are however deserved, in terms of both software and hardware sides. Vuzix Blade allows an easy development, as the application is Android-based and does not require particular skills. The Vuzix also provides a SDK (not available for Unity) with specific libraries but most of the features are already exposed. Hand gestures can be implemented for a friendly interaction, and this aspect is very important for workers, as they can exert their job hand-free. Another important aspect that cannot be underestimated is the connectivity. Our architecture is designed to send and receive information in real time, and this represent the main contribution of the proposed system. Being the glass able to communicate with the cloud, it has been fundamental for receiving alerts in real time and to use the same system to develop the remote operator task, in a all-in-one solution. Despite the positive aspects above mentioned, it is fair to say that Vusix Blade suffer some technical limitations: (i) The smart classes are prone to overheating, and this aspect can hamper the operational conditions for the worker. (ii) w.r.t. previous models, the application runs quite smooth, marker recognition is fast and in

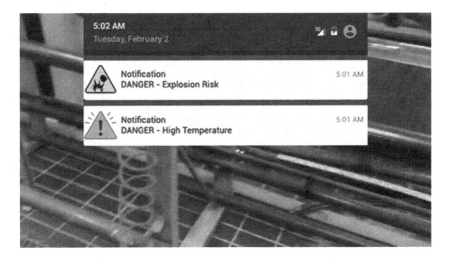

Fig. 8. Alerting task. Example of notifications sent by the cloud system in real time.

Fig. 9. Remote operator function running.

terms of frame-coherency it can be state that the hardware is mature enough to deploy real-world applications. (iii) another limitation is the battery duration, as it is limited to one hour (even less for the remote operator functionality). (iv) For safety and security purposes, it would be useful to develop a localisation system to deliver location-based services but, with the current version, the alerting system is only entrusted on notification and marker recognition. This aspect represent a limitation for the deploy of such solution in I4.0 real environments.

5   Conclusion and Outlook

In this work, an AR application for safety and security purposes has been presented. It is well known that the aid that AR can bring in the world of Industry

4.0 is invaluable. However, different functions has been developed in order to assess and validate how AR can make I4.0 environments more safe for the workers. The experiments have been conducted into our laboratories, in order to set up a system that is now ready to be used in real I4.0 environments. The literature proposes application developed for training and/or for the smart operator, but few has been done in terms of safety and security. The developed system can be seen as a proof of concept, which can be a baseline for future experiments. In fact, despite the system has been developed together with expert of safety and security, the requirements of a multimedia approach to this issue are not still widespread. The cloud based infrastructure proved to be the key solution for exchanging information between the machinery and the smart device; it can be extended to any environment, making the application scalable to other machinery and case studies. This test was also useful as a benchmark for the research community, since the application is paired in real time and provide different functionalities in the same application. The User Interface and the usability of the application gave us promising insights, but no user tests have been conducted; we expect that in the upcoming future, the application can be test by both experts and non experts in order to update the current version. By performing more test with real user, we are confident that it will be possible to draw guidelines and protocols for the development of AR applications for safety and security. The low performance of the camera does not allow to get a robust tracking of the scene, so that the use of real time notification can be useful, but it requires a location-based service that we foresee to develop in the next release of the application. Finally, it is fair to say that, due to the COVID-19 lock down, the activities has been delayed, and the validation of the application still requires an in-depth analysis.

Acknowledgments. Special thanks is dedicated to the Spin-off of Polytechnic University of Marche, Syncode Scarl, for having supported an important research project and for accepting to integrate our AR device functionality in its Cloud infrastructures.

Funding. This research was funded by INAIL (Istituto Nazionale per l'Assicurazione Contro gli Infortuni sul Lavoro), the Italian National Institute for Insurance against Accidents atWork grant number BRIC 2018 project titled "Sviluppo di soluzioni smart attraverso metodologie Digital Twin per aumentare la sicurezza degli operatori durante i processi di manutenzione degli impianti produttivi" ("Development of smart solutions through Digital Twin methodologies to increase operator safety during production plant maintenance processes")—BRIC ID12.

References

1. Azuma, R.T.: A survey of augmented reality. Presence Teleoper. Virt. Environ **6**(4), 355–385 (1997)
2. Bekele, M.K., Pierdicca, R., Frontoni, E., Malinverni, E.S., Gain, J.: A survey of augmented, virtual, and mixed reality for cultural heritage. J. Comput. Cult. Heritage (JOCCH) **11**(2), 1–36 (2018)

3. Chang, Y.J., Liu, H.H., Kang, Y.S., Kao, C.C., Chang, Y.S.: Using augmented reality smart glasses to design games for cognitive training. In: 2016 13th International Conference on Remote Engineering and Virtual Instrumentation (REV), pp. 252–253. IEEE (2016)
4. Clini, P., Frontoni, E., Quattrini, R., Pierdicca, R.: Augmented reality experience: from high-resolution acquisition to real time augmented contents. Adv. Multimedia **2014**, 18 (2014)
5. De Paolis, L.T., Ricciardi, F., Manes, C.L.: Augmented reality in radiofrequency ablation of the liver tumors. In: Computational Vision and Medical Image Processing V: Proceedings of the 5th ECCOMAS Thematic Conference on Computational Vision and Medical Image Processing, VipIMAGE 2015, Tenerife, Spain, October 19–21, 2015, p. 279. CRC Press (2015)
6. Kim, S., Nussbaum, M.A., Gabbard, J.L.: Augmented reality "smart glasses" in the workplace: industry perspectives and challenges for worker safety and health. IIE Trans. Occupat. Ergon. Hum. Factors **4**(4), 253–258 (2016)
7. Kim, W., Kerle, N., Gerke, M.: Mobile augmented reality in support of building damage and safety assessment. Nat. Hazards Earth Syst. Sci. **16**(1), 287 (2016)
8. Langfinger, M., Schneider, M., Stricker, D., Schotten, H.D.: Addressing security challenges in industrial augmented reality systems. In: 2017 IEEE 15th International Conference on Industrial Informatics (INDIN), pp. 299–304. IEEE (2017)
9. Liu, C., Huot, S., Diehl, J., Mackay, W., Beaudouin-Lafon, M.: Evaluating the benefits of real-time feedback in mobile augmented reality with hand-held devices. In: Proceedings of the 2012 ACM Annual Conference on Human Factors in Computing Systems - CHI 2012. Association for Computing Machinery (ACM) (2012). https://doi.org/10.1145%2F2207676.2208706
10. Pierdicca, R., Frontoni, E., Pollini, R., Trani, M., Verdini, L.: The use of augmented reality glasses for the application in industry 4.0. In: De Paolis, L.T., Bourdot, P., Mongelli, A. (eds.) AVR 2017. LNCS, vol. 10324, pp. 389–401. Springer, Cham (2017). https://doi.org/10.1007/978-3-319-60922-5_30
11. Pierdicca, R., et al.: Smart maintenance of riverbanks using a standard data layer and augmented reality. Comput. Geosci. **95**, 67–74 (2016)
12. Remondino, M.: Applicazioni delle tecnologie immersive nell'industria e realtà aumentata come innovazione di processo nella logistica: stato dell'arte ed implicazioni manageriali
13. Salah, H., MacIntosh, E., Rajakulendran, N.: Wearable tech: leveraging Canadian innovation to improve health. MaRS Discovery District (2014)
14. Talmaki, S.A., Dong, S., Kamat, V.R.: Geospatial databases and augmented reality visualization for improving safety in urban excavation operations. In: Construction Research Congress 2010: Innovation for Reshaping Construction Practice, pp. 91–101 (2010)
15. Tatić, D.: An augmented reality system for improving health and safety in the electro-energetics industry. Facta Universitatis, Ser. Electr. Energet. **31**(4), 585–598 (2018)
16. Tatić, D., Tešić, B.: The application of augmented reality technologies for the improvement of occupational safety in an industrial environment. Comput. Ind. **85**, 1–10 (2017)
17. Vignali, G., Bertolini, M., Bottani, E., Di Donato, L., Ferraro, A., Longo, F.: Design and testing of an augmented reality solution to enhance operator safety in the food industry. Int. J. Food Eng. **14**(2) (2017)

Evaluating the Suitability of Several AR Devices and Tools for Industrial Applications

Edoardo Battegazzorre⬤, Davide Calandra⬤, Francesco Strada⬤,
Andrea Bottino⬤, and Fabrizio Lamberti$^{(\boxtimes)}$⬤

Politecnico di Torino, Dipartimento di Automatica e Informatica, Turin, Italy
{edoardo.battegazzorre,davide.calandra,francesco.strada,
andrea.bottino,fabrizio.lamberti}@polito.it

Abstract. In recent years, there has been an increasing interest in Industrial Augmented Reality (IAR) due to its prominent role in the ongoing revolution known as Industry 4.0. For companies and industries it is essential to evaluate carefully which of the developed AR-based technologies to adopt, and when, for tasks such as training, maintenance, assistance, and collaborative design. There is also a wide array of hardware and software alternatives on the market, characterized by a significant heterogeneity in terms of functionalities, performance and cost. With this work, our objective is to study and compare some widely available devices and Software Development Kits (SDKs) for AR by leveraging a set of evaluation criteria derived from the actual literature which have been deemed capable to qualify the above assets as suitable for industrial applications. Such criteria include the operative range, robustness, accuracy and stability. Both marker-based and marker-less solutions have been considered, in order to investigate a wide range of possible use cases.

Keywords: Augmented Reality · Industrial Augmented Reality · Evaluation · Marker detection · Positional tracking

1 Introduction

The last years have been characterized by a growing interest in Industrial Augmented Reality (IAR) applications, mainly because of their key role in the ongoing developments framed under the Industry 4.0 umbrella [2,7]. Moreover, the continuous advancements in the field of Augmented Reality (AR) translate into an ever-broader choice of devices characterized by progressively a lower cost, higher performance, and a growing set of capabilities that can be relevant for

This work has been supported by a study funded by SIPAL Spa under the research project titled "Cantiere Tecnologico per infrastrutture militari e civili (Unmanned vehicles and Virtual facilities)", Regione Puglia, and by the VR@POLITO initiative.

L. T. De Paolis and P. Bourdot (Eds.): AVR 2020, LNCS 12243, pp. 248–267, 2020.
https://doi.org/10.1007/978-3-030-58468-9_19

industrial scenarios. However, these hardware and software solutions are characterized by significant heterogeneity in terms of technical specifications and features offered. Therefore, it is essential to provide methods for comparing them and assessing their behavior in industrial settings. In [3], Duenser et al. investigated, through a literature survey, different techniques for performing evaluations in the context of AR, providing an overview of each technique and discussing how they were used in the specific study. They also proposed a taxonomy of such techniques, which classifies them into objective measures, subjective measures, qualitative analyses, usability evaluations, and informal evaluations. In particular, objective measures appeared to be the most adopted evaluation technique over the time-span considered in [3]. As an example, the authors of [1] presented an objective evaluation of different IAR tools and Software Development Kits (SDKs) for a specific industrial setting, namely the shipyard. The research focused on evaluating marker-based detection techniques; the authors intentionally disregarded marker-less 3D model-based tracking approaches, stating that they would not satisfy the minimum requirements for industrial applications in terms of hardware performance, storage, and robustness in highly dynamic environments.

Despite the effectiveness of objective measures, investigating specific characteristics of selected devices and tools requires the use of other evaluation approaches. For example, the authors of [5] leveraged a subjective evaluation protocol for assessing the capabilities of Mixed Reality (MR) in the field of production and logistics. Users involved in the study were first asked to engage in an "item-picking" scenario (using the Microsoft HoloLens^{TM}) and then to fill in a questionnaire investigating aspects such as realism of the projection, visibility of the holograms, ease of interaction, comfort, ergonomics, and satisfaction.

The evaluation protocol should also take into account the specific requirements of the industrial context, as done in [8,10]. Although requirements such as cost-effectiveness, data security, and applicable regulations have to be partially or totally addressed at the software level, the device to use still plays an essential role in terms of set-up time, system reliability, quality of presentation, real-time capabilities and ergonomics. To this end, the possibility to use, in industrial contexts, devices and technologies coming from the entertainment sector (like in [6,11]) requires careful analyses. If it is true that these devices are generally quite affordable and offer a broad set of general-purpose features, they are also characterized by lower precision, reliability, and employability compared with solutions specifically designed for the industry. For instance, in [9], the authors proved that Lighthouse 1.0[1] (the tracking technology exploited by some HTC® Vive^{TM} devices) is unsuitable for a particular class of scientific tasks involving the accurate visual stimulation of self-motion in a virtual environment.

The present work provides an objective evaluation of three AR devices, namely the Microsoft HoloLens^{TM}, the Samsung® Galaxy Tab S4 Android^{TM}, and the DreamWorld DreamGlass (each combined with different AR libraries) to assess the viability of such technologies in industrial applications and

---

[1] https://www.vive.com/us/accessory/base-station/.

Table 1. Marker-based configurations (devices and libraries) considered in the study.

Device	Library	Type of marker	Marker sample	Maximum number of markers
HoloLens^{TM} / Android^{TM}	Vuforia	ArMarker		2.147.483.648
HoloLens^{TM}	SpectatorView Marker Detection	ArUco 6×6		1.000
Android^{TM} Tablet	ARCore	ArMarker		2.147.483.648

Table 2. Marker-less configurations (devices and libraries) considered in the study.

Device	SDK	Tracking technology
DreamGlass + NOLO	DreamWorld + NOLO VR	Outside-in
HoloLens^{TM}	Holo-Toolkit	Inside-out

environments. In particular, we focused on different tracking methods available for each of the considered device-SDK pairs. Hence, we first assessed the performance of the different marker detection techniques, and then we moved to analyze the marker-less sensor-based tracking techniques (either inside-out or outside-in) offered by these devices. Table 1 and Table 2 summarize the different configurations (device, SDK, type of marker, etc.) considered in the evaluation. The methodology used to assess marker-based IAR was inspired by the work reported in [1], extending the previous analysis to encompass also different marker types and sizes, more evaluation metrics, and a larger number of devices/SDKs. The sensor-based analysis applied the same methodology exploited in [9] to different positional tracking techniques. It should be noted that, following the approach in [1], we did not consider the 3D model-based tracking techniques because of their poorer suitability for the context of interest.

2 Selected Hardware and Software

This section illustrates the different hardware and software solutions included in the evaluation, which were selected to cover a broad set of characteristics. Thus, the analysis included devices that are both enterprise-grade and consumer-grade, head-mounted and hand-held, tethered and untethered, etc. On the software side, native solutions provided through the official SDKs were considered when available, and the Unity game engine (2018.4) was leveraged to implement the measuring tools required for the experiments.

2.1   Microsoft HoloLens™

The Microsoft HoloLens™ (1ˢᵗ generation) is an optical see-through AR Head-Mounted Display (HMD). The device uses an inside-out SLAM (Simultaneous Localization And Mapping) positional tracking to register the virtual contents with the surrounding (real) space. The principal method for aligning virtual and real contents is based on so-called spatial "anchors", i.e., geometric descriptors attached to specific points that help the device to track them over time. Another tracking possibility relies on the front-mounted RGB camera of the HMD for detecting fiducial markers, with different approaches detailed in the following.

ArUco Marker Detection. The HoloLens™ supports an official marker tracking solution based on the ArUco markers [4,12]. The plug-in provides two different detection strategies:

- *stationary*, for markers that are known to be fixed in space; this strategy applies heuristics to filter out noisy detections;
- *moving*, for non-stationary markers; this strategy averages multiple observations and does not apply any noise reduction filter.

In the evaluation, both strategies were separately analyzed using the default algorithms configuration provided by the vendor.

Vuforia. This library[2] probably represents the simplest method to implement the marker detection with the HoloLens™, since it is officially supported and allows for the combination of marker detection capabilities with the device's spatial mapping in a modality named Extended Tracking. The Extended Tracking feature was intentionally disabled in our evaluation. Regarding the implementation details, in the analysis, Vuforia 8.3.8 was used, generating the markers with the ArMarker[3] tool.

2.2   Android™

Android™ devices can exploit AR through the native ARCore SDK or a set of third-party libraries (e.g., Vuforia, Wikitude[4], Kudan AR SDK[5]). In this work, the native AR solution was tested against the Vuforia library using an Android-based tablet device, namely, a Samsung® Tab S4).

---

[2] https://www.ptc.com/en/products/augmented-reality/vuforia.
[3] https://github.com/shawnlehner/ARMaker.
[4] https://www.wikitude.com/.
[5] https://www.xlsoft.com/en/products/kudan/ar-sdk.html.

ARCore. This library offers a series of tools to implement a marker-based tracking solution through the Augmented Images API[6]. The API can recognize a maximum of 20 concurrent reference images providing as output position, rotation and size of each image. The trackable images must be included in an internal database that has a maximum size of 1000 elements. Similarly to the HoloLens, ARCore can also perform SLAM to infer the device's position in the real environment and, thus, use it to improve the robustness and stability of the marker-based tracking. However, to better characterize the API, this feature was disabled in the evaluation. Again, ArMarker was used for generating ARCore-specific markers.

Vuforia. The Vuforia library for Android[TM] is the same used for the HoloLens[TM]. Thus, the same settings were used (i.e., version 8.3.8, Extended Tracking turned off and markers generated with ArMarker).

2.3   DreamWorld DreamGlass[TM] and NOLO[TM]

The DreamGlass[TM] is an optical see-through AR HMD characterized by a native 3-DOF (Degrees of Freedom) tracking. Opposite to the HoloLens[TM], this is a tethered device and, thus, requires an external computation unit (a personal computer running Windows or an Android[TM] smartphone). The device is equipped with two front cameras, an IR camera used for gesture recognition, and a RGB one. According to the vendor, these cameras can be enabled simultaneously only in Android[TM]. This fact, along with the lack of support for native marker detection and the impossibility to deploy Vuforia applications as Windows stand-alone executables, make it particularly hard to support marker-based tracking. To cope with this limitation, the vendor suggests to integrate the headset with the NOLO[TM] 6-DOF optical-inertial motion tracking system. The NOLO[TM] kit includes a single table-top base station, a wired HMD tracker, and two wireless controllers. In the evaluation, the DreamGlass[TM] and the NOLO[TM] were used in combination with a backpack laptop (precisely, the MSI VR One 7RE) in order to eliminate the encumbrance of the wired components (i.e., the HMD and its tracker).

3   Methodology

The definition of the evaluation methodology was preceded by an investigation phase aimed to identify the basic requirements for industrial AR applications. As reported in [13], IAR applications can be subdivided in many use cases: manual assembly, robot programming and operations, maintenance, process monitoring, training, process simulation, quality inspection, picking process, operational setup ergonomics and safety. Some features may be more or less relevant in relation to the various industrial activities. For example, the device field of view

---

[6] https://developers.google.com/ar/develop/c/augmented-images.

(FOV) may be a key factor for the maintenance/assembly of large elements (e.g. vehicles), but it may be less relevant for other activities (e.g. item picking). As a result of the investigation, the need for a proper tracking technology to register virtual contents with real objects proved to be the most common requirement among all the use cases. Based on this consideration, the initial focus was put on marker detection techniques, considering alternative methods when the former were unavailable or not applicable.

3.1 Marker-Based AR

We defined the following four metrics for assessing the viability of each device or SDK in an IAR context: *Detection Distance* (DD), *Loss Distance* (LD), *Detection Rate* (DR) and *Stability* (ST). The experimental setup for the evaluation of each metric is illustrated hereinafter.

Detection Distance (DD) and Loss Distance (LD). When focusing on the evaluation of a marker detection technique, one of the first aspects to consider is the maximum distance at which the device is capable of tracking a marker (DD distance). To measure this distance, we placed a marker on a tripod at the same height as the device tested. Then, the experimenter began to walk towards the marker, starting from a distance at which the marker detection was not occurring and stopping when the first detection was registered (Fig. 1 and 2, left). Afterwards, the experimenter measured the LD distance by slowly walking backward while keeping the marker in the device's FOV until the tracking was lost. It is worth noting that we could measure the LD metric only for the Vuforia and ARCore configurations. The reason is that, after detection, both SDKs exploit tracking techniques to maintain marker identification as long as possible even for considerable distances. On the contrary, ArUco Marker Detection is characterized by a completely different behavior since it only provides information about marker detection and lacks a tracking component. Hence, in order to filter out spurious or unrepeatable detection events, the ArUco DD value was measured as the distance at which the detection occurs steadily with at least a frequency of 1 Hz. In contrast, LD was measured as the first sampled distance at which the above requirement was not fulfilled.

For all the SDKs, DD and LD measures were repeated with different configurations of three parameters, as summarized below (Fig. 1, right):

- four angles of approach (0°, 30°, 45° and 60°);
- three marker sizes (5, 10 and 20 cm);
- two lighting conditions (artificial and natural light).

Detection Rate (DR). A further metric considered in the evaluation refers to the marker identification capabilities of the considered devices and SDKs within a given time interval measured at predetermined distances (Table 3). The DR metric is computed as:

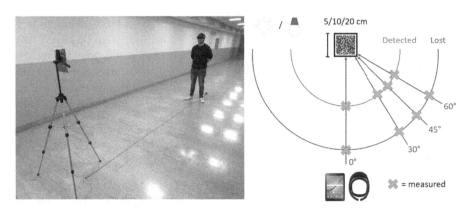

Fig. 1. Setting for DD/LD/DR/ST with artificial light using the HoloLens™ (left) and experimental setup for DD/LD (right)

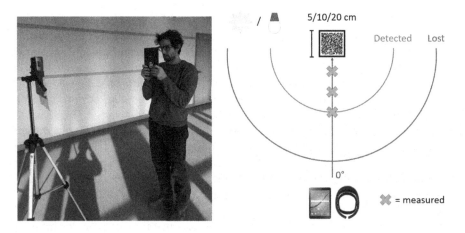

Fig. 2. Setting for DD/LD/DR/ST with natural light using an Android tablet (left) and experimental setup for DR/ST (right)

$$DR(\%) = \frac{N_D}{N_T} \tag{1}$$

where N_D is the number of times the detection occurred in less than 5 seconds, and N_T is the number of detection attempts (10 in the evaluation). The setup of this experiment is similar to the first one, but using a single angle of approach (namely, $0°$, see Fig. 2, right).

Stability. This metric represents the capability to detect the same position and rotation of a static marker over time. The setup used for this experiment was the same used for the DR metric (Fig. 2, right). After detecting the marker with an angle of approach of $0°$, the detected positions and rotations along all the

Table 3. Distances for DR and ST measures: ✓ indicates a distance included in the analysis, (✓) a distance included only if necessary (DD < 0.625 m or DD > 15 m).

Measure	Distance (m)										
	<0.625	0.625	1.25	2.5	3.75	5	7.5	10	12.5	15	>15
DR	(✓)		✓	✓		✓	✓	✓			(✓)
ST	(✓)	✓	✓	✓	✓	✓	✓	✓	✓	✓	(✓)

three axes were sampled for 5 seconds at 50 Hz. Measurements were repeated at multiple fixed distances (Table 3) for the three marker sizes (5, 10 and 20 cm), and with both natural and artificial lighting. Positional Stability (PS) is computed as the pooled standard deviation of all samples on each axis as:

$$PS = \sqrt{\frac{\theta_x^2 + \theta_y^2 + \theta_z^2}{3}} \tag{2}$$

where θ_x, θ_y and θ_z represent the samples' variances for each axis. Assuming a completely static marker, the ideal PS should be 0, meaning that all registered values are equal. Angular Stability (AS) is measured as the average of the angular dispersion on all the three axes which, for a given axis, is computed as:

$$R = \sqrt{\left(\frac{\sum cos\alpha}{n}\right)^2 + \left(\frac{\sum sin\alpha}{n}\right)^2} \tag{3}$$

where AS $\in$ [0,1]. The upper bound indicates the concentration of all the samples in the same direction and represents the optimal AS behavior, whereas the lower bound indicates uniform dispersion.

3.2 Marker-Less AR

When marker detection is not available (or not suitable) for a given application, other techniques have to be considered. If the device supports positional tracking, this feature can be exploited to align the virtual content with its real counterpart over time. Hence, *Tracking Accuracy* (TA) becomes an essential metric for studying the suitability of a given configuration for the applications of interest.

Tracking Accuracy. The evaluation of the TA for HoloLens[TM] and NOLO[TM] was based on collecting positional and rotational data on a grid of known reference points and comparing them with a ground truth.

The grid for the NOLO[TM] devices was composed of cells of size 60×60 cm included in the active tracking area specified by the vendor. This area has a range of 5 m and a FOV of 100° from the base station, resulting in a total of 60 valid points for the evaluation (Fig. 4, left). The base station was positioned on a stand at 53.3 cm from the floor. During the experiment, the tracker under

Fig. 3. Measurements of TA for the NOLO^{TM} HMD (left) and controller (right).

testing was placed in each point of the grid, and its position was recorded for 1 second at a 50 Hz frequency to minimize possible jittering effects. This procedure was repeated separately for the HMD tracker (installed on the DreamGlass^{TM}) and for one of its controllers in three different configurations:

– *front*: the controller is pointed towards the base station, parallel to the bisector of its FOV;
– *top*: the controller is pointed towards the ceiling;
– *side*: the controller is pointed sideways to the right (from the point of view of the base station).

To ensure the stability of the trackers during measurements, the HMD was placed on the ground (Fig. 3, left), whereas the controllers were mounted on an adjustable tripod at 1.5 m from the floor (Fig. 3, right), which is the height suggested by NOLO^{TM} for the calibration of the device. The mean positional and rotational errors for each axis (X, Y, and Z) were computed for each grid point by first collecting measurements over one second and then subtracting the ground truth. Finally, these differences were averaged again to obtain the mean positional and rotational errors for each configuration. We underline that, as detailed in Sect. 4.5, the controllers seem to suffer from a notable rotational drift during regular use (probably due to issues with sensor fusion between optical data from the base station and inertial data coming from the gyros/accelerometers). Thus, we tried to minimize this effect by re-calibrating the controllers every three measurements following the procedure suggested by the vendor.

A similar procedure was then adopted for the TA evaluation of the HoloLens^{TM} tracking. Since this tracking does not require any external sensors, the user could theoretically move and operate in an arbitrarily large area. With this fact in mind, in order to guarantee the same experimental conditions used to evaluate the NOLO^{TM} TA, a rectangular reference grid of 77 points superimposed to the previous one was drafted (Fig. 4, right). An experimenter

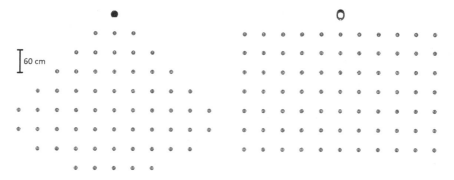

Fig. 4. Grids used to evaluate the TA for the NOLO^{TM} (left) and HoloLens^{TM} (right).

wearing the HoloLens^{TM} carefully stepped onto each of the grid points, where the position and orientation of the headset were sampled, like before, at 50 Hz for 1 s.

4 Experimental Results

In this section, the results of the experimental activities are presented, firstly focusing on the marker-based evaluation metrics described in Sect. 3.1, then concluding with the marker-less metric introduced in Sect. 3.2.

4.1 Detection Distance

Plots in Figs. 5, 6, 7 and 8 summarize the data collected for four of the pairs device/SDK under analysis. Data concerning Android^{TM}/Vuforia have not been reported since the behavior was substantially similar to the HoloLens^{TM} counterpart (Fig. 5) in both lighting conditions. Results obtained with artificial lighting will be firstly exposed, followed by a discussion of the meaningful differences in comparison with natural lighting. In general, the plots show fairly predictable trends, in which the DD increases with the marker size and decreases with the angle of approach.

The pair showing the best performance was the HoloLens^{TM}/ArUco Moving (Fig. 6), which reaches a DD of 16.85 m under the most favorable conditions (20 cm marker, angle of approach of 0°) and 1.96 m in the least favorable one (5 cm marker, angle of approach of 60°). The worst performing pair was Android^{TM}/ARCore (Fig. 8), with a DD of 0.86 m under the most favorable conditions, and a complete detection failure in every test performed at 60°. All the other pairs showed maximum DD values between 2 and 3 m.

HoloLens^{TM}/ArUco Moving (Fig. 6) had the most linear trend, while its Stationary counterpart (Fig. 7) behaved very erratically as, counter-intuitively, the 0° angle of approach showed the worst performance. This result could be attributed to how the tracking algorithm works. One could speculate that, due

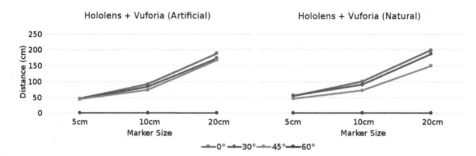

Fig. 5. DD for HoloLens^{TM}/Vuforia with artificial (left) and natural lighting (right).

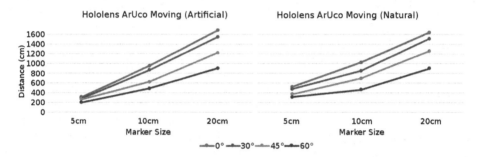

Fig. 6. DD for ArUco Moving with artificial (left) and natural lighting (right).

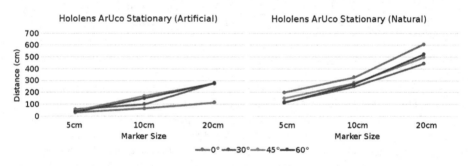

Fig. 7. DD for ArUco Stationary with artificial (left) and natural lighting (right).

to the filtering behavior of the given detection strategy, the framing of the full marker at 0° yields a substantial number of noisy samples, which are then discarded when filtering is applied on position and rotation. When the experimenter approaches the marker at a wider angle, actual detections are less frequent so that they could appear as more precise from the heuristics' perspective and, thus, less prone to be discarded.

Vuforia (Fig. 5) showed difficulties in detecting markers at the steepest angle (60°) in almost every case except for a few detections obtained on Android^{TM} in artificial lighting conditions. The different specifications of the cameras on the

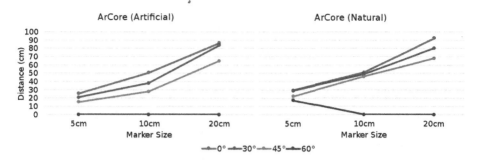

Fig. 8. DD for Android^{TM}/ArCore with artificial (left) and natural lighting (right).

various devices (including their distinct distortion parameters and sensitivity to light) could explain this behavior.

With natural lighting, the trends remained the same for all the pairs. Again, the best performance was obtained by HoloLens^{TM}/ArUco Moving with DD values of 16.38 m and 3.1 m under the most/least favorable conditions. Android^{TM} with ArCore still scored the lowest distances with 0.92 m under the best conditions and a complete failure under the worst ones. However, it can be observed that, under these conditions, only the smallest 5 cm marker was detected at 60°. This result can be explained by the fact that distances were so short (15.5 cm) that camera distortion could play a significant role, making it impossible to recognize larger markers. The only pair that showed improvements with the brighter, natural lighting was the HoloLens^{TM}/ArUco Stationary pair, having its DD values doubled (3 to 6 m in the best case scenario). Still, this SDK behaved oddly as the DD does not seem to be inversely proportional to the angle of approach. Again, this result underlines the sensibility of the algorithm to minimal lighting variations, possibly tied to the behavior of the filter that discards noisier detections.

4.2 Loss Distance

As previously mentioned, only Vuforia and ARCore were able to preserve the tracking farther than the initial DD thresholds, as shown in Figs. 9, 10 and 11. The blue part of each glyph represents the initial DD, whereas the orange part shows the threshold at which the tracking is lost (LD). In all the figures, data collected with both artificial (left) and natural lighting (right) are reported.

From the plots, it is evident that Vuforia outperforms ARCore, showing improvements that go from 92% to 338% of the initial DD. For ARCore, the improvements are more marginal, ranging from 15% to 96% of the initial DD. It is worth pointing out that natural lighting has a negative effect on the average range extension, especially for Vuforia, for which the average improvement decreases from 261% to 162%. It should be noted, however, that there is a tradeoff between tracking distance and tracking stability, as illustrated in the following sections.

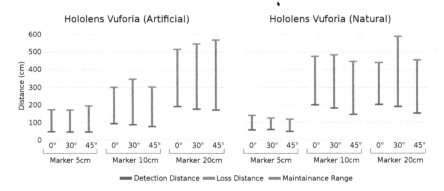

Fig. 9. DD and LD for HoloLens^TM/Vuforia with artificial (left) and natural (right) lighting. (Color figure online)

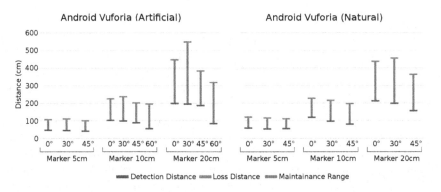

Fig. 10. DD and LD for Android^TM/Vuforia with artificial (left) and natural (right) lighting. (Color figure online)

4.3 Detection Rate

The results for this metric are reported in Fig. 12. Two very distinct behaviors can be observed. DR for Vuforia and ARCore immediately go from 100% to 0% as soon as the measurement is performed at distances larger than the DD threshold (Sect. 4.1). On the contrary, all the ArUco detections were successful (100%) when attempted at distances smaller than the DD, and DR continuously decreases as the HoloLens^TM moves away from the DD threshold. This degradation is more evident under natural lighting conditions.

4.4 Stability

Overall, both PS and RS showed no remarkable differences between artificial and natural lighting. For this reason, the discussion will focus on the behavior of PS and AS in artificial lighting conditions. In Fig. 13, PS (top) and AS (bottom) are presented as a function of distance for all the five configurations. Measurements

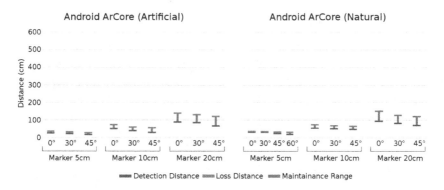

Fig. 11. DD and LD for Android^{TM}/ArCore with artificial (left) and natural (right) lighting. (Color figure online)

were performed at fixed distances (Table 3), not exceeding the measured LD for the specific device/SDK pair; for this reason, some lines in the plots fall straight to zero over a certain distance.

PS is significantly low, generally under 0.02, and presents a stable behavior independent of the distance at which it was measured. Nonetheless, HoloLens^{TM} ArUco Moving was the only pair capable of detecting markers at a distances larger than 5 m. Over this threshold, PS starts to increase notably, deteriorating up to 30 times (at 12.5 m) compared to the closest point (62.5 cm). Finally, PS values are comparable also across different marker sizes. However, the number of measurable PS is smaller, given the shorter range in which the marker was detectable (Sects. 4.1 and 4.2).

Similarly, AS results were very stable when observed at close distances, with an average angular dispersion close to 1 for all devices/SDKs, except for Android^{TM} ARCore, which never reached a value higher than 0.7. The deterioration of AS at increasing distances follows, in general, a linear behavior with a 20 cm marker. Contrary to PS, degradation is more evident reducing the marker size. However, AS for HoloLens^{TM} ArUco Moving remains higher than 0.5, whereas the AS values of the other pairs fall in the [0.2, 0.4] range.

A general exception regards HoloLens^{TM} ArUco Stationary with artificial lighting, for which a true range does not exist (DD values were always below 1.25 m). For this reason, it was possible to sample PS and AS only at a single point, at which the device/SDK showed again the best performance among all the five configurations.

4.5 Tracking Accuracy

The plots in Figs. 14, 15, 16, 17 and 18 present the differences between the average measured positions and rotations and the ground truth. Both the single points and their interpolation surfaces are shown, providing an overview of the topology of the plane reconstructed by the tracking devices. An illustration of the rotational errors is also provided to the right.

Configuration			< 1.25	1.25	2.5	5	7.5	10	> 10
HoloLens ArUco STAT	5	N	100%	30%	0%	0%	0%	0%	0%
		A	100% (29.3)	0%	0%	0%	0%	0%	0%
	10	N	100%	100%	50%	20%	0%	0%	0%
		A	100% (62.5)	0%	0%	0%	0%	0%	0%
	20	N	100%	100%	100%	80%	60%	30%	0%
		A	100% (114)	0%	0%	0%	0%	0%	0%
HoloLens ArUco MOV	5	N	100%	100%	100%	100%	0%	0%	0%
		A	100%	100%	100%	0%	0%	0%	0%
	10	N	100%	100%	100%	100%	90%	80%	0%
		A	100%	100%	100%	100%	100%	90%	0%
	20	N	100%	100%	100%	100%	100%	100%	50% (18)
		A	100%	100%	100%	100%	100%	100%	100% (17)
HoloLens Vuforia	5	N	100% (0.55)	0%	0%	0%	0%	0%	0%
		A	100% (46)	0%	0%	0%	0%	0%	0%
	10	N	100% (1.0)	0%	0%	0%	0%	0%	0%
		A	100% (92)	0%	0%	0%	0%	0%	0%
	20	N	100%	100%	0%	0%	0%	0%	0%
		A	100% (189)	0%	0%	0%	0%	0%	0%
Android Vuforia	5	N	100% (0.56)	0%	0%	0%	0%	0%	0%
		A	100% (44.5)	0%	0%	0%	0%	0%	0%
	10	N	100% (1.17)	0%	0%	0%	0%	0%	0%
		A	100% (50)	0%	0%	0%	0%	0%	0%
	20	N	100%	100%	0%	0%	0%	0%	0%
		A	100% (86)	0%	0%	0%	0%	0%	0%
Android ARCore	5	N	100% (0.29)	0%	0%	0%	0%	0%	0%
		A	100% (25.4)	0%	0%	0%	0%	0%	0%
	10	N	100% (0.51)	0%	0%	0%	0%	0%	0%
		A	100% (50.6)	0%	0%	0%	0%	0%	0%
	20	N	100% (0.92)	0%	0%	0%	0%	0%	0%
		A	100% (196)	0%	0%	0%	0%	0%	0%

Fig. 12. DR values for all the marker sizes (5, 10 and 20 cm) and both lighting conditions (natural and artificial). In brackets, under the DR value, the distance at which DR has been additionally sampled (cm below the minimum, m above the maximum).

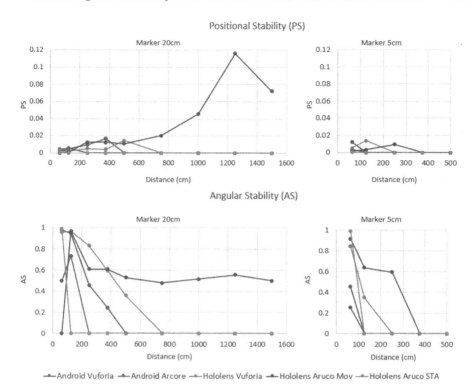

Fig. 13. PS (top) and AS (bottom) for markers sized 20 cm (left) and 5 cm (right) under artificial lighting conditions.

NOLO^{TM}. For the NOLO^{TM} HMD, the calibration procedure suggested by the vendor was strictly followed. However, this calibration method did not take into account the height of the DreamGlass^{TM}, resulting in a collection of samples having a constant offset on both height (Y axis) and pitch (rotation around the Z axis). Thus, raw data were later compensated using these known offsets (13 cm and 23.9°). Figure 14 shows a variable positional error (especially in the area to the left of the base station close to the limits of the FOV), which generally gets worse moving away from the base station. The average positional error is 9.5 cm and 6.9 cm on the X and Z axis, respectively; the Y axis is the most critical, with an average error of 16.8 cm. The rotational tracking is relatively accurate (especially compared to the NOLO^{TM} controllers, as discussed in the following paragraphs) with an average error of 1.6°, 3.46° and 0.76° on the X, Y and Z axis respectively.

Before examining the data gathered with the controller (Fig. 15, 16 and 17), it is worth recalling that the controller was tested in three different configurations. The average positional errors for these configurations were:

– *front*: 6.7 cm (X), 4.6 cm (Y), 12.2 cm (Z);
– *top*: 5.1 cm (X), 8.0 cm (Y), 7.3 cm (Z);

NOLO (HMD)

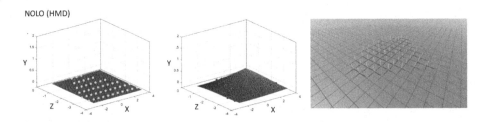

Fig. 14. TA results: actual positions on the grid (left) for the NOLO™ HMD, measured positions (center), and measured rotations (right).

NOLO Controller (Front)

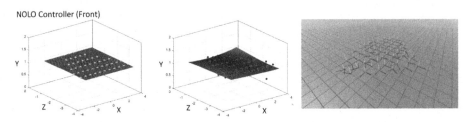

Fig. 15. TA results: actual positions on the grid (left) for the NOLO™ controller (front), measured positions (center), and measured rotations (right).

– *side*: 24.6 cm (X), 14.6 cm (Y), 66.2 cm (Z).

While these errors are comparable for the first two configurations, there is a substantial decay in accuracy for the last one, especially on the Z axis with an average error of 66.2 cm (more than one whole square on the grid).

Data also indicate considerable errors for the measured rotations. In some specific cases, the errors are almost 180° away from the actual rotation. The average rotational errors were:

– *front*: 4.3° (X), 99.9° (Y), 5.3° (Z);
– *top*: 6.9° (X), 52.2° (Y), 23.6° (Z);
– *side*: 4.5° (X), 29.6° (Y), 3.7° (Z).

It can be noticed that the performance of the controller appears to be dramatically worse than that of the HMD. These errors could be ascribed to a drift caused by issues in sensor fusion of optical and inertial data. This can justify the frequent necessity of a controller re-calibration, in order to keep it aligned to the virtual counterpart.

HoloLens™. As ut can be observed from the interpolation surface (Fig. 18, center), the HoloLens™ appears to be more accurate than the NOLO™; the average error is 2.7 cm on the X axis, 0.9 cm, on the Y axis and 2.8 cm on the Z axis. The same consideration applies to rotations, whereby discrepancies from the real values are contained (1.1°, 0.6°, Z: 0.5° for the X, Y and Z axis, respectively).

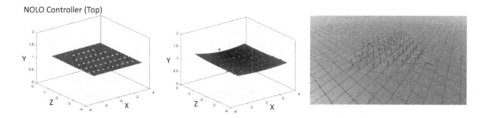

Fig. 16. TA results: actual positions on the grid (left) for the NOLO^{TM} controller (top), measured positions (center), and measured rotations (right).

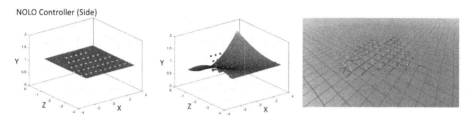

Fig. 17. TA results: actual positions on the grid (left) for the NOLO^{TM} controller (side), measured positions (center), and measured rotations (right).

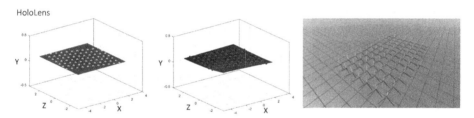

Fig. 18. The real positions on the grid (left) for the HoloLens^{TM}, the measured positions (center) and rotations (right)

5   Conclusions

The objective evaluation described in this work highlighted a series of different behaviors across the considered devices and SDKs. These differences can help in guiding the choice of the specific hardware or library with the aim to ensure a reliable and usable AR experience in industrial environments.

When the capability to detect markers from large distances is required, the ArUco library proved to outperform the alternatives (detection up to 16 m). However, at such distances, tracking stability is quite low. On the contrary, Vuforia requires first to detect the marker at a close distance (always below 2 m), but after detection, it can maintain the tracking up to four times that distance. Moreover, for distances between DD and DL, only the angular tracking stability deteriorates as the device gets farther from the marker, whereas the positional tracking remains stable. This behavior is similar to the one observed for the Hololens^{TM} ArUco Moving configuration.

Overall, no remarkable differences were detected in the two analyzed lighting conditions, with the exception of the ArUco Stationary configuration. In this case, the tracking algorithm seems to suffer from artificial lighting. Under such conditions, marker detection was affected by a strange behavior, showing better performance with a wider angle of approach, probably ascribable to the effects of the noise detection filter.

Regarding detection rate, results did not provide particularly relevant information, except that Vuforia and ArCore probably hide spurious detections, signaling a detection event only when it happens with a given degree of reliability. For this reason, measured values were always equal to 100% when sampled below the DD threshold, and to 0% above. Instead, for ArUco, a progressive degradation for the metric was observed.

Concluding, considering the investigated configurations, only HoloLens^{TM} can provide effective support for both long-range (ArUco Moving) and short-range (Vuforia/ArUco Stationary) scenarios. The ArUco Moving configuration is characterized by the widest ranges, but at the expense of tracking stability. Vuforia is probably the best trade-off between range and stability, whereas ArUco Stationary offers the best stability performance but in very short ranges. ARCore, instead, resulted as unsuitable for the investigated scenarios.

When marker-based tracking is not feasible, other solutions have to be considered. Regarding the comparison between the HoloLens^{TM}'s SLAM and the NOLO^{TM}'s outside-in tracking, the results highlighted that the first one achieves the best performance in terms of positional tracking. The DreamGlass^{TM} with NOLO^{TM}, on the other hand, proved to be dramatically less accurate (especially in terms of the rotational errors of the controllers), thus resulting in an impractical solution for tracking real objects in AR scenarios.

Future development will focus on the creation of a test scenario covering all those aspects that can be investigated only through a subjective evaluation, like, e.g., presentation quality, usability, and comfort. Moreover, further devices and libraries will be included in the evaluation, together with other tracking techniques like the vision-based, marker-less ones.

References

1. Blanco-Novoa, O., Fernández-Caramés, T.M., Fraga-Lamas, P., Vilar-Montesinos, M.A.: A practical evaluation of commercial industrial augmented reality systems in an industry 4.0 shipyard. IEEE Access **6**, 8201–8218 (2018)
2. De Pace, F., Manuri, F., Sanna, A.: Augmented reality in industry 4.0. Am. J. Comput. Sci. Inf. Technol. **06**, 17 (2018)
3. Duenser, A., Grasset, R., Billinghurst, M.: A survey of evaluation techniques used in augmented reality studies. In: ACM SIGGRAPH ASIA 2008 (2008)
4. Garrido-Jurado, S., Muñoz Salinas, R., Madrid-Cuevas, F., Medina-Carnicer, R.: Generation of fiducial marker dictionaries using mixed integer linear programming. Pattern Recogn. **51**, 481–491 (2015)

5. Lang, S., Kota, M.S.S.D., Weigert, D., Behrendt, F.: Mixed reality in production and logistics: Discussing the application potentials of microsoft hololens^{TM}. Procedia Comput. Sci. **149**, 118–129 (2019)

6. Liagkou, V., Salmas, D., Stylios, C.: Realizing virtual reality learning environment for industry 4.0. Procedia CIRP **79**, 712–717 (2019). 12th CIRP Conference on Intelligent Computation in Manufacturing Engineering, 18–20 July 2018. Gulf of Naples, Italy

7. Masood, T., Egger, J.: Adopting augmented reality in the age of industrial digitalisation. Comput. Ind. **115**, 103112 (2020)

8. Navab, N.: Developing killer apps for industrial augmented reality. IEEE Comput. Graphics Appl. **24**(3), 16–20 (2004)

9. Niehorster, D., Li, L., Lappe, M.: The accuracy and precision of position and orientation tracking in the HTC VIVE virtual reality system for scientific research. i-Perception 8 (2017). https://journals.sagepub.com/doi/full/10.1177/2041669517708205

10. Quandt, M., Knoke, B., Gorldt, C., Freitag, M., Thoben, K.D.: General requirements for industrial augmented reality applications. Procedia CIRP **72**, 1130–1135 (2018). 51st CIRP Conference on Manufacturing Systems

11. Roldán, J.J., Crespo, E., Martín-Barrio, A., Peña Tapia, E., Barrientos, A.: A training system for industry 4.0 operators in complex assemblies based on virtual reality and process mining. Robot. Comput. Integr. Manuf. **59**, 305–316 (2019)

12. Romero-Ramirez, F., Muñoz Salinas, R., Medina-Carnicer, R.: Speeded up detection of squared fiducial markers. Image Vis. Comput. **76** (2018)

13. de Souza Cardoso, L.F., Mariano, F.C.M.Q., Zorzal, E.R.: A survey of industrial augmented reality. Comput. Ind. Eng. **139**, 106–159 (2020)

Industrial Training Platform Using Augmented Reality for Instrumentation Commissioning

Gustavo Caiza[1] , Jennifer K. Bologna[2] , Carlos A. Garcia[2] ,
and Marcelo V. Garcia[2,3](✉)

[1] Universidad Politecnica Salesiana, UPS, 170146 Quito, Ecuador
`gcaiza@ups.edu.ec`
[2] Universidad Tecnica de Ambato, UTA, 180103 Ambato, Ecuador
`{jbologna7458,ca.garcia,mv.garcia}@uta.edu.ec`
[3] University of Basque Country, UPV/EHU, 48013 Bilbao, Spain
`mgarcia294@ehu.eus`

Abstract. Augmented reality (AR) platforms are poised to have great potential for industries when it comes to complex processes like maintenance or instrument commissioning in the Oil and Gas industry. The human-centered technology displays context-specific 3-D information in a real environment related to a specifically targeted object. Immersive experiences are expected to boost task efficiency, the quality of training, and maintenance purposes. This research shows an AR system that allows users to train in the calibration of HART instrumentation, using the Unity 3D platform and Meta 2 glasses. This application offers a platform that has advantages for users since it can train in the operation of expensive industrial equipment in an error-prone system. The validation of the system was carried out through an evaluation module, which allows the user to determine the level of training and autonomously build their own learning, obtaining positive responses that show that around 82% of the population evaluated.

Keywords: Industrial training applications · Augmented Reality · Unity 3D · Human-centered smart systems

1 Introduction

The applications that are developed in Virtual Reality (VR) or Augmented Reality (AR) can be oriented to the processes of teaching-learning [6], in the academic part and to the training - qualification in the industrial scope, these processes previously mentioned can be applied individually or in collaborative works between users, for which it is considered: (i) environments with a user in which tasks that can be performed individually are considered such as assembly of mechanical parts, doors [4], spot welding, precision welding [17,19], electronic control units [3], electric motors, among others.

© Springer Nature Switzerland AG 2020
L. T. De Paolis and P. Bourdot (Eds.): AVR 2020, LNCS 12243, pp. 268–283, 2020.
https://doi.org/10.1007/978-3-030-58468-9_20

The use of intelligent instruments for process control and for the detection of problems in the industry is increasingly necessary to avoid production outages or work accidents and to provide intrinsically safe environments within processes. However, it is good to keep in mind what are the effects of lack of employee training in the handling of these instruments?. When workers are not trained, the actions and protocols they should follow are not clearly defined, creating an atmosphere of conflict and confusion. Training has, therefore, become a necessity, in order to reduce risks and prevent damage to equipment and workers. Industries are looking for powerful innovative tools for learning and training [5].

In recent years, information technologies have become present in several engineering fields and the training and learning areas have not been an exception. Several studies have been done on the benefits of virtual environments for training, due to their relationship to the concept of experiential learning. Virtual reality offers many resources for such training and involves lower costs and risks of both personnel and equipment, physical equipment is not needed (often expensive), the possibility of training in undeveloped equipment [18].

In addition, the design of interactivity allows active learning, providing to users security and a sense of control, because they can repeat the training as many times as necessary and progress in their own way, actions that are not possible in the real world [1,13].

In the Industrial field, the virtual reality is quite unconnected to technological advances and therefore it is difficult for employers and workers to understand how this tool would contribute to training. However, experts say the potential of 3D virtual worlds is rooted in the possibility of offering more student-centered learning processes, which requires students to be more committed to relying on interaction activities [10].

From the problem described above arises the need to design an innovative AR system for industrial training applications, which allows reproducing computer-generated images for interactive viewing of an industrial instrument with virtual sequences designed to train a user in the setting up of HART instruments. Because experimentation will allow the user to acquire skills that they will use in the real workplace, getting familiar with the use of the instrument, both in its function and in its operating principles and procedures.

The design of the document is as follows, Sect. 2 shows some related works that have been used as a starting point for this research. Section 3 describes the state of the art that introduce the elements used in the methodology of this research Sect. 4 illustrates a case study of AR for industrial training. The proposed solution for the case study is presented in Sect. 5. Finally, some conclusions and future work are established in Sect. 6.

2   Related Works

Since the purpose of a training system is to help users to acquire skills used in the real workplace, it is important that the simulation of realistic scenes of the real workspace provide the same work interfaces used in a real situation and make them fit into the training methods. Based on this premise, work involving training, whose focus is on the Industrial area, was analyzed.

In [2], provides an introduction to virtual reality technology (VR) and its possibilities for training. Focuses on immersion as the key added value of virtual reality, and analyses the cognitive variables connected to it, how it is generated in synthetic environments, and what are its benefits. Based on this perspective, the different requirements of a Virtual Training Environment (VET) for different applications can be determined.

Regarding the development of virtual environments at an industrial level, there are works in different areas such as the Nguyen and Meixner research [12], which present a gamified augmented reality environment to fulfill an industrial assembly task, focused on the user participation where is represented by an avatar, which performs the operation in a similar way to the real world. As in the proposed environment, this application has a 3D interface, and learning is generated due to the active and protagonist participation of the user in a highly individualized system that adapts to his learning pace.

The proposed virtual system provides the simulation of purely industrial equipment using an interactive AR environment development platform for training and industrial education applications, very useful and complete, where through a visual editor the user can import 3D models, textures, etc, and then work on them. The system has a high level of immersion because using an Immersive Virtual Reality (RVI) headset, where the user can get more interaction with the environment and the perception of different stimuli that intensify the feeling of reality.

3   State of Technology

This section will explain all the concepts that will be applied for the development of the research proposal.

3.1   Augmented Reality and Education

Within the incorporation of new tools in training environments, AR is one of the most outstanding and important technologies developed for this purpose. Currently, there are some AR applications that are used for content teaching. In general, the contents that have been addressed using this technology are those in which the user requires the ability to handle a high level of abstraction to understand them [20].

This is related to the characteristics of AR as a technology, particularly of generate an immersive and interactive environment; a feeling that for users has important consequences in digital educational contexts [7]. In essence, users could apply their acquired knowledge in new contexts or situations, generating a phenomenon of content transfer or learning. In addition, due to its high interactivity as a technology and methodology, it adapts very well to paradigms such as Problem Based Learning or Action-Oriented Teaching [9].

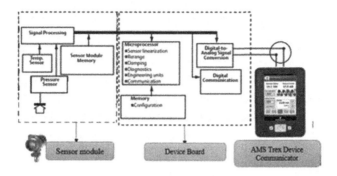

Fig. 1. Rosemount 2088 block diagram

3.2   Industrial Instruments with HART Protocol

HART is a communication protocol for field devices, designed for control and measurement applications of the industrial process. This standard transforms the analog signal of 4 to 20 mA into a digitally modulated signal suitable for industrial use [8]. HART devices indicate if they are configured correctly and if they are being operated correctly, allowing them to remove the necessity of routine revisions and helping to detect failure conditions before they cause further problems in the process. The configuration of an instrument is done by a programmer which acts as a secondary master.

The simulated secondary master in the AR system for device configuration is the Rosemount factory's AMS Trex which allows the detection of HART equipment problems and can diagnose instruments in the field while these are installed. The equipments to be simulated for their configuration are the Rosemount 2088 transmitters that perform gauge pressure (GP) and absolute pressure (AP) measurements and the temperature transmitter model 648 that offers a wireless solution in the verification of industrial processes. (See Fig. 1).

3.3   Meta 2 Development Kit AR Glasses

Meta 2 glasses are currently one of the most recognized hardware platforms for augmented reality [11]. These glasses were selected due to they have a high immersion level, because they have integrated sensors for motion tracking and manual interaction that creates depth impression, and parallax and includes surface tracking, which is a big advantage for the project as the user will be able to reach and move virtual objects in the real world through hand interaction, and will be able to interact with the system so that he feels like is part of the environment, and this makes the training more friendly and immersive.

3.4   Unity 3D

Unity 3D [16], is a multiplatform video game engine that thanks to its versatility allow working with both User Interface (UI) elements that are 2D elements and allows to integrate 3D objects to develop virtual learning environments, also due to a set of features that compared to other engines like Unreal Engine and Gamemaker presents advantages such as ease of use since it has an intuitive interface and allows to work with different practical tools that make work easier, as it is mainly based on dragging and dropping objects and writing codes.

Another important approach is coding because by working with C#, it is only necessary to have a basic knowledge of programming, In addition, its compatibility with a lot of platforms makes it easy to use with the selected Augmented Reality glasses as it is only necessary to add the pertinent Software Development Kit (SDK) to the viewer to allow interaction.

4   Case Study

The augmented reality system for training of HART instrumentation calibration is going to be developed for instrumentation technicians that work in the Oil and Gas field in Ecuador. The design of the AR interface is made by the collaboration of interns and technicians who evaluate the usefulness provided by the system to users.

The hardware architecture is the conceptual design and the fundamental operational structure of the system. It is the physical support where the software resides. The hardware architecture consisting of a Meta 2 glasses [14] as the AR device. Meta 2 is a stand-alone device that has an own graphic processor that runs the processes natively on its hardware. These glasses provide real-time tracking, stable and accurate.

Meta 2 glasses are connected to the computer through communication cables that will allow interaction with the developed AR system. As shown in Fig. 2, once a precise location of the space is achieved and maintained, the user just by putting on the viewer will already have the reach to the virtual objects and the virtual training sequences that will be overlaid on the real environment through the computer that contains the application and because the device maps the environment and tracking the user's actual location, the user can use defined hand movements to interact with the 3D images.

The software architecture provides a general reference necessary to guide the construction of the augmented reality system for user training, allowing all application objectives and restrictions to be covered.

This way, as shown in Fig. 2, the system design has an interface level at which the previously selected development engine will design the graphical interface and the set of instructions with which the user can interact. It also has a development level that will allow the encoding of the top-level instructions, and where the user interface and general development libraries of the application will be added, and then compiled them, all this will be done using Unity 3D software and Visual Studio. Finally, the base level will allow managing the communication channels of the Hardware architecture with the system.

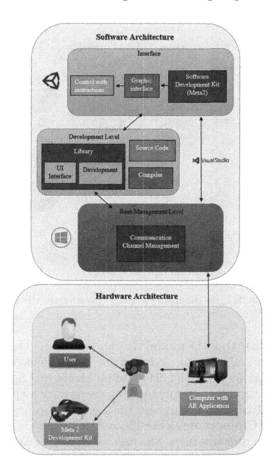

Fig. 2. AR training system architecture

5 Implementation of the Solution Proposal

This stage defines both the user requirements and the aspects concerning the design and animation of objects and elements that would make up the learning system, for this purpose the information on the functioning of the HART equipment.

5.1 Augmented Reality System User Cases

This section explains the interactions between the user and the system in detail. The use case diagram shown from the user's perspective allows analyzing the interaction options presented to you at the start of the application. The following is a detailed analysis of each case (See Fig. 3):

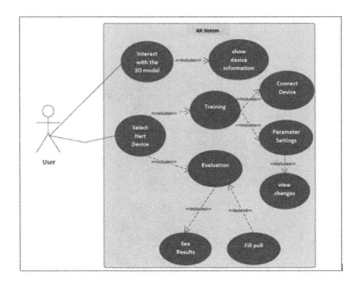

Fig. 3. Case diagram by actor (user perspective)

(i) **Interact with the 3D model**: In this case of use the user will be able to grab, rotate and scale the 3D models of the HART devices, in addition, the user will get information from the device of his choice. (ii) **Select the HART device:** The user selects the type of HART device to work with either pressure or temperature. (iii) **Training:** In this case, the user can be trained in the use of the HART device. (iv) **Connect devices:** The user must have selected the training option. (v) **Setting parameters:** The user accesses this case of use and from this can configure the basic parameters of the selected device. (vi) **Evaluation:** Allows the user to enter a practice mode where tests what has learned. (viii) **Survey:** Allows the user to validate the functionality of the application

5.2   Augmented Reality System Design

The AR application within the Unity engine features an internal component-based architecture. Figure 4 describes the physical elements of the system and its relations.

The application at a general level uses components of Unity and C# to develop each interface within it. Having as its main component the desktop application, which has the internal method called *"Initialize"*, which is associated with the *"Game Engine"* component to load the application, which is linked to the working interface at Unity within which the project is developed.

The C# components that are associated with the working environment are the class *"Monobehaviour"* which is the core of the API (Application Programming Interface) in Unity, because all the object-linked scripts within the project are derived from this class that provides various useful events and functions.

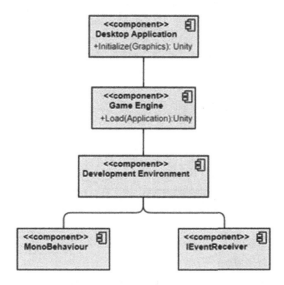

Fig. 4. Design of application components in Unity

Besides, the *"IEventReceiver"* component is used to integrate the functions of the augmented reality viewer into the program.

The augmented reality application is made by a group of interfaces which correspond to the components, the connector assembles a required interface of one component with the interface provided by another, and the relations of dependence indicate that one component refers to services offered by another. The diagram of components of the application is defined in Fig. 5, which shows the different modules of the application. An approximation to these modules is described below:

Overview. The system has an introduction and familiarization module about the equipment. Users can use this space to become familiar with the function of the equipment without having to have the physical device, therefore helps to reduce the time spent on training. It also allows interaction with the equipment, through the AR.

Training Module. The training mode interface is divided into two main areas:

1. **Device Connection:** As the user follows the instructions provided in the application and clicks on the connection options, animations are displayed showing how the elements should be connected. In addition to adapting to different learning styles, the information in the AR system is presented in written form as animations are generated and the user can access a video of the connection of the devices.

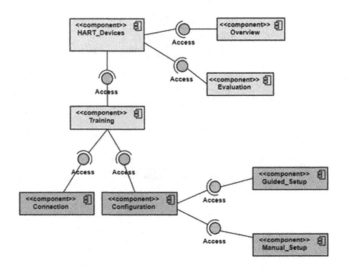

Fig. 5. AR application component diagram

2. **Device Configuration:** Once the connection of the equipment is complete, the configuration begins. In the first part of this mode, it is a guided setup and offers more help to users, but it is not very flexible because users have to follow a rigid set of instructions. The second part is a manual setup, which allows users to freely navigate during the procedure and make changes according to their own judgment.

Evaluation Module. At the end of the training module, the application presents the option to make an evaluation, which consists of a set of questions referring to what was learned in the previous module. In each question, the user is given instructions on what to do in a given time and at the end of all the questions, a table of results can be displayed in a summary mode of the failures and successes.

5.3   Class Diagrams of the Developed AR Application

Class diagrams base their operation on the manipulation of elements, which are inside of scenes that interact with each other to give movement to the application. The encoding required for this system is done using C Sharp language scripts. The operation of such scripts in Unity is based on the fact that each of them implements a class, with their attributes and methods. Therefore this approach leads to consider the scenes of the application as classes and the elements within them as attributes. The main class diagrams are presented below.

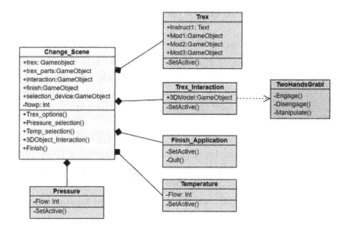

Fig. 6. Class diagram of the overview module

Device Overview Module. Figure 6 presents the classes used in the device overview module with their attributes, methods and the type of relationship that exists between them which is of composition because this describes the relationship between a set of parts and a part of it all, This means that if the system removes the whole "Change_Scene", the other classes cannot function independently. The description of the function of each class is presented below in the Table 1.

Training Module: Pressure Transmitter Connection. As shown in Fig. 7, the classes used in the connection phase of the pressure transmitter training module are presented; it is important to note that the type of relation between the main class "ChangeEsc_Press" and those linked to it, is of composition, and the relationship between the class "Int_3D_Model" with the classes provided by the SDK of the augmented reality glasses for the manipulation of objects is dependence type because it needs the methods provided by those classes to perform interaction tasks. The description of the function of each class is presented below in the Table 2.

5.4   Designed Interfaces

The graphical user interface (GUI) is the environment that manages the interaction with the user based on visual relations, to represent the information and actions available from the virtual application, and is used for the user to establish easier and intuitive contact with the system.

The interfaces developed in the Unity 3D [15] software are presented, these interfaces were modeled based on the diagrams presented in the previous section.

Table 1. Description of the overview module class

Class name	Description
Change_Scene	Main class of the module, because it is the one that allows to access to each "GameObject" element that represent a scene inside the application, for this it has methods that allow to make this change like TrexOptions(), PressureSelection(), TempSelection(), among others
Trex	Class that contain Text-type instructions that describe the operation of the equipment and the main elements of the communication module, associated to the main class by the SetActive() method, for access
Trex_Interaction	Class that allows you to observe and manipulate the device modeled in 3D
Pressure	Class that allows to access to pressure transmitter options
Temperature	Class that allows to access to temperature transmitter options
TwoHandsGrabI	Class provided by the SDK of the augmented reality viewer that allows you to hold the 3D model with both hands
End_Application	Class that allows closing the augmented reality application, using the Quit() method

Training Module: Device Connection. The interfaces designed within the training module in the first phase corresponding to the device connection are those shown in Fig. 8 where (A) corresponds to the interface of connection components that shows each one of the parts necessary to make the connection of the equipment and also adds a video demonstration of connection. (B) Connection of the transmitter and (C) Connection of the Trex programming device, both

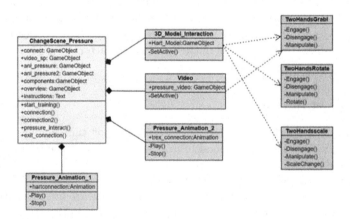

Fig. 7. Training-connection module class diagram

Table 2. Description of the training module classes (Connection) Class Description

Class name	Description
ChangeEsc_Press	Class that allows to access to each public element "GameObject" that make up the user interface, where for each element there is an access method
Int_3D_Model	By using this class it is possible to observe and manipulate the 3D modeled pressure transmitter
Video	Within the connection a demonstration video is offered, the private method SetActive() is used to access it
Animation_Press1, Animation_Press2	Both classes allow the visualization of the animations that show the connections of the TREX field programming device with the HART equipment. It has the Play(), and Stop() methods to play and stop the animation respectively
TwoHandsGrabI, TwoHandsRotate, TwoHandsScale	Public classes provided by the SDK of the augmented reality viewer that allow to grab the 3D model with both hands, rotate and scale it respectively

shown the connection instructions and reproduce the animations of the way the devices are connected.

It is important to mention that as an example only the transmitter interfaces were selected, however, the temperature transmitter interfaces have the same components and interaction characteristics.

Training Module: Device Configuration. For the training module in its second phase which is the configuration of the device, Fig. 9 details the main initial configuration options in the pressure device as they are (A) The Trex communicator home screen, which is the same as presented in the actual device interface, (B) HART device selection screen, to connect to the device (C) the device panel menu with the main navigation options (D) the device configure the screen to access "Guided Setup" or "Manual Setup" and start the parameter configuration.

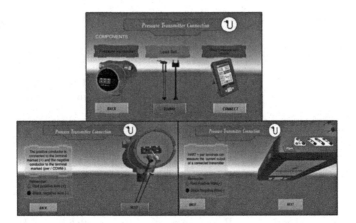

Fig. 8. Training module interfaces-Connection (pressure)

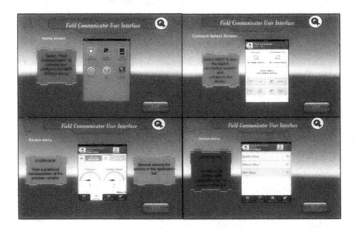

Fig. 9. Training module interfaces-Configuration (pressure)

The AR system for training is evaluated through several attempts in real-time by some different kinds of users such as industrial technicians and students (See Fig. 10). The AR platform gets satisfactory evaluation results. When users tested the application, the developers had the opportunity to ask them a series of open questions as an interview about their perception of the developed system. The users said that they found the application interesting and that they found it innovative and interactive to be able to see the 3D models on the screen and to be able to move them. The users also commented that the application proved to be intuitive and very useful to know the operation of HART instruments.

Fig. 10. Validation by user of AR platform

6   Conclusions and Future Work

The AR system for training was developed based on the specifications of a software architecture using different UI elements of the interface in the creation of virtual scenes to expose theoretical content, 3D models, multimedia content, and instructions under which the user performed their training, so the application proved to be intuitive navigation and very useful for user learning because, by using the augmented reality glasses obtained greater compression of content, presented in a new and more immersive way, differentiating it from the conventional way of receiving training in the handling of industrial equipment.

The interaction between the user and the proposed AR system was established through the design of the architecture, both hardware and software of the system, which allowed to constitute the fundamental organization, the detailed structure and the set of relations between each of the parts of the application, which were necessary to define the behavior of each component, module, and class, and in this way it was possible to optimize times of creation of scenes, 3D models and multimedia resources, in addition, it provided a general reference necessary to guide the construction of the system, covering all the objectives and restrictions of the application.

Future work should include a "real industry scenario practice module" where the user is exposed to workplace situations regarding the operation of HART transmitters and must make a decision regarding virtually generated solution options.

References

1. del Amo, I.F., Galeotti, E., Palmarini, R., Dini, G., Erkoyuncu, J., Roy, R.: An innovative user-centred support tool for Augmented Reality maintenance systems design: a preliminary study. Procedia CIRP **70**, 362–367 (2018). https://doi.org/10.1016/j.procir.2018.02.020
2. Bernal Zamora, L., Ballesteros-Ricaurte, J.A.: Metodología para la construcción de objetos virtuales de aprendizaje, apoyada en realidad aumentada. Sophia **13**, 4–12 (2017). publisher: scielo
3. Cardoso, A., et al.: VRCEMIG: a virtual reality system for real time control of electric substations. In: 2013 IEEE Virtual Reality (VR), pp. 165–166, March 2013. https://doi.org/10.1109/VR.2013.6549414
4. Dodoo, E.R., et al.: Evaluating commodity hardware and software for virtual reality assembly training. Electr. Imaging **2018**(3), 468-1–468-6 (2018). https://doi.org/10.2352/ISSN.2470-1173.2018.03.ERVR-468
5. Garcia, C.A., Caiza, G., Naranjo, J.E., Ortiz, A., Garcia, M.V.: An approach of training virtual environment for teaching electro-pneumatic systems. IFAC-PapersOnLine **52**(9), 278–284 (2019). https://doi.org/10.1016/j.ifacol.2019.08.221. 12th IFAC Symposium on Advances in Control Education ACE 2019
6. Garcia, C.A., Naranjo, J.E., Ortiz, A., Garcia, M.V.: An approach of virtual reality environment for technicians training in upstream sector. IFAC-PapersOnLine **52**(9), 285–291 (2019). https://doi.org/10.1016/j.ifacol.2019.08.222. 12th IFAC Symposium on Advances in Control Education ACE 2019
7. Labovitz, J., Hubbard, C.: The use of virtual reality in podiatric medical education. Clin. Podiatr. Med. Surg. **37**(2), 409–420 (2020). https://doi.org/10.1016/j.cpm.2019.12.008
8. Li, T., Dong, Z.: Design and implementation of field bus device management system based on hart protocol. In: 2018 2nd IEEE Advanced Information Management, Communicates, Electronic and Automation Control Conference (IMCEC), pp. 2221–2225, May 2018. https://doi.org/10.1109/IMCEC.2018.8469220
9. Lopez-Faican, L., Jaen, J.: Emofindar: Evaluation of a mobile multiplayer augmented reality game for primary school children. Comput. Educ. **149** (2020). https://doi.org/10.1016/j.compedu.2020.103814
10. Mendoza, L.I.U.: Uso de la realidad virtual, en la educación del futuro en centros educativos del ecuador. J. Sci. Res.: Revista Ciencia e Investigación **1**(4), 26–30 (2016)
11. Meta 2 development kit (2020). https://www.schenker-tech.de/en/meta-2/
12. Nguyen, D., Meixner, G.: Gamified Augmented Reality Training for An Assembly Task: A Study About User Engagement, pp. 901–904, September 2019. https://doi.org/10.15439/2019F136, https://fedcsis.org/proceedings/2019/drp/136.html
13. Palmarini, R., Erkoyuncu, J.A., Roy, R., Torabmostaedi, H.: A systematic review of augmented reality applications in maintenance. Robot. Comput.-Integr. Manuf. **49**, 215–228 (2018). https://doi.org/10.1016/j.rcim.2017.06.002, http://www.sciencedirect.com/science/article/pii/S0736584517300686
14. Schenker-tech: META 2 - Exclusive Augmented Reality Development Kit, December 2020. https://www.schenker-tech.de//en/meta-2/
15. Unity, T.: Unity3d (2020). https://unity3d.com/es/unity
16. Unity 3d (2020). https://www.unity.com/
17. Wallace, M.W., Zboray, D.A., Aditjandra, A., Webb, A.L., Postlethwaite, D., Lenker, Z.S.: Virtual reality GTAW and pipe welding simulator and setup, October 2014. uS Patent 8,851,896

18. Wild, F.: The Future of learning at the workplace is augmented reality. Computer **49**(10), 96–98 (2016). https://doi.org/10.1109/MC.2016.30, http://ieeexplore.ieee.org/document/7598181/

19. Zboray, D.A., et al.: Virtual reality pipe welding simulator, 23 December 23 2014, uS Patent 8,915,740

20. Zinchenko, Y., et al.: Virtual reality is more efficient in learning human heart anatomy especially for subjects with low baseline knowledge. New Ideas Psychol. **59** (2020). https://doi.org/10.1016/j.newideapsych.2020.100786

AugmenTech: The Usability Evaluation of an AR System for Maintenance in Industry

Daniel Brice$^{(\boxtimes)}$, Karen Rafferty, and Seán McLoone

Queen's University Belfast, Belfast, UK
`dbrice01@qub.ac.uk`

Abstract. Maintenance tasks are common operations in manufacturing environments. However, it is becoming increasingly challenging for companies to recruit personnel with adequate skills and tacit knowledge to perform them. This paper proposes the use of augmented reality (AR) as a solution to provide contextually relevant guidance as a method to upskill a user performing a task. However, implementing a disruptive tool such as AR into the workforce requires considerations for acceptability and compliance amongst employees. AugmenTech is a proposed AR guidance application which was designed and tested with a strong focus on usability. Due to issues with the HoloLens native input modalities in the application area, a tactile input module has been designed and integrated with the system. A mock-up bearing replacement maintenance procedure, based on a real-world use case provided by a local manufacturer, has been designed as a platform for evaluation. Using this task and AugmenTech a between-subjects experiment was conducted, comparing the system with a traditional paper documentation approach. Overall workload, quantified using the NASA-TLX, was similar when using AR. Likewise, the use of AR also had minimal effect on time needed to complete the task. The usability of AugmenTech has been quantified, scoring highly, (M = 79.5, SD = 16.13), using the System Usability Scale (SUS) questionnaire.

Keywords: AR training · Maintenance · Usability testing

1 Introduction

The manufacturing sector faces a shortage in labour with the skills and tacit knowledge required for maintenance of workshop machinery [9]. This is a shortage which is expected to increase [4,13] with the continued use of costly to replace legacy systems and increasingly complex modern day machines.

Augmented Reality (AR) may provide a solution to this problem and is already expected to play a strong role in the future of human machine interfaces [3,10,21]. With Industry 4.0 and Internet Of Things (IoT) we see greater

© Springer Nature Switzerland AG 2020
L. T. De Paolis and P. Bourdot (Eds.): AVR 2020, LNCS 12243, pp. 284–303, 2020.
https://doi.org/10.1007/978-3-030-58468-9_21

connectivity of diagnostic tools and machines in manufacturing. However, frequently resources for maintenance procedures are found lagging in the form of outdated paper documentation. It is therefore fitting that we investigate the capabilities of a digital solution such as AR to provide real-time maintenance operation parameters and procedural knowledge for the user.

We introduce AugmenTech, a proof of concept AR system designed primarily to guide a technician in carrying out a maintenance procedure. The system utilises the Microsoft HoloLens to provide the user with guidance in the form of videos, pictures and animations in 3D space overlaid on the real environment.

The HoloLens comes with the native ability to use speech and gesture as input modalities. However, during discussions with industry it became clear that during previous attempts to use the system, there had been issues implementing these modalities in the application area due to use of gloves, dust masks and loud environments. An application specific tactile input module (TIM) was developed and integrated with the Hololens to provide a solution.

A local manufacturing company provided a definition of a use case in the form of a maintenance procedure. The operation was an infrequent bearing replacement procedure for a low pressure pump. For the purpose of demonstration and evaluation in a controlled environment, a non-functional low-fi prototype of the low pressure pump was created.

Implementation of AR into the workplace requires compliance and acceptability from users. We therefore focus our attention on the usability of the system. If a system such as AugmenTech were to be used in real-world applications instead of traditional methods it must be easy to use and cannot afford to lead to an increase in workload.

AugmenTech was used to conduct a controlled, between-subjects experiment comparing utilising the system with a traditional paper instructions approach to conducting a maintenance procedure. The primary goal of the study was to gain feedback on the usability of an AR system for guidance in a task. Both qualitative and quantitative feedback were gained through short interviews and System Usability Scale (SUS) questionnaires. Secondary goals of the study involved measuring the effect of using the AR system on time taken and workload perceived for the task, which was quantified by the NASA-TLX. Usages of different forms of instructions and input modalities were observed. Correlations between instruction type usage and time taken to complete the procedure were also derived.

In our paper we present an AR guidance system featuring different forms of instructions. The user is able to use pictures, videos or animated virtual models interchangeably. We have developed a controlled laboratory mock-up of a real-world bearing replacement maintenance procedure to investigate the effectiveness of AR as a guidance tool. To ensure the task was as realistic as possible it was designed to be identical to the definition use case. UI modalities have been developed by integrating our TIM with the HoloLens to facilitate simple and robust control by a technician. The system usability has been assessed by users in the form of SUS questionnaires and qualitative feedback. A user study has also been conducted on the system to investigate its effects on time taken for task completion and subjective workload.

The key contributions of our work are:

1. A user study to determine the usability of AR for guidance in performing a hands-on task. Additionally workload is measured and compared for the use of AR and printed instructions as guidance formats.
2. The development of a proof of concept AR assistance system using video, image and animations as media to provide guidance during a maintenance procedure and enable evaluation of its usability.

2 Related Work

AR provides the user with useful information overlaid virtually in the real-world 3D environment. This is one of the reasons it is becoming an area of great interest in human factors, with researchers demonstrating its effectiveness in real time training across many application areas [4,16,18].

The powerful ability of AR guidance systems to develop strong memory of task procedure has been shown in an evaluation study by Gavish et al. [7]. In their work they compared AR with virtual reality (VR) for a group of technicians carrying out an assembly task on an electronic actuator. They found receiving guidance whilst performing the task using AR resulted in the greatest skill retention.

A recent review of the application of AR in industrial maintenance applications was conducted by Palmarini et al. [11]. In their review the majority of AR applications had used only static images as instructions. One of their suggested areas for future work was determining the best form of presenting information in AR. This provides motivation for the multi-media instruction form design of AugmenTech.

In the work of Westerfield et al. [23] AR was used to assist users in performing a motherboard assembly. They show the performance that can be gained in reduced time and reduced errors when using adaptive instructions in AR. The effectiveness of animations in their system further warrants their implementation in AugmenTech.

Research into the capabilities of AR to provide guidance in assembly with the use of an interactive tool was conducted by Yuan et al. [24]. They claimed that assembly tasks are one of the most promising for AR. They found that those using the AR system took longer to complete their tasks, due to limitations in the technologies used.

Webel et al. [22] developed a handheld, multimodal AR system for guidance in maintenance. In their findings they demonstrate the ability for such systems to develop operator sensorimotor skills due to the ability to access virtual information whilst interacting with objects. They also found that traditional training results in greater numbers of unsolved errors. One of their suggestions for further work is determining the best method for presenting information in AR.

The findings of Siew et al. [17] emphasised the importance of user accept-ability of an AR maintenance system. In their work they utilise a bracelet haptic interface and demonstrate good usability through success in their user satisfac-tion questionnaires. Video and animation were not available as forms of visual feedback in their system.

An assistive, hand held AR system for aeronautic applications was developed and compared against traditional methods by Rios et al. [12]. In their small sample evaluation they had participants carry out drilling procedures for over 4 h. Participants reported greater understanding of the process for the AR condition.

Tumler et al. [20] recognised the significance of user comfort in AR for task guidance. In their research they conducted a study where participants received guidance in a pick and place task. Throughout the procedure they recorded heart rate variance to determine stress caused by the system vs a traditional paper instruction approach. Their findings and conclusion indicate the large potential for AR usage to reduce stress and strain in the workplace, suggesting further work should be carried out to look at the same effects across alternative tasks.

The effect of AR instructions vs traditional methods on mental workload was an area of interest for Tang et al. [19]. In their research they use the NASA TLX and determine mental workload to be lowered when receiving AR instructions in a complex assembly task, compared to paper instructions. They account this to the users not needing to mentally transform instruction objects to understand their physical position.

In the work of Schlagowski et al. [15] the design of an AR system is proposed. They emphasise the importance of effects on workload in their design specifica-tion. They specifically emphasise the need for adaptive instructions to ensure the user mental workload is not too low or too high.

Sanna et al. [14] developed an AR maintenance system using static images on a handheld device for instructions. Qualitative feedback from their user study was that users also desired the ability to watch videos of the subtasks in AR. The study also showed people performed tasks faster with the assistance of AR, though statistic significance was not determined.

Botto et al. [5] demonstrate an AR tablet based guidance system to show users how to complete designs of Meccano models. The system is also used in a study where both AR and printed paper instructions are used as guides to design Meccano models. In their study it is shown that participants took less time to perform tasks using paper instructions, than they did using the AR system. Our user study also investigates the effect guidance medium has on time taken for task completion. However, our study looks into this effect during a task of longer duration, as the tasks performed in the study conducted by Botto et al. were usually less than 2 min.

The suitability of the Microsoft HoloLens for industrial procedures is evalu-ated by Aleksy et al. [1]. In their study they investigated user feedback on an AR system for maintenance. Findings regarding user input techniques showed that users preferred to use the clicker or voice control over gestures. The use of the clicker in an industrial environment could be problematic however, due to its small size. AugmenTech features the HoloLens, but with an input modality interface that doesn't fully depend on gestures.

3   The AugmenTech System

3.1   Virtual Positioning

AugmenTech uses the Vuforia software development kit (SDK) in combination with a single marker and the HoloLens front facing camera for localisation. This enables positioning of virtual models alongside their physical counterparts and provides anchors in 3D space for the different UI elements, such as the task bar or gesture buttons.

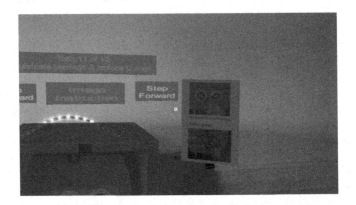

Fig. 1. View of image instructions in AugmenTech.

3.2   Instructions

The instructions take three forms. Image instructions are similar to conventional instructions, making use of photos combined with brief written instructions. This is displayed on a fixed 2D plane approximately 30 cm x 50 cm in size adjacent to the workstation. This can be seen in Fig. 1. Video instructions consist of example recordings of the subtask playing on a loop. The length of the demonstrator subtask recordings range from 10–40 s. Videos are displayed on a 2D plane similar in size to the image instructions plane, in a fixed position adjacent to the workstation. Animation instructions entail full-scale virtual models of physical parts animated to illustrate movements of the components and indicate actions to be performed. These animations occur in the same location as the real world parts in 3D space. This enables the location of unseen parts to be known to the user.

All 3 forms of instruction are displayed in 3D space with proximity to the components relevant to the step in the task. These can be used interchangeably by the user to facilitate different skill levels or subtask complexity. The images based instructions provide information which can be taken in quickly by the user. Videos on the other hand help provide tacit knowledge by allowing the user to see exactly how the task can be performed. Animations provide high level guidance with clear identification of relevant components in 3D space imposed against the physical maintenance assembly. The ability for users to easily select between instruction forms mid-task ensures the user can view instructions based on their needs, resulting in less frustration and improved overall usability.

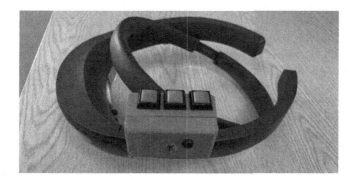

Fig. 2. Tactile input module (TIM) attached to HoloLens.

3.3   Multi-modal Input

The input interface is kept minimal to reduce complexity whilst still enabling control of the application by the user. The 3 actions a user is required to make are: step forward a task, step backwards a task and change the instruction form. These actions were mapped to three different input modalities: speech recognition, HoloLens gesture and button presses on the TIM.

The HoloLens natively provides the speech and gesture modalities. Separate keywords are associated to each of the actions for the speech commands. Saying, "next" steps the task forwards, "back" steps the task backwards and "type" changes instruction type. A fourth speech command, "follow", is used to toggle the HUD mode for instructions. The user can also use the HoloLens "select" gesture to select virtual buttons associated to each action which are positioned above the task components.

Industry feedback was presented during discussions on issues regarding previous attempts to implement the HoloLens native input modalities in tests. It was reported that there were frequent unintended gesture recognitions and difficulty in performing gestures by the technicians wearing gloves. To provide an appropriate solution to the concern regarding technicians input to the system a module is presented with tactile switches, a battery and an ESP-8266 microcontroller in a 3D printed casing, see Fig. 2. The TIM can be easily attached to either side of the HoloLens to facilitate handiness of the user or removed entirely from the HMD and placed with the user's preference. The mass of the TIM is 64 g and no users have yet reported comfort issues whilst wearing it on the HoloLens. The module communicates with the HoloLens via the message queuing telemetry transport (MQTT) publish and subscribe protocol over Wi-Fi. The input modality is robust and provides an interface for HoloLens usage in an industrial setting.

3.4 Scheduling and Training

AugmenTech provides the ability to passively record times taken for individual subtasks within the maintenance procedure, an ability which is not available with conventional approaches. Sub task times can be compared across operators to develop understanding in the procedure and highlight difficult sections. Sub task times taken by operators can be compared to the average durations for the procedure to assist in identifying suitable candidates to train others or be trained. During maintenance operation the operator's progress and previously recorded times provide the opportunity to forecast task completion time for scheduling of both the machine and technician in real-time. A LED strip of individually controllable coloured segments is connected by Wi-Fi (via a Raspberry Pi) to the HoloLens. This is used to signal subtask progress in real-time to people nearby.

4 Experiment Design

In order to evaluate AugmenTech, a maintenance procedure was set-up in the lab. A controlled between-subjects experiment was conducted where participants carried out the procedure with a single independent variable of using either AugmenTech for guidance or a traditional, paper-based control.

4.1 Goals

The primary goal of the study was to determine the usability of AR in the context of guidance in a maintenance task. This was assessed within a controlled environment as a precursor to industrial implementation and case study.

Additional goals in the study were:

- To highlight areas for improvement in the system design and any concerns with usability.
- To determine the effect on workload of using the AR system vs traditional methods.
- To determine the effect of using the AR system vs traditional methods on task duration.
- To observe user usage of different forms of instructions and determine its relationship on time taken for the task.

4.2   Hypotheses

We formed two hypotheses for the comparisons between using the AugmenTech system and the control:

- **H1** – Participants in the AR group would report similar workload to those using the traditional method.
- **H2** – The time taken to complete the task would be similar for both conditions.

Additional hypotheses and questions were based on the usage of the AR system:

- **H3** – Usability would be evaluated highly with minimal issues.
- **H4** – There would be a relationship between instruction form usage and task duration for AugmenTech users.

4.3   Independent Variables

Control. Participants were split across two conditions. As documented printout instructions are commonly used in industry it was decided they would be suitable as the control for the study. Participants in this condition performed the task by following a set of paper instructions designed to mimic those used in the real-world case. These instructions were formed of photos and written sentences delivered in a stapled booklet. The booklet was not fixed to the environment and could be freely moved by participants throughout the task.

AR System. The other condition consisted of using AugmenTech for guidance whilst completing the task. Participants had the ability to change the form of instructions throughout the task, as per the design feature of AugmenTech. It is acknowledged that this meant participants could experience the AR system differently to one another. However, instruction changes can be performed in less than a second and make use of AR capabilities to help maximise usability.

4.4   Dependent Variables

Time. The full duration of time taken to complete the task was recorded. This was carried out by the study administrator using an electronic timer.

Workload. Workload was assessed by administering the NASA-TLX questionnaire after completion of the task. The NASA-TLX is commonly used for its strengths in quantifying the individual elements of workload [8] for a task. A combined workload score was created for comparison by summing the individual workload components. A shortened version of the NASA-TLX, named the

RAW-TLX, was used during the study as workload weightings were not considered important for the purpose of the study. The RAW-TLX has been used by many and has also shown identical results to the full version on many occasions [8].

Usability. The subjective usability of the only the AR system was quantified by using the highly robust and versatile System Usability Scale (SUS) questionnaire [2]. Participants in the control group were given 5 min to use the AugmenTech system at the end of the study and also completed a SUS questionnaire for it.

Assessing the usability of the AugmenTech system would also require qualitative feedback to provide insight where the SUS could not. All participants were interviewed post study to discuss areas for improvement on the usability of the system, as well as the aspects of it which they appreciated.

Instruction Form Usage for AR. Usage of the image, video and animation instruction mediums was recorded across the 10 participants who used the AR system as guidance for the task procedure. Only one form of instruction could be used at a time and participants had the ability to freely change this throughout the task.

4.5 Participants

A total of 20 participants were recruited. The gender composition for the participants was 16 males and 4 females split evenly across the two conditions. The mean ages of the participants were 33.5 (SD = 15.0) and 36.9 (SD = 12.9) years old for the control and AR systems, respectively. Out of the 20 participants, 18 of them were students or staff members of the school of Electronics, Electrical Engineering and Computer Science. Many of the participants had previously tried the HoloLens at demonstrations around the university.

4.6 Task

With the intention of the system ultimately being usage in a factory setting, an exemplar maintenance procedure and accompanying documentation were provided by a local company. The task consisted of a partial disassembly and reassembly of a low-pressure pump to replace a worn bearing. The entire procedure was recreated in a total of 16 steps. The steps within the task were non-complex, but still required instructions for completion. These are briefly described in Table 1.

Table 1. Table showing brief definitions for steps in the maintenance task.

Step #	Definitions of task steps
1	Unscrewing of front bolt and separation of front panel
2	Detachment of hidden earth wire from panel
3	Disassembly of left hand side bearing housing
4	Disassembly of right hand side bearing housing
5	Removal and set down of dowell pins
6	Removal of o rings from bearings
7	Removal of bearings
8	Removal of spacers
9	Placement of new spacers
10	Placement of new bearings
11	Lubrication of bearings and replacement of o rings
12	Dowell pins replacement
13	Loctite application to bolts
14	Assemblies of bearing housings
15	Attachment of earth wire
16	Replacement and fixing of front panel

Fig. 3. Replica of low-pressure bearing pump.

4.7 Apparatus

For the AR system the Microsoft HoloLens (first generation) was used to provide visualizations of instructions. Input modalities were provided in the form of speech commands, gestures and the developed TIM attached to the HMD.

A raspberry pi 3 development board was used to host an MQTT server passing messages between the ESP-8266 (01-module) microcontroller within the TIM and the HoloLens.

All HoloLens development was carried out in C# using Unity 3D (v2018.4.6) and the Mixed Reality ToolKit (v2), with additions from the Vuforia SDK (v8.3.8) and the M2Mqtt GitHub project (v4.3). The ESP-8266 module firmware was developed using the Arduino IDE (v1.8.9) using embedded C.

The pump was recreated in a controlled environment using low-fidelity prototyping techniques; 3D printing, CNC cut foam and laser cut MDF with off-the-shelf fixings. The replica of the pump, shown in Fig. 3, used was approximately $0.6\,m \times 0.6\,m \times 0.6\,m$ and was placed on a desk. The tools used to perform the procedure included a screwdriver, small spanner, large rachet spanner, needle-nose pliers, an empty of lubricant dispenser and an empty bottle of Loctite.

4.8   Protocol

All participants were asked to read over and sign a consent form approved by the faculty ethics board detailing the study protocol. An overview on the research project and maintenance task was provided. The tools used within the procedure were explained to each participant and Personal Protective Equipment (PPE) gloves were optionally provided.

Introductions to the HoloLens and the software application were provided for the participants who used the AR system whilst performing the task. Before beginning the task these participants were provided an AR training environment to learn how to use the different input modalities to control the app. Once the controls were understood the study administrator launched the study application and scanned the marker for localization before handing over to the participant to begin the task sequence. Participants were able to change freely between input modalities throughout the task.

Once the task had been completed a NASA TLX questionnaire was answered by each participant using pen and paper. Following the NASA-TLX, participants who used the AugmenTech system during the task were also given a SUS questionnaire to complete with pen and paper. This was followed up by participants discussing how they felt about the usability of the system. This was achieved by prompting them with open ended questions such as, "What did you like or dislike about using the system?".

For the participants in the control group introductions to the HoloLens and the application were provided. They were then provided the same training environment to learn how to use the different input modalities as controls for the app. Once satisfied with the controls participants were shown the different forms of instruction and given 5 min to explore the app. Once this time was up each participant completed a SUS questionnaire followed up by a short interview for feedback on the system usability.

5   Results and Discussion

Hypotheses testing was carried out using SPSS Statistics for statistical tests and data plots. Box and whisker plots are used throughout this section to illustrate comparisons. Within the plots; the T-bars indicate 95% confidence interval extents, the edges of the box represent the upper and lower quartiles and the line within the box represents the median. All data used in independent sample t tests met the necessary assumptions, including the Shapiro-Wilk test for normality and Levene's test for homogeneity of variance.

5.1   H1: Participants in the AR Group Would Report Similar Workload to Those Using the Traditional Method

Results – H1. Individual workload elements were scored between 1–21 using individual questions in the NASA-TLX questionnaire. These scores were then scaled to a new range from 0–100. In the NASA-TLX higher scores mean greater amounts of effort, frustration, etc. An overall score was calculated for each participant by taking an average across the different forms of workload.

The mean scores for mental workload were close with 38.0 (SD = 19.46) and 36.5 (SD = 3.92) for the AR and traditional guidance methods, respectively. An independent sample t test showed the difference was not statistically significant, $F(1, 18) = 0.03$, $p = 0.866$.

For physical demand participants, mean scores were 27.5 (SD = 25.19) and 43.0 (SD = 12.74) for the AR and printout conditions, respectively. This difference was shown to not be significantly different in an independent sample t test, $F(1, 18) = 17.24$, $p = 0.100$.

Temporal demand mean scores were 28.5 (SD = 20.42) and 37.5 (SD = 14.19) for the AR and printout conditions, respectively. This difference was shown to not be significantly different in an independent sample t test, $F(1, 18) = 2.28$, $p = 0.267$.

The mean scores for performance were 17.5 (SD = 13.18) for the AR condition and 27.0 (SD = 20.17) for the paper condition. This difference was shown to not be significantly different in an independent sample t test, $F(1, 18) = 3.31$, $p = 0.228$.

The mean effort score for the AR system was 34.9 (SD = 20.92) and for the traditional approach, 41.5 (SD = 26.36). This difference was shown to not be significantly different in an independent sample t test, $F(1, 18) = 1.22$, $p = 0.490$.

For the AR system the mean score for frustration was 31.0 (SD = 20.92), for the traditional method it was 50.5 (SD = 18.78)). An independent t teset on the frustration scores showed this difference to be significant, $F(1, 18) = 1.64$, $p = 0.042$.

An overall score for workload was determined by taking an average across each form of workload. The combined workload scores for the AR system and traditional approach were 29.4 (SD = 11.95) and 39.3 (SD = 14.54), respectively. The difference was shown to be not statistically significant, $F(1, 18) = 0.529$, $p = 0.113$.

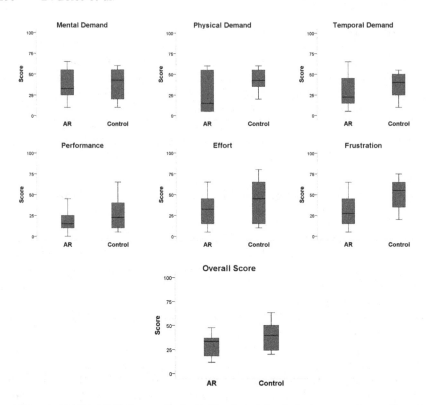

Fig. 4. NASA-TLX Scores for individual workload elements and overall score.

Discussion – H1. We have demonstrated that mental workload when using the AugmenTech system for guidance was similar to that of the traditional approach. The closeness in mental workload between the conditions indicates there were no issues in interpreting the AR instruction or challenge in using the UI.

There was no statistically significant difference in physical demand between the conditions. Particularly physically challenging subtasks could be performed with more ease when seeing the technique exhibited in the videos within the AR system. However, it was expected that the effect of conditions on physicality would be negligible.

It was assumed that using AR would have minimal effect on temporal demand. This was due to the fact that using AR did not introduce, nor remove, any elements creating temporal pressure.

It can be seen from the scoring of the performance that most of the participants felt they had performed well. Both the AR system and printout instructions are sufficient to performthe procedure, there are very few options to perform the task incorrectly. We therefore believe that the participants using the AR system felt a greater sense of confidence in their performance due to being able to confirm their actions across multiple instruction forms.

It had been anticipated that using the AR system would reduce effort and frustration in cases where the participant needed guidance on technique in the form of video demonstration. However, it was also assumed that if there were any issues with the system UI these would reflect badly on the effort and frustration scores. We believe that the simplicity of UI design for AugmenTech can be credited for it not leading to an increase in either effort or frustration. In short interviews many participants indicated that they enjoyed using the AR system for the task. We believe this to be the reason why using the system would lead to lower effort & frustration.

An overall workload score was created by averaging across individual workload elements, as shown in Fig. 4. The results clearly demonstrate that using the AR system did not contribute to an increase in workload overall. We attribute this reduction to the AR system's ease of use and participants being able to watch videos with demonstrations of technique. The authors believe that if the task were more complex there would be greater potential for the AR system to reduce workload.

5.2 H2: The Time Taken to Complete the Task Would Be Similar for Both Conditions

Results – H2. There was no cut off time limit set for the task, all participants managed to complete the task. The mean total time taken for the task was 18 min and 18 s (SD = 244) and 17 min and 36 s (SD = 188) for the AR and control groups, respectively. An independent t test showed the difference was not statistically significant, $F(1, 18) = 0.19$, $p = 0.671$.

Discussion – H2. No difference in time taken was observed between the two conditions. There was a greater difference in times taken between subjects than between conditions, see Fig. 5. Feedback from short interviews with the participants indicated that the majority of time was spent on performing the tasks, as opposed to interpreting the instructions. During short interviews none of the AR group participants claimed to have wasted time due to issues with the system. It was typical that participants across both conditions who took a long time to complete the task had physical challenges with performing one specific subtask; removing the o rings. We believe that the variability in skill level of the participants in performing the dexterous tasks required of them had a greater effect on the time taken than the format of guidance used.

5.3 H3: Usability Would Be Evaluated Highly with Minimal Issues

Results – H3. The SUS questionnaire consists of 10 questions revolving around usability scaled between 1–5, where a score of 1 means strongly disagree and a score of 5 means strongly agree. The individual questions can be calculated and combined for an overall score ranging between 0–100, as shown in [6]. It was clear that completing a SUS for the paper instructions method would not

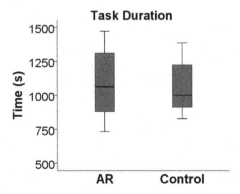

Fig. 5. Time taken for task completion.

be appropriate. Instead, the control group were able to evaluate AugmenTech with a SUS questionnaire after using it for 5 min at the end. It was decided appropriate to combine the scores from both groups after an independent sample t test showed there to be no statistically significant difference between them, $F(1, 18) = 0.02$, $p = 0.894$.

A Shapiro-Wilk test, $W(20) = 0.891$, $p = 0.028$, showed the combined results of the total SUS scores were non-normally distributed. The data was negatively skewed with a moderate skew value to of -0.71 (SE = 0.512). The mean score was 79.5 (SD = 3.61), median was 87.5, 95% CI [71.95, 87.05].

Discussion – H3. In a study by Bangor et al. [2] guidance on interpreting the usability of a tested system was provided. In their work they determined that a system with a SUS score of 70 or over is ready for implementation. They also state that better products would score high 70 s and low 80 s. Work carried out by Sanna et al. [14] demonstrated an AR system with a SUS score of 76. Based on SUS scores AugmenTech has been positively evaluated, with a mean score of 79.5 and a median of 87.5. The authors are pleased that 85% of the participants agreed when asked if they would like to use the system frequently.

The qualitative feedback gained from post study interviews of the participants was in agreement with the quantitative feedback from the SUS questionnaires. The following summaries were made from the discussions:

- The majority of participants enjoyed using the system and were comfortable with the newly introduced controls.
- Animation was a very aesthetically pleasing form of instruction. Though it was not the most capable of the instruction forms the visualisation of moving component parts proved to be appealing.
- When asked for ideas for improvement to the system a common area of interest was auditory feedback.

5.4   H4: There Would Be Relationship Between Instruction Form Usage and Task Duration for AugmenTech Users

Results – H4. Whilst participants in the AR condition were performing the task they could freely change the mode of instruction in the app from the default which was randomly assigned on each instance. Once the task had been completed the time spent on each instruction form was calculated as a percentage of overall task completion time. Image, video and animation mean usages were 36.4% (SD = 38.4), 38.4% (SD = 37.0) and 25.2% (SD = 32.0), respectively.

Tests for Pearson's correlation were conducted to determine correlations between instruction usage and total time taken. Image usage was shown to have a strong negative correlation with time taken, $r = -0.807$, $p < 0.01$. There was a strong positive correlation between video usage and time taken, $r = 0.902$, $p < 0.01$. Animation usage showed no correlation with time taken, $r = -0.069$, $p = 0.85$ (Figs. 6 and 7).

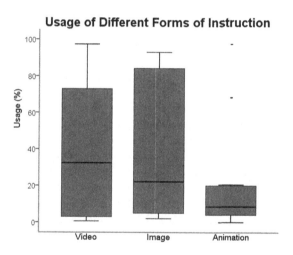

Fig. 6. Box plots showing the usage, based on time, of each form of instruction. Dots represent outliers.

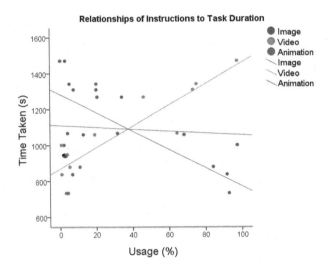

Fig. 7. A scatter plot showing correlations between the different forms of instruction and total task time taken.

Discussion – H4. During interviews many of the participants claimed to have enjoyed using the animations. However, the mean scores for usage showed animation to be the least used across participants. The assumption is that although the participants enjoyed using the animation instructions, they still needed to use the video or images regularly to verify there weren't any actions being missed.

We did not expect any correlations between animation or image usage and time taken. Neither form require much time to interpret actions from. We believe the reason for correlation between image instruction and time could be that using the images enables the user to interpret the key points necessary to complete the task step in the shortest time. Although the animations are short loops (<5 s) they do not convey technique to be used in completing the task step, which can lead to a longer amount of time being spent trying to execute the action with poor form. It was clear that watching videos would take longer than reading the image instruction.

We believe that the relationships expressed in these findings should be taken into consideration when designing an AR assistive system. If urgency is required the option to use video feedback within the app can be an attractive one which results in slower progression. The effect of this relationship could be decreased by granting control of the playback to the users, our system utilises looping videos as part of a theme of simplistic user interface.

6   Limitations and Future Work

There were a few limitations identified during the study. These form the basis for recommendations for future work.

The maintenance procedure provided by industry was not a very complex one and did not require precise actions or techniques for its completion. Similarly, as the majority of the task entailed straightforward assembly and disassembly where there weren't many opportunity for mistakes to be made. The consequence of this was that participants did not need to avail of the additional functionality provided by AugmenTech. A recommendation for further work would be to use a more mentally challenging maintenance procedure as a means of demonstrating the capabilities of AR for guidance.

One of the drawbacks from using participants from the university was the variety in technical skill level for completing the task. This disparity in skill set made it difficult to measure the effect of using AugmenTech on time taken for the procedure. Those who were more naturally skilled required no technique demonstration to quickly perform difficult subtasks. Individuals with less technical skill sometimes struggled on physical steps for a long time regardless of the technique shown in the instructions. It would be recommended to perform a similar study from a population with less variance in skill levels, such as a group of industry technicians of similar experience.

For the study presented in this paper it was important to validate the overall usability of AugmenTech, therefore participants were able to change between instruction forms. However, the authors recognise that AugmenTech provides a platform for work to be carried out to investigate the differences between different instruction forms in AR. A future within-participants study will be carried out to look at the usability of the instruction forms specifically in comparison with one another.

7 Conclusion

AugmenTech was developed to determine feasibility of utilising AR for guidance in a maintenance procedure. The system's usability has been tested within a controlled environment and has proven to be of a high standard through both quantitative and qualitative feedback. Participants with no prior experience in a task procedure were able to perform it using AugmenTech. The system is now ready to be tested in an industrial setting, as no major concerns regarding the UI or system robustness have arisen during testing.

Workload has shown to be similar when using the AR system as it is when following instructions on paper. It is quite common for those not accustomed with the state-of-the-art AR technologies to be impressed by them due to novelty. However, we feel for many people this novelty would have worn off during the course of the study. Instead many participants expressed pleasure in using the system, a promising sign which helps to alleviate concerns regarding acceptability during real world implementation. It is important that workload for tasks in industry are not increased by poor UI design when implementing AR systems such as AugmenTech.

Users of the system have enjoyed using animated instructions in AR, but results show how they still turned to video and image modes to complete maintenance tasks. There were strong correlations with usage of video and image forms and the time taken to complete the procedure. Participants using mainly video took longer to complete the task, whilst those who used image instructions took less time.

References

1. Aleksy, M., Troost, M., Scheinhardt, F., Zank, G.T.: Utilizing hololens to support industrial service processes. In: 2018 IEEE 32nd International Conference on Advanced Information Networking and Applications (AINA), pp. 143–148, May 2018. https://doi.org/10.1109/AINA.2018.00033
2. Bangor, A., Kortum, P.T., Miller, J.T.: An empirical evaluation of the system usability scale. Int. J. Hum. Comput. Inter. **24**(6), 574–594 (2008). https://doi.org/10.1080/10447310802205776
3. Billinghurst, M., Clark, A., Lee, G.: A survey of augmented reality. Found. Trends®R Hum. Comput. Inter. **8**(2–3), 73–272 (2015). https://doi.org/10.1561/1100000049
4. Bottani, E., Vignali, G.: Augmented reality technology in the manufacturing industry: a review of the last decade. IISE Trans. **51**(3), 284–310 (2019). https://doi.org/10.1080/24725854.2018.1493244
5. Botto, C., et al.: Augmented reality for the manufacturing industry: the case of an assembly assistant. In: 2020 IEEE Conference on Virtual Reality and 3D User Interfaces Abstracts and Workshops (VRW), pp. 299–304 (2020)
6. Brooke, J.: SUS-A quick and dirty usability scale. Usability evaluation in industry. CRC Press (1996). https://www.crcpress.com/product/isbn/9780748404605, iSBN: 9780748404605
7. Gavish, N., et al.: Evaluating virtual reality and augmented reality training for industrial maintenance and assembly tasks. Inter. Learn. Environ. **23**(6), 778–798 (2015). https://doi.org/10.1080/10494820.2013.815221
8. Hart, S.G.: Nasa-task load index (NASA-TLX); 20 years later. Proc. Hum. Fact. Ergon. Soc. Ann. Meet. **50**(9), 904–908 (2006). https://doi.org/10.1177/154193120605000909
9. Healy, J., Mavromaras, K., Sloane, P.J.: Adjusting to skill shortages in Australian SMES. Appl. Econ. **47**(24), 2470–2487 (2015). https://doi.org/10.1080/00036846.2015.1008764
10. Ong, S., Yuan, M., Nee, A.: Augmented reality applications in manufacturing: a survey. Int. J. Prod. Res. **46**(10), 2707–2742 (2008)
11. Palmarini, R., Erkoyuncu, J.A., Roy, R., Torabmostaedi, H.: A systematic review of augmented reality applications in maintenance. Robot. Comput. Integr. Manuf. **49**, 215–228 (2018). https://doi.org/10.1016/j.rcim.2017.06.002. http://www.sciencedirect.com/science/article/pii/S0736584517300686
12. Rios, H., Hincapié, M., Caponio, A., Mercado, E., González Mendívil, E.: Augmented reality: an advantageous option for complex training and maintenance operations in aeronautic related processes. In: Shumaker, R. (ed.) VMR 2011. LNCS, vol. 6773, pp. 87–96. Springer, Heidelberg (2011). https://doi.org/10.1007/978-3-642-22021-0_11
13. Sandborn, P.A., Prabhakar, V.J.: The forecasting and impact of the loss of critical human skills necessary for supporting legacy systems. IEEE Trans. Eng. Manage. **62**(3), 361–371 (2015). https://doi.org/10.1109/TEM.2015.2438820

14. Sanna, A., Manuri, F., Lamberti, F., Paravati, G., Pezzolla, P.: Using handheld devices to sup port augmented reality-based maintenance and assembly tasks. In: 2015 IEEE International Conference on Consumer Electronics (ICCE), pp. 178–179, January 2015. https://doi.org/10.1109/ICCE.2015.7066370

15. Schlagowski, R., Merkel, L., Meitinger, C.: Design of an assistant system for industrial maintenance tasks and implementation of a prototype using augmented reality. In: 2017 IEEE International Conference on Industrial Engineering and Engineering Management (IEEM), pp. 294–298, December 2017. https://doi.org/10.1109/IEEM.2017.8289899

16. Schmorrow, D., Cohn, J., Nicholson, D.M.: The psi handbook of virtual environments for training and education [three volumes]: Developments for the military and beyond (2008)

17. Siew, C., Ong, S., Nee, A.: A practical augmented reality-assisted maintenance system framework for adaptive user support. Robot. Comput. Integr. Manuf. **59**, 115–129 (2019). https://doi.org/10.1016/j.rcim.2019.03.010. http://www.sciencedirect.com/science/article/pii/S0736584518306318

18. Stanney, K.M., Mourant, R.R., Kennedy, R.S.: Human factors issues in virtual environments: a review of the literature. Presence Teleoper. Virtual Environ. **7**(4), 327–351 (1998). https://doi.org/10.1162/105474698565767. http://dx.doi.org/10.1162/105474698565767

19. Tang, A., Owen, C., Biocca, F., Mou, W.: Comparative effectiveness of augmented reality in object assembly. In: Proceedings of the SIGCHI Conference on Human Factors in Computing Systems, CHI 2003, pp. 73–80. ACM, New York (2003). https://doi.org/10.1145/642611.642626, http://doi.acm.org/10.1145/642611.642626

20. Tumler, J., et al.: Mobile augmented reality in industrial applications: approaches for solution of user-related issues. In: 2008 7th IEEE/ACM International Symposium on Mixed and Augmented Reality, pp. 87–90, September 2008. https://doi.org/10.1109/ISMAR.2008.4637330

21. Wang, X., Ong, S.K., Nee, A.Y.C.: A comprehensive survey of augmented reality assembly research. Adv. Manuf. **4**(1), 1–22 (2016). https://doi.org/10.1007/s40436-015-0131-4

22. Webel, S., Bockholt, U., Engelke, T., Gavish, N., Olbrich, M., Preusche, C.: An augmented reality training platform for assembly and maintenance skills. Robot. Auton. Syst. **61**(4), 398–403 (2013). https://doi.org/10.1016/j.robot.2012.09.013. http://www.sciencedirect.com/science/article/pii/S0921889012001674, models and Technologies for Multi-modal Skill Training

23. Westerfield, G., Mitrovic, A., Billinghurst, M.: Intelligent augmented reality training for motherboard assembly. Int. J. Artif. Intel. Educ. **25**(1), 157–172 (2015). https://doi.org/10.1007/s40593-014-0032-x

24. Yuan, M.L., Ong, S.K., Nee, A.Y.C.: Augmented reality for assembly guidance using a virtual interactive tool. Int. J. Prod. Res. **46**(7), 1745–1767 (2008). https://doi.org/10.1080/00207540600972935

WAAT: A Workstation AR Authoring Tool for Industry 4.0

Pierre Bégout[1,2,4], Thierry Duval[2,3(✉)], Sébastien Kubicki[3,4],
Bertrand Charbonnier[2,3], and Emmanuel Bricard[1]

[1] elm.leblanc, Drancy, France
[2] IMT Atlantique, Brest, France
`thierry.duval@imt-atlantique.fr`
[3] ENIB, Brest, France
[4] Lab-STICC, UMR CNRS 6285, Brest, France

Abstract. In this paper, we present WAAT, an AR authoring tool dedicated to industrial environments. The interest of such a tool in an industrial context is to allow non-expert users to quickly create and dynamically modify 3D models of workstations, and also test the AR guidance placement. WAAT makes on-site authoring possible, which should really help to have an accurate 3D representation of assembly lines. The verification of AR guidance should also be very useful to make sure everything is visible and doesn't interfere with technical tasks. We deployed WAAT in an assembly line of an elm.leblanc/Bosch boiler factory to assess its features in an ecological context. We also made a comparison to another AR authoring tool to better estimate its advantages.

Keywords: 3D authoring · AR authoring tool · Virtual reality ·
Augmented reality · Mixed reality · AR training · AR guidance ·
Virtual environment · Industry 4.0 · Human-computer interaction · 3D
interaction

1 Introduction

In a context of constant industrial evolution and a need of more industrial agility to answer the increasingly unpredictable customer requests, having well trained assembly line operators is extremely important. This operator training problematic is well known by manufacturers such as elm.leblanc, a boiler manufacturer for which this training problem is very important during each winter, when boiler orders rise a lot, as many temporary workers must be hired for a few months. The training of these new operators is an important process that involves a lot of time and human resources. For instance, one experimented operator is dedicated to the training of one new operator. During this time, the production lines output is not optimal because of the learning curve of the new operators as well as the attention they require from permanent staff decreasing the overall capacity.

One solution to this training issue is the use of AR in the factory (*cf.* Fig. 1), to train new operators directly on the assembly line with less supervision from

© Springer Nature Switzerland AG 2020
L. T. De Paolis and P. Bourdot (Eds.): AVR 2020, LNCS 12243, pp. 304–320, 2020.
https://doi.org/10.1007/978-3-030-58468-9_22

experimented operator. This tool could also be used by an experimented operator to train on a new position of the assembly line or a different assembly line.

Indeed, in the industrial context, AR can be used in many different ways. It can be used to make expert remote guidance, create new products using collaborative engineering methods, or realize digital inspection of new prototypes [6]. AR is also used to test the ergonomics of the workstations and the reachability of some equipment [2]. Error and default detection using AR are possible and very useful in Airbus factories [1]. These different uses have a lot of potential, but the most interesting feature of AR in our case and the most used is the assembly assistance, for training purpose [1,19]. Actually, assembly tasks training using AR has been researched for a long time, with the comparison of paper instructions sheets with VR and AR instructions, showing that AR instructions were the most efficient [3]. More recently, new ways of using AR for assembly training are researched, by combining AR and other tools. It can be an intelligent tutoring system for error detection [23] or data from the factory [4,17].

Fig. 1. Operator on an assembly line using AR guidance to select components

These AR environments are created with AR authoring tools, and most of them are dedicated to 3D CAD experts or 3D AR experts. So, even if the end-users can participate to the modelling of the AR environment during its user-centered design with such authoring tools, they cannot use them to evolve the AR representation according to the real environment changes.

This is why we make the assumption that to be efficient and to provide feedback on the operator in training, such authoring tools should be dedicated to line managers. It would permit the users with the real knowledge of the assembly line to model its different elements. These elements could be, for instance, 3D models or anchors[1].

In our industrial context, which can occur quite often for factories, the 3D models of the parts of the assembly line are not available or could change dynamically according to the needs of the production. This is why we cannot use a

---

[1] detailed in Sect. 3.2.

classical 3D CAD tool to manage the placement of the augmentation relatively to the parts of the assembly line and we need an authoring tool to facilitate the configuration of the AR training tool.

Our contribution is to improve AR authoring by proposing a tool allowing line managers, who are not familiar neither with AR technology nor 3D CAD tools, to quickly create a 3D representation of the assembly line, by placing and manipulating 3D elements easily without the need of long training time to be efficient with AR technology.

The remaining of this paper is organized as follows: in Sect. 2 we explain the industrial constraints for the use of this authoring tool. Section 3 contains the related work, justifying the choices made in Sect. 4 which describes WAAT, our authoring tool. Section 5 describes the comparison between WAAT and Microsoft Guides on an authoring task. Finally, Sect. 6 concludes this paper and discusses about future developments.

2   Industrial Context

In an industrial context, we have a lot of constraints related to the nature of the workstations and the way boiler assembling is done. We have many problematic to take into account in order to make an authoring tool that allows line managers to quickly and easily create a 3D representation of the assembly line.

2.1   Time Management

When working on an assembly line, every gesture is thought to accomplish the technical action in the smallest amount of time possible. Every workstation is thought to accomplish a certain number of technical tasks, the placement of each equipment is well thought. Therefore the authoring tool should help gaining time in the factory by quickly configuring the training tool. The final user of this authoring tool should be able to perform the authoring task quickly, otherwise the tool won't be used.

2.2   Managing Evolution

The elm.leblanc company assembly lines are manageable and can be changed during the day to correspond with the current boiler model. Each workstation can be rearranged (some parts are on wheels to be easily movable). Some tasks can pass from a workstation to another when changing the boiler model currently assembled on the line.

This leads to the need of regular updates of the 3D model of the assembly line to correspond to the state of the real one and/or to new boilers models. The most suitable user to perform these updates is the line manager, who knows the assembly line state and each workstation very well.

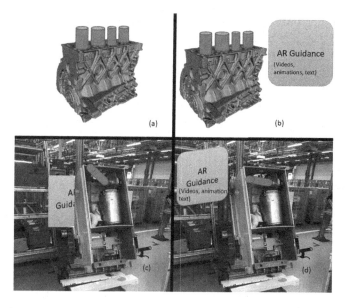

Fig. 2. Needed features of the authoring tool. (a) 3D models placement with a motor. (b) AR guidance placement on the motor. (c) AR checking of 3D models and AR guidance on a real boiler. (d) AR validation of the placement on a real boiler

2.3   Main Features

Knowing these requirements, we have several uses for our authoring tool. First, the authoring tool must allow fast and easy placement of 3D models of the workstation (*cf.* Fig. 2a). The AR guidance could consist of an information panel containing text, videos, pictures, or it could also be highlights of 3D models. This AR guidance must also be placed easily (*cf.* Fig. 2b). The AR part of the tool must allow the user to compare the 3D models and the real objects (*cf.* Fig. 2c), and to move or resize the 3D objects to match the real scene and the objects, and also to make sure the operator guidance panel is visible (*cf.* Fig. 2d). The next section presents the state of the art about 3D authoring tools that we could use to meet all our requirements.

2.4   Tool Evaluation Criteria

Knowing our constraints and our context, we defined criteria to evaluate the different tools we studied. First, the tool must allow the placement of 3D models, and also the placement of AR guidance (3D animation, text, video) to check its placement and its visibility. As seen previously, the workstations can change quite often so we need to be able to do live edit while in AR. The industrial context prevents us to put tracking markers (detailed in Sect. 3.2) everywhere to track the workstation elements, so we need to use only one marker for the whole workstation. The training required to use the authoring tool must be fast and simple. The tool's interface must be simple, a GUI authoring is preferable. Our final users are the line managers and experimented operators, so the authoring tool needs to be easy to use, and the AR part must be usable hands free to enable users to perform the technical tasks (head mounted display are probably the best solution to do that).

3   Related Work

3.1   3D Authoring Tools

3D models of components and workstations are widely used in the industry. Most of the time they are used to create the full product, change the layout of the factory, test the ergonomics of the workstations [2]. To design these 3D models, many tools are available since the 70's. Some of the most used tools to model industrial component are SolidWorks[2], Inventor[3], CATIA[4], Pro/ENGINEER[5] and AutoCAD[6]. These tools offer precise modeling features. The problem with these CAD (Computer Aided Design) tools is that their learning curve is very steep and require dozens of hours to properly use them [14]. It is also difficult to export files to AR engines like Unreal[7] or Unity[8] without the use of an other software. Usually, the exported object are opened in a DCC (Digital Content Creation) tool (Blender[9] for example) to be converted in a suitable format for AR engines.

Other digital content creation tools, such as 3dsMax[10], Maya[11], Blender, can be used to model our workstation, but just as the previous CAD softwares seen previously, their interface is very complicated, and the learning time is very high. They offer lots of options to create very precise 3D models. SketchUp[12], another DCC tool, is easier to learn since it is based on line drawing but the 3D models obtained this way are less accurate than with the other tools [20].

These 3D modeling tools are great when accurate 3D models are required, but they target professional designers who can spend time to learn a new tool and realize accurate 3D models of industrial components and workstations. In our case, we don't need such accurate 3D models. Indeed we only need to represent the components of the workstation and their position to the AR guidance tool.

---

[2] https://www.solidworks.com/.
[3] https://www.autodesk.com/products/inventor/overview.
[4] https://www.3ds.com/products-services/catia/.
[5] https://www.ptc.com/en/products/cad/pro-engineer.
[6] https://www.autodesk.com/products/autocad/overview.
[7] https://www.unrealengine.com/en-US/.
[8] https://unity.com/.
[9] https://www.blender.org/.
[10] https://www.autodesk.com/products/3ds-max/overview.
[11] https://www.autodesk.com/products/maya/overview.
[12] https://www.sketchup.com/.

3.2   AR Authoring

To be able to use AR authoring tools in our assembly lines, we have to know where to locate the 3D models in the space, to place them at the right position, and which graphical assets to use. To achieve that goal, several tracking techniques are used, and several recommendations exists. These are detailed in the next subsection.

Graphic Elements. To use AR in an industrial context, we have to adapt our graphical assets to be easy to understand, create and render, and avoid occlusion [7]. To achieve that goal, it is better to use symbols and simple models [22] to guide the user and represent instructions. Text can be used but has to be simplified [8] and write in a billboard to have contrast between the text and the background.

Tracking Methods. Tracking is a fundamental issue when using AR. Accurate and stable tracking techniques are important for using AR in an industrial environment. Most of the time, markers are used to locate the real objects and help positioning 3D objects. The capture of the marker is made by image recognition. After recognition, the 3D object linked with the marker appears [10,12,18,21,23–25]. Markers can be pictures, QR code, colored paper, any kind of 2D unique-looking object. This technique is easy to implement and useful in an environment that can change depending on the assembly task such as our assembly line. An other tracking technique uses object recognition by comparing a 3D model of the object to the real object captured by the camera [5]. This technique requires precise 3D models of our objects and is useful in a static environment, which is not the case with our assembly line.

AR Authoring Tools. With the emergence of AR, many tools have appeared to build AR applications such as ARToolkit [13] that provides a marker-based registration using computer vision. ARToolKit and its variations all require the user to have C/C++ skills. More recently, Vuforia[13] a software development kit, provides computer vision technology to recognize and track planar images and 3D objects in real time. To use Vuforia, C# skills are necessary. This is the main problem with creating AR content. Most of the time low level AR libraries are used, requiring programming skills from the user.

The need for High level AR authoring tools for non-programmers is important. The earlier frameworks were often a plug-in of an other software, like DART [16], a plug-in for Adobe Director[14] (not supported anymore). DART was supporting the 3D editing part of the software with visual programming, such as dragging a 3D object in a scene and adding behavioral scripts to the object. Another GUI-based visual AR authoring tool, AMIRE [11] allows the

---

[13] https://developer.vuforia.com/.
[14] https://www.adobe.com/products/director.html.

user to describe interactions between objects with visual representations, which can become complex. An other approach with a more rigid framework was APRIL [15] based on XML descriptions. APRIL is a plug-in of their own platform containing XML parser. Using XML can be quite difficult for a user with no programming skills at all.

More recently, 3D GUI-based authoring tools have been studied. In ACARS [25] the authoring part is realized on desktop using a 3D model of the equipment. The maintenance technician can do on-site authoring using a tangible object to change the information's position. The authoring in SUGAR [10] is also realized on desktop. The maintenance expert can place AR information around the equipment using depth map of the factory. The authoring is also made by an expert in ARAUM [5], he gives information to the authoring tool about the procedures to perform, which will place automatically the AR content around the equipment using spatial, time and user context. Some authoring tools include the final user in the authoring process. In ARTA [8], an experienced worker is recorded performing a task using eye-tracking and a camera, but he also has to learn how to use Unity3D to split the recording in different steps. The final user can also intervene to verify the quality of the modeling in AR [9], to add details in the instructions or edit the models, but the original modeling is done by an engineer. The target devices for these authoring tools are HMD (Head Mounted Display) devices, but a mobile platform (tablet or phone) can also be a good alternative. Using the VEDILS framework [18] allows any user to create AR content for mobile using a desktop application. It uses visual programming and behavioral blocks to add interactions to the 3D objects, but it requires knowledge in algorithmic to be used properly.

Using mobiles to visualize AR content leads to research on mobile AR authoring tools, reducing the material needed for the authoring task, allowing in-situ authoring, which can be really interesting in some situations where we don't have access to a computer. HARATIO [21] allows the user to add 3D objects from a library in a scene, including behavior scripts. All actions are made with a radial menu. We can see limitations with mobile authoring tools like in [12] or [24]. In the first one, the user interacts with the 3D object on the touch screen, whereas in the second one the interactions are done directly with the markers which can be combined. With these tools we can only associate one marker with one 3D object.

It seems that authoring tasks made using desktop applications are often realized by an expert on the industrial procedure or a designer while we need our tool to be usable by line managers. It also seems that most authoring tools don't allow users to directly edit the content while in AR to better match the real objects. Mobile authoring can be interesting in our case but the interaction limitations and the marker/3D object limit is a problem because we will have multiple 3D objects per workstation.

Table 1. Table summarizing the main features of 3D authoring tools suited for AR authoring.

	3D model placement	AR guidance placement	Live AR authoring	Modular tracking	learning time	GUI-based	HMD use	Usable by operators
SolidWorks		X	X	X	X		X	X
Inventor		X	X	X	X		X	X
CATIA		X	X	X	X		X	X
Pro/ENGINEER		X	X	X	X		X	X
AutoCAD		X	X	X	X		X	X
Blender		X	X	X	X		X	X
3dsMax		X	X	X	X		X	X
Maya		X	X	X	X		X	X
SketchUp		X	X	X	X		X	X
ARToolKit			X		X	X		X
Vuforia			X		X	X		X
DART			X		X			X
AMIRE			X		X			X
APRIL			X		X	X		X
ACARS					X			X
SUGAR			X		X		X	X
ARAUM			X	X	X			X
VEDILS			X		X			X
ARTA			X	X	X			
Geng et al.					X			X
HARATIO				X			X	
Jung et al.				X			X	
Yang et al.				X			X	

4 WAAT (Workstation AR Authoring Tool)

To meet all the requirements presented in Sect. 2 and summarized in Table 1, we propose WAAT: an authoring tool designed to allow users to create 3D scenes of workstations by placing 3D objects representing the workstation. The originality of WAAT is that it makes it possible for the user to compare the 3D model with the real workstation. The authoring task in WAAT is easy to perform by production staff, only need a few 3D models, and does not require any engineer or designer.

4.1 System Overview

WAAT is composed of two modules, a desktop 3D authoring module and an AR authoring module, as illustrated Fig. 3. The desktop authoring module (see Fig. 4) is used to create the 3D scene whereas the AR authoring module is used to modify and validate the placement and/or size of the 3D models. The two modules are connected by the server, with a JSON file for each scene allowing the user to modify the scene either on desktop or AR.

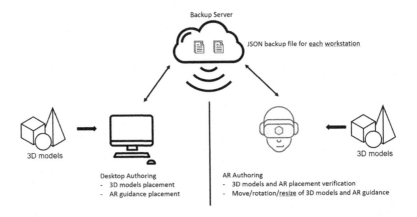

Fig. 3. WAAT system overview

WAAT is developed with Unity using Vuforia for the marker tracking in the AR module. The AR hardware currently used is the Microsoft Hololens 2[15].

To deploy WAAT on another AR device such as the Magic Leap[16] we would just have to add to our system the Magic Leap extension of the SDK (Software Development Kit) we currently use.

4.2 3D Authoring of the Assembly Line

The authoring task on the desktop application is done with simple interactions using a mouse and a keyboard. To select which object the user wants to add, he just has to choose the object in the bottom interface (*cf.* Fig. 4) and define its position in the scene (we get the 3D objects from any 3D modelling or CAD tool). He can then move the objects to place them more precisely and change

---

[15] https://www.microsoft.com/en-us/hololens.
[16] https://www.magicleap.com/.

some of their properties (*e.g.*, name, scale, ...). We chose **drag and drop** as the interaction method but it is not the only one available (*i.e.*, keyboard or a graphic overlay for the axis and rotation), and testing will help to choose the best suited one. Then the user can save the scene he created or load a scene previously created.

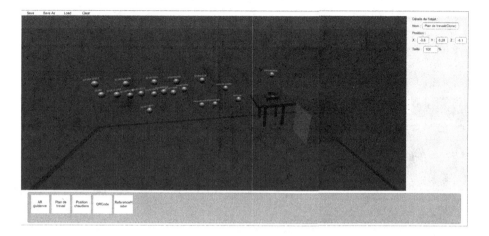

Fig. 4. WAAT desktop module

We tested WAAT on a workstation from the factory (*cf.* Fig. 5). We used 3D models to represent the workstation and the placement of the boiler. We represented the boxes where the parts to assemble are kept and the tools to use with "spatial anchors", a 3D object allowing the AR training tool to know the position of the different part to pick (see Fig. 8). We also placed the panel used to display AR assembly guidance.

We conceived WAAT to also be usable in an immersive mode, but we focused on the main features of the tool and our users want to use it in non-immersive mode for the moment.

4.3   Using AR to Check the 3D Modeling

To make sure the 3D model of the assembly line is on par with the real assembly line, the user will use the AR part of the tool and compare the position, rotation, size of the 3D objects with their corresponding real object.

If it is not on par with the real objects (as illustrated in Fig. 6), the user can move the 3D objects by grabbing them and placing them at the correct position. Each 3D object refers to a real object and must be placed, rotated and scaled as its real counterpart to allow the AR guidance system to be well configured (as illustrated in Fig. 9). The AR guidance system will use the position of the 3D objects to tell the operator where to grab or place technical parts.

After finishing all his modifications, the user can save his work, which updates the 3D model of the assembly line in the WAAT system. He can now load another scene to check the 3D modeling.

Fig. 5. The workstation we want to model

Fig. 6. Bad placement and size of the 3D models

4.4 WAAT and AR Guidance

WAAT is also used to place the marker position for further AR guidance of the operators. Each scene is associated to a marker allowing the system to load the correct objects related to a workstation. The 3D objects in WAAT are then used for the training or as anchors for the AR guidance system.

Placing AR Markers in the Model of the Assembly Line. After the 3D modeling of the assembly line, the final step is to place the markers positions in the virtual scenes. This virtual marker is used to show the user in AR the position where he is supposed to place the real marker to use the system. It is placed in the same way than any other 3D object.

Placing AR Markers in the Real Assembly Line. To be able to test the AR guidance (and to use it during the operator formation) the user has to place real markers at the same place as the "virtual" markers in the real assembly line. For every workstation, a specific marker is placed in a specific position. If the real marker is not at the same position as the virtual one, as illustrated Fig. 7, all the 3D objects will be misplaced compared to the real objects. If the position of the virtual marker is too difficult to use in the assembly line, the user can move it to match the correct position and obtain the situation illustrated in Fig. 8.

Fig. 7. Bad marker placement on the real object

AR Checking of the AR Guidance. The AR scene is also used to verify the positioning of the "operator guidance": the panels where the training instructions will be shown. The user can move these panels to make sure the instructions are visible and that there is no occlusion or other problems. The user will also check the positioning of all markers and objects and move them if needed since they will also be used by the AR guidance system.

Here again, after finishing all his modifications, the user can save his work, this will update the assembly line model globally, and more precisely, the markers positions and AR guidance panels positions.

Fig. 8. Good placement of the AR Guidance

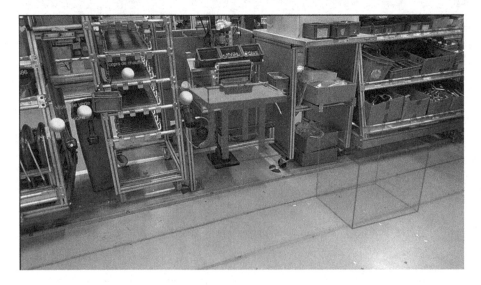

Fig. 9. Good placement of the 3D models

5   Comparison with Microsoft Dynamics 365 Guides

We compared the use of our tool WAAT with the solution from Microsoft[17]. This solution is similar to ours, it is separated in two modules: the desktop module and the AR module. The desktop module is the place where the user creates the instructions and add the 3D models tied with these instructions. The difference with WAAT is that there is no placement of the 3D models with Microsoft Dynamics 365 Guides. The AR module is used for the placement of the 3D models in the real environment and to create the AR assistance (*i.e.*, arrows showing what to do at each instruction, where to place the element). The tracking is made with a QR code.

We compared the authoring time to place the 3D models of the workstation at the right position between WAAT and Microsoft Guides. We evaluated the total authoring time (desktop + AR), with the same number of 3D models to place on the same workstation.

Table 2. Table summarizing the time (minutes) for the authoring of a workstation using WAAT or Guides.

Tool	Desktop	AR	Total
WAAT	6'30"	1'50"	8'20"
Guides	3'19"	5'10"	8'29"

The desktop authoring is faster with Guides, since there is no placement of the 3D objects in a virtual world. The 3D models are linked to a task and their characteristics can't be changed (position, name, scale).

For the AR authoring, our tool is much faster because the 3D models are already placed almost at the right position. The movement to achieve the right positioning is minimal. In Guides, however, the user has to get the 3D models in the instructions panel, requiring a lot of movement, and taking a lot of time.

As summarized in Table 2, we can see that WAAT is slightly faster than Guides on the environment authoring task. To improve our tool and reduce the authoring time, we have to improve the desktop authoring, and more precisely the placement of the 3D models. One of the considered solution is workstation templates placing the anchors automatically with only the references in entry. However in WAAT, knowing the names and positions of the 3D models and anchors allows the AR assistance creation tool to generate automatically the placement instructions by collision detection.

More testing is required, in which we will evaluate the authoring time, the number of error, the accuracy and fidelity. We will also evaluate the usability with the System Usability Scale, and a workload test with the Nasa TLX.

---

[17] https://dynamics.microsoft.com/en-us/mixed-reality/guides/.

6   Conclusion

In this paper, we have presented WAAT, a 3D authoring tool allowing untrained users to create 3D models of the assembly line in a boiler factory. WAAT allows fast creation and AR comparison of the virtual and the real model. In case of a mismatch between both virtual and real models, the user can easily and quickly move the 3D virtual components to match the components of the real workstation. He can test the AR guidance used to train assembly line operators to make sure that everything is fully visible and doesn't interfere with the realization of the technical tasks.

Improving desktop authoring will be an important part of our future work to reduce the time spent on the desktop part. First, to adapt the interactions used to move/rotate/resize the 3D objects to our users, adding accessories such as a 3D controller will be explored. We will also test new AR systems to test their usability and native interactions to see if we can use them, or if we can adapt them to our users. Second, we have to make other tests with the line managers from the factory to enhance the usability and the intuitiveness of WAAT. Last, using 3D models of the workstations will also allow us to test the ergonomics of new workstations during the creation process with the use of a posture capture outfit.

Finally, the immersive mode of WAAT will allow us to visualize the augmented environment and test the placement of the operator guidance, even if it's not the focus right now. We will be able to simulate the AR test of the scenes without the need to be in the factory all the time.

Acknowledgements. This work is possible thanks to the workers of the Drancy elm.leblanc factory and of Saint-Thégonnec elm.leblanc factory for exchanging with us on the problematic of their work and helping us to better understand their needs in 3D modeling and AR guidance.

References

1. Barbosa, G.F., Frigo, M.A., Da Silva, E.C.C., Barbosa, G.F.: Augmented reality in aerospace manufacturing: a review. J. Ind. Intell. Inf. **4**(2), 125–130 (2016)
2. Berg, L.P., Vance, J.M.: Industry use of virtual reality in product design and manufacturing: a survey. Virtual Reality **21**(1), 1–17 (2016). https://doi.org/10.1007/s10055-016-0293-9
3. Boud, A.C., Haniff, D.J., Baber, C., Steiner, S.J.: Virtual reality and augmented reality as a training tool for assembly tasks. In: Proceedings of the International Conference on Information Visualisation, vol. 1999, pp. 32–36. Institute of Electrical and Electronics Engineers Inc. (1999)
4. Danielsson, O., Syberfeldt, A., Holm, M., Wang, L.: Operators perspective on augmented reality as a support tool in engine assembly. In: Procedia CIRP, vol. 72, pp. 45–50. Elsevier B.V. (2018)
5. Erkoyuncu, J.A., del Amo, I.F., Dalle Mura, M., Roy, R., Dini, G.: Improving efficiency of industrial maintenance with context aware adaptive authoring in augmented reality. CIRP Ann. Manuf. Technol. **66**(1), 465–468 (2017)

6. Fraga-Lamas, P., Fernandez-Carames, T.M., Blanco-Novoa, O., Vilar-Montesinos, M.A.: A review on industrial augmented reality systems for the industry 4.0 shipyard. IEEE Access **6**, 13358–13375 (2018)
7. Gattullo, M., Scurati, G.W., Evangelista, A., Ferrise, F., Fiorentino, M., Uva, A.E.: Informing the use of visual assets in industrial augmented reality. In: Rizzi, C., Andrisano, A.O., Leali, F., Gherardini, F., Pini, F., Vergnano, A. (eds.) ADM 2019. LNME, pp. 106–117. Springer, Cham (2020). https://doi.org/10.1007/978-3-030-31154-4_10
8. Gattullo, M., Scurati, G.W., Fiorentino, M., Uva, A.E., Ferrise, F., Bordegoni, M.: Towards augmented reality manuals for industry 4.0: a methodology. Robot. Comput. Integr. Manuf. **56**, 276–286 (2019)
9. Geng, J., et al.: A systematic design method of adaptive augmented reality work instruction for complex industrial operations. Comput. Ind. **119**, 103229 (2020)
10. Gimeno, J., Morillo, P., Orduña, J., Fernández, M.: A new AR authoring tool using depth maps for industrial procedures. Comput. Ind. **64**(9), 1263–1271 (2013)
11. Grimm, P., Haller, M., Paelke, V., Reinhold, S., Reimann, C., Zauner, R.: AMIRE-authoring mixed reality. In: Proceedings of the 1st IEEE International Augmented Reality Toolkit Workshop, ART 2002. Institute of Electrical and Electronics Engineers Inc. (2002)
12. Jung, J., Hong, J., Park, S., Yang, H.S.: Smartphone as an augmented reality authoring tool via multi-touch based 3D interaction method. In: Proceedings of the 11th ACM SIGGRAPH International Conference on Virtual-Reality Continuum and its Applications in Industry, VRCAI 2012, p. 17. ACM Press, New York (2012)
13. Kato, B.: Marker tracking and HMD calibration for a video-based augmented reality conferencing system. In: Proceedings 2nd IEEE and ACM International Workshop on Augmented Reality, IWAR 1999 (1999)
14. Kostic, Z.: Comparative study of CAD software, Web3D technologies and existing solutions to support distance-learning students of engineering profile. Int. J. Comput. Sci. Issues **9**(4), 181–187 (2012)
15. Ledermann, F., Schmalstieg, D.: APRIL: a high-level framework for creating augmented reality presentations. In: 2005 IEEE Proceedings of the Virtual Reality, VR 2005, pp. 187–194. IEEE (2005)
16. MacIntyre, B., Gandy, M., Dow, S., Bolter, J.D.: DART. In: Proceedings of the 17th Annual ACM Symposium on User Interface Software and Technology, UIST 2004, p. 197. ACM Press, New York (2004)
17. Makris, S., Karagiannis, P., Koukas, S., Matthaiakis, A.S.: Augmented reality system for operator support in human-robot collaborative assembly. CIRP Ann. Manuf. Technol. **65**(1), 61–64 (2016)
18. Mota, J.M., Ruiz-Rube, I., Dodero, J.M., Arnedillo-Sánchez, I.: Augmented reality mobile app development for all. Comput. Electr. Eng. **65**, 250–260 (2018)
19. Paelke, V.: Augmented reality in the smart factory: supporting workers in an industry 4.0. environment. In: Proceedings of the 2014 IEEE Emerging Technology and Factory Automation (ETFA), pp. 1–4. IEEE (2014)
20. Parisi, T.: Programming 3D Applications with HTML5 and WebGL: 3D Animation and Visualization for Web Pages. O'Reilly Media (2014)
21. Sambrooks, L., Wilkinson, B.: Designing HARATIO: a novice AR authoring tool. In: Proceedings of the 28th Australian Computer-Human Interaction Conference, OzCHI 2016 (2016)
22. Scurati, G.W., Gattullo, M., Fiorentino, M., Ferrise, F., Bordegoni, M., Uva, A.E.: Converting maintenance actions into standard symbols for Augmented Reality applications in Industry 4.0. Comput. Ind. **98**, 68–79 (2018)

23. Westerfield, G., Mitrovic, A., Billinghurst, M.: Intelligent augmented reality training for motherboard assembly. Int. J. Artif. Intell. Educ. **25**(1), 157–172 (2015)
24. Yang, Y., Shim, J., Chae, S., Han, T.D.: Mobile augmented reality authoring tool.
In: Proceedings of the 2016 IEEE 10th International Conference on Semantic Computing, ICSC 2016, pp. 358–361. Institute of Electrical and Electronics Engineers
Inc. (2016)
25. Zhu, J., Ong, S.K., Nee, A.Y.: An authorable context-aware augmented reality
system to assist the maintenance technicians. Int. J. Adv. Manuf. Technol. **66**(9–
12), 1699–1714 (2013)

Cinematic Space in Virtual Production

Katriina Ilmaranta[(✉)] [iD]

University of Lapland, Rovaniemi, Finland
katriina.ilmaranta@saunalahti.fi

Abstract. In this article, I aim to examine the ways virtual technologies have affected on the arrangement of the cinema space. Virtual technologies are eventually referenced here as virtual production (VP), which makes it possible for filmmakers to mix live footage and computer graphics interactively while filming on set. The cinema space, respectively, is delineated along the views provided by the enactive approach and neuroscience of emotion. The enactive approach in cognitive science describes the relationship of a human being to her environment as an embodied experience, and neuroscience of emotion bridges the gap needed to understand the role of an enactive system in meaning-making. I will also focus on how the concept of digital cinema has evolved since its beginning from the perspective of both practice and theory. I render how digital cinema first resembled in its functions the traditional glass matte paintings behind the character and gradually turned into manifesting an essential hookup between the filmmakers and digital content. I wish to abandon the idea that digital image just represents a pictorial illusion of reality and instead see it making possible a lifelike simulation of the digital environments throughout the filmmaking process, eventually blending the borders of pre-, production and postproduction phases. This weaving of interactive digital tools into cinema practice has created new approaches, which tend to emphasize intense body-related experiences, thus conveying a thickened sense of immersive presence in the film experience.

Keywords: Digital cinema · Virtual production · Simulation-based filmmaking practices · Enactive film experience · Embodied cognition · Narrative space

1 Introduction

"We're in 100% digital film space now. I think the industry has to accept that this is like the transition to talkies—it's massive and it's game-changing and it's happening", insists the famous production designer and director of the USC World Building Media Lab (WBML), Alex McDowell, and continues further to elaborate the new role of digital technology in the filmmaking by claiming: "I expect it can do anything I imagine" [1]. While I believe this argument describes the excitement within the film industry on the doorstep of digital technologies, the possibility to create anything imaginable seems plausible considering the strength of the current visual effects (VFX) industry. However, a question remains, what "100% digital film space" might mean? In McDowell's own words, we can define this concept as "a non-linear workflow within an immersive technology-driven space" [2].

© Springer Nature Switzerland AG 2020
L. T. De Paolis and P. Bourdot (Eds.): AVR 2020, LNCS 12243, pp. 321–332, 2020.
https://doi.org/10.1007/978-3-030-58468-9_23

The development of digital cinema has been noticeably fast. I am writing this paper driven by my own artistic experiences within the field of film production design. I started my career in the 80s by hauling the huge glass sheets with matte paintings on the roof of an old factory building since the visual effects (VFX) were finalized on the actual filming site. I gradually proceeded through the years to use the computer-generated imagery (CGI) in my designs for the first time and was happy enough to add simple flowers on the grass field in a single film scene. However, the possibility to retouch a static image soon developed towards more sophisticated use of camera tracking systems allowing the CGI in the moving shot. Even though the budgets in my country do not allow the filmmakers to use similar comprehensive applications as in blockbuster movies, I eventually could do my filmmaking experiments with extensive use of virtual applications.

Having witnessed this evolution from a personal viewpoint of a practitioner has led me to delve deeper into digitalization. The rapidly changing arena of CGI has undoubtedly provided an escalating amount of techniques to produce and manipulate film image assets, but what about cinema as a whole, as an artform mimicking life itself? As McDowell's words hint, filmmaking has been transferred from an arduous world of physical limitations into the universe, where only bits matter. Most likely, this crucial change has profound level effects not only on the practice itself, but also on how we establish our presence in the cinematic story worlds, that are essentially synthetic, and thus isolated from the physical experience.

In the following article, I wish to reflect on this transition, where new technologies and artistic expression are intertwined. First, I will be discussing digital cinema from contrasting perspectives. Each of them provides some cue, how CGI related film environments can be understood. However, traditional film theories (such as realist or structuralist film theories) or even the early views on digital cinema seem not to provide sufficient explanation, what does it mean to be in 100% digital film space – practice wise and artistically. Therefore, I proceed to contemplate whether the relatively new approach, enactive cognitive science could provide a novel way to scrutinize digital cinema. As an example, I will introduce the idea of virtual production.

Digital cinema in my mind tends to problematize such concepts as reality, illusion (as false perception), and simulation (as an imitation of reality), so they will be in focus in this essay. The characterization of cinema as moving-image art will also be emphasized since through movement, the cinematic worlds are explored and substantiated.

2 Camera Viewing Space

The cinema as an eye, or a kino-eye, a man seeing through the camera the world, implicating the essence of real, is well expressed through Jean-Luc Godard's famous analogy suggesting cinema as "truth 24 frames per second" [3]. This notion of film recording the real and experienced is a central argument of the realist film theory, and forcefully put forward by one of its central thinkers, André Bazin. He saw the ontology of a photographic image as a derivative of a technological process incapable of deceiving:

> "This production by automatic means has radically affected our psychology of the image. The objective nature of photography confers on it a quality of credibility

absent from all other picture-making. Despite any objections our critical spirit may offer, we are forced to accept as real the existence of the object reproduced, actually re-presented, set before us, that is to say, in time and space. Photography enjoys a certain advantage in virtue of this transference of reality from the thing to its reproduction" [4].

However, how ontologically oriented Bazin might have seemed to be, he ambiguously fluctuated between ideas of reality and illusion implying that "the perfect illusion of outside world" [5] in cinematic reproduction could be "composed of a complex of abstraction (black and white, plane surface), of conventions (the rules of montage, for example), and of authentic reality" [6]. The unavoidable consequence of this was, that the awareness of reality, in the end, could be lost, while watching a film. Thus, Bazin saw illusion as a necessary element in cinema, and further speculated that the spectator's engagement with the pseudorealistic illusion was based on her existential engagement with the lived reality [7].

The paradigm of indexical image depended on the production process of a cine-matographic image during the pre-digital time when there seem not to be a reason to raise questions of content manipulation: what was once filmed, was there on the film, as a proof, as an exact composition of an authentic situation. As film theorist Stephen Prince has brought up, the existing postproduction methods of that time were far more limited. While there were some, they relied on altering the photographic development process, which naturally led to partially uncontrolled results, since this method affected the entire film image. Digital cinema, with its wide variety of control on film footage, meant quite a revolution in this respect. As Prince delineates, "in regard to color timing and the control of many other image variables, digital methods now offer filmmakers greatly enhanced artistic powers compared with traditional photo-mechanical methods" [8].

The emergence of digital technologies within the film industry forced both practi-tioners and theorists to re-evaluate Bazin's idea of the realist film image. Media theorist Lev Manovich was one to early dig into the question, what is digital cinema. To briefly summarize his viewpoint, he immediately recognized the ontological shift taking place when the live-action film shot got digitalized[1], thus meaning its "privileged indexical relationship to pro-filmic reality" to be lost, when the newly pixelated image became subject to endless modifications, with no respect of origin [9]. Manovich went quite far by suggesting the film image eventually was "reduced to just another graphic" [9]— which is precisely the impression you get while working on a complicated composite shot during the postproduction of the film. In his quest for digital cinema, he completed the following explanation: "Digital cinema is a particular case of animation that uses live-action footage as one of its many elements" [10].

Manovich bowed here to formalism. While for Bazin the film image metaphorically stood for a window into the imaginary world, for Manovich it seemingly represented active framing of the view through a process of selection and combination. Therefore, a single shot within the finished film product could comprise quite contradicting elements,

---

[1] Digitalization was needed before the introduction of the 4K digital cameras such as RED One in 2006. However, many filmmakers still use traditional film cameras for expressive reasons.

some live-action, some CGI. The result, essentially a collage, also alluded an idea of spatial montage, as "an alternative to traditional cinematic montage, replacing traditional sequential mode" [11]. The central task of digital filmmaking seemed now straight forward. It laid in compositing seamlessly together different image sources, in the manner equal to the temporal montage techniques, providing the coexistence of images in space, like layers on the top of each other, visible simultaneously.

However, as insightful as Manovich's argumentation is, it does leave one fundamental aspect of cinema almost overlooked, namely the question of movement. Admittedly, Manovich did recognize the difference between illusion and simulation but could not fully articulate the meaning of this division in digital cinema. Instead, he urged digital image—or digital frame—could be categorized as a deceiving impression of space in the sense of renaissance trompe l'oeil. This proposition describes an important function of digital cinema as misleading the perception but does not analyze further, what makes us immerse in cinematic worlds. To fully understand this problem, we might look, how cinema sequences 'move' or how they mimic or reproduce the life-like constantly changing situations, and what does this movement stands for.

3 Camera Structuring Space

As opposed to the realist film theories, there have been so-called structural-psychoanalytic premises revered by screen theorist Stephen Heath in his famous essay Narrative Space (1976) [12]. Heath scrutinizes here the essence of narrative space as control of movement required to maintain the story and restrict its single character perspective. In other words, the camera, along with its moving position, confronts by framing the space exploring character, and this way refines the spectator's possibility to depict these same cinema events from her perspective. He describes this idea in the following way:

> "The figures move in the frame, they come and go, and there is then need to change the frame, reframing with a camera movement or moving to another shot. The transitions thus effected pose acutely the problem of the filmic construction of space, of achieving a coherence of place and positioning the spectator as the unified and unifying subject of its vision" [13].

Heath also adapted film theorist Christian Metz's view of cinema space as "a trick effect": "if several successive images represent a space under different angles, the spectator, victim of the 'trick effect', spontaneously perceives the space as unitary" [13]. Noteworthy, the cinema space prior the digital era gets specified. Despite the availability of various cinematic techniques (i.e., editing, the use of off-screen space), the eventual spatial scheme of the film results from an active reorganization of what is seen in the series of separate shots.

Thus, for Heath, the moving position of the frame in the first place provides a spatial schema required for a narrative to happen, but, equally important, it allows a pattern of observation, thus constituting film spectatorship as participatory. Despite unified as a whole, Heath's narrative space consists of fragments, or in other words, of sequential shots and eventually frames. It is noteworthy to recognize, that here the concept of space by no means involves the idea of a single shot as a possible collage – or as a spatial montage as suggested by Manovich. As film critic Matthew Croombs points out, "Heath, for all of his claims about the discursive nature of the image, was highly attentive to what was before the camera, and even to the so-called indexical qualities of the image" [14]. Interestingly, Heath's model of cinematic space creation relies on real camera 'replacing' the imaginary witness of events. By doing so, he seemingly implied that the arrangement of time and space in cinema would 'inherit' the limitations that cinematography as a craft poses for filmmaking. Although many impressive camera equipment (such as Steadicam used for handheld shots) were not invented [15], when Heath wrote his essay, the pre-digital era of filmmaking was unquestionably labeled by the restrictions in cinematography stemming from the mere nature of physics.

An early indication that the traditional concept of coherent real-like cinema space has started to collapse emerged alongside non-linear editing tools. As Heath has proposed, the movement in cinema relates not only to the movement of the camera but also to the movement from one shot to another. The possibility to try cuts in an uninhibited way, and still be able to return to the earlier versions seemed to create cinematic sequences in which the old bylaws simply did not matter anymore. The cultural critic and post-cinema theorist Steven Shaviro described this change by noting, "there no longer seems to be any concern for delineating the geography of action, by clearly anchoring it in time and space" [16]. The continuity rules are continuously disregarded, eventually leading to combining even mismatching shots. In this "post-continuity" situation, "continuity has ceased to be as important as it used to be" [17]. Shaviro's account indicates, there is some ongoing discussion, whether the emerging tendency towards post-continuity means that the role of the narrative is "diminished" in the film entirely. However, I would like to think the mind is flexible enough to learn new ways to perceive and interpret spatial schemas suggested by the cinematic movement.

Partially, the development Shaviro describes originates also from the emergence of the CGI. In postproduction, a considerable amount of the total footage can consist of blue or green screen shots. Thus, they do not necessarily include any cues of the geography of the imaginary story space since the character is staged in front of the monochromatic single-color background. When filming on the soundstage with actual scenery or on real locations you are to a great extent faced with the real-world plans of space, but in postproduction, while compositing matte shots, you basically are allowed to choose the placement and the view of the camera and even an idea of camera lens purely based on your inner vision. As a result, the arrangement of space exemplifies something I would like to call a loosened logic of cinematic space, which results in the disconnection of the embodied experience of space.

4   Camera Immersing in Digital Space

To fully understand the narrative space in the digital era, we might now focus on the digital image in its fully immersive power, not only from the viewpoint from practice but also as a space-creating medium allowing the spectator to get absorbed. The most immediate model for this purpose is made available by virtual reality (VR).

There are several ways to characterize VR, however, let us look at the one film critics Thomas Elsaesser, and Malte Hagener have suggested. They describe the variety of VR technologies mainly from a pragmatic viewpoint: 1. VR can simulate real-like environments for diverse purposes, such as learning, training, or therapy 2. VR can make visible such abstract systems that otherwise would be difficult to show, for instance, because they are invisible to eye 3. VR can be used in art and entertainment as a by-product of directly useful applications in the military field, in architectural design, medicine, or the modeling of systems, whose 3-D visualization facilitates the purpose of remote control or tele-action [18].

What is not emphasized here is that VR does produce not only simulative environments but also *a virtual camera*, through which we can perceive those environments. I believe it is genuinely revolutionizing, to be able to witness film events in any imaginable place, in any imaginable way. This specific quality of digital cinema has started to mold the film making process fundamentally, meaning the whole idea of CGI just belonging to the postproduction phase of the filmmaking process has gradually become outmoded. The ways VR technologies have sneaked into the filmmaking process are all-encompassing. The idea of "100% digital film space" has affected on all cinema practices. For example, the art of production design, which traditionally has been associated with the pre- and production phases of filmmaking, eventually partakes in completing the overall look of the film during the postproduction. The same applies to cinematography. Cinematographers, who as the heads of camera crew were most urgently involved in the production phase of filmmaking, have also recognized their practice turning into "a new kind of unity of art and technology". Consequently, "the conversion of existing crafts and the activities of cinematography, design, art direction, visual effects, virtual lighting, previsualization, as well as emerging visual practices" forming a new profession of "Cinematographer-Artist-Designer-Technologist" [19].

This is especially true in the new form of film production, namely a virtual production (VP), defined by David Morin, Head of Epic Games' L.A. Lab, as:

"The ability to mix live footage and computer graphics at once, to get real-time feedback, and to make decisions on set about the VFX and animation. It's real-time computer graphics on set, where real-time computer graphics can, and do, inform your decisions as a filmmaker. VP is also the process of creating the digital world, beginning with the inception of the movie and ending with the final VFX, centered around the real-time interaction on set. VFX is no longer considered post. The order of production is no longer in order" [20].

Understood this way, virtual production paves the way to the digital cinema as the particular computer-generated simulation, comprising sights and sounds, thus being a real like three-dimensional environment that someone using special electronic equipment might interact *in a seemingly physical way*. Furthermore, this arrangement differs from seeing a digital image as a representational surface, delivering an illusion of a spatial world. To put it merely, via virtual production, we simulate not just the narrative surroundings, but on some level, the circumstances of filmmaking itself.

5   Enactive Approach

The notion of VP invites us to contemplate further the codependency of movement and space in digital cinema. Here, I aim to refer to the recent cognitive film studies, especially the enactive turn. I can see this turn structuring our understanding of a cinematic experience, which in this case is not just seeing and hearing, but holistically throwing oneself into a simulation of life-like situation. On a common level, an enactive approach describes a human being's relationship to her environment, especially as an embodied experience: the individual rather lives her environment through the action than experiences it mediated as mental representations. The most basic anchors in this discussion are provided by cognitive linguists George Lakoff and Mark Johnson in Metaphors We Live By (1980) presenting the Conceptual Metaphor Theory (CMT) [21], and by cognitivists Francisco Varela et al. in The Embodied Mind (1991) developing the enactive perspective on cognition [22].

Some revelatory work in film is also presented by Pia Tikka, a brain researcher in neurocinematics and the founder of the Enactive Virtuality Lab in Tallinn. In her Enactive Cinema: Simulatorium Eisensteinense (2008) [23], she explores the psychophysiological grounds of the film experience, and envisions, how the involvement in the world of film is an all-compassing process depending on similar responses arisen while we encounter our daily socio-emotional situations. Thus, a scene of a story can now be understood as a playground of meaningful human interaction, employing the spectator's specific emotional participation. Much of this view is understood due to the discovery of mirror neurons, which offers a novel view to understand the basis of our engagement with the cinema narrative as the compassion for the film protagonist. Also, film researcher Steffen Hven [24] has offered some valuable viewpoints by considering narrative structures as essentially enactive and experiential. According to him, narratives arise along the continuously evolving affective and intellectual states embodied while watching a film, and thus, can be explored in spatial terms as "our surrounding environment" [24].

Enactivism is also associated with such grand ideas as neuroscientist Antonio Damasio's theory of consciousness, where the emotion is understood as a response to any change of the bodily state. We see here the core consciousness as a non-cognitive part of the psyche, interacting continuously with its environment and tracking on a momentary basis the bodily changes. The extended consciousness, based on the core self, is the entity that enables the personal identity and memory and makes, for instance, possibly the complex individual goals [25]. As Tikka notes, any cinema experience can be concluded in the Damasian way as "the conscious oscillation between emotional immersion (core consciousness) and back-to-reality (expanded consciousness)" [26].

While it is important to remember that the enactivist movement in its essence is anti-representational, we can complete it with the Damasian idea of mental images. These images are a refinement of the mapping structures and "represent physical properties of entities and their spatial and temporal relationships, as well as their actions" [27]. Maps, on the other hand, "are constructed when we interact with objects, such as a person, a machine, a place, from the outside of the brain toward its interior" [28]. Damasio writes:

> "The fact that neurons and brains are about the body also suggests how the external world would get mapped in the brain and mind. ... when the brain maps the world

external to the body, it does so thanks to the mediation of the body. When the body interacts with its environment, changes occur in the body's sensory organs, such as the eyes, ears, and skin; the brain maps those changes, and thus the world outside the body indirectly acquires some form of representation within the brain" [29].

This process of body vs. world interaction will lead to naturally emerging narratives, not in the sense that a self-conscious mind tells her story, but in the middle of ongoing events, lives it. As Heath earlier in his category of thinking posed filmmaking as an intentional process, we are here provided an alternative way to approach the process of composing cinematic narratives involving imaginary spaces. The films are created both on the conscious and unconscious level, inherently by manipulating the very same maps—eventually developed into images accompanying reasoning [28]—prompted while enacting the real world. Like Kaipainen et al. suggest, to evaluate the role of the enactive system in content creation, the framework of metaphor theories such as CMT is needed [30], especially when establishing an understanding of how embodied spatial metaphors deliver meanings.

From the viewpoint of this paper, what could this all mean? I feel confident to summarize, from the viewpoint of the enactive cognitive science, the movement in cinema equals the movement of mind. To make humanly sense, any camera, real or digital, must carry the qualities of our body tied existing [31]. Nevertheless, how does digital cinema meet this requirement? Does it mimic the functions of the traditional camera tied to the limitations of the real world – thus reproducing certain cinematic conventions – or does it invent new ways to enjoy unlimited being within a new realm fully?

6   The Movement of the Digital Camera Becomes Cinema

To clarify the question, how do we experience presence in cinematic worlds, I discuss some practical examples of how new digital cinematography aims to simulate intense spatio-physical experiences. I am starting one of the earliest films using CGI. Visualizing Lord of the Rings Trilogy (2001–03) [32] involves quite a variety of digital technologies such as creating computer-generated characters, comprehensive digital sceneries, armies of soldiers programmed to move and behave itself, and making full-size actors appear at hobbit scale [33].

While the range of digital components here is broad, a more important viewpoint concerning digital cinema is provided by the trilogy's cinematography. Here individually, the CGI scenery has turned out to be a powerful asset in the way it enables the animated camera to express a new kind of movement while exploring the imaginary digital spaces. Thus, the digital environment behind the character remains not a mere moveless background but inherently reveals to possess all the possibilities of digital 3D-animation. The animated camera in the trilogy wanders on some occasions like a bird through the scenery, providing breathtaking moments no physical camera equipment is capable of. In film researcher Kristen Moana Thompson's word, the camera "thrusts the spectator through dizzying heights, skimming up or down the sides of the two towers, and often moving rapidly from the micro to macro-level or from extreme heights to depths" [34].

Another landmark in digital filmmaking is Minority Report (2002) [35] set in future Washington, DC, in the year 2054. McDowell, who designed the film, has spoken in many contexts of the diverse digital applications developed during the filmmaking process, which in the first place was unusual in the sense that the actual design work was started before the script was even near being completed. McDowell felt it had some extraordinary influence on the eventual narrative, the design consequently representing a strong storytelling aspect [36]. Again, one might easily get overwhelmed by the uttermost detailed look of the scenery based on the almost 'systemic' research of the outlook of the future environment [36]. However, the consequences of McDowell's approach were much more far-reaching. A new film making tool called "previs" was developed, and McDowell describes director Steven Spielberg's spontaneous reaction:

> "He immediately saw that he could direct the prototype of a complex sequence in the same way he would use storyboards, except now he was 'boarding' with a moving camera with a prime lens pointing at a low resolution but scale-accurate character traversing designed narrative space, months before shooting.—The same impetus—to be able to direct a camera frame within the virtual world—later developed into the Virtual Camera which now allow a director or key to move through dimensionally accurate designed virtual cinema space in real-time, at multiple scales, with prime lenses, constrained focus, dolly track, atmospherics, and lighting" [36].

Some mind-blowing cinematography was evolved in Minority Report, like in the scene where the main character John Anderton is hiding from the government officials in a large, murky apartment building. An army of spider-like robots are let out to search him, and these nasty creatures crawl through every door crack of the entire building. Based on experiments with previs, the camera brilliantly choreographs through this dynamically complex scene by using the cut-out sections in the ceiling [37]. It also uses embodied patterns to express the role of an above watching eye, seeing through the structures meant to be shielding, being a relentless follower of throughout the long scene eventually stating that I will see everything.

The development is going towards the direction where filmmakers truly wish to interact with the digital content, the emphasis of expression, thus being in providing even more sensual experiences. This means an innovative use of digital technologies emphasizing the embodied-like movement as a storytelling asset, as in Gravity (2013) [38], a film directed by Alfonso Cuarón. Gravity is almost all about the presence, and we have throughout a film a hovering feeling of floating in the space just as weightless as its characters. The actual gravity or the lack of it orients all the action in the imaginary world we are immersed and "all of the physical demands are effectively transmitted to the viewer who experiences immersion in fictional space, therefore empathetically experiencing character's difficulty in moving or breathing" [39].

The cinematographer Emmanuel Lubezki describes a ravishing moment in the film, which reflects the digital cinema experience almost *uniting in the character's body*. The camera's empathic vision, first perceiving the character within the frame, gradually drifts into seeing the space through her eyes:

"Something very exciting for me to see is Sandra Bullock spinning out of control. We designed all this equipment that allows us to spin the environment around her and give the impression that she is spinning. You can see that in the reflections in her eyes and the visor as the shot is going from an objective shot, where you see her spinning, and then suddenly it becomes this subjective shot, and you start to see what she's looking at while spinning out of control. I think it's beautiful!" [40]

7 Conclusion

Ultimately, digital cinema seems to depend on what mind is capable of recognizing as *meaningful* since there are no restraints that a digital camera can theoretically do. The camera can fly like a bird or flow in the cosmos in a relentlessly complicated way, but at the same time, it balances with the idea, in which manner we can imagine our bodies to move. While the purpose of these existentially oriented functions is solely to enhance presence in the cinematic world, to achieve this, the practitioners are paradoxically faced with an even more complex structure of the film image.

Naturally, in the usual case of filmmaking, the virtual tools are accompanied by the traditional ones, but the pure existence of them seems to have provided quite radical ways to explore the imaginary space. As suggested, the results aim to imply diegetic space structures, even though the filmmaking practices in the digital age are far from using such during the pro-filmic phase. Instead, they rely on the process, which is not only about the film being fragmented into sequential shots but also the shot being fragmented to various assets of diverse origin, layered on the top of each other via parallax multi-channeling. Following, we might even speak of pseudo-diegetic experiences. At the same time, it seems that space continuity is a more complicated question since, especially in post-cinema age, there is a tendency towards lack of cohesion concerning a space represented in successive shots.

As film researcher Kathrin Fahlenbrach has noted, the cinema space is rarely recognized consciously by the viewers. However, at the same time, the interpretation of the narrative is highly guided by the way this space is bodily experienced [41]. The enactive ideas discussed in this paper aim to explore the very basis of this process, where bodily changes lead to the forming of space-related mental images that precede the narrative. The current digital cinema has noticeably advanced in its practice of harnessing interactive technologies. We can see the narratives told by these technologies creating some new storytelling aspects, emphasizing the character's sensual interplay with her environment. Gravity provides an example here, providing "a minimalist set with maximum effects" [42]. As an intimate film, Gravity's most ultimate task seems to be in establishing a thickened sense of immersive presence in the film experience.

References

1. Halligan, F.: FilmCraft: Production Design [Kindle DX version] Loc 2457 (2012). http://amazon.com
2. Dempsey, M.: Designers in Film: Production Designer Alex McDowell in conversation with Mike Dempsey (December 2018). https://filmandfurniture.com. Accessed 3 Jan 2020

3. Le Petit Soldat. Directed by Godard, J.-L. [Film] France, Les Productions Georges de Beauregard & Société Nouvelle de Cinématographie (SNC) (1963)
4. Bazin, A.: The ontology of the photographic image. Film Q. **13**(4), 4–9 (1960). https://doi.org/10.2307/1210183
5. Bazin, A.: What is Cinema? vol. II, p. 20. University of California Press, Berkeley and Los Angeles (2004). [Originally published in 1971]
6. Bazin, A.: What is Cinema? vol. II, p. 27. University of California Press, Berkeley and Los Angeles (2004). [Originally published in 1971]
7. Tröhler, M.: Film – movement and the contagious power of analogies: on André Bazin's conception of the cinematic spectator. Stud. Fr. Cine. **14**(1), 40 (2014). https://doi.org/10.1080/14715880.2014.891314
8. Prince, S.: The emergence of filmic artifacts: cinema and cinematography in the digital era. Film Q. **57**(3), 27 (2004). https://doi.org/10.1525/fq.2004.57.3.24
9. Manovich, L.: Language of New Media, p. 300. Mit Press, Cambridge (2001)
10. Manovich, L.: Language of New Media, p. 302. Mit Press, Cambridge (2001)
11. Manovich, L.: Language of New Media, p. 322. Mit Press, Cambridge (2001)
12. Heath, S.: Narrative space. Screen **17/3**, 68–112 (1976)
13. Heath, S.: Narrative space. Screen **17/3**, 85 (1976)
14. Croombs, M.: Pasts and futures of 1970s film theory. Scope Online J. Film Telev. Stud. **20**, 1–18 (2011). https://www.nottingham.ac.uk/scope/documents/2011/june-2011/croombs.pdf
15. Kenigsberg, G.: The Invention That Shot Rocky Up Those Steps (December 2016). https://www.nytimes.com. Accessed 7 Dec 2019
16. Shaviro, S.: Post-continuity: an introduction. In: Leyda, J., Denson, S. (eds.) Post-Cinema: Theorizing 21st-Century Film, vol. 52. Reframe, Sussex (2016). https://reframe.sussex.ac.uk/post-cinema/
17. Shaviro, S.: Post-continuity: an introduction. In: Leyda, J., Denson, S. (eds.) Post-Cinema: Theorizing 21st-Century Film, vol. 56. Reframe, Sussex (2016). https://reframe.sussex.ac.uk/post-cinema/
18. Elsaesser, T., Hagener, M.: Film Theory: An Introduction through senses, pp. 176–177. Routledge, New York (2010)
19. Leon, G.: The Evolving Role of the Cinematographer (July 2013). http://filmcastentertainment.blogspot.com. Accessed 7 Feb 2020
20. What is Virtual Production? [Podcast] Visual Disruptors podcast series ep. 1 (October 2018). https://www.unrealengine.com. Accessed 7 Feb 2020
21. Lakoff, G., Johnson, M.: Metaphors We Live By (1980)
22. Varela, F., Thompson, E., Rosch, E.: The Embodied Mind (1991)
23. Tikka, P.: Enactive Cinema: Simulatorium Eisensteinense. Gummerus, Jyväskylä (2008)
24. Hven, S.: Cinema and Narrative Complexity: Embodying the Fabula, p. 16, 34. Amsterdam University Press, Amsterdam (2017)
25. Damasio, A.: The Feeling of What Happens: Body and Emotion in the Making of Consciousness, pp. 170–176. Harcourt Brace and Co., New York (1999)
26. Tikka, P.: Enactive Cinema: Simulatorium Eisensteinense, p. 193. Gummerus, Jyväskylä (2008)
27. Damasio, A.: Self Comes to Mind: Constructing the Conscious Brain, p. 60. Pantheon, New York (2010)
28. Damasio, A.: Self Comes to Mind: Constructing the Conscious Brain, p. 55. Pantheon, New York (2010)
29. Damasio, A.: Self Comes to Mind: Constructing the Conscious Brain, p. 38. Pantheon, New York (2010)
30. Kaipainen, M., et al.: Enactive Systems and Enactive Media: Embodied Human-Machine Coupling beyond Interfaces. Leonardo **44**(5), 436 (2011)

31. Sobchack, V.: The scene of the screen: envisioning photographic, cinematic, and electronic "presence". In: Post-Cinema: Theorizing 21st-Century Film, vol. 52, pp. 107–108. Reframe, Sussex (2016). https://reframe.sussex.ac.uk/post-cinema/. [Originally published in Sobchack, V.: Carnal Thoughts, pp. 135–162. University of California Press, Los Angeles (2004)]
32. Lord of The Rings Trilogy. Directed by Jackson, P. [Film] New Line Cinema, New Zealand and United States (2001–2003)
33. Jackson, P.: Lord of the rings: the fellowship of the ring. In Proceedings of the 29th International Conference on Computer Graphics and Interactive Techniques. Electronic Art and Animation Catalog, SIGGRAPH 2002 (2002). https://doi.org/10.1145/2931127.2931219
34. Thompson, K.M.: Scale, spectacle and vertiginous movement: massive software and digital special effects in the lord of the rings. In: Mathjis, E., Pomerance, M. (eds.) From Hobbits to Hollywood: Essays on Peter Jackson's Lord of The Rings, p. 291. Editions Rodopi, The Netherlands (2006)
35. Minority Report. Directed by Spielberg, S. [Film] 20th Century Fox and Dreamwork Pictures, United States (2002)
36. McDowell, A.: PD4C21 - Production Design for the 21st Century (June 2017). https://www.kosmorama.org. Accessed 17 Jan 2020
37. McDowell, A.: The Impact of Tradition and New Digital Technology in Film Design. A presentation at the Cilect Conference (May 2004)
38. Gravity. Directed by Cuarón, A. [Film] Warner Bros. Pictures (2013)
39. D'Aloia: The character's body and the viewer: cinematic empathy and embodied simulation in the film experience. In: Coëgnarts, M., Kravanja, P. (eds.) Embodied Cognition and Cinema, p. 192. Leuven University Press, Leuven (2015)
40. Moakley, P.: Behind the Moving Image: The Cinematography of Gravity (February 2014). https://time.com. Accessed 14 Feb 2020
41. Fahlenbrach, K.: Embodied spaces: film spaces as (leading) audiovisual metaphors. In: Anderson, J.D., Fisher Anderson, B. (eds.) Narration and Spectatorship in Moving Images, p. 105. Cambridge Scholars Publishing, Newcastle (2007)
42. Seymour, M.: Gravity: Vfx that's Anything but Down to Earth (October 2013). https://www.fxguide.com. Accessed 9 Feb 2020

Augmented Reality Application in Manufacturing Industry: Maintenance and Non-destructive Testing (NDT) Use Cases

Fakhreddine Ababsa$^{(\boxtimes)}$

Arts et Metiers Institute of Technology, LISPEN, HESAM University, Paris, France
Fakhreddine.Ababsa@ensam.eu

Abstract. In recent years, a structural transformation of the manufacturing industry has been occurring as a result of the digital revolution. Thus, digital tools are now systematically used throughout the entire value chain, from design to production to marketing, especially virtual and augmented reality. Therefore, the purpose of this paper is to review, through concrete use cases, the progress of these novel technologies and their use in the manufacturing industry.

Keywords: Augmented Reality · Industry 4.0 · Manufacturing · Human-machine interaction · Maintenance and quality monitoring

1 Introduction

We are in the era of the fourth industrial revolution after that of mechanization, mass-production and automation. Thanks to the digital transformation, factories are more and more connected and appear as part of a global ecosystem that includes the entire production chain. This new paradigm is called Industry 4.0, it aims to maintain and develop a strong and innovative industrial activity. Factories become smarter, more competitive because they are more efficient and safe; their production processes are completely changing. This transformation is mainly based on new technologies such as robotics, virtual and augmented reality, sensor networks, Internet of Things (IoT), data processing, big data, etc. It is a new model that puts the human at the heart of business and organization. Thus, the operator in his factory will accomplish his daily tasks in a different way; he will be equipped with wearable and intelligent devices that allow him to communicate and collaborate with other operators, and to assist him in carrying out his task. At the same time, customer expectations are changing much faster than before. To cope with this, companies need to be able to detect weak signals and feedback this information to anticipate changes in customer behavior. They must also be able to innovate much more quickly, to adapt their offer by adopting an agile organization allowing flexible and therefore completely reconfigurable production modes [1], able to deliver customized and competitive products. Virtual and Augmented Reality is one of the key components in achieving the goals of the industry 4.0. For example, virtual reality is used during the product creation process to optimize and prototype experiments in order to test new

© Springer Nature Switzerland AG 2020
L. T. De Paolis and P. Bourdot (Eds.): AVR 2020, LNCS 12243, pp. 333–344, 2020.
https://doi.org/10.1007/978-3-030-58468-9_24

products "in near-use situations". It also allows employees to receive hands on training thanks to virtual environments, which mimic production equipment in a very realistic manner [2]. This prevents expensive down time and disruptions in normal operations, and improve the efficiency of skills transfer and increased knowledge retention. On the other hands, augmented reality is a powerful tool that allows operators to better undertake tasks on site, thanks to its ability to visualize virtual objects in the real word. This is the case for tasks such as parts assembly [3, 4], maintenance [5], quality control or material management [6]. The goal of this paper is to show the practical uses of augmented reality in the manufacturing industry. We will present two innovative solutions to answer the maintenance problem encountered in the manufacturing industry. The paper is organized as follows. Section 2 describes the related projects. Section 3 introduces the Key technologies on augmented reality currently used in the manufacturing industry. Section 4 shows two practical applications of this technology and provides a detailed analysis of its usability in an industrial setting. In Sect. 5, we present the conclusions and future work.

2 Related Works

The use of Augmented Reality in industry goes back to the 1990s. In 1993 [7] Boeing engineers presented one of the first see-through displays integrating a head position estimation approach and a real/virtual registration system, and allowing to increase the operator's vision with digital information relevant to the job he is performing. On the other hand, several companies (EADS, BMW, Airbus, etc.) participated in the ARVIKA project (1999–2003), which aimed to study the capacity of augmented reality to support work processes in the design, production and service for complex industrial products and plants [8, 9]. The project STARMATE, funded by the EU (2000–2003), provided two main functionalities: User assistance during assembling task of complex mechanical parts and increasing the operator's skills to carry out such processes by passing them training scenarios in augmented reality. The ARTESAS project led by Siemens (2004–2006) aimed to develop an augmented reality system for aeronautical and automotive maintenance [10]. AVILUSplus (2009–2011) is a collaborative project that brought together German basic industries and research institutes to develop innovative systems in the areas of Virtual and Augmented Reality for products life cycle (PLM) services. The main areas are information management, simulation and rendering, tracking, interaction and geometry acquisition [11]. Testia, a subsidiary of Airbus, has developed the SART (Smart Augmented Reality Tool) system for the aerospace industry. A system that allows inspection personnel, as part of quality control, to establish a digital model of the actual part on a tablet or PC, and thus reliably identify non-conforming parts [12]. The European project REPLICATE [13] has improved the human creative process by integrating new user experiences in mixed reality. Thus, experimental solutions such as 3D/4D story-boarding in unconstrained spaces and the expression of new ideas by manipulating objects (assembly/disassembly) in a co-creative workspace, have been developed and tested in an industrial context. In the same way, the European project SPARK (Spatial Augmented Reality as a Key for co-creativity) (2016–2019) aims to realize an intuitive ICT platform based on spatial augmented reality (SAR) in order to show designers and customers new products/concepts in the form of mixed prototypes during brainstorming sessions, with the aim of enriching the design process. It is a collaborative platform that allows users to work freely together, promoting open innovation and creative thinking [14]. In 2017 Safran Landing Systems launched the Argo (Augmented Reality for Ground Operations) project [15], which aims to deploy augmented reality on an industrial scale at Safran's various MRO sites to help operators with aircraft maintenance tasks and automate the writing of technical operating reports. In this way, Safran hopes to reduce intervention times, which would give a considerable competitive edge as an increase in air traffic goes hand in hand with an increase in MRO activities. In addition, several research works have been conducted over the last years to develop AR systems dedicated to the industry. For example, in [16] the authors propose the ACAAR system (Authoring for Context-Aware AR) which allows users to add and organize digital content (text, images, CAD) in 3D space and specify its relationship with the maintenance context. In [17] the authors give a thorough state of the art on the use of AR in industrial maintenance. Future research directions are also proposed, including hardware, monitoring and user interaction. Other studies, such as in [18], have focused on the use of mobile devices such as smartphones and tablets to perform maintenance and assembly procedures with augmented reality (AR). They evaluated performance by comparing the execution times and errors made when performing a maintenance procedure with an augmented reality tool and paper-based instructions.

3   Augmented Reality Technologies for Industrial

3.1   Applications

Traditionally, augmented reality has been seldom used in the manufacturing industry due to the lack of maturity of the technology, computational and hardware were limited and visualization devices uncomfortable. The advent of tablets and smartphones (Fig. 1) with more capabilities have enabled the development of the first augmented reality applications in industrial environments.

Fig. 1. AR mobile device

However, these devices have not been as successful as expected, as they can divert attention of the operators, who need to have their hands free to perform their tasks. The head-mounted displays (HMDs) developed in recent years overcome these limitations.

The operator equipped with such a device can view spatialized information/instructions in hands-free mode while performing his task. In addition, these helmets over automatic gesture recognition allowing interaction with 3D holograms. Furthermore, the performance of HMDs continues to improve with each release, offering increasingly attractive functionalities for creating immersive and personalized user experiences, which makes it easier to integrate them into industrial processes [19]. This explains the new craze for Augmented Reality in the industry in recent years. HMDs are now able to detect information coming from the environment and process/interpret them in real-time. They are more comfortable, less heavy, and easy to use and have a larger field of view.

Fig. 2. Microsoft HoloLens 2

Figure 2 shows the Microsoft HoloLens 2 headset released in 2019, which has the following characteristics:

- A diagonal field of view (FoV) of 52°, improving over the 34° field of view of the first generation of HoloLens headset, while maintaining image fidelity at 47 pixels per degree of sight. In practice this, will ensure a better user experience.
- An integrated finger and hand movement recognition and tracking system with greater accuracy. This is what makes it possible for users interact directly with 3D content with more natural gestures.
- A powerful eye tracking software, allowing users to interact efficiently with the GUI.
- The battery is made of carbon fiber and therefore lighter compared to the HoloLens 1, it is positioned behind the head. It allows 2 to 3 h of active use. The total weight of the helmet is 566 g.
- A voice-based interaction thanks to command and control on-device and Cortana natural language with internet connectivity.

Thanks to all these improvements, the Hololens 2 headset is now considered the reference device for the implementation of augmented reality applications in industrial environments.

3.2 Programming Library

The development of an industrial application based on augmented reality requires the use of high-performance software capable of tracking 3D objects, reconstructing and understanding the often cluttered and changing work environment. The most frequently used libraries are:

- ArtToolKit: open-source marker-based video tracking library that displays virtual 3D models in the real world. It consists in estimating in real time the pose (position + rotation) of the camera in regard to a planar marker placed into the physical environment. It was originally developed by Hirokazu Kato of Nara Institute of Science and Technology in 1999 [20]. The main characteristics of this library are the possibility to customize the targets as long as they remain square in shape, a simplified approach to calibrate the camera, the availability of several platform distributions and to be an open-source system giving access to the whole image processing algorithms.
- ArUco Markers: a binary square fiducial markers that can be used for camera pose estimation. ArUco markers are small planar targets containing 2D binary code. Each marker is encoded thanks to the grid which composes it and whose cells are colored in black and white. The ArUco recognition algorithm allows to extract, identify and estimate the pose of the different ArUco markers seen by the camera [21].
- Vuforia SDK: Uses image processing and computer vision approaches to detect and track on the y planar targets and 3D objects. It enables precise alignment of virtual objects to real-world objects. It allows to track several targets simultaneously. It is multi-platform (Windows, Android, IOs) and well suited for mobile devices [22].
- ARCore: is the platform developed by Google to provide augmented reality on mobile devices without using markers. The embedded motion tracking technology uses the phone's camera to detect and track the interesting points identified in the surrounding environment. The combination of the movement of these points with data from the phone's inertial sensors allows real-time estimation of the phone's position and orientation as it moves through space. In addition, ARCore can detect at surfaces and estimate the average lighting in its close vicinity [23].
- ARKit: allows to build high-detail AR experiences for iPad and iPhone devices. As the device moves, it maps the environment using data coming from on-board sensors (camera, gyroscope accelerometers). The inertial sensor data is fused with the camera information to accurately estimate the location of the device. In addition, ARKit can detect visual characteristics of the environment like planes and tracks motion in conjunction with information from the inertial sensors [24]

Moreover, compatibility with the Unity 3D game engine is an advantage and should be examined. Indeed, Unity 3D is currently one of the most advanced games on the market and is often used to develop industrial applications using virtual and augmented reality. For example SDKs such as Vuforia, ARCore and ARKit are fully compatible with Unity 3D.

4 Industrial Augmented Reality Applications

4.1 Visualization of NDT Measurements Using Augmented Reality

Non-destructive testing (NDT) is an analytical method used in industry to evaluate the properties of a material, component or system without employing processes that could destroy or affect its properties. NDT is used to detect defects within a component and determine whether the component is damaged or in need of repair. Ultrasonic transducers are often used for NDT of industrial parts in their volume or surface. This consists of emitting acoustic waves and detecting their interaction with defects present in the part. The transmitted waves, like an echo, are then converted, in real time, into a digital image of the defect thus located and characterized. One of the problems of this task concerns the visualization of the measurements in an intuitive and unequivocal way. It is clear that the use of 2D images remains insufficient to illustrate and explain the results of NDT tests. Therefore, more appropriate 3D visualization tools and methods need to be developed in order to improve the understanding and interpretation of NDT data. The objective of this project is to develop an augmented reality interface allowing visualizing directly on the part the measurements resulting from the non-destructive testing. Thus, the operator will be able to visualize the areas requiring further investigation for example. This visualization mode, which is more intuitive than simple numerical data, saves time and significantly reduces the complexity of the inspection task.

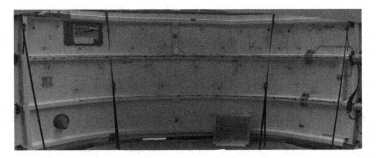

Fig. 3. Airbus A380 Nacelle

The part studied in our case is a nacelle of an Airbus A380 (Fig. 3) for which we have a set of data including:

- The nacelle CAD file (Fig. 4-a).

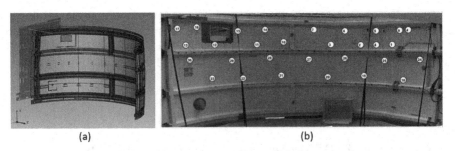

(a)   (b)

Fig. 4. Example of available data

- The coordinates of the ultrasonic transducers and their locations on the nacelle (Fig. 4-b).
- The simulation files containing defect coordinates.

Based on this data, our augmented reality application therefore aims to visualize:

- On the real structure, the sensors used for the NDT measurements.
- The structure area with a defect. Sensors whose measurements indicate the presence of a defect will delimit an area.
- The precise localization of the defect.

Our Approach. The proposed solution was developed under unity 3D and Vuforia, then deployed and tested on a tablet and a HoloLens 1 headset.

Fig. 5. 3D positioning of transducers

The first difficulty we encountered concerns the import of the nacelle 3D model under unity 3d. Indeed, the provided file is in Catia format which is incompatible with Unity 3D. A step of tessellation and simplification of the model was necessary to avoid overloading the computations of the augmented scene. The second step consists in creating, under 3D unity, the augmented scene. We started by positioning the sensors on the 3D model of the nacelle. It is necessary that this positioning be precise enough to allow the shown result to be coherent with the real measurements. However, the coordinates of these sensors are given in a 2D coordinate system. So, in order to represent them in 3D space, we have implemented a function that projects these positions on the surface of the nacelle whose geometry is known precisely (Fig. 5). The next step is to visualize the defect areas on the 3D model. For this purpose, we have used the NDT measurement results provided by the maintenance department, which indicate the active sensors that have detected a defect. Figure 6 shows an example of this functionality in case four sensors (symbolized here by blue dots) are active. The defect area is displayed as a polygon that passes through all four sensors. In order to reduce the defect search area, we propose to only display the areas generated by at least three and at most five active sensors.

We used Vuforia markers to implement the augmented reality part, a simple and fast solution given the complex geometry of the nacelle (large size and non-textured surface). We used Vuforia's extended tracking which, thanks to the sensors of the mobile device, continues to accurately place the virtual model in the real environment even if

Fig. 6. Example of a defect area

the marker is lost while moving through the scene. The marker is placed in the center of the horizontal axis of the workpiece, but also on the lower part, which has no sensors. Finally, the interactive interface of the final application allows the user to select one or more sensors in order to view various information such as coordinates or temperature. The user can also choose the defect areas present in the scenario in order to visualize them in augmented reality on the real nacelle. Figure 7 shows an example of a rendering of the latest version of our application.

Fig. 7. View of the final version of our application

Discussion. The first experimental tests have shown that this application works well. Nevertheless, we have noticed that the tracking sometimes becomes unstable, especially when we are very close to the structure or when the marker becomes invisible. To avoid this instability, we have to be at a minimum distance of 2 m from the nacelle, which is not practical for the maintenance technician who has to be as close as possible to the structure. An interesting way to solve this problem is to use markerless tracking based on a simultaneous localization and mapping system (SLAM) to create a geometric reconstruction of the world while estimating the location of the camera [25, 26]. In this case, SDKs such as Google ARCore or ARKit would be more appropriate. In addition, an in-depth study of the usability of the application in real conditions will be carried out. This will enable us to obtain more refined feedback from maintenance operators, particularly on the interface's ergonomics, the affordance of augmented reality interactions, and the contribution of the proposed functionalities to the practical execution of the task. This study would make it possible to improve the application by taking into account the industrial constraints of the project.

4.2   Implementation of AR Application in Aeronautical Maintenance

This project is being carried out in collaboration with Safran Landing Systems (SLS) in France. Its objective is to study the feasibility and usability of augmented reality in aeronautical maintenance. Thus, we conducted an experiment on an assembly task to observe the impact of Augmented Reality under industrial conditions. The use case corresponds to the assembly of workpieces or axles, the tightening of individual bolts and the protection of unpainted areas (Fig. 8). The participants in this experiment carried out the task under real working conditions, using two operating modes, the first one using only paper supports according to the classical process, and the second one with an augmented reality support installed on a mobile workstation. The time required to complete the task was registered and the participants' feedback was evaluated by means of questionnaires immediately after the task. We used Diota software [27] to create our augmented reality solution which was then installed on a Windows 10machine equipped with a high-definition industrial camera. This workstation is placed on a mobile trolley allowing it to be moved as required and easily installed on the assembly line. Thus, the operators involved in the experiment can test the scenario "with augmented reality" in real working conditions without being disturbed. This is important in order not to bias the results of the experiment.

Fig. 8. The use case equipment

Measurement Protocol 9 maintenance operators were enrolled to take part in the experiment. None of them have any prior knowledge of augmented reality technologies. We took into account the level of expertise and knowledge of the participants regarding the task to be performed and aeronautical maintenance in general. We therefore divided them into three groups: Beginner, Confirmed and Expert. The participant begins the experiment using the classical procedure, which consists in searching on the paper support for the relevant information to carry out the assembly of the workpiece. The experiment is repeated with the augmented reality support. For each participant we measure the time needed to understand and achieve the task. We set up two questionnaires that the participants fill in at the end, the NASA-TLX [28] to subjectively evaluate the quality of the experience, notably the mental demand necessary to perform the task with

or without augmented reality, and the SUS [29, 30] to evaluate the degree of facility in using the augmented reality support. The analysis of the quantitative and qualitative results allows, firstly, to measure the impact of augmented reality on the performance of the participants, and secondly, to evaluate the usability of the augmented reality application as well as the cognitive load induced on the participants.

Discussion. The obtained results clearly demonstrate that augmented reality improves performance for all three user profiles. the "with augmented reality" scenario got the best usability score thanks to a better distribution of time between the comprehension phase and the action phase during the assembly task. We have found that augmented reality, because of its ability to facilitate the understanding of the assembly instructions, allows users to concentrate more on the action phase. This is confirmed by the decrease in the cognitive load score of the task and by a better execution time. This supports our hypothesis on the added value of augmented reality in the completion of an industrial process. Furthermore, we have noted that the impact of Augmented Reality is different depending on the level of expertise of the user. Thus, the "Beginner" users benefit the most from augmented reality which considerably reduces their cognitive load, making a strong contribution to their learning. We also noted that these augmented reality tools increase productivity when used by "Confirmed" operators but they have no effect on "Expert" users who have a perfect knowledge of the assembly process. This first experimentation has allowed us to identify and measure the added value of augmented reality on an assembly task. The obtained SUS score shows that users preferred to work with AR rather than with the reference handbook that details the maintenance process. In addition, the execution time for assembly tasks has been reduced by 74% when the AR procedure is carried out, demonstrating that AR has a direct and significant impact on the execution of maintenance tasks. The next step is to extend the experiment to other tasks related to aeronautical maintenance so that the obtained results can be generalized. You can find more details on this study in the paper we presented in 2019 at the EuroVR conference [31]. Thus, thanks to this pilot project, Safran plans to deploy Augmented Reality in other MRO departments in Asia and the Americas, and to extend it to other services such as quality control.

5   Conclusion and Future Directions

The purpose of this study was to present the current state of augmented reality and their practical application in the manufacturing industry. We first outlined a brief history of industrial projects that used augmented reality, we found that such technology is often used in maintenance, training and upstream design in product development. Its use continues to increase, particularly in the context of Industry 4.0, where it represents one of the cornerstones of this paradigm. Then, the paper give the most relevant hardware and software technologies of Augmented Reality actually used in industrial applications. We presented two industrial projects in which we collaborate and whose objectives are the development of augmented reality solutions for aeronautical maintenance, and the study of the usability of such technology in MRO department, taking into account industrial constraints. We have thus implemented a methodology allowing to integrate augmented reality in an industrial task and to measure its added value in a qualitative and quantitative way. Further work will consist on extending these results to evaluate augmented reality on the whole aeronautical maintenance process. Furthermore, in order to address future challenges for the industry 4.0 efforts should focus on improving Augmented Reality HMIs by developing new user-centric approaches that integrate workers into the design loop, and enable on-site and remote collaboration.

References

1. Kang, H.S., et al.: Smart manufacturing: Past research, present findings, and future directions. Int. J. Precis. Eng. Manuf. Green Technol. **3**(1), 111–128 (2016). https://doi.org/10.1007/s40 684-016-0015-5
2. Fischer, C., Lusic, M., Faltus, F., Hornfeck, R., Franke, J.: Enabling live data controlled manual assembly processes by worker information system and near field localization system. Procedia CIRP **55**, 242–247 (2016). https://doi.org/10.1016/j.procir.2016.08.013
3. Wang, X., Ong, S.K., Nee, A.Y.C.: A comprehensive survey of augmented reality assembly research. Adv. Manuf. **4**(1), 1–22 (2016). https://doi.org/10.1007/s40436-015-0131-4
4. Loch, F., Quint, F., Brishtel I.: Comparing video and augmented reality assistance in manual assembly. In: 12th International Conference Intelligent Environments (IE), pp. 147–150 (September 2016)
5. Paelke, V.: Augmented reality in the smart factory: supporting workers in an industry 4.0. environment. In: IEEE Emerging Technology and Factory Automation (ETFA), pp. 1–4, (September 2016)
6. Munera, E., Poza-Lujan, J.L., Posadas-Yagüe, J.L., Simo, J., Blanes, J.F., Albertos, P.: Control kernel in smart factory environments: Smart resources integration. In: 2015 IEEE International Conference on Cyber Technology in Automation, Control, and Intelligent Systems (CYBER), pp. 2002–2005 (June 2015)
7. Caudell, T.P., Mizell, D.W.: Augmented reality: an application of heads-up display technology to manual manufacturing processes, In: 25th International Conference System Sciences, vol. 2, pp. 659–669. IEEE Press, Hawaii (1992)
8. Wohlgemuth, W., Triebfürst, G.: ARVIKA: Augmented reality for development, production and service. In: Proceedings of DARE 2000 on Designing Augmented Reality Environments, pp. 151–152, (2000)
9. Friedrich, W.: ARVIKA-augmented reality for development, production and service. In: International Symposium on Mixed Augmented Reality, pp. 3–4 (2002)
10. ARTESAS (Advanced Augmented Reality Technologies for Industrial Service Applications) Project. https://www.tib.eu/en/search/id/TIBKAT%3A52755300X/
11. AVILUSplus. Applied Virtual Technologies Focused Long-range on the Product and Production Equipment Life Cycle. http://www.avilusplus.de
12. TESTIA, an Airbus Compagny. https://www.testia.com
13. REPLICATE - cReative-asset harvEsting PipeLine to Inspire Collective AuThoring and Experimentation. https://tev.fbk.eu/projects/replicate
14. SPARK. Spatial Augmented Reality as a Key for co-creativity. https://cordis.europa.eu/pro ject/id/688417
15. ARGO. Augmented Reality for Ground Operations. https://www.safran-group.com/media/augmented-reality-welcome-maintenance-40-20190117
16. Zhu, J., Ong, S.K., Nee, A.Y.: A context-aware augmented reality assisted maintenance system. Int. J. Comput. Integr. Manuf. **28**(2), 213–225 (2015)
17. Palmarini, R., Erkoyuncu, J.A., Roy, R., Torabmostaedi, H.: A systematic review of augmented reality applications in maintenance. Robot. Comput. Integr. Manuf. **49**, 215–228 (2018)
18. Sanna, A., Manuri, F., Lamberti, F., Paravati, G., Pezzolla, P.: Using handheld devices to support augmented reality-based maintenance and assembly tasks. In: 2015 IEEE International Conference on Consumer Electronics (ICCE), pp. 178–179 (2015)

19. Bach, B., Sicat, R., Beyer, J., Cordeil, M., Pfister, H.: The hologram in my hand: how effective is interactive exploration of 3D visualizations in immersive tangible augmented reality? IEEE Trans. Vis. Comput. Graph. **24**(1), 457–467 (2018)

20. Kato, H., Billinghurst, M.: Marker tracking and HMD calibration for a videobased augmented reality conferencing system. In: the 2nd International Workshop on Augmented Reality, IWAR 1999, San Francisco, USA (October 1999)

21. Garrido-Jurado, S., Muñoz-Salinas, R., Madrid-Cuevas, F.J., Marin-Jiménez, M.J.: Automatic generation and detection of highly reliable fiducial markers under occlusion. Patt. Recogn. **47**(6), 2280–2292 (2014)

22. Vuforia. https://developer.vuforia.com/

23. ARCore. https://developers.google.com/ar

24. ARKit. https://developer.apple.com/augmented-reality/

25. Ababsa, F.: Robust Extended Kalman Filtering for camera pose tracking using 2D to 3D lines correspondences. In: IEEE/ASME International Conference on Advanced Intelligent Mechatronics, pp. 1834–1838 (2009)

26. Maidi, M., Ababsa, F., Mallem, M.: Vision-inertial tracking system for robust fiducials registration in augmented reality. In: IEEE Symposium on Computational Intelligence for Multimedia Signal and Vision Processing, pp. 83–90 (2009)

27. Diota. Solutions 4.0 for Industry. http://diota.com/index.php/en/

28. Hart, S.G., Staveland, L.E.: Development of NASA-TLX (task load index): results of empirical and theoretical research. Adv. Psychol. **52**, 139–183 (1988)

29. Brooke, J.: SUS - A Quick and Dirty Usability Scale (1996)

30. Bangor, A., Kortum, P., Miller, J.: Determining what individual SUS scores mean: adding an adjective rating scale. J. Usability Stud. **4**, 114–123 (2009)

31. Loizeau, Q., Danglade, F., Ababsa, F., Merienne, F.: Evaluating added value of augmented reality to assist aeronautical maintenance workers—experimentation on on-field use case. In: Bourdot, P., Interrante, V., Nedel, L., Magnenat-Thalmann, N., Zachmann, G. (eds.) EuroVR 2019. LNCS, vol. 11883, pp. 151–169. Springer, Cham (2019). https://doi.org/10.1007/978-3-030-31908-3_10

Industrial Control Robot Based on Augmented Reality and IoT Protocol

William Montalvo[1] , Pablo Bonilla-Vasconez[2] , Santiago Altamirano[2],
Carlos A. Garcia[2] , and Marcelo V. Garcia[2,3(✉)]

[1] Universidad Politecnica Salesiana, UPS, 170146 Quito, Ecuador
wmontalvo@ups.edu.ec
[2] Universidad Tecnica de Ambato, UTA, 180103 Ambato, Ecuador
{pbonilla8622,santiagomaltamirano,ca.garcia,mv.garcia}@uta.edu.ec
[3] University of Basque Country, UPV/EHU, 48013 Bilbao, Spain
mgarcia294@ehu.eus

Abstract. The use of robotic systems into production processes has resulted in the reduction of manufacturing costs and an improvement in product quality, However, as technologies advance, complex and high-cost control systems are required, hence the need to create low-cost and efficient control systems, with low complexity when operating them. For these reasons, the research presents a control system for the Scorbot ER 4U manipulator arm using a low-cost embedded board and augmented reality platform that brings to the users a real experience with virtual add-ons, thus facilitating the training and management of robotic equipment. A virtual control proposed in Unity 3D allowing the application to be much more interactive and very easy for the user. For the validation of the system, operating tests were carried out, resulting in movements with great precision and in a very simple way without having greater complexity when indicating positions to which the manipulator must reach.

Keywords: Industry 4.0 · Cyber-Physical Production Systems (CPS) · Robotics · Embedded systems · Augmented Reality · Unity 3d

1 Introduction

The applications that are developed in Virtual Reality (VR) or Augmented Reality (AR) can be oriented to the processes of teaching-learning [4,5], in the academic part and to the training - qualification in the industrial scope, these processes previously mentioned can be applied individually or in collaborative works between users, for which it is considered: (i) environments with a user in which tasks that can be performed individually are considered such as assembly of mechanical parts, doors [3], spot welding, precision welding [17,18], electronic control units [2], electric motors, among others.

In recent years, robotics has aimed to find solutions to the needs of all indus-trial fields. Technological evolution influences developing more research topics in

© Springer Nature Switzerland AG 2020
L. T. De Paolis and P. Bourdot (Eds.): AVR 2020, LNCS 12243, pp. 345–363, 2020.
https://doi.org/10.1007/978-3-030-58468-9_25

the robotics community. This evolution has been dominated by human needs, mainly in works that are high risk to man, hence the idea of replacing them with industrial robots [7].

In the current context of the technological world, robotic systems have had a significant advance in cost and implementation, with the emergence of low-cost Single Board Cards (SBC) that can be developed efficient control systems for robotic automation to really low prices compared to the systems that are handled in the robotics and automation market [1]. However, despite being a major breakthrough, these new technologies have only taken place in the major world powers, there is limited knowledge of them in less industrialized countries.

The main goal of this research is the development of augmented reality (AR) platform for the control and handling of a robotic manipulator such as the Scorbot ER 4U, using low-cost microcontrollers or so-called low-cost embedded cards. The first step is performed the cinematic analysis of the robotic arm, and thus define the method of control of the manipulator, which will be designed in an AR environment using the Unity 3D engine, together with the Meta 2 glasses increases for interaction with the user, finally, the users can send messages to the embedded card using the Message Queuing Telemetry Transport (MQTT) protocol, and in turn, the low-cost controller card control the robotic arm, finally, these messages will be validated checking that the robot's movement is the desired one.

The design of the document is as follows, Sect. 2 shows some related works that have been used as a starting point for this research. Section 3 describes the state of art that introduce the elements used in the methodology of this research. Section 4 illustrates a case study of AR for industrial training. The proposed solution for the case study is presented in Sect. 5. Finally, some conclusions and future work are established in Sect. 8.

2   Related Works

This section highlights the importance of using systems based on industry 4.0, for the control of robotic joints from virtual environments using low-cost cards, this is what details McLin et al. research [9], where an approach is proposed to establish bidirectional interactions between robots in the physical and virtual worlds, allowing changes that occur in a physical robot to be automatically reflected by its virtual counterpart, and vice versa, based on this research can be established what are the requirements to create a virtual environment that reflects the physical robot.

Similarly in the research developed by Yoshiaki et al. [11], where he explains about a new software architecture for a Human-Robot Interaction simulator (HRI) in virtual environments, a cloud-based virtual reality platform, called "SIGVerse", which reduces costs to develop real robots and real-world interaction experiments with the help of the virtual. This information underpins the understanding of how virtual platforms are generated to generate movements in physical devices achieving synchronization between the two.

Similar research shows that efficient control systems can be designed for manipulators such as SCORBOT, so, it is exposed by Mota Muoz in [12], which explains the implementation of a Proportional Derivative Gravitational (PD+ G) controller for the second and third articulation of the SCORBOT ER-4u robot. For which the dynamic parameters of the robot were calculated through laboratory measurements and calculations in a CAD model. The dynamic model was got by Euler Lagrange method, based on this the authors of this paper can perform the study of the behavior of the robot and how to set the parameters that should be considered to create a controller of the Scorbot manipulator.

According to recent advances in hardware technology he describes that new interfaces can be created with Augmented Reality (AR) for the control and manipulation of robotic systems, as Courtney Hutton states in [6] which refers to the new technologies that are present in activities for defining task-oriented robots, the research explains how to start developing an AR system in Unity 3D^{TM} software to control robots, under the simple "point where to move" system.

On the other hand, AR can also be used for data visualization as explained by Florian Leutert et al. in [8] who exposes on AR as a form of Mixed Reality that is a technique that improves the natural environment of the user with additional useful virtual information to help the user with their tasks; details the correct way in how information should be integrated and oriented within the environment, which must be dynamic, interactive and real-time in the user's workspace. Under this consideration, efficient reality environments can be designed, where there is a virtual environment with augmented reality support for user interaction.

With the support of the researches above addressed, it becomes feasible the development of the proposed topic, since, supported by the topics developed by the different authors can be developed a control method for the manipulator SCORBOT-ER 4U, from an environment virtual with augmented reality support which is interactive and intuitive and using low-cost devices as hardware means for physical communication.

3   State of Technology

This section will explain all the concepts that will be applied for the development of the research proposal.

3.1   Augmented Reality (AR)

It is a technology that allows to add layers of visual information about the real world around us, using devices such as mobile phones, technological glasses, tablets, computers, camera, among others. This helps us generate experiences that provide relevant knowledge about our environment, and we also receive that information in real time. Among its main features are the ease of interacting in the real world with elements of the virtual world, thus mixing the best of both and the inclusion of information in real time.

AR has brought with it a great contribution to various fields such as: medicine, education, entertainment and in recent years various applications have been developed for the industrial field, brings great advantages to the various fields between the which highlight the optimization of times on daily tasks of many workers, implement new channels to show information to people and ease for training staff [3].

3.2 Unity 3D™

Unity 3D™, created by Unity Technologies [16], is a powerful cross-platform 3D engine and easy-to-use development environment. For 3D interfaces, Unity enables specification of texture compression, mipmaps, and resolution settings for each platform supported by the game engine, and provides support for embossed mapping, reflection mapping, parallaeude mapping, occlusion screen space (SSAO), dynamic shadows using shadow maps, texture rendering, and full-screen post-processing effects.

It's cross-platform, supporting C-programming and Visual Studio integration. Unity also offers JavaScript as an assembly language and MonoDevelop as an IDE for those who want an alternative to Visual Studio. It comes with powerful animation tools that simplify creating 3D scenes or creating 2D animations from scratch.

3.3 SCORBOT ER 4U

The SCORBOT-ER 4u [15] robot is an industrial robot, a general purpose programmable machine that has certain anthropomorphic characteristics. This arm along with the robot's ability to be programmed makes it ideal for a variety of production tasks. The SCORBOT-ER 4u robot is a versatile and reliable system for educational use. The robot arm can be mounted on a table, a pedestal or a linear sliding base.

The specifications are as follows: It is a 5-axis vertical articulated robot, the maximum operating radius is 610 mm, at the end it has a clamping clamp whose maximum aperture is 75 mm. The actuators are servo motors of 12 v in direct current whose maximum weight capacity is 15 oz and a speed of 600 mmsec also has optical feedback sensors on each axis. The transmission is by gear and timing belt. The weight of the robot is 10.8 gk

3.4 META 2 Development Kit

Technical features of Meta 2 Development [10] include a transparent AR headset that displays digital content or holograms with a 90-degree field of view and a high-resolution 2550x1440 display. Designed for comfort, the headphones allow the user to unobstructed everything under the eyebrows so they can easily make eye contact with other people or wear lenses comfortably. The kit also includes a 720p front camera, a four-speaker audio system near the ear, brightness and volume control, and a sensor array for hand interactions and positional tracking. There is also a 9-foot video cable (HDMI 1.4b), data and power.

3.5   Raspberry PI (RPi) 3B+ Card

Among its main features we can mention the speed of its processor that is 1.4 GHz which makes its data processing capacity very high, indispensable to control a process or system in real time. By possessing physical and wireless USB, Ethernet, Bluetooth and wifi communication ports allow the possibility to develop a number of applications under most communication protocols (MQTT, TCPIP, AMQP. Works with operating systems such as Windows and Linux derived systems (Raspbian) [13].

Raspbian is a free Debian-based operating system optimized for Raspberry Pi hardware. The RPi card is used for the creation of the Scorbot manipulator control system, possesses digital input/output pins (GPIOS), necessary to operate the servo motors and read the feedback devices (encoders) of the Scorbot arm, and thus give movement to the robot joints, RPI will be the controller of the robotic arm in the proposed project.

3.6   Message Queuing Telemetry Transport (MQTT) Protocol

MQTT is an application layer protocol that works above the TCP/IP transport layer protocol for transferring messages. It is a suitable protocol for devices with limited resources and was invented by Dr. Andy Standford-Clark and Arlen Nipper in 1999. It's a lightweight, open, simple, and easy-to-use protocol, making it ideal for communication in resource-constrained environments like IoT.

The protocol works under the publisher-subscriber mode through the creation of a broker, to filter messages, these are arranged in topics organized hierarchically. Figure 1 illustrates the working method of mqtt. The communication parameters are as follows: (i) Broker Address, (ii) Define topic name and (iii) Define the communication port.

MQTT PUBLISHER   BROKER   MQTT SUBSCRIBER

Fig. 1. MQTT Architecture

4   Case Study

The hardware architecture is the conceptual design and the fundamental operational structure of the system. It is the physical support where the software resides. The hardware architecture consisting of a Meta 2 glasses [14] as the AR device. Meta 2 is a stand-alone device that has an own graphic processor that runs the processes natively on its hardware. These glasses provide real-time tracking, stable and accurate.

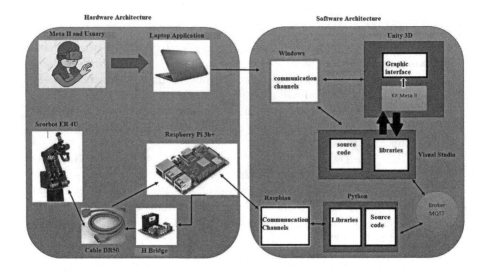

Fig. 2. Software and Hardware Architecture

Meta 2 glasses are connected to the computer through communication cables that will allow interaction with the developed AR system. As shown in Fig. 2, once a precise location of the space is achieved and maintained, the user just by putting on the viewer will already have the reach to the virtual objects and the virtual training sequences that will be overlaid on the real environment through the computer that contains the application and because the device maps the environment and tracking the user's actual location, the user can use defined hand movements to interact with the 3D images.

The main goal of this research is the development of a control system for the Scorbot ER 4U robotic arm, from an augmented reality environment platform created in Unity 3D and with the use of Meta II augmented reality goggles, a low-cost arm controller is designed used the RPI card which interacts with the robotic manipulator through the GPIO inputoutput pins. The MQTT communication protocol is used for communication between the virtual environment and the controller.

The software architecture provides a general reference necessary to guide the construction of the augmented reality system for user training, allowing all application objectives and restrictions to be covered.

This way, as shown in Fig. 2, the system design has an interface level at which the previously selected development engine will design the graphical interface and the set of instructions with which the user can interact. It also has a development level that will allow the encoding of the top-level instructions, and where the user interface and general development libraries of the application will be added, and then compiled them, all this will be done using Unity 3D software and Visual Studio. Finally, the base level will allow managing the communication channels of the Hardware architecture with the system.

5 Implementation of the Solution Proposal

This stage presents the design of the system architecture both at the hardware and software level, describes all the components that will be part of the control system, for the description Unified Modelling Language (UML) diagrams, are used.

5.1 Hardware Architecture

The hardware architecture consists of the design of a physical communication network that allows the interaction of all hardware components of the system supported in the software. Figure 3 has a diagram of components of the hardware that are part of the proposed control system.

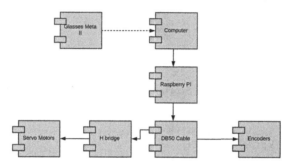

Fig. 3. Diagram of Physical Components Control System Scorbot ER 4U

For user interaction with the system the Meta 2 augmented reality goggles is used, these smart glasses offer the ability to track in real-time, stable and accurate, provide a mapping of the environment and follow the actual location of the user. The glasses interact with the virtual world through the computer by using communication channels such as the HDMI port and the USB3.0 port. In this way the user when placing the virtual reality glasses will be able to visualize the Scorbot robot in 3D, having the possibility to change the position of the effector of the robot indicating where it should go simply by moving its hand.

RPI interacts with the Scorbot arm to drive the servo motors and receive the signal coming from the encoders, for such interaction the boards use the GPIO input/output pins. The embedded card is also connected to the virtual world via the computer, through the ethernet or wifi communication ports and supported by the MQTT data transmission and reception protocol receives all the signals coming from the PC where the META 2 goggles are connected.

Between RPI, the Scorbot arm actuators and sensors have two additional peripherals for communication. The H-bridges chip needed to raise the current and voltage of the signal sent by the embedded card, and the DB50 cable that connects directly with the elements of the robot, it should also be mentioned that to have sufficient supply of current and voltage it is essential to use an auxiliary source.

Figure 4 provides the hardware architecture between RPI and the Scorbot manipulator arm.

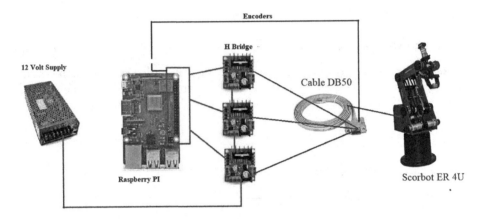

Fig. 4. Raspberry pi and Scorbot hardware architecture proposed

6 Software Architecture

It consists of two levels of assembly, the first, is developed in Visual Studio and allows the coding of the instructions in the language C# for the control and movement of the 3D model of Scorbot which was previously designed, instructions to communicate under the MQTT protocol and code to interact with the META 2 glasses, in addition, at this level also add all the libraries necessary for the user interface, control of objects in the workspace and communications.

The second level of assembly is developed in the Thonny Raspbian IDE which is a code manager for Python language, in this assembler are encoded the instructions for sending and receiving signals through the GPIO pins, thus managing to interact with the robot Scorbot. Also, there are a C# code to establish communication through the MQTT broker, and finally, all the libraries necessary for the use of raspberry GPIO pins and MQTT libraries are added.

6.1 Virtual Environment

The virtual environment component diagram shows the different objects that the application has (see Fig. 5).

(i) **Scorbot ER 4U model**: Inside the graphical interface the user can display the 3D model of Scorbot, which through the augmented reality device can be interacted with. (ii) **Home button:** A button labeled "Home Position" can be displayed, which when pressed sends the robot to its home position.

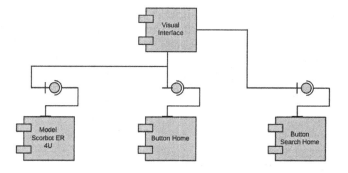

Fig. 5. Virtual interface component diagram

(iii) **Search Home button:** Inside the interface is a button labeled "Search Home" that when pressed sends a message to the microcontroller for the physical robot to start its search for the home position.

6.2   Human-Robot Interface (HRI) Design

It bases its operation on the manipulation of 3D objects, which are contained within a scene, in order to manipulate the objects that require script coding C# Sharp language. These scripts implement a class with attributes and methods. For the development of the proposed control system, scripts have been developed for both the control and handling of the robot and for communication with the embedded card. This interface is programming used 5 different classes which are detailed below:

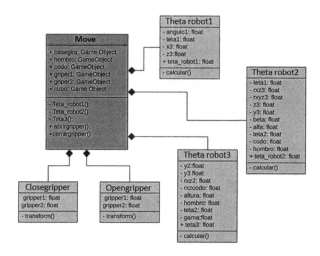

Fig. 6. Scorbot Movement Class Diagram

Scorbot ER 4U Movement Design. Figure 6 shows the classes used for Scorbot arm control, each class has their attributes and methods.Furthermore, there is a composition relationship between the classes. As the "movement" class can be observed predominates over the others i.e. without the "movement" class the others cannot continue to function independently. The description of each class is presented in the Table 1:

Table 1. Description of the Scorbot Er 4U movement classes

Class name	Description
Move	Is the main class for scorbot arm control, this class is able to access each element of type Game Object that is in the scene of the application. Each Game Object element provides attributes to subclasses, these attributes are required to perform the calculation of the values that the arm joints should take based on the kinematics
Theta_robot1	It contains the encoding of the calculations needed to find the value that joint 1 should take
Theta_robot2	Calculates the value that joint 2 should take, all its attributes are of type float, and like the previous class its attributes are taken from the main class
Theta_robot3	A class that calculates the value that joint 3 should take, based on the attributes of type float provided by the main class
Opengripper	Class that contains the encoding to open the gripper. Its attributes are of type float provided by the main class
Closegripper	A class that contains the encoding to close the gripper. Its attributes are of type float provided by the main class

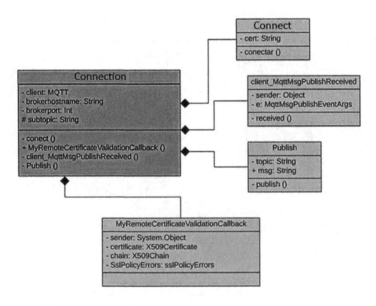

Fig. 7. Scorbot Movement Class Diagram

Communication Implementation in Unity 3D Software. Figure 7 shows the classes that are used for MQTT communication protocol implementation in Unity 3D software. The MQTT communication stack used is Mosquitto Broker. Each class has their respective attributes and methods, it is important to note that there is a composition relationship between the "communication" class and the other classes, i.e. the classes they cannot function independently without the "communication" class. Each class is described below in the Table 2:

Main Scene Class Diagram. Figure 8 shows the classes that are used for the main scene, each class has their respective attributes and methods, it is important to note that there is a composition relationship between the "main" class and the other classes, the classes do not can operate independently without the "main" class. Each class is described below in the Table 3:

6.3   Raspberry Software Interface Design

Figure 9 shows the classes that are used for the control of General Purpose Input/Outputs (GPIO) pins in RPI, each class has their respective attributes and methods, it is important to note that there is a composition relationship between the "control" class and the other classes. In Table 4 is presented the description of the all classes used:

Table 2. Description of MQTT communication classes for Unity 3D

Class name	Description
Connection	It is the main class for establishing MQTT communication, makes the connection to a Broker and subscribes to a topic
Connect	The class which sets the necessary parameters to communicate using MQTT protocol. Requires attributes of type string, MQTT, and int, which the main class provides, performs a single action that is to initialize the MQTT protocol communication
Client_MqttMsg Publish Received	A Class to receive messages that comes from the topic to which have been connected requires attributes of type object and MQTT
Publish	A class that allows messages to be sent to a topic, requires string-type attributes
MyRemote Certificate Validation Callback	A class that provides security and encryption parameters for messages that are exchanged within a topic in MQTT communications, requires private attributes of the MQTT class

Table 3. Description of the main classes

Class name	Description
Main Class	The main class of the module, because it is the one that allows me to access each "GameObject" element that represents a scene within the application
Interaccion_Trex	Class that allows the user to manipulate the Scorbot 3D arm
Finish	Class that allows the user to close the application
Home	Class that allows the message to be sent to the robot's home position
Position Home	Class that allows the message to be sent so that the robot searches for its position at home

MQTT Communication Implementation in Raspberry Pi. Figure 10 depicts the class diagram of the MQTT communication in RPI. This class has attributes of type MQTT like client, and the userdata, also attributes of type String that are what define the Broker's IP address, the name of the topic, and the message that is received. The methods used are to create connection (on_conecct), to receive the message (on_message), and to initialize the client (mqtt.client). The MQTT communication stack used is Mosquitto Client. These are the parameters required to communicate under the MQTT protocol with the Unity environment.

6.4 Interface Development in Unity

Within the virtual environment should be positioned the 3D model of Scorbot which is built in the Blender software. With the model already in the workspace, the authors proceed to give physical and kinematic characteristics for the

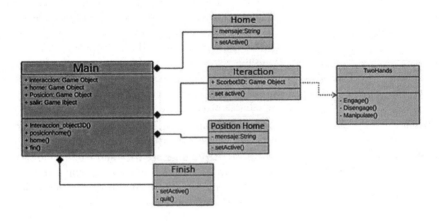

Fig. 8. Scorbot Movement Class Diagram

Table 4. Description of the control GPIOs classes

Class name	Description
Control	Main class that provides subclasses with all the attributes needed for GPIO pin control
Motor Turn Base positive	A class that drives the motor at the base of the Scorbot manipulator in clockwise direction
Motor Turn Base negative	A class that drives the Scorbot robot base motor counter to the previous class
Motor Turn Elbow positive	A class that drives the Scorbot arm elbow motor in clockwise direction
Motor Turn Elbow negative	A class that drives the Scorbot manipulator elbow motor in the opposite direction to the previous class
Motor Turn Shoulder positive	A class that drives the Scorbot arm shoulder motor in clockwise direction
Motor Turn Shoulder negative	A class that drives the Scorbot manipulator's shoulder motor in the opposite direction to the previous class
Motor Turn Gripper positive	A class that drives the gripper engine of the Scorbot manipulator in clockwise direction
Motor Turn Gripper negative	A class that drives the scorbot manipulator's gripper motor in the opposite rotation to the previous one

movement of each part of the robot. In addition, is inserted into the scene a small white cube that is a pointer that indicates where the end of the robot should be placed. Finally, buttons and labels are created that will be inside the scene, a background image has also been added to give the scene a pleasant look according to the situation. Figure 11 shows the design of the virtual environment.

The AR system for robot control is evaluated through several attempts in real-time by some different kind of users such as industrial technicians and students (See Fig. 12). The AR platform gets satisfactory evaluation results. When users tested the application, the developers had the opportunity to ask them a series of open questions as an interview about their perception of the developed system. The users said that they found the application interesting and that they found it innovative and interactive to be able to see the 3D models on the screen and to be able to move them.

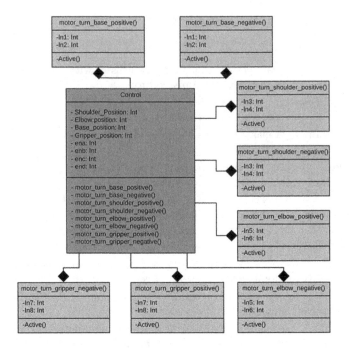

Fig. 9. Scorbot Movement Class Diagram

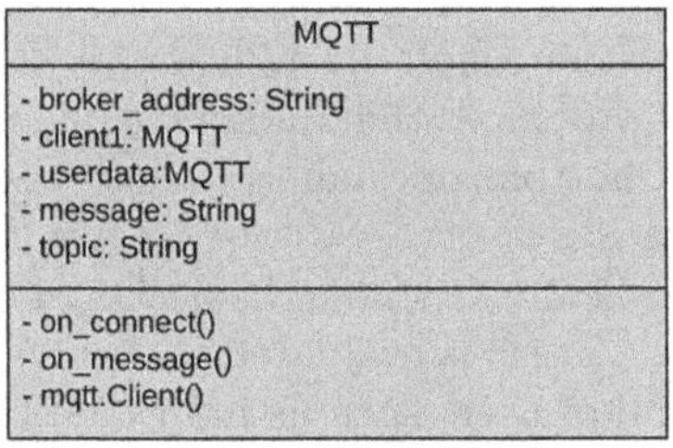

MQTT
- broker_address: String - client1: MQTT - userdata:MQTT - message: String - topic: String
- on_connect() - on_message() - mqtt.Client()

Fig. 10. MQTT into Raspberry Pi Class Diagram

7   Analysis and Discussion of Results

This section explains different tests that are conducted with the designed AR applications on the local machine connected to the Meta II glasses and RPI for a time of 10 min the following. The results of the different test are detailed below:

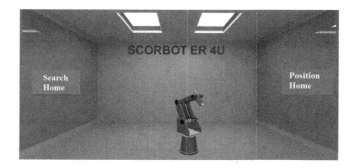

Fig. 11. HRI Virtual Environment

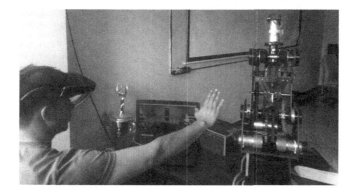

Fig. 12. HRI Virtual Environment Evaluation by Users

7.1 MQTT Network Latency Test

In this test can be observed that network latency remains constant with an average of 45.42 ms on most of the connection for the time evaluated, there are constantly high and low peaks having an upper limit value of 60 ms and a lower limit value of 1 ms (See Fig. 13).

The results show low network latency, which denotes that the established communication protocol is fast enough to perform processes in real-time, being the constant graph in most of the process ensures that the response of the low-cost hardware responds according to the virtual medium by having a synchronization between the virtual robot and the physical robot.

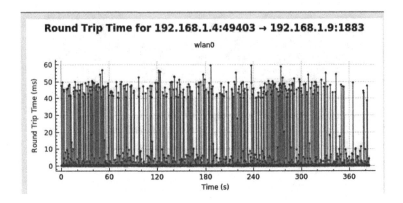

Fig. 13. MQTT Network latency

7.2 Throughput

The results for MQTT Throughput reflect that there is sufficient bandwidth for data transmission between unity and raspberry pi, having a bandwidth in megabits ensures that there has not been lost data since the data to be transmitted does not exceed kilobits, this ensures that all data sent from the virtual environment arrives complete to the embedded card thus having the desired movement in the Scorbot robot.

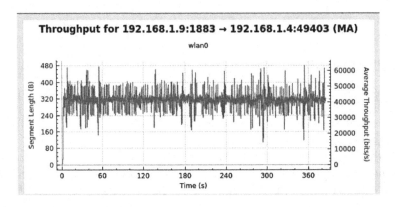

Fig. 14. MQTT Network Throughput

7.3 Raspberry PI Temperature

For RPI temperature data was taken from both the GPU and the processor, it should be noted that the data recorded was before and after communicating with unity, this to better appreciate how the percentage increases in the work card when the control system is launched.

The results obtained reflect the use of card resources when the control system is put into action because for the initial stage of the graph the RPI is on but without communicating with the unity application, for the second stage communication with unity was launched, and it can be seen that the recessed card minimally increases its temperature indicating that the resources it occupies are very low, and as time goes on it keeps the temperature ensuring that in no Time the card comes to use a lot of resources (See Fig. 15).

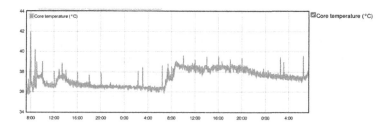

Fig. 15. RPI Temperature

8   Conclusions and Future Work

The use of the Raspberry Pi card as the controller of the Scorbot ER 4U robotic arm is an effective means of giving movement and control to the manipulator, as it adapts perfectly to the vast majority of communication protocols and thus interacts with different platforms and environments. The processing speed it offers is industrial-type giving open up the development of fairly robust cyberphysical systems and this, in turn, supports the needs of Industry 4.0, finally working with an open-source system and free software which it is important because it gives the possibility of to operate with cross-platform systems and does not require any software developed by private entities making it a great reliable and low-cost alternative for process control anywhere in the industry.

Establishing communication with the controller under MQTT parameters ensure success in the Control System of the Scorbot manipulator, currently, a number of communication protocols are handled that use different parameters and provide certain advantages to when it comes to establishing communications, the Internet of Things has come in with great force in recent years and new communications have been developed that are mainly based on the quality of data and the security with which they are transmitted from one place to another, MQTT is one of these protocols, the use of this communication system makes that the goal achieve successfully because it provides security and quality in the transmission of the message from the virtual environment to the controller card, there is no loss of information and its method of operating under hierarchical topics ensures that only clients connected to the topic receive the information thus avoiding diverting or hiding messages.

From this research can be developed applications for monitoring parameters in real-time control systems since by integrating augmented reality can be displayed on the work screen important information, in addition, you can be able to develop a system for handling loads through manipulative arms in hazardous environments without the need for the person to undergo these conditions as with the use of a low-cost controller and using the communication system implemented you can manipulate the robotic arm remotely and if you add augmented reality in a very easy and intuitive way.

References

1. Caiza, G. et al.: Industrial shop-floor integration based on AMQP protocol in an IoT environment. In: 2019 IEEE Fourth Ecuador Technical Chapters Meeting (ETCM), pp. 1–6 (2019). https://doi.org/10.1109/ETCM48019.2019.9014858
2. Cardoso, A. et al.: VRCEMIG: A virtual reality system for real time control of electric substations. In: 2013 IEEE Virtual Reality (VR), pp. 165–166 (2013). https://doi.org/10.1109/VR.2013.6549414
3. Dodoo, E.R., Hill, B., Garcia, A., Kohl, A., MacAllister, A., Schlueter, J., Winer, E.: Evaluating commodity hardware and software for virtual reality assembly training. Electronic Imaging **2018**(3), 468-1–468-6 (2018). https://doi.org/10.2352/ISSN.2470-1173.2018.03.ERVR-468
4. Garcia, C.A., Caiza, G., Naranjo, J.E., Ortiz, A., Garcia, M.V.: An approach of training virtual environment for teaching electro-pneumatic systems. IFAC-PapersOnLine **52**(9), 278–284 (2019).https://doi.org/10.1016/j.ifacol.2019.08.221. 12th IFAC Symposium on Advances in Control Education ACE 2019
5. Garcia, C.A., Naranjo, J.E., Ortiz, A., Garcia, M.V.: An approach of virtual reality environment for technicians training in upstream sector. IFAC-PapersOnLine **52**(9), 285–291 (2019).https://doi.org/10.1016/j.ifacol.2019.08.222. 12th IFAC Symposium on Advances in Control Education ACE 2019
6. Hutton, C., Sohre, N., Davis, B., Guy, S., Rosenberg, E.S.: An augmented reality motion planning interface for robotics. In: 2019 IEEE Conference on Virtual Reality and 3D User Interfaces (VR), pp. 1313–1314 (2019). https://doi.org/10.1109/VR.2019.8798010
7. Ivorra, E., Ortega, M., Alcañiz, M., Garcia-Aracil, N.: Multimodal computer vision framework for human assistive robotics. In: 2018 Workshop on Metrology for Industry 4.0 and IoT, pp. 1–5 (2018). https://doi.org/10.1109/METROI4.2018.8428330
8. Leutert, F., Herrmann, C., Schilling, K.: A spatial augmented reality system for intuitive display of robotic data. In: 2013 8th ACM/IEEE International Conference on Human-Robot Interaction (HRI), pp. 179–180 (2013). https://doi.org/10.1109/HRI.2013.6483560
9. McLin, J., Hoang, N., Deneke, W., McDowell, P.: A mirror world-based robot control system. In: 2017 Second International Conference on Information Systems Engineering (ICISE), pp. 74–77 (2017). https://doi.org/10.1109/ICISE.2017.10
10. Meta 2 development kit (2020). https://www.schenker-tech.de/en/meta-2/
11. Mizuchi, Y., Inamura, T.: Cloud-based multimodal human-robot interaction simulator utilizing ROS and unity frameworks. In: 2017 IEEE/SICE International Symposium on System Integration (SII), pp. 948–955 (2017). https://doi.org/10.1109/SII.2017.8279345

12. Munoz, F.M., Martinez de la Piedra, S., Moctezuma, M.V.: PD+G set-point controller for the second and third joint of a ER-4u scorbot robot. In: 2014 International Conference on Mechatronics, Electronics and Automotive Engineering, pp. 173–178 (2014). https://doi.org/10.1109/ICMEAE.2014.36
13. Raspberry pi card (2020). https://www.raspberrypi.org/
14. Schenker-tech: META 2 - Exclusive Augmented Reality Development Kit (2020). https://www.schenker-tech.de//en/meta-2/
15. Scorbot er-4u educational robot (2020). https://www.intelitek.com/robots/scorbot-er-4u/
16. Unity 3d (2020). https://www.unity.com/
17. Wallace, M.W. et al.: Virtual reality GTAW and pipe welding simulator and setup. US Patent 8,851,896, 7 Oct 2014
18. Zboray, D.A. et al.: Virtual reality pipe welding simulator. US Patent 8,915,740, 23 Dec 2014

Generating Synthetic Point Clouds of Sewer Networks: An Initial Investigation

Kasper Schøn Henriksen[ID], Mathias S. Lynge[(✉)][ID], Mikkel D.B. Jeppesen[ID],
Moaaz M. J. Allahham[ID], Ivan A. Nikolov[ID], Joakim Bruslund Haurum[ID],
and Thomas B. Moeslund[ID]

Visual Analysis of People (VAP) Laboratory, Aalborg University, Aalborg, Denmark
{kshe16,mlynge16,mjeppe15,mallah16}@student.aau.dk,
{iani,joha,tbm}@create.aau.dk

Abstract. Automatic robot inspections of sewer systems are progressively becoming more used for extending the lifetime of sewers and lowering the costs of maintenance. These automatic systems rely on machine learning and the acquisition of varied training data is therefore necessary. Capturing such data can be a costly and time consuming process. This paper proposes a system for generation and acquisition of synthetic training data from sewer systems. The system utilizes Structured Domain Randomization (SDR) for the generation of the sewer systems and an approximated model of a Pico Flexx Time-of-Flight camera for capturing depth and point cloud data from the generated sewer network. We evaluate the proposed system by comparing its output to ground truth data acquired from a Pico Flexx sensor in sewer pipes. We demonstrate that on average our system provides an absolute error of 5.78 ± 8.92 and 7.58 ± 8.68 mm, between data captured from real life and our proposed system, for two different scenarios. These results prove satisfactory for capturing training data. The code is publicly available at https://bitbucket.org/aauvap/syntheticsewerpipes/src/master/.

1 Introduction

The sewerage infrastructure is an essential part of modern society consisting of huge pipe networks hidden under the ground. This system is normally not a concern for the general public, but it is indispensable. To reduce maintenance costs, regular inspection of the entire sewer system is important. With today's methods this is not feasible, as inspection of sewer systems is a laborious task, carried out manually by skilled operators [3]. This is done by sending a remote-controlled platform with a camera through a section of the sewer system while an operator monitors the live video feed from this camera. As a result, pipes are often replaced prematurely to avoid older pipes causing issues. Pipes with an expected lifetime of 75 years are replaced after just 50 years, causing several hundred million DKK in expenses for the Danish state [5]. To improve this

© Springer Nature Switzerland AG 2020
L. T. De Paolis and P. Bourdot (Eds.): AVR 2020, LNCS 12243, pp. 364–373, 2020.
https://doi.org/10.1007/978-3-030-58468-9_26

lack of inspection, an ongoing research project, the Automated Sewer Inspection Robot (ASIR) project, intends to develop an autonomous robot, that will roam the sewers and utilise machine learning to identify defects [5]. For a machine learning algorithm to properly identify defects and landmarks such as joints and branch pipes in a sewer network, the algorithm that is utilised by the robot requires training, and for this, an annotated data set is desired. The intended plan of collecting data from the sewers is using depth- and RGB cameras. Currently, only databases with RGB images from CCTV inceptions are available, and a data set consisting of depth information is needed. As capturing data from real sewers can be a huge and expensive task, an alternative could be generating synthetic data.

Different types of depth sensors can be utilised for capturing depth information, such as Time of Flight (ToF)[7,11], stereo cameras [8], and structured light [21]. The ToF sensor Pico Flexx by Camboard is chosen as the sensor to be implemented as part of the proposed system. The sensor is chosen because of its small size, high resolution and low power consumption. It is also shown by [9] that ToF sensors are ideal for use in inspection of hazardous and hard to reach places. The Pico Flexx outputs point clouds, which offers more depth information that can help identify defects in the sewer network. This sensor will be implemented and will be the focus of this paper.

Contributions. Our contribution is a novel system, making the first foray into generating Synthetic Point Clouds (SPC) in the sewer domain. This system consists of two parts;

- Generate virtual sewer networks which are based on the method Structured Domain Randomization (SDR) method.
- Generate SPCs, approximating the Pico Flexx output, that can be used for training machine learning algorithms.

2   Related Work

We will be looking at the state of the art for both the sewer generation and ToF simulation.

Depth Sensors: Bulczak et al. [2] suggests a method for simulating amplitude modulated continuous wave (AMCW) ToF sensors including the artefacts caused by multi-path interference (MPI). MPI is of particular interest for simulating sewer inspection in textured pipes, which could be of interest even in smoother plastic pipes, as it could model reflections. This method increases computational costs, however, it is specifically designed for GPU execution to allow fast processing.

Sarbolandi et al. [18] compares structured light and ToF depth sensing in detail, specifically comparing the two different versions of the Microsoft Kinect sensors that employ these different technologies. They found that the ToF variant performed better at rejecting background illumination, motion, highly translucent objects, and at large incident angles.

Sarker et al. [19] explores the use of a stereo vision based depth camera for the use of crack detection in concrete, showing the ability to detect and classify variants of cracks.

Synthetic Generation of Environments: In recent years the interest in generating annotated synthetic data has been steadily increasing, as to meet the demands of more complex deep learning architectures in an inexpensive manner [1,6,10,16]. Tobin et al. [20] presents a method for computer generation of synthetic data, called Domain Randomization (DR), which is achieved by generating structured variations of a chosen scenario, such that a machine learning algorithm would process real images as if they were another variation of the scenario. The work was further developed by Prakash et al. [14], into an expanded version of DR: Structured Domain Randomisation (SDR). Instead of placing objects by a uniform random distribution with DR, context of the scene is considered. This structures the randomisation by a set of rules that corresponds to the intended environment. This allows machine learning algorithms to train not only on the virtual objects placed in the scene, but also on the context of where these objects are positioned in relation to each other. The SDR method is found to fit the focus of our solution, and it will be used for generating the environment that will later be used for the 3D data acquisition.

3   Methods and Material

The proposed solution is implemented in Unity, which consists of two parts: *Environment Generator* and *Data Generator*. The overall structure of the system is shown in Fig. 1.

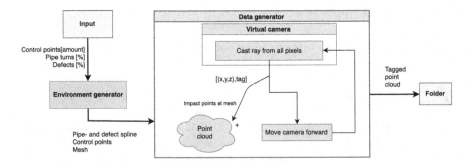

Fig. 1. Structure of the proposed solution.

The *Environment Generator* dynamically generates a virtual sewer network consisting of splines, control points and pipe meshes based on given parameters.

These are passed to the *Data Generator* that generates point clouds based on them and two additional parameters: folder path and number of point clouds. Folder path: defines the output folder for point cloud data. Number of point clouds: defines how many point clouds to create. The camera moves forward until this parameter is satisfied.

3.1   Pico Flexx

Camboard Pico Flexx, is a joint production by PMD Technologies and Infineon. It is based on PMD ToF technology (AMCW-ToF), which uses Near Infrared (NIR) laser to determine the distance from the sensor to the impact points of objects. The small size and the low power consumption enhances the number of possible applications. To mimic the Pico Flexx, its parameters should be implemented for the synthetic sensor. Because the information available from PMD [13] only shows camera characteristics such as field of view and aspect ratio, a complex ToF simulation can be difficult to be implemented as more information is required. The sensor approximation in this paper is therefore estimated using ray casting.

3.2   Environment Generator

The gap between the real- and the virtual domain can be reduced using 3D models that mimic physical models and utilize SDR to generate the environment. 3D models and environment generator will be explored in the upcoming sections.

Pipes and Defects: To mimic the physical environment, 3D representations of physical pipes and defects are utilised. The system generates points along the network, where handmade defects can spawn.

Generator: To enhance the generator, the structure of how objects are generated should be acknowledged by utalizing SDR. As the sewer system domain differs to the domain in the SDR paper, other contexts such as rubber rings mostly occurring at pipe displacements should be considered. SDR proposes a taxonomy which covers the following four principles. *Scenario:* determines general parameters to generate the domain such as length of the sewer network and defect probability. *Global Parameters:* generates contextual splines based on parameters from the scenario. *Context Splines:* instantiate objects based on given probabilities and context. *Objects:* contain a transform, 3D mesh, collider, and defect- or fine tag.

3.3   Data Generator

Without extensive information about the Pico Flexx, an approximated virtual camera in Unity is set up to mimic the output of the Pico Flexx. The virtual camera utilises the same resolution and focal length. Moreover, to detect depth in a scene, rays are cast up to the distance of the detectable depth of the Pico

Flexx. These rays are cast from each pixel of the virtual camera in the direction of the viewport in normalized coordinates. Figure 2 shows a comparison of 2D depth images from the data generator and Pico Flexx. However, to evaluate the data generation, comparing point clouds is preferred to avoid dimensionality reduction.

In a simulated environment, a physics engine can utilise ray casting to determine impact positions at 3D meshes. This provides additional information for each ray which can label the points within the point cloud. For each ray, random noise from a Gaussian distribution is added with a range of $\pm 1\%$ from the true value, based on the datasheet from PMD [13].

(a) Synthetic   (b) Pico Flexx

Fig. 2. Output image from the image generator, compared to the Pico Flexx, where white indicates missing points.

4   Results

To evaluate the solution, point clouds from both Pico Flexx and the system using similar setups are acquired.

4.1   Data Gathering from Pico Flexx

To gather Pico Flexx data, a controlled environment was set up, and an already built robot with a mounted Pico Flexx was used, as shown in Fig. 3a. It is preferred to get data around pipe connections, as displaced pipes are the most common defect[1]. Physical pipes were set up inside a windowless room, to avoid external light sources disturbing the Pico Flexx sensor that was attached to a small remote controlled mobile platform. Based on the setup in Fig. 3b, two scenarios were arranged; the first setup without displacement and second with displacement. In the first scenario (**S1**), the robot was placed at the start of the pipe and programmed to move forward through the pipe. In the second scenario (**S2**), the robot was placed 50 cm from both the first pipe connection and a misplaced rubber ring, and programmed to move through the connection. The outcome from these scenarios was point cloud data sequences split by time

---

[1] Based on unpublished works.

stamps. In order to evaluate the Pico Flexx data, the sewer system and scenarios of the physical setup were mimicked for the virtual setup, as shown in Fig. 3c where the Pico Flexx's orientations were mimicked by approximately transforming the virtual camera. Using these virtual scenarios, SPCs were extracted to be compared to the Physical Point Clouds (PPC).

(a) The robot   (b) Physical setup   (c) Virtual setup

Fig. 3. The figures represent the robot's placement, the physical- and virtual setup, respectively. Note: The branch pipe is not within the sensor's FoV.

4.2 Point Cloud Comparison

To evaluate the simulation performance, differences and similarities between the PPCs and SPCs were compared, which allows a per point distance calculation. For this, the widely used software CloudCompare [4], which has been tested by several studies [12,15], is utilised. The PPC will be used as the ground truth whilst the SPC will be used to compare with. Before comparing the point clouds, they are aligned using the fine registration method, Iterative Closest Point (ICP) [17], which aligns the desired point clouds to the ground truth, by minimizing the distance error between them. As missing points exist in the PPCs, local modelling is utilised to approximate planes based on least square to estimate the pipe geometry. This minimizes the distance between point clouds, as approximated planes can cover holes in the PPCs.

The absolute distances distribution of the compared point clouds for the two scenarios is presented in Fig. 5. The results show a difference of 5.78 ± 8.92 mm for **S1** and 7.58 ± 8.68 mm for **S2**.

4.3 Accuracy of Point Clouds

To ensure both the synthetic- and physical data give correct measurements of the real pipe, the diameter error is calculated. This is done on **S1** as this is the scenario with the longest straight section. Each point cloud is sliced into overlapping segments of 100 mm, using a step size of 10 mm. At each segment, the distance from each point to its most distant point is calculated, and the mean of these distances are then used as the diameter for that section.

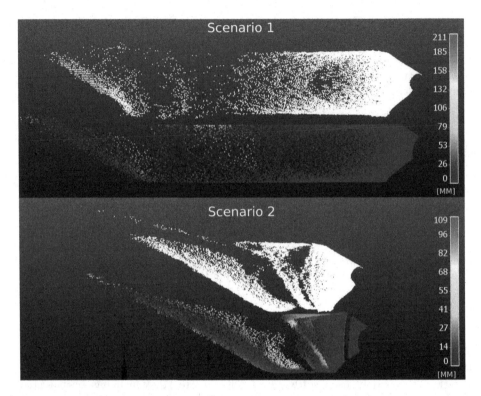

Fig. 4. This figure represents the two scenarios, where the white point clouds are PPCs and the colored point clouds are SPCs. Moreover, the legend indicates the absolute distance error value for the gradient colors in the SPCs. (Color figure online)

5   Discussion

In the point cloud comparison, some of the error described by the mean in both scenarios, may be caused by a difference in placement of the Pico Flexx and the virtual camera, as the placement of the virtual camera was done by hand, as close to the Pico Flexx positioning as possible. As seen in Fig. 5, outliers are present, with the largest occurrence is in **S1**. The outliers appear at the pipe connection of the pipes which can be seen in Fig. 4, by the yellow and red colors. The remaining outliers in **S1** are located at the end of the point cloud, likely caused by the lower point density. In **S2**, the outliers are most noticeable around the pipe connection point, but in this case they seem to be caused by the shadow cast by the rubber ring in **S2**. This can be seen in Fig. 4 as a lack of points. Considering the mean for all evaluations, in regards to the size of the pipes, the error rate is considered acceptable in order to classify e.g. displacements.

Figure 6 shows the diameter size along the point clouds from the accuracy of point cloud comparison. The first 25 cm section of both the point clouds shows a diameter of 0 mm, and that is due to the distance between the sensor and

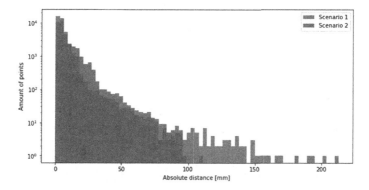

Fig. 5. Histogram of the absolute distances from points in the SPC, to the corresponding calculated least square plane in the PPC. Note the y-axis is log-scaled. Scenario 1 mean: 5.78 ± 8.92 mm. Scenario 2 mean: 7.58 ± 8.68 mm.

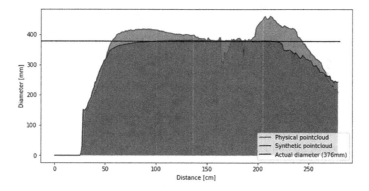

Fig. 6. Error rate compared to the specified diameter of the real pipe from **S1**.

the pipe surface. The next 35 cm section has increasing diameters size due to the slanted shape of the point cloud at the beginning as can be seen in Fig. 4, which results in a non-circular slice. From 60 until 150 cm, the mean diameter is 405 mm for the PPC and 376 mm for the SPC, which shows a small error in the PPC, believed to be caused by the lack of points in that area of the point cloud. However, the SPC shows almost a diameter size that matches the real pipe diameter for the majority of the pipe length. After 160 cm, major errors occur in both point clouds, which starts around the bend of the pipe, this is not of interest as the test assumes the pipe is straight. The point cloud comparison test indicates that the Pico Flexx yields more noise than expected, but to clarify this, further research is required. The accuracy of the point clouds test, indicates that the imperfections can be caused by the textures, imperfectness of the surfaces, dirt in the pipes or lighting that could reflect within the pipes' internal surfaces. All these characteristics define the appearance of real surfaces, which can have an impact on other elements when implemented in computer graphics.

6   Conclusion

This paper has introduced a system which is capable of generating annotated SPCs based on the characteristics of the Pico Flexx in a synthetic sewer environment. Through experiments, it is concluded that the difference of the two point clouds is mainly caused by the lack of points in areas of the PPC. Furthermore, it is found that regions of the point clouds have points that approximately match the real data. Using a moving robot, a continuous good point cloud could be stitched together from multiple instances of the good section. However, if a larger portion of the point cloud is to be used, a more accurate simulation of the sensor might be required, for example an implementation of the MPI simulation as mentioned in related work Sect. 2. Considering the simplicity of the calculation behind the SPCs, the result seems promising. This especially applies in relation to the first part of the point clouds in **S1**. It should be noted that this is a controlled environment, and entering more realistic scenarios, that contain water, dirt etc. might challenge the Pico Flexx and therefore it yields noisier data. Here the solution might perform poorly due to it being too idealised, therefore reflection, refraction etc. need to be taken into considerations. Overall the solution is able to generate randomised sewer systems that contain defects using SDR. Moreover, SPCs can be generated which can potentially be used to accelerate the data acquisition process for machine learning algorithms.

Acknowledgment. This work is supported by Innovation Fund Denmark [grant number 8055-00015A] and is part of the Automated Sewer Inspection Robot (ASIR) project. The authors declare no conflict of interests.

References

1. Bruls, T., Porav, H., Kunze, L., Newman, P.: Generating all the roads to rome: Road layout randomization for improved road marking segmentation. In: 2019 IEEE Intelligent Transportation Systems Conference (ITSC), pp. 831–838 (2019). https://doi.org/10.1109/ITSC.2019.8916785
2. Bulczak, D., Lambers, M., Kolb, A.: Quantified, interactive simulation of AMCW ToF camera including multipath effects. Sensors **18**(1), 13 (2018). https://doi.org/10.3390/s18010013
3. DTVK: TV-H, Håndbog for TV-inspektion (2019)
4. ENST, EDF, Daniel Girardeau-Montaut: Cloud compare. http://www.cloudcompare.org/. Accessed 01 Feb 2020
5. EnviDan: Envidan er med i nyt udviklingsprojekt, hvor robotter i kloakken vil spare samfundet for kæmpe millionbeløb! (2019). https://www.envidan.dk/cases/asir-udviklingsprojekt
6. Fang, J., et al.: Augmented lidar simulator for autonomous driving. IEEE Robot. Autom. Lett. **5**(2), 1931–1938 (2020). https://doi.org/10.1109/LRA.2020.2969927
7. Gokturk, S.B., Yalcin, H., Bamji, C.: A time-of-flight depth sensor - system description, issues and solutions. In: 2004 Conference on Computer Vision and Pattern Recognition Workshop, p. 35 (2004). https://doi.org/10.1109/CVPR.2004.291
8. Hamzah, R.A., Ibrahim, H.: Literature survey on stereo vision disparity map algorithms. J. Sens. **2016**, 1–23 (2016). https://doi.org/10.1155/2016/8742920

9. Jans, R.M., Green, A.S., Koerner, L.J.: Characterization of a miniaturized IR depth sensor with a programmable region-of-interest that enables hazard mapping applications. IEEE Sens. J. **20**, 1 (2020). https://doi.org/10.1109/JSEN.2020.2971595
10. Kamilaris, A., van den Brink, C., Karatsiolis, S.: Training deep learning models via synthetic data: Application in unmanned aerial vehicles. In: Vento, M., Percannella, G., Colantonio, S., Giorgi, D., Matuszewski, B.J., Kerdegari, H., Razaak, M. (eds.) CAIP 2019. CCIS, vol. 1089, pp. 81–90. Springer, Cham (2019). https://doi.org/10.1007/978-3-030-29930-9_8
11. Lange, R., Seitz, P.: Solid-state time-of-flight range camera. IEEE J. Quantum Electron. **37**(3), 390–397 (2001). https://doi.org/10.1109/3.910448
12. Oniga, E., SAVU, A., Negrila, A.: The evaluation of cloudcompare software in the process of tls point clouds registration. RevCAD J. Geodesy Cadastre **21**, 117–124 (2016)
13. pmd: Development kit brief camboard pico flexx. https://pmdtec.com/picofamily/wp-content/uploads/2018/03/PMD_DevKit_Brief_CB_pico_flexx_CE_V0218-1.pdf. Accessed 13 Dec 2019
14. Prakash, A., Boochoon, S., Brophy, M., Acuna, D., Cameracci, E., State, G., Shapira, O., Birchfield, S.: Structured domain randomization: Bridging the reality gap by context-aware synthetic data. https://arxiv.org/abs/1810.10093 (2018). Accessed 28 Feb 2020
15. Rajendra, Y., et al.: Evaluation of partially overlapping 3d point cloud's registration by using ICP variant and cloudcompare (2014)
16. Ros, G., Sellart, L., Materzynska, J., Vazquez, D., Lopez, A.M.: The synthia dataset: A large collection of synthetic images for semantic segmentation of urban scenes. In: 2016 IEEE Conference on Computer Vision and Pattern Recognition (CVPR), pp. 3234–3243 (2016). https://doi.org/10.1109/CVPR.2016.352
17. Rusinkiewicz, S., Levoy, M.: Efficient variants of the ICP algorithm (2001)
18. Sarbolandi, H., Lefloch, D., Kolb, A.: Kinect range sensing: Structured-light versus time-of-flight kinect (2015). https://arxiv.org/abs/1505.05459
19. Sarker, M., Ali, T., Abdelfatah, A., Yehia, S., Elaksher, A.: A cost-effective method for crack detection and measurement on concrete surface. Int. Arch. Photogrammetry Remote Sens. Spat. Inf. Sci. **42**, 237 (2017). https://doi.org/10.5194/isprs-archives-XLII-2-W8-237-2017
20. Tobin, J., Fong, R., Ray, A., Schneider, J., Zaremba, W., Abbeel, P.: Domain randomization for transferring deep neural networks from simulation to the real world (2017). https://ieeexplore.ieee.org/abstract/document/8202133
21. Valkenburg, R., McIvor, A.: Accurate 3d measurement using a structured light system. Image Vis. Comput. **16**(2), 99–110 (1998). https://www.scopus.com/inward/record.uri?eid=2-s2.0-0032000083&partnerID=40&md5=af7a27632873263c1d548f1cd6c8c948. cited By 220

Author Index

Printed in the United States
By Bookmasters